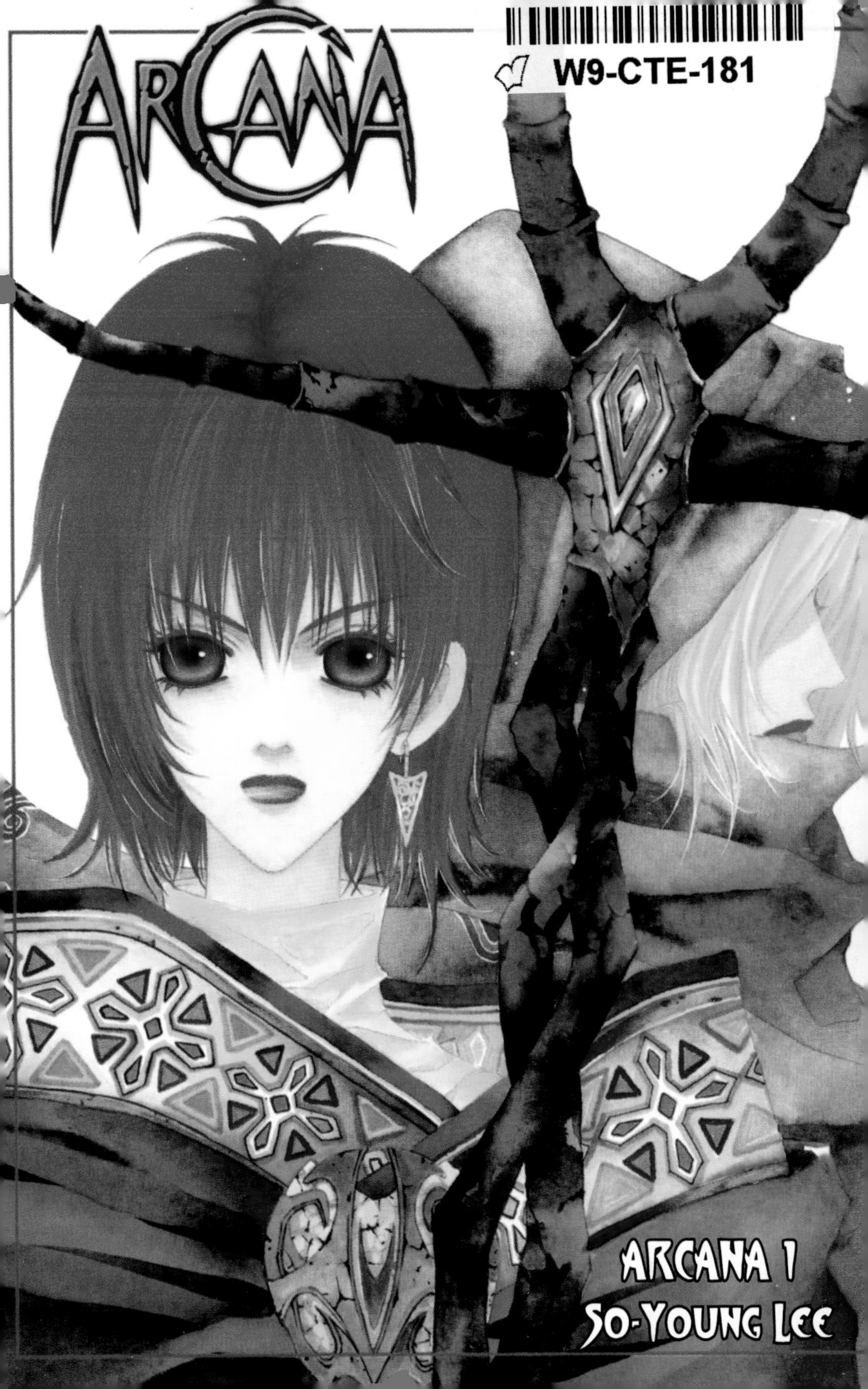
ARCANA
ARCANA 1
SO-YOUNG LEE

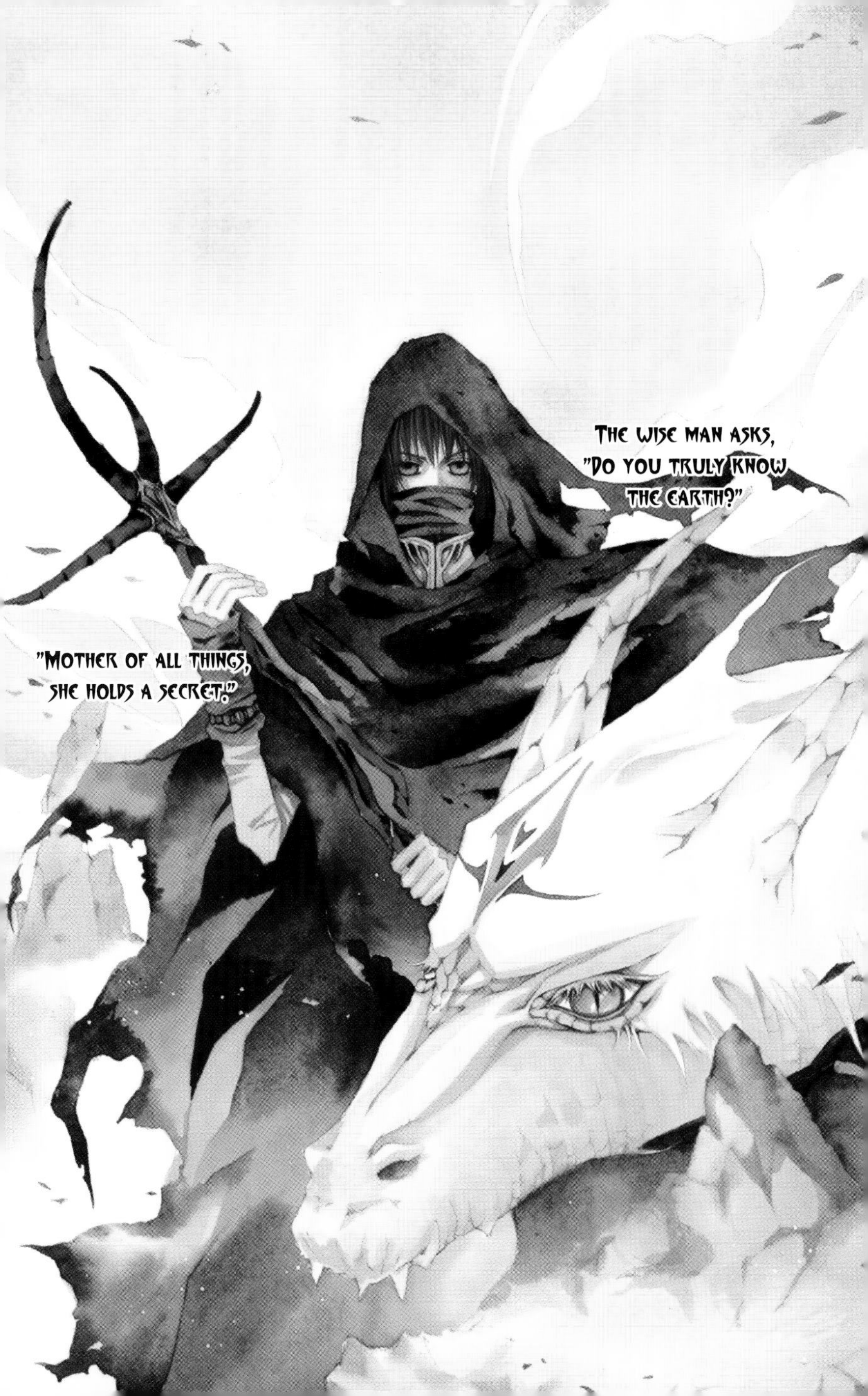
THE WISE MAN ASKS, "DO YOU TRULY KNOW THE EARTH?"
"MOTHER OF ALL THINGS, SHE HOLDS A SECRET."

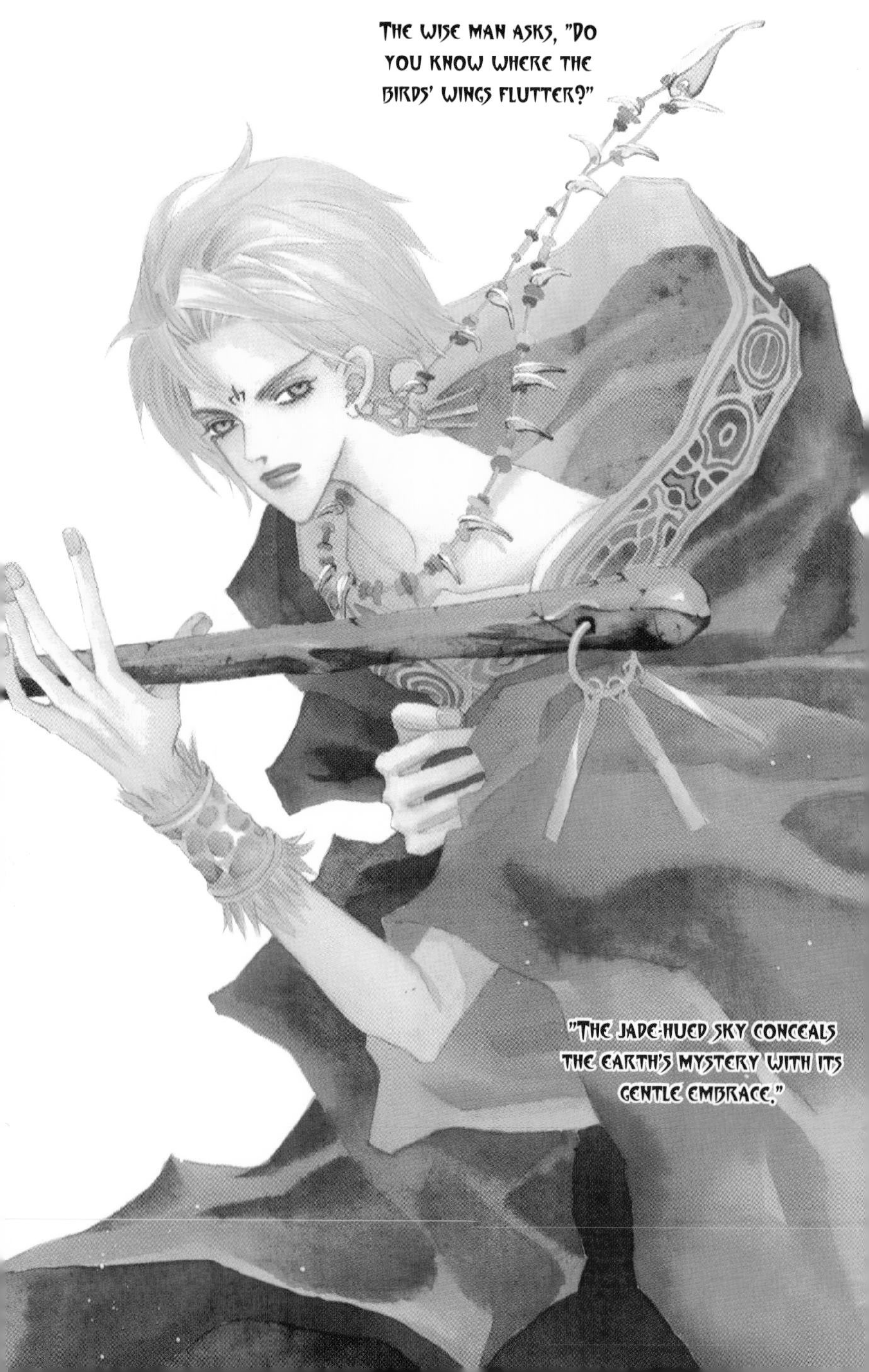
THE WISE MAN ASKS, "DO YOU KNOW WHERE THE BIRDS' WINGS FLUTTER?"
"THE JADE-HUED SKY CONCEALS THE EARTH'S MYSTERY WITH ITS GENTLE EMBRACE."

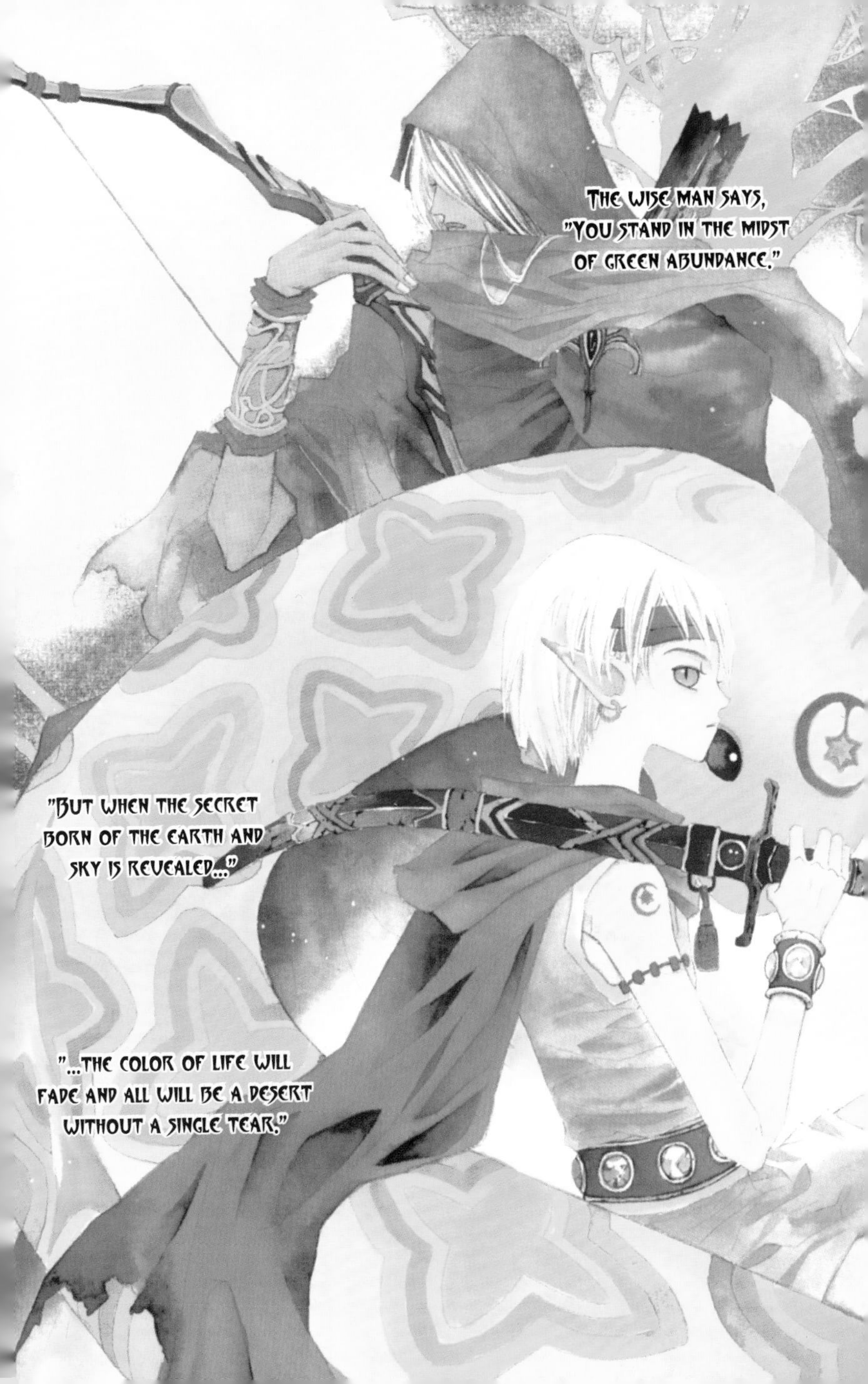
THE WISE MAN SAYS, "YOU STAND IN THE MIDST OF GREEN ABUNDANCE."
"BUT WHEN THE SECRET BORN OF THE EARTH AND SKY IS REVEALED..."
"...THE COLOR OF LIFE WILL FADE AND ALL WILL BE A DESERT WITHOUT A SINGLE TEAR."

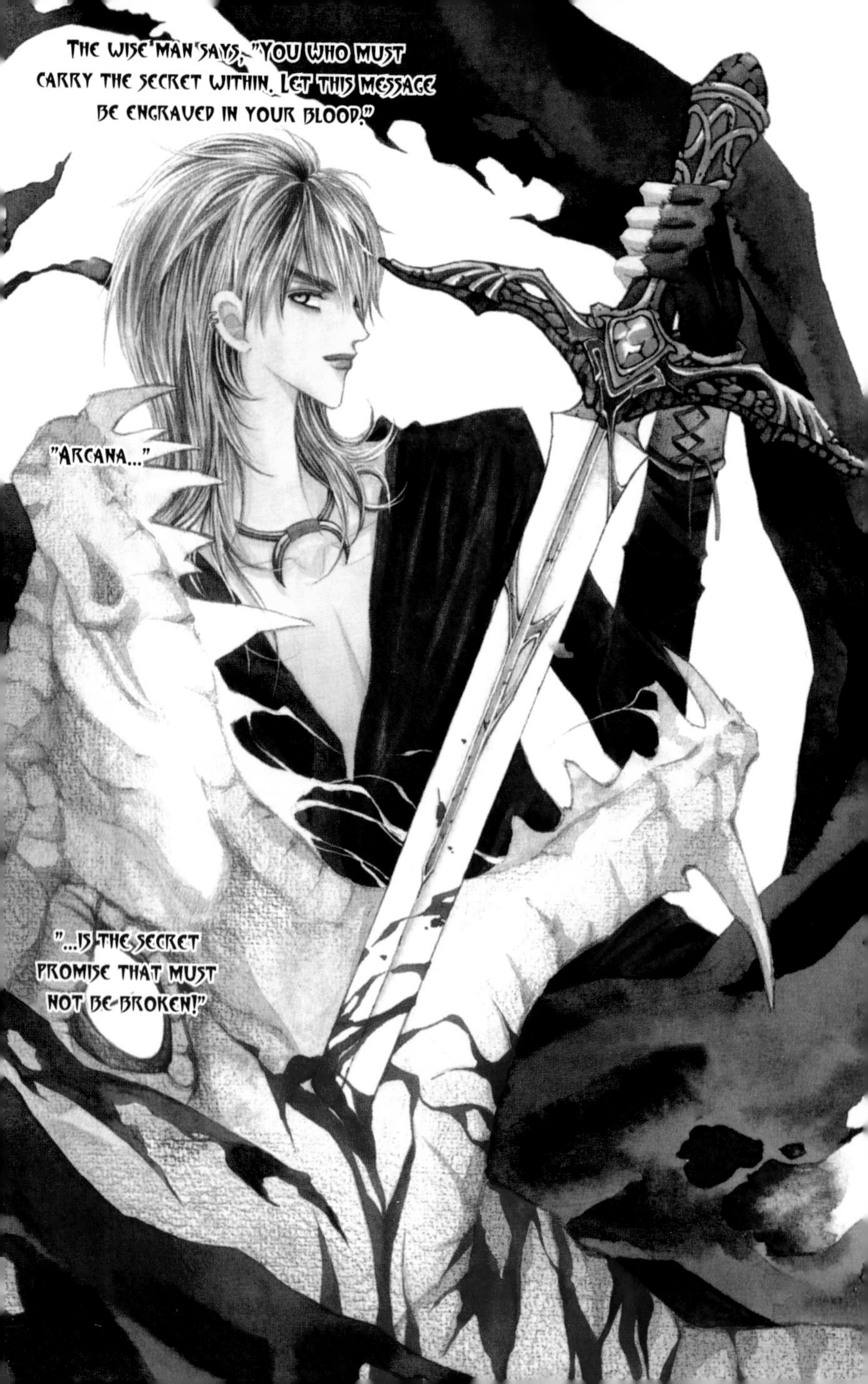
The wise man says, "You who must carry the secret within. Let this message be engraved in your blood."
"Arcana..."
"...is the secret promise that must not be broken!"

VOLUME 1
SO-YOUNG LEE

HAMBURG // LONDON // LOS ANGELES // TOKYO

Arcana Vol. 1
Created by So-Young Lee

Translation - Youngju Ryu
English Adaptation - Barbara Randall Kesel
Copy Editor - Suzanne Waldman
Retouch and Lettering - Eva Han
Production Artist - Vicente Rivera, Jr.
Cover Design - Thea Willis

Editor - Bryce P. Coleman
Digital Imaging Manager - Chris Buford
Pre-Press Manager - Antonio DePietro
Production Managers - Jennifer Miller and Mutsumi Miyazaki
Art Director - Matt Alford
Managing Editor - Jill Freshney
VP of Production - Ron Klamert
Editor-in-Chief - Mike Kiley
President and C.O.O. - John Parker
Publisher and C.E.O. - Stuart Levy

A  Manga

TOKYOPOP Inc.
5900 Wilshire Blvd. Suite 2000
Los Angeles, CA 90036

E-mail: info@TOKYOPOP.com
Come visit us online at www.TOKYOPOP.com

ISBN: 1-59532-481-X

First TOKYOPOP printing: June 2005
10 9 8 7 6 5 4 3 2 1
Printed in the USA

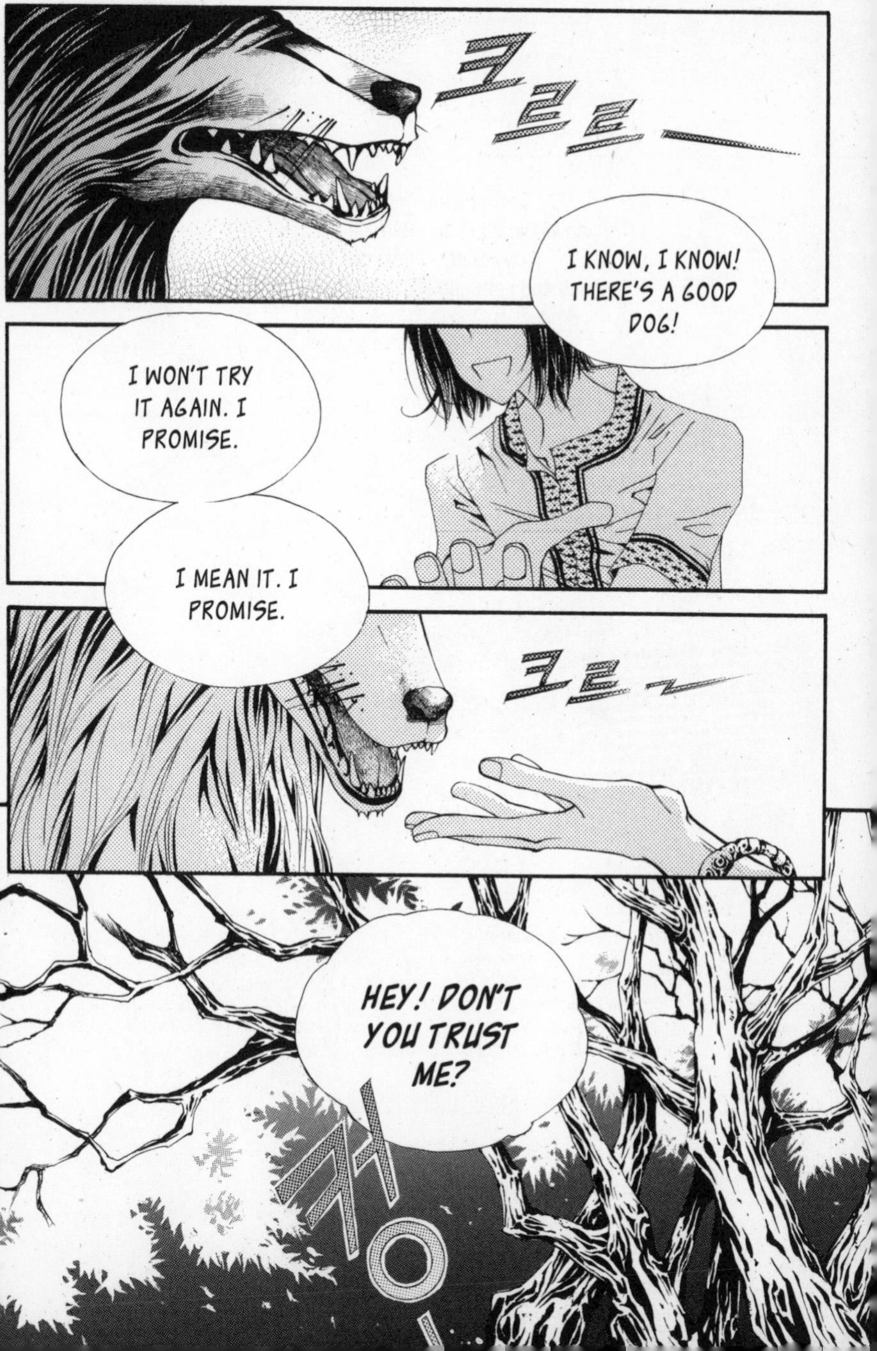
크르르
I KNOW, I KNOW! THERE'S A GOOD DOG!
I WON'T TRY IT AGAIN. I PROMISE.
I MEAN IT. I PROMISE.
크르
HEY! DON'T YOU TRUST ME?

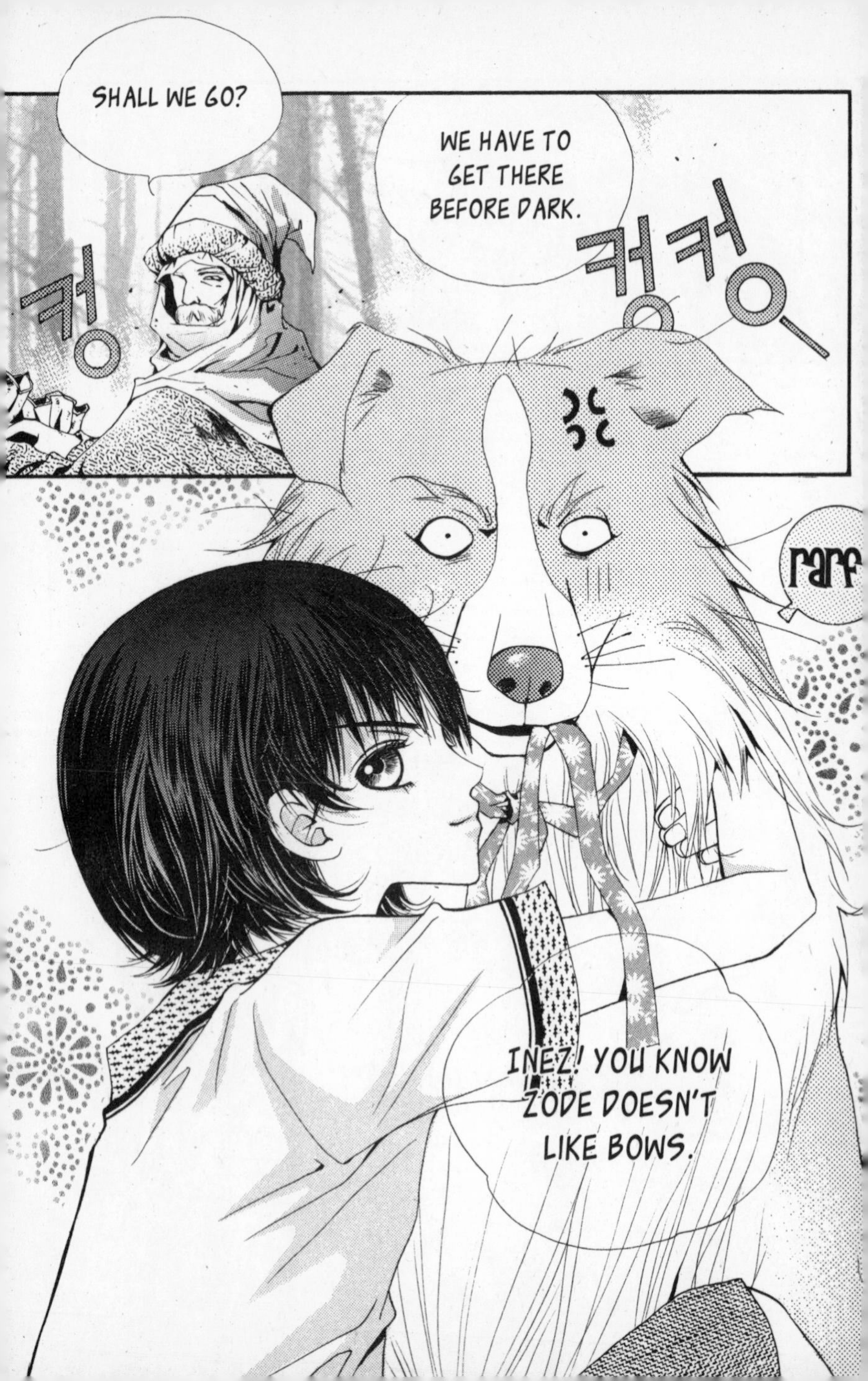
SHALL WE GO?
컹
WE HAVE TO GET THERE BEFORE DARK.
컹컹
rarf
INEZ! YOU KNOW ZODE DOESN'T LIKE BOWS.

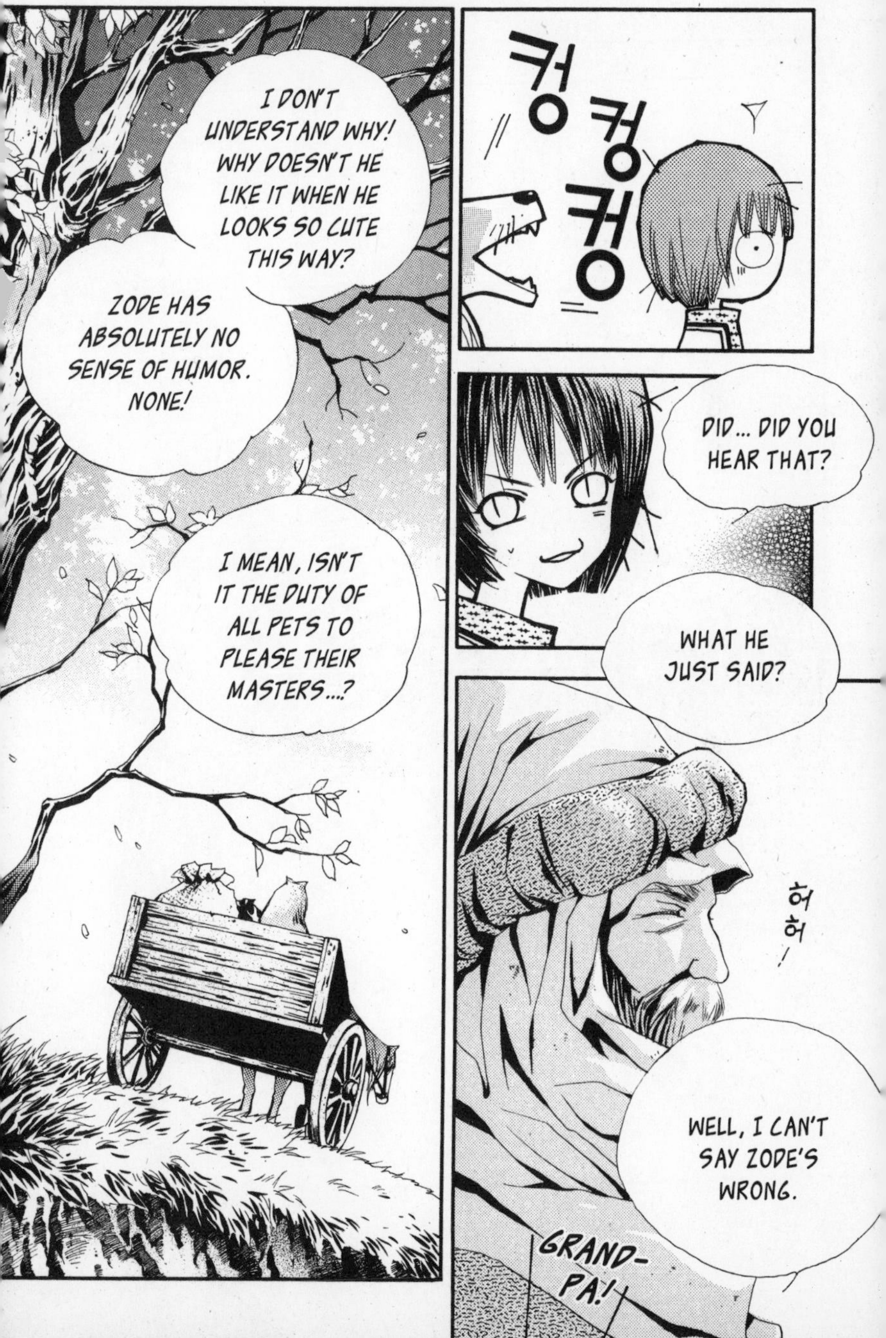
I DON'T UNDERSTAND WHY! WHY DOESN'T HE LIKE IT WHEN HE LOOKS SO CUTE THIS WAY?
ZODE HAS ABSOLUTELY NO SENSE OF HUMOR. NONE!
I MEAN, ISN'T IT THE DUTY OF ALL PETS TO PLEASE THEIR MASTERS...?
컹 컹 컹
DID... DID YOU HEAR THAT?
WHAT HE JUST SAID?
허허
WELL, I CAN'T SAY ZODE'S WRONG.
GRAND-PA!

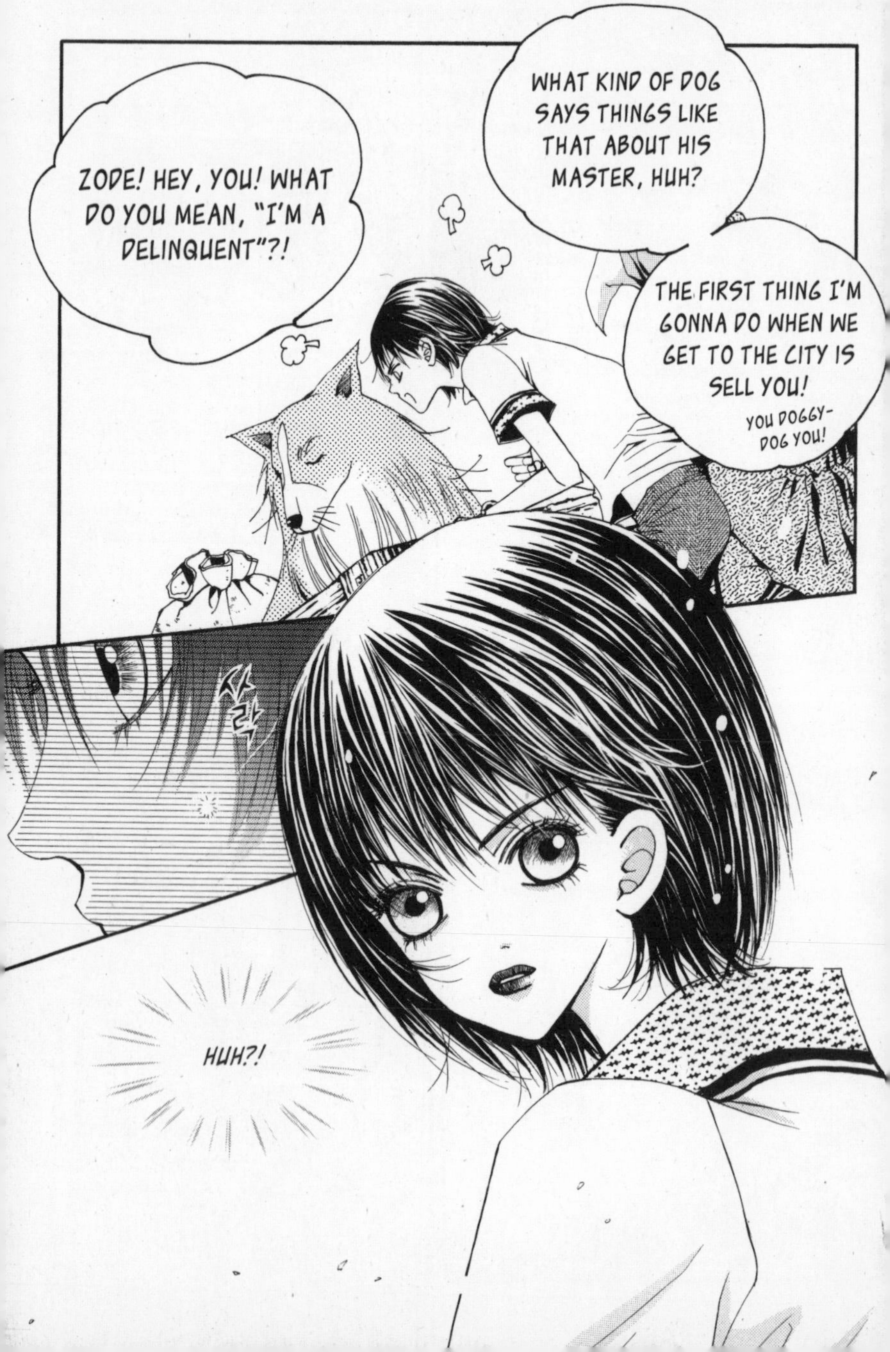
ZODE! HEY, YOU! WHAT DO YOU MEAN, "I'M A DELINQUENT"?!
WHAT KIND OF DOG SAYS THINGS LIKE THAT ABOUT HIS MASTER, HUH?
THE FIRST THING I'M GONNA DO WHEN WE GET TO THE CITY IS SELL YOU!
YOU DOGGY-DOG YOU!
HUH?!

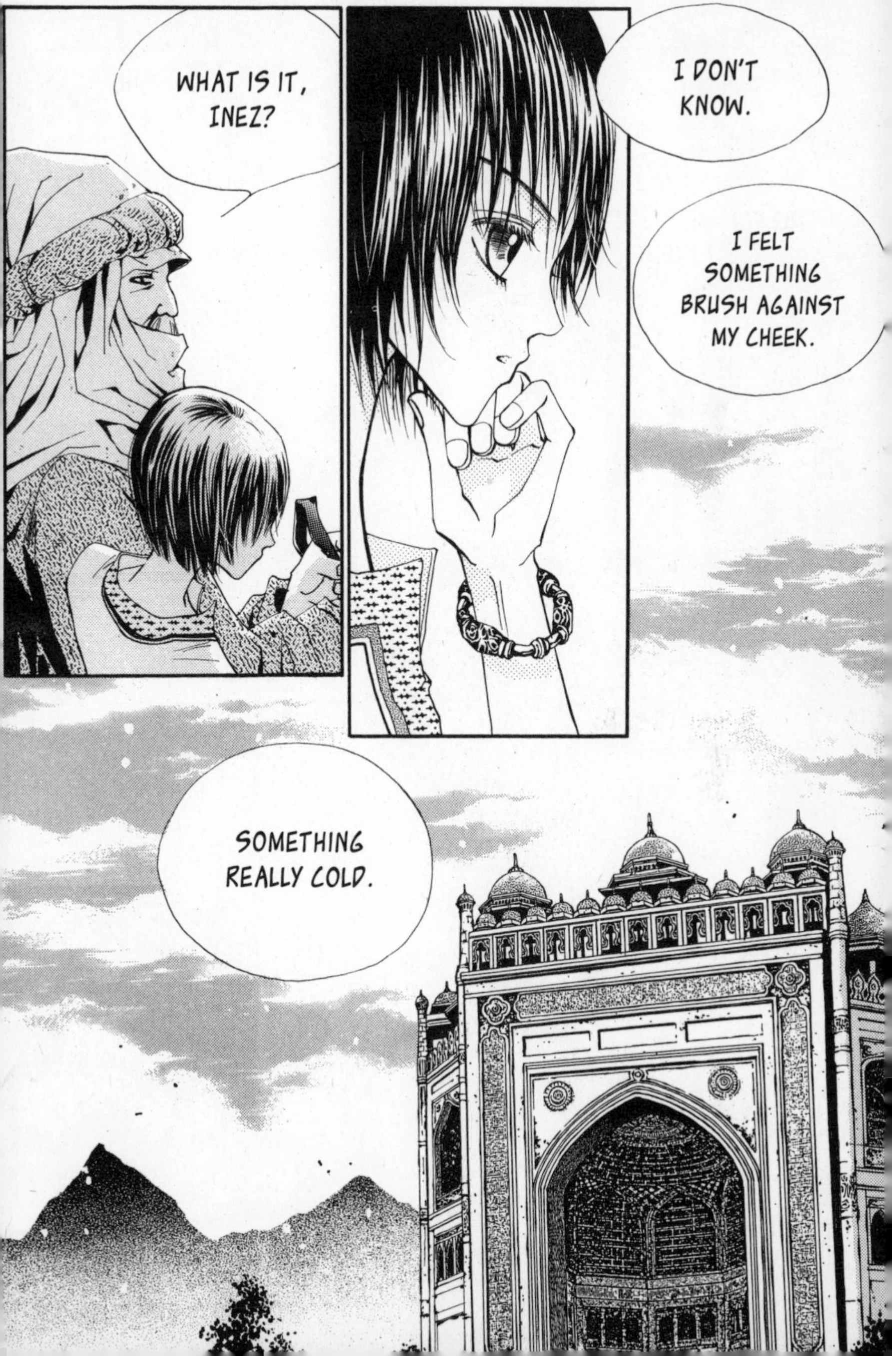
WHAT IS IT, INEZ?
I DON'T KNOW.
I FELT SOMETHING BRUSH AGAINST MY CHEEK.
SOMETHING REALLY COLD.

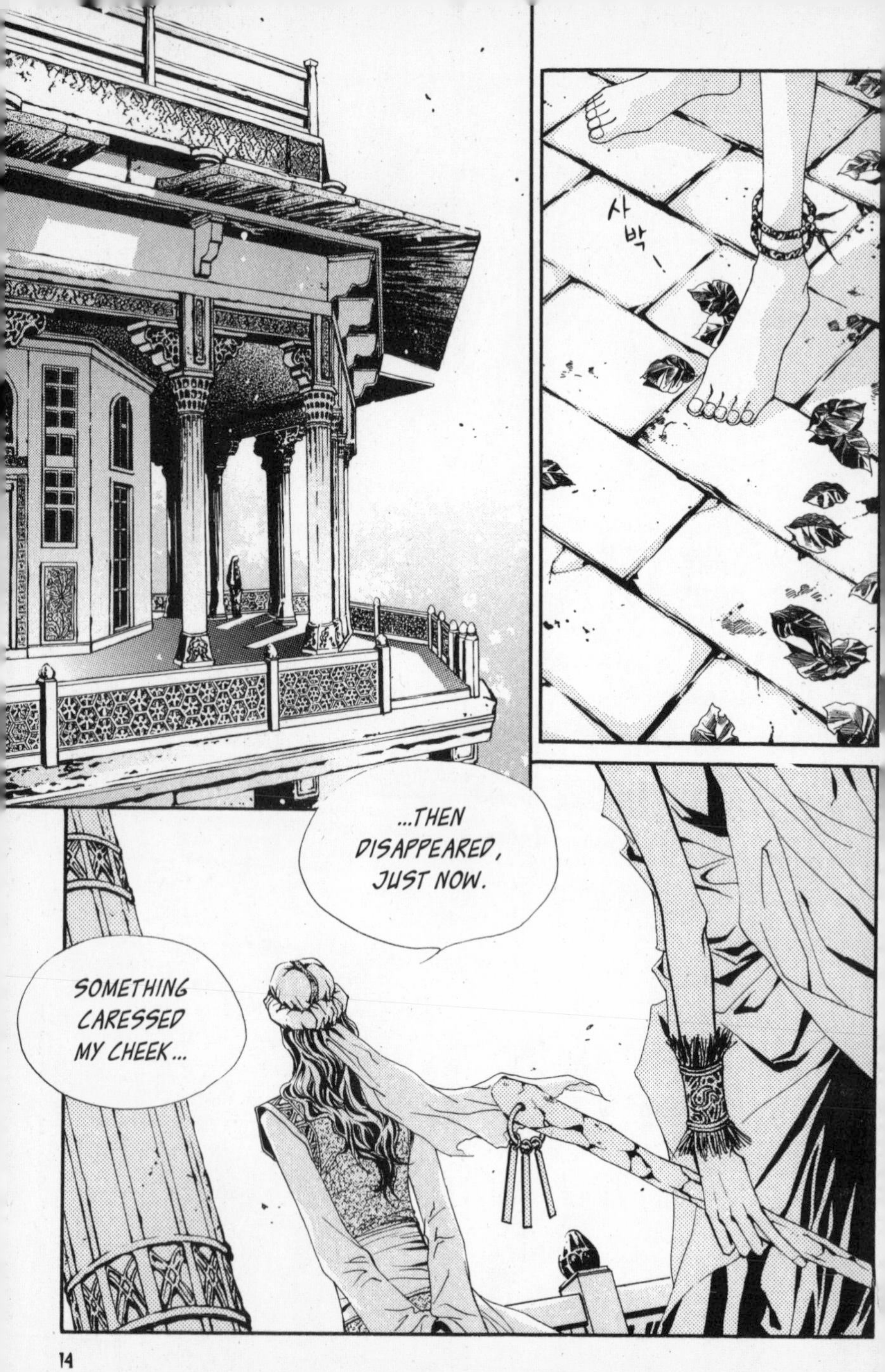
사박
SOMETHING CARESSED MY CHEEK...
...THEN DISAPPEARED, JUST NOW.

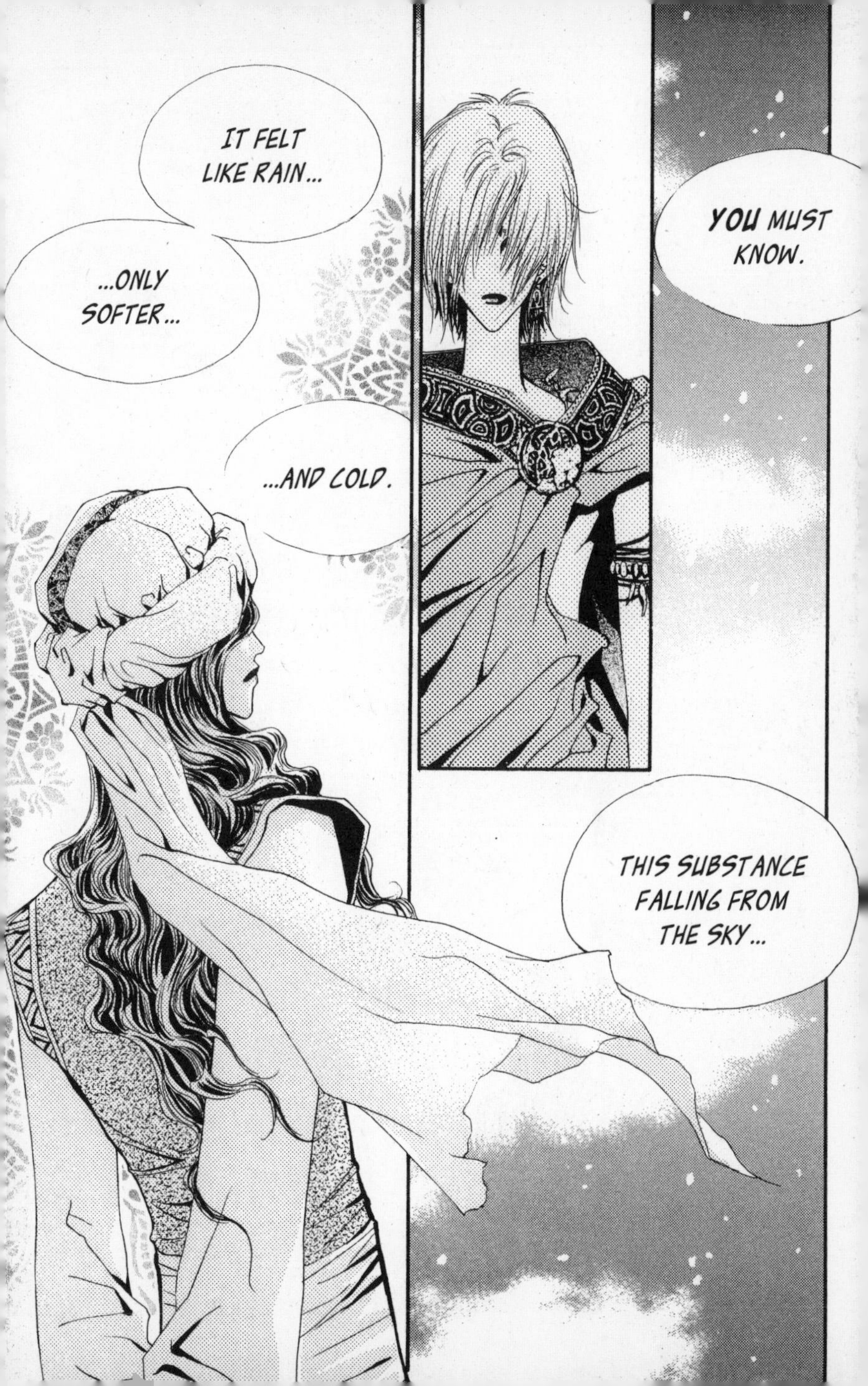
IT FELT LIKE RAIN...
...ONLY SOFTER...
...AND COLD.
YOU MUST KNOW.
THIS SUBSTANCE FALLING FROM THE SKY...

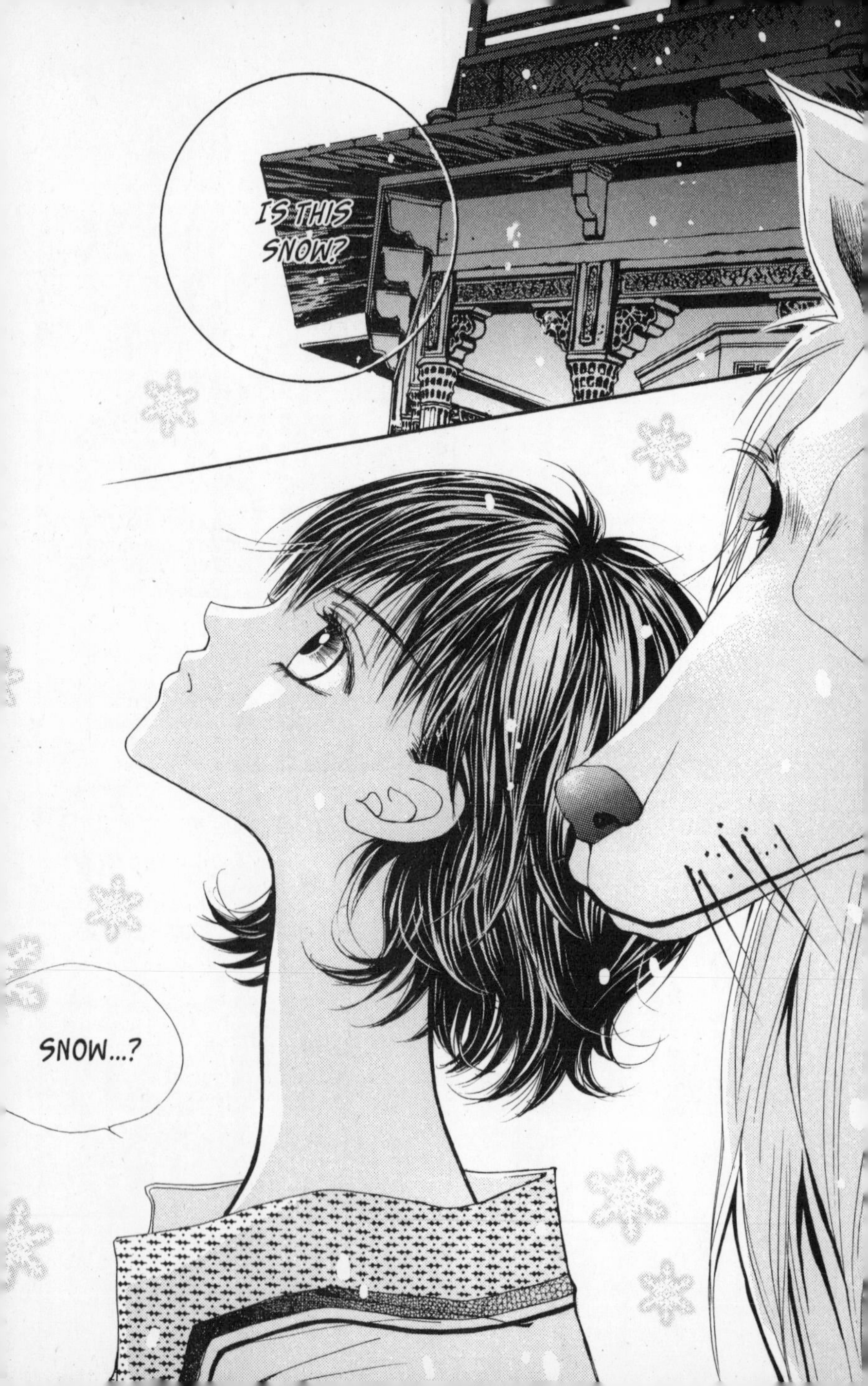
IS THIS SNOW?
SNOW...?

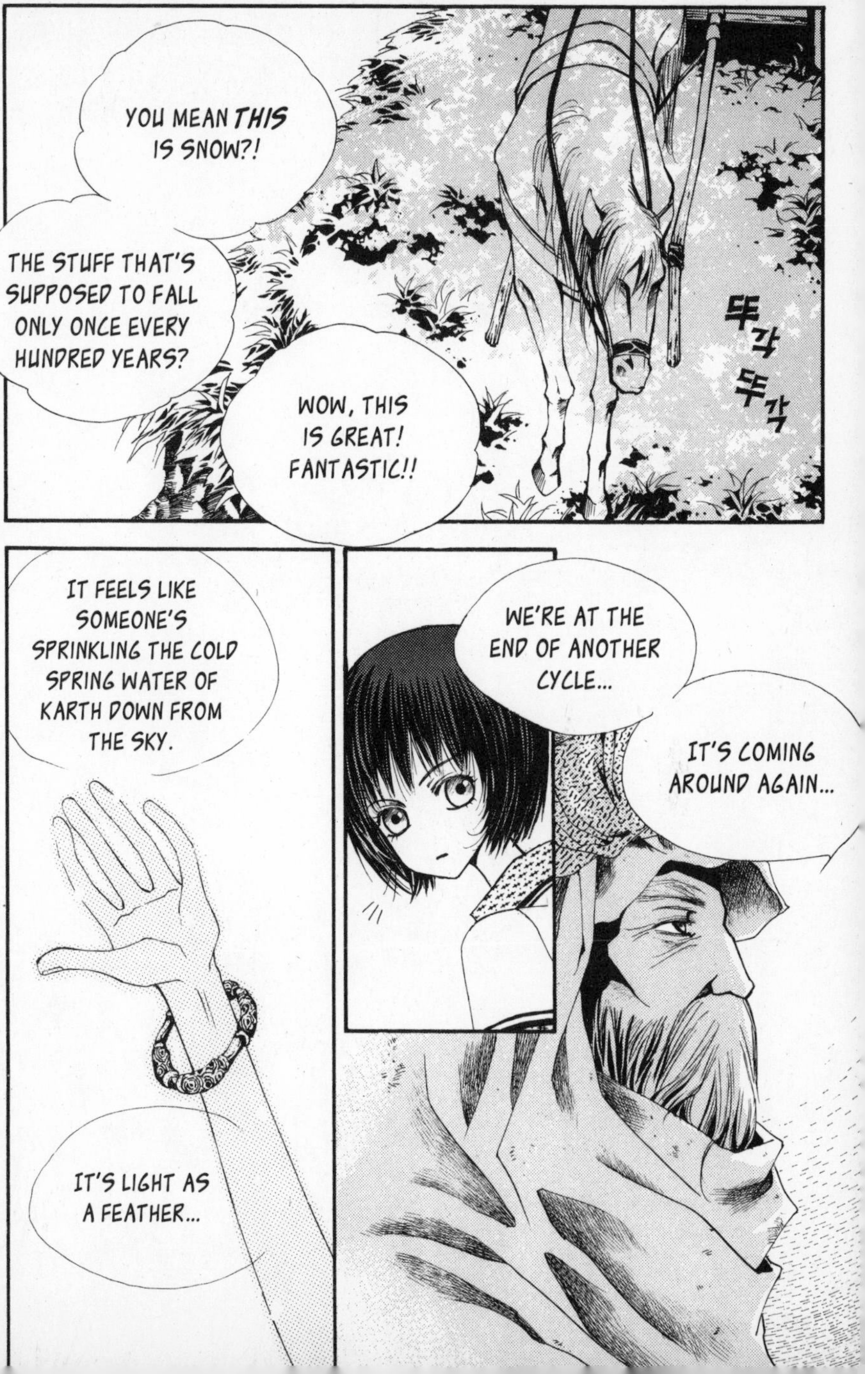
YOU MEAN *THIS* IS SNOW?!
THE STUFF THAT'S SUPPOSED TO FALL ONLY ONCE EVERY HUNDRED YEARS?
WOW, THIS IS GREAT! FANTASTIC!!
뚜각 뚜각
IT FEELS LIKE SOMEONE'S SPRINKLING THE COLD SPRING WATER OF KARTH DOWN FROM THE SKY.
IT'S LIGHT AS A FEATHER...
WE'RE AT THE END OF ANOTHER CYCLE...
IT'S COMING AROUND AGAIN...

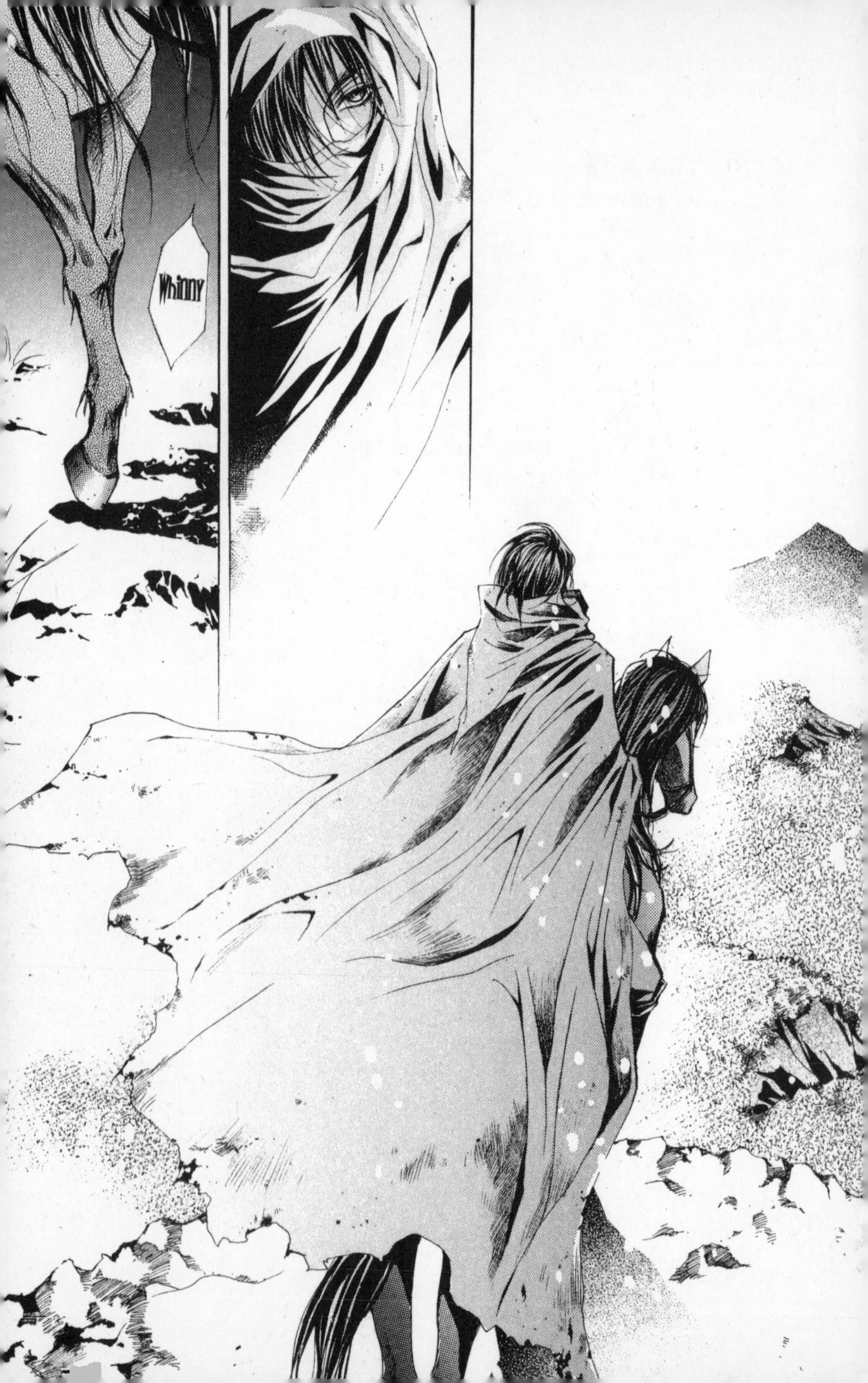
Whinny

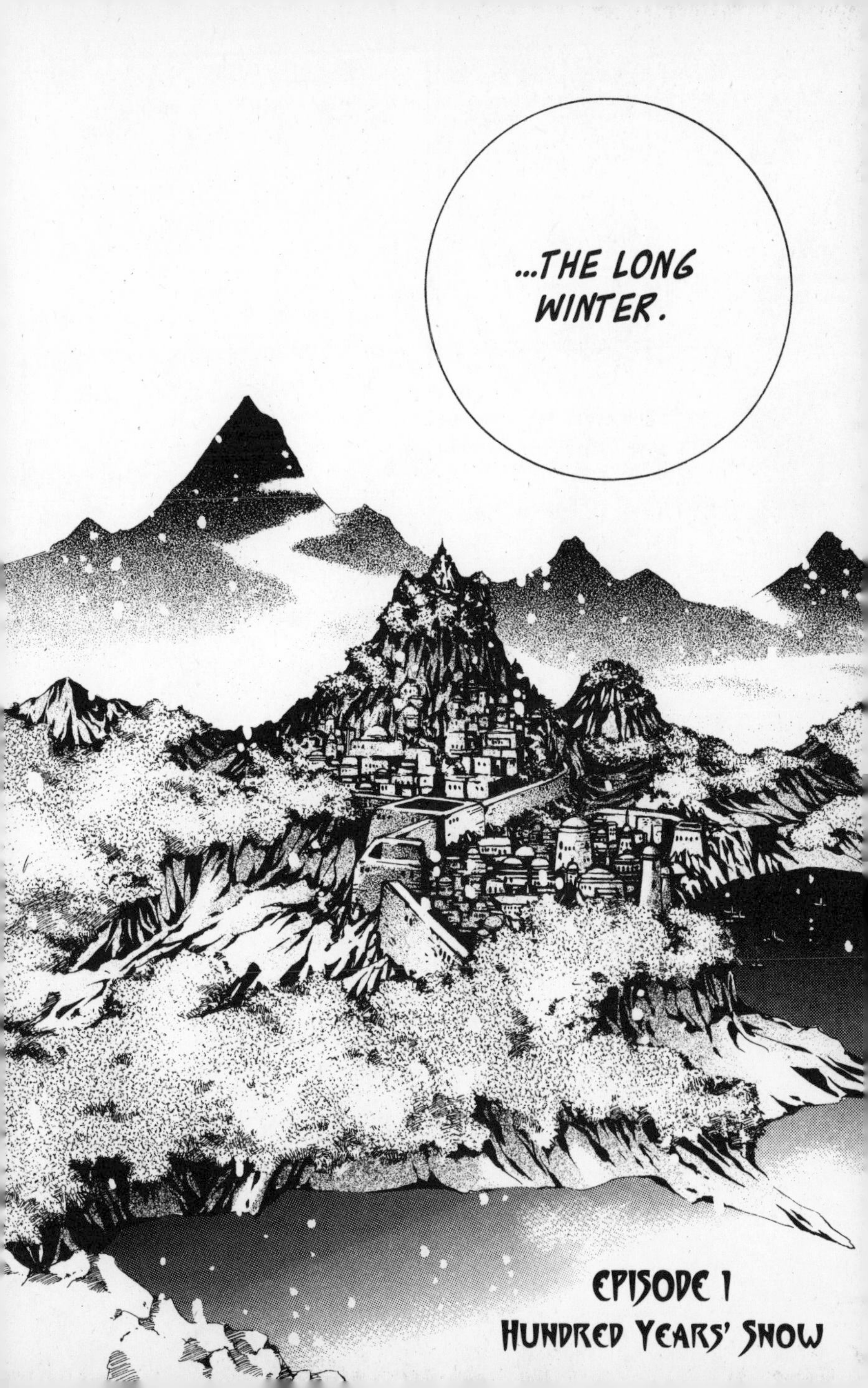
...THE LONG WINTER.
EPISODE 1
HUNDRED YEARS' SNOW

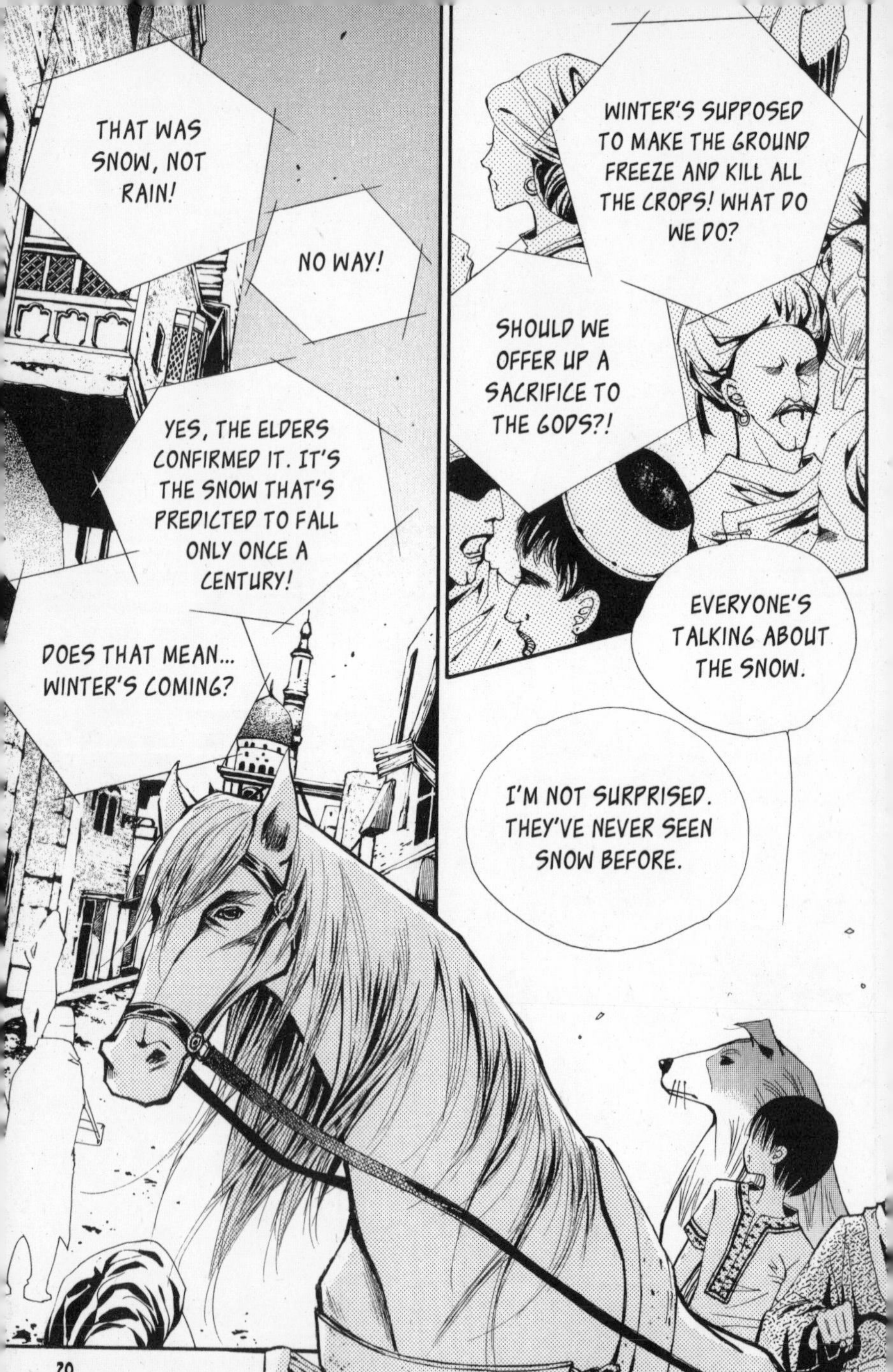
THAT WAS SNOW, NOT RAIN!
NO WAY!
YES, THE ELDERS CONFIRMED IT. IT'S THE SNOW THAT'S PREDICTED TO FALL ONLY ONCE A CENTURY!
DOES THAT MEAN... WINTER'S COMING?
WINTER'S SUPPOSED TO MAKE THE GROUND FREEZE AND KILL ALL THE CROPS! WHAT DO WE DO?
SHOULD WE OFFER UP A SACRIFICE TO THE GODS?!
EVERYONE'S TALKING ABOUT THE SNOW.
I'M NOT SURPRISED. THEY'VE NEVER SEEN SNOW BEFORE.

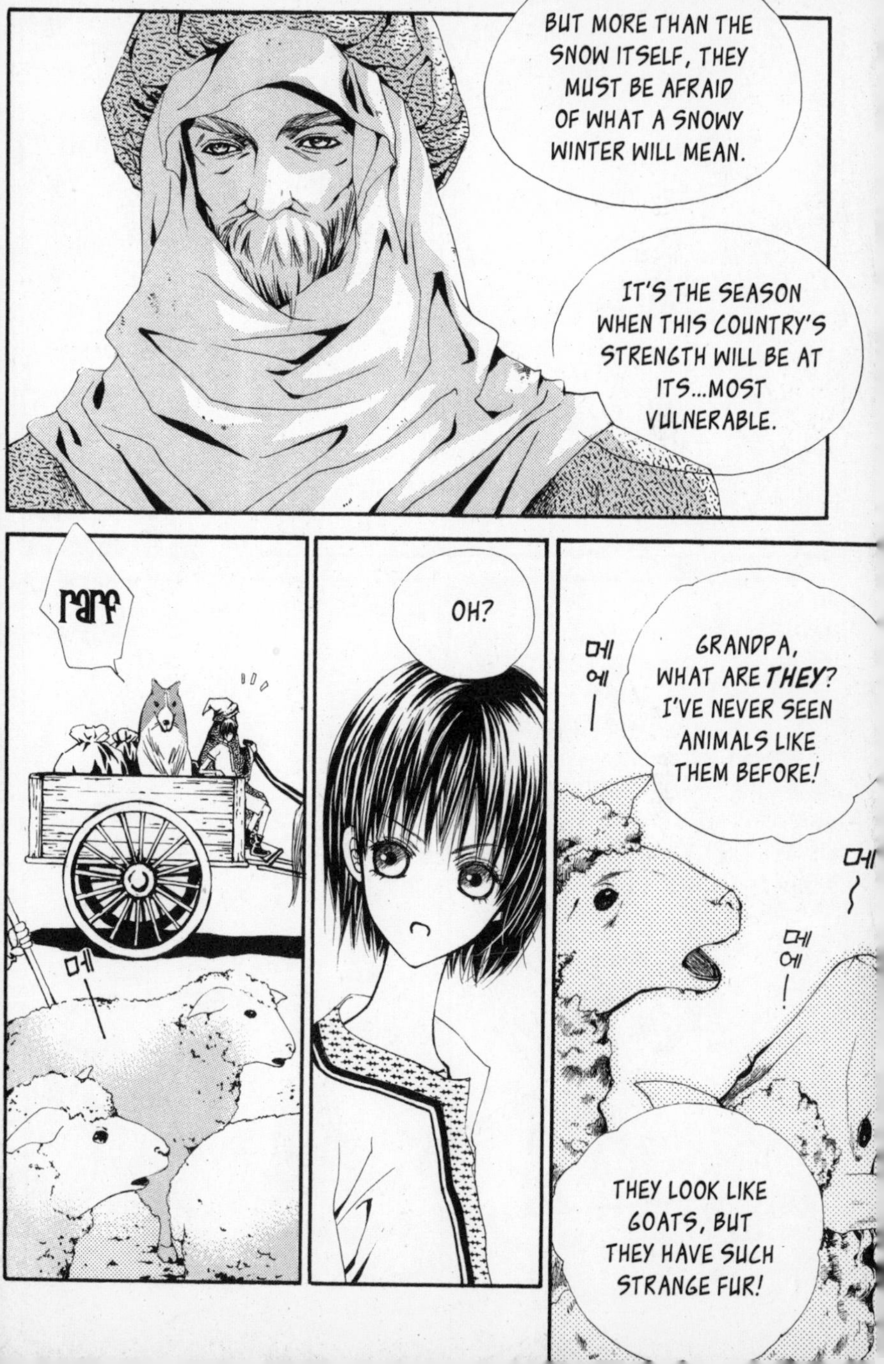
BUT MORE THAN THE SNOW ITSELF, THEY MUST BE AFRAID OF WHAT A SNOWY WINTER WILL MEAN.
IT'S THE SEASON WHEN THIS COUNTRY'S STRENGTH WILL BE AT ITS...MOST VULNERABLE.
rarf
매 |
OH?
매에 |
GRANDPA, WHAT ARE *THEY*? I'VE NEVER SEEN ANIMALS LIKE THEM BEFORE!
매 ~
매에 !
THEY LOOK LIKE GOATS, BUT THEY HAVE SUCH STRANGE FUR!

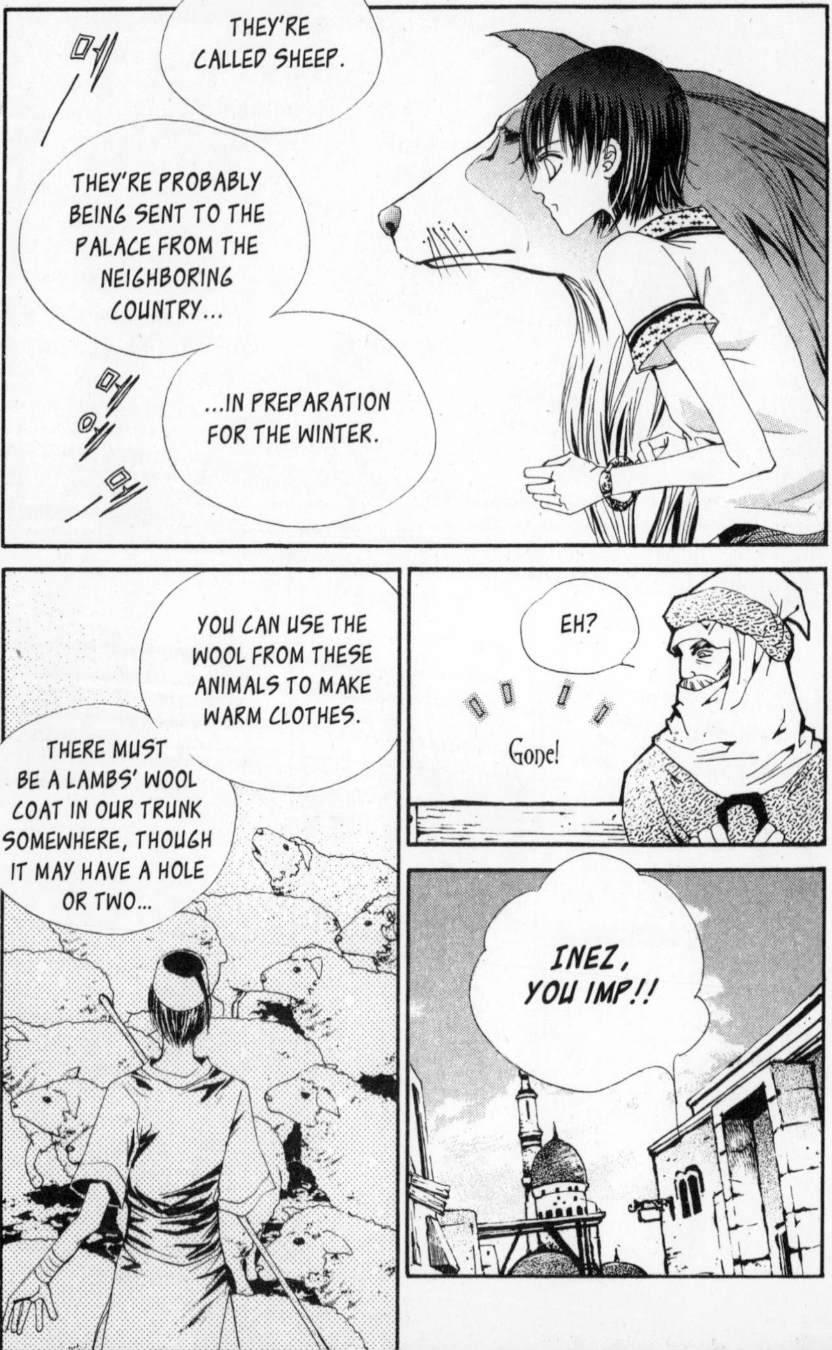
THEY'RE CALLED SHEEP.
메
THEY'RE PROBABLY BEING SENT TO THE PALACE FROM THE NEIGHBORING COUNTRY...
...IN PREPARATION FOR THE WINTER.
메에
메
YOU CAN USE THE WOOL FROM THESE ANIMALS TO MAKE WARM CLOTHES.
THERE MUST BE A LAMBS' WOOL COAT IN OUR TRUNK SOMEWHERE, THOUGH IT MAY HAVE A HOLE OR TWO...
EH?
Gone!
INEZ, YOU IMP!!

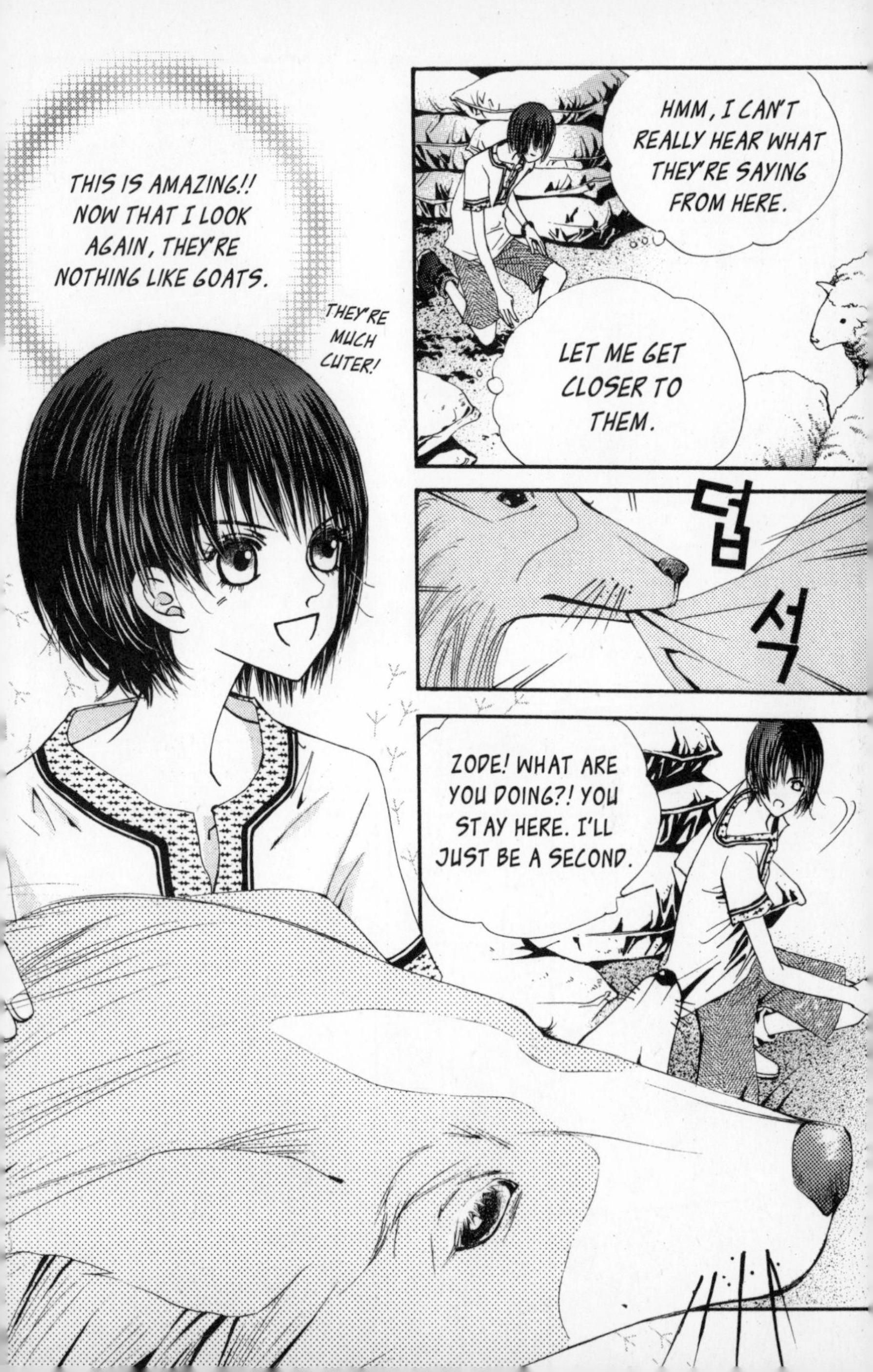
THIS IS AMAZING!! NOW THAT I LOOK AGAIN, THEY'RE NOTHING LIKE GOATS.
THEY'RE MUCH CUTER!
HMM, I CAN'T REALLY HEAR WHAT THEY'RE SAYING FROM HERE.
LET ME GET CLOSER TO THEM.
덥석
ZODE! WHAT ARE YOU DOING?! YOU STAY HERE. I'LL JUST BE A SECOND.

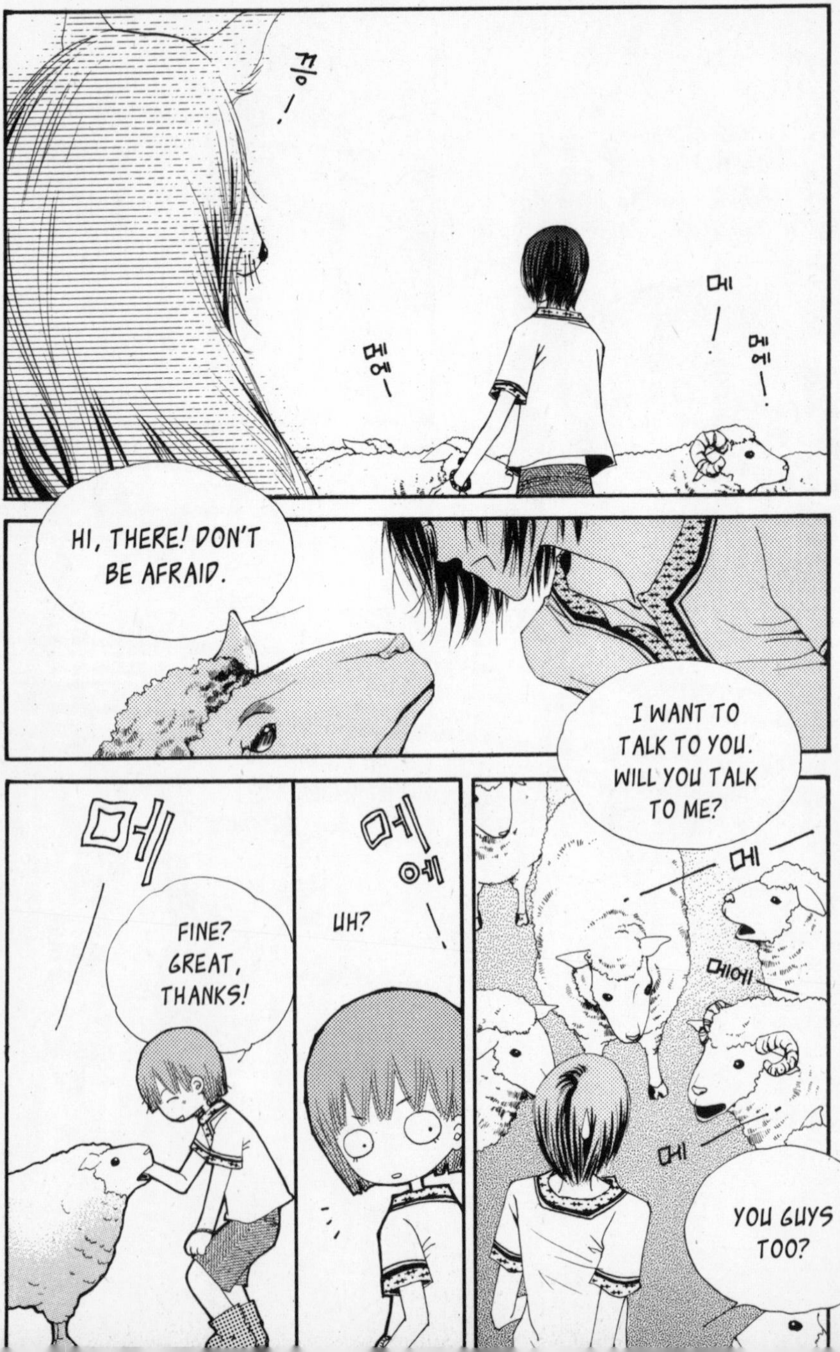
끙-!
메에-
메-!
메에-!
HI, THERE! DON'T BE AFRAID.
I WANT TO TALK TO YOU. WILL YOU TALK TO ME?
메에-
FINE? GREAT, THANKS!
메에-!
UH?
메
메이이
메
YOU GUYS TOO?

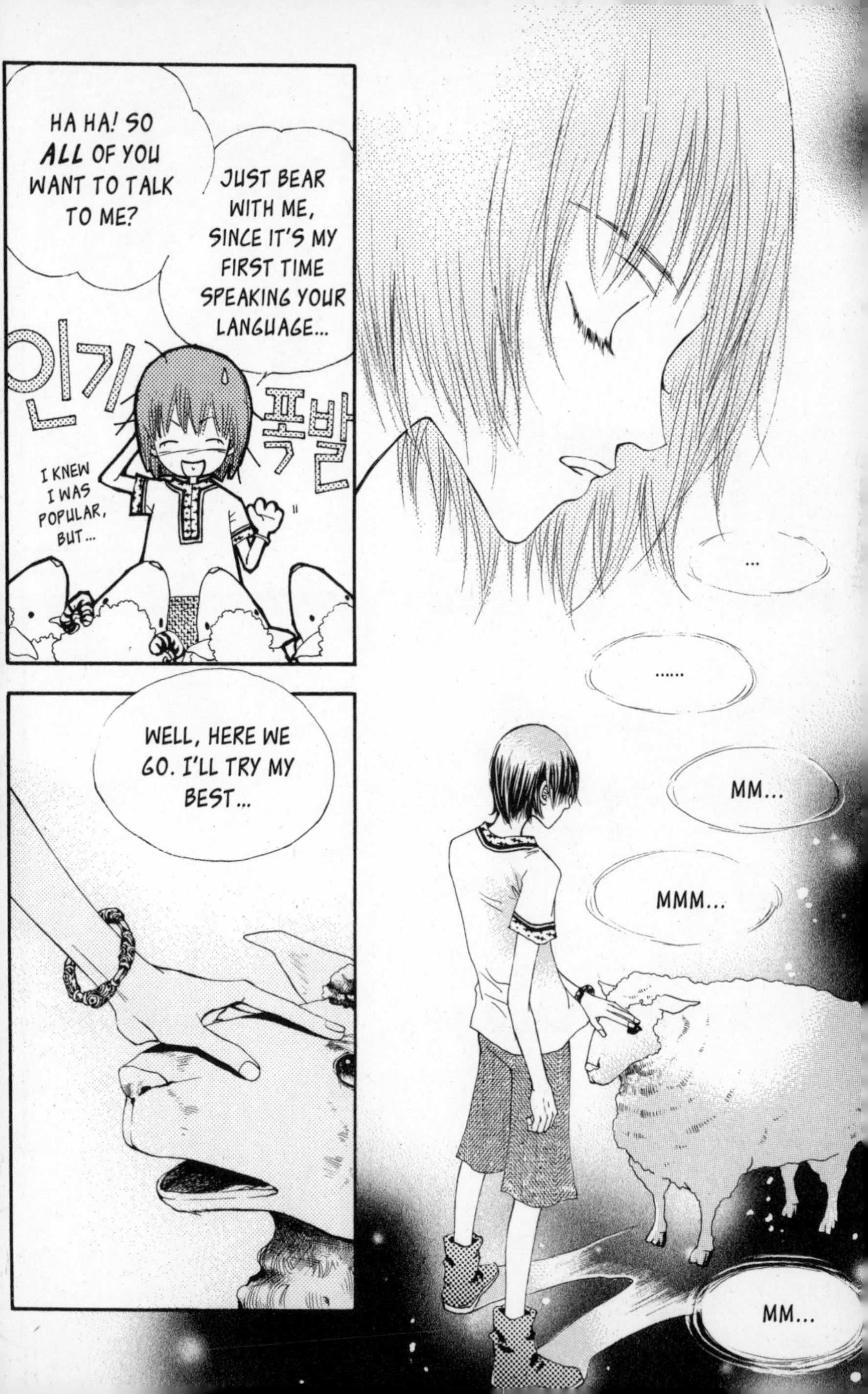
HA HA! SO **ALL** OF YOU WANT TO TALK TO ME?
JUST BEAR WITH ME, SINCE IT'S MY FIRST TIME SPEAKING YOUR LANGUAGE...
인기 폭발
I KNEW I WAS POPULAR, BUT...
WELL, HERE WE GO. I'LL TRY MY BEST...
...
......
MM...
MMM...
MM...

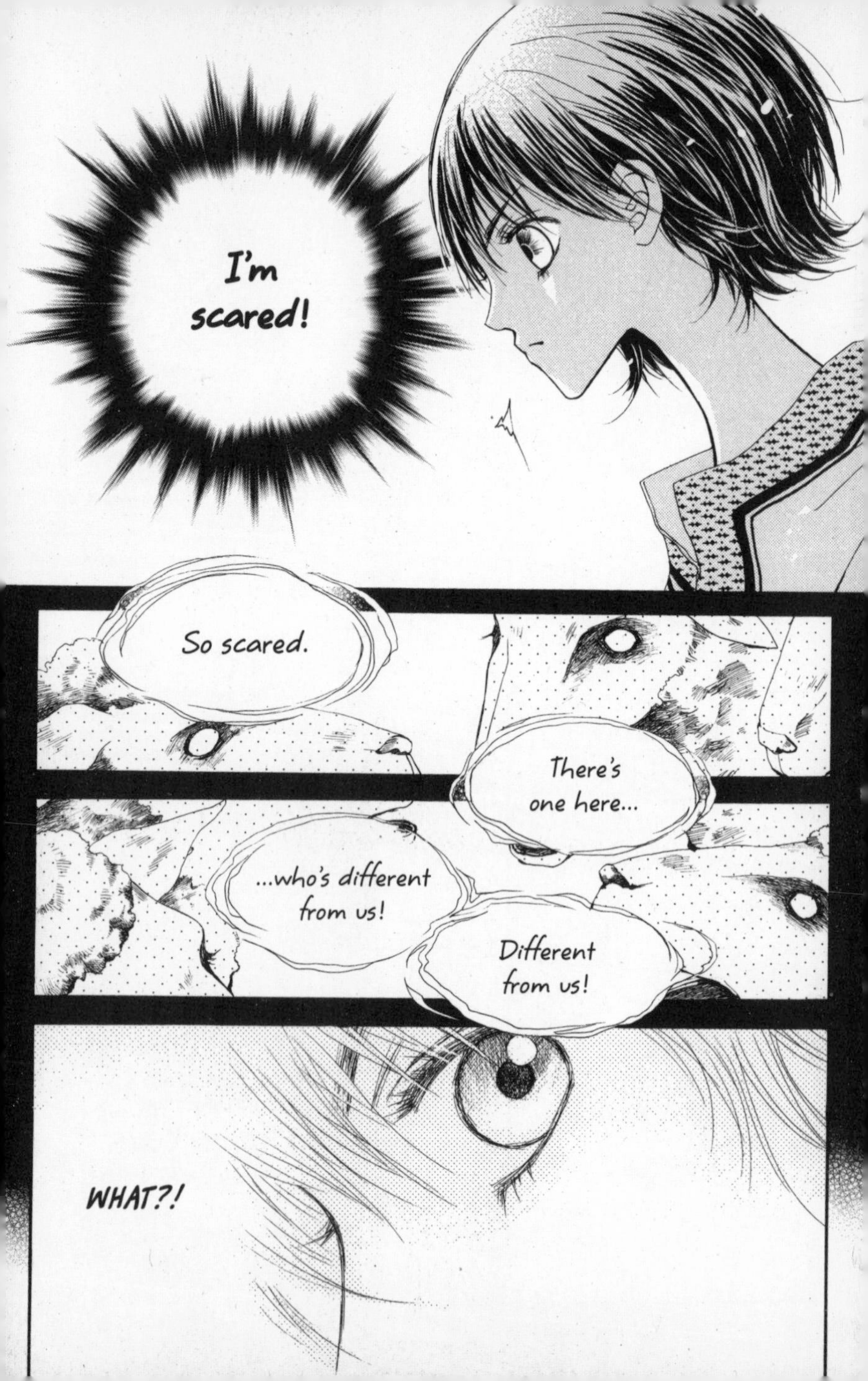
I'm scared!
So scared.
There's one here...
...who's different from us!
Different from us!
WHAT?!

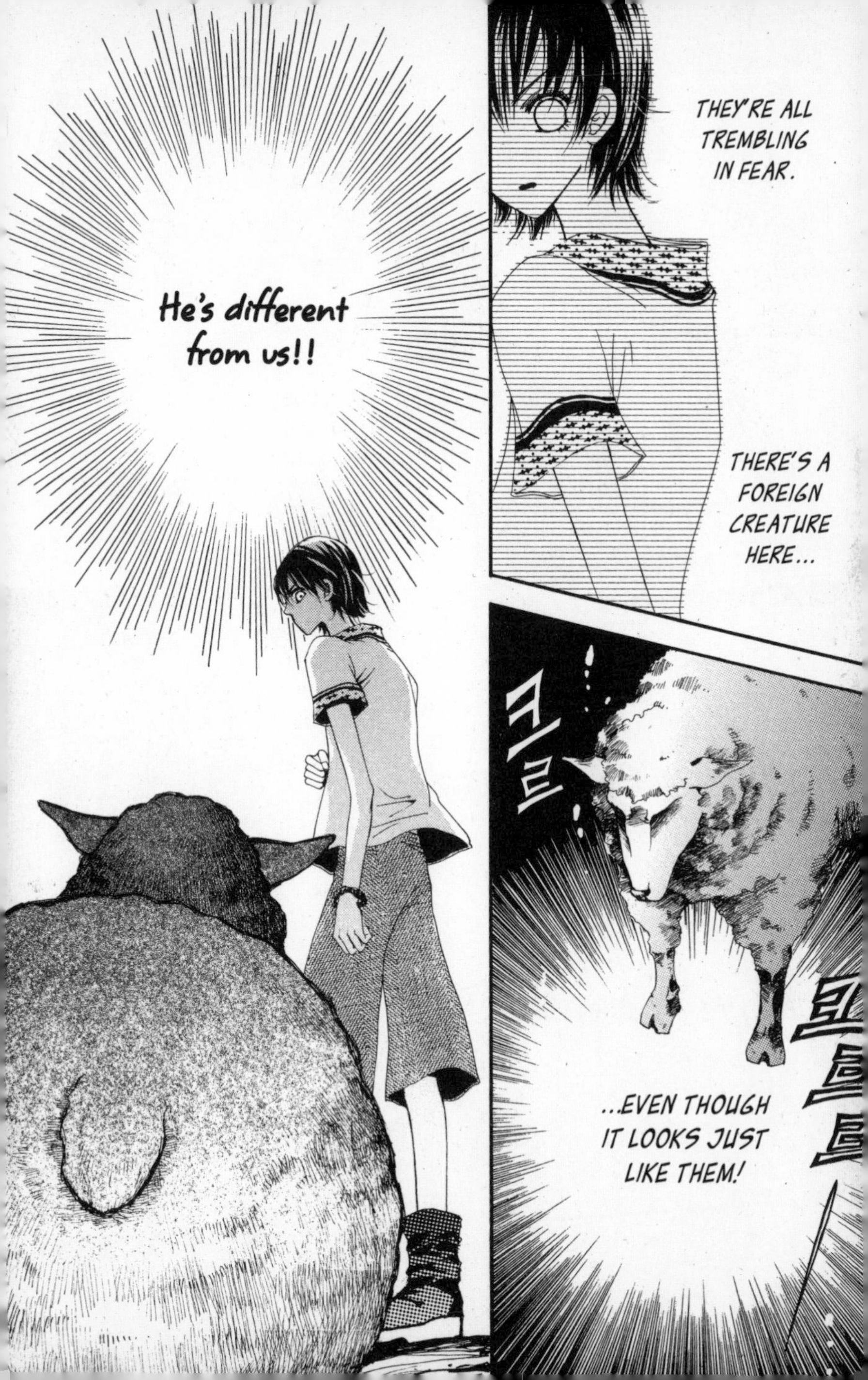
He's different from us!!
THEY'RE ALL TREMBLING IN FEAR.
THERE'S A FOREIGN CREATURE HERE...
...EVEN THOUGH IT LOOKS JUST LIKE THEM!

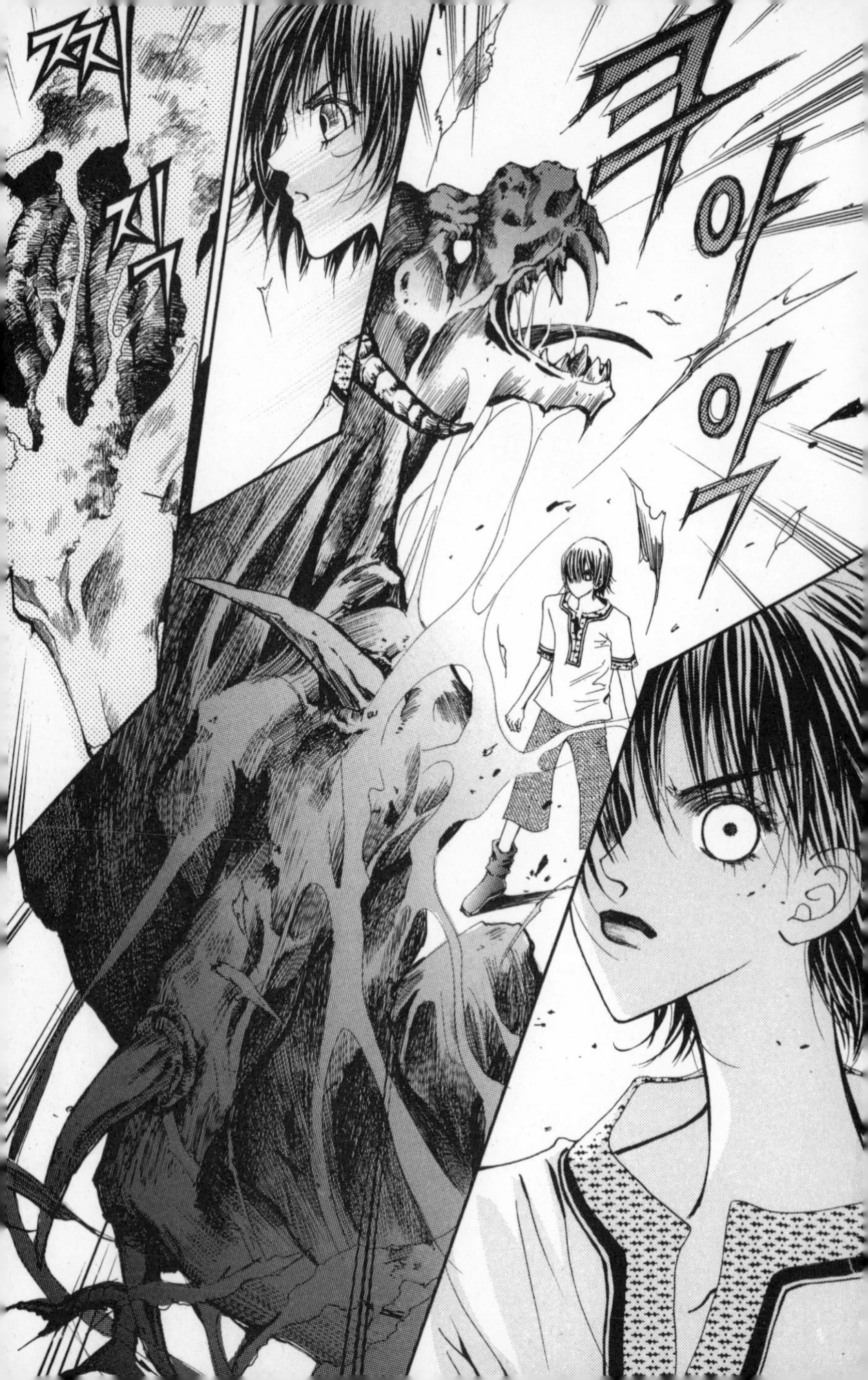
쿠아악

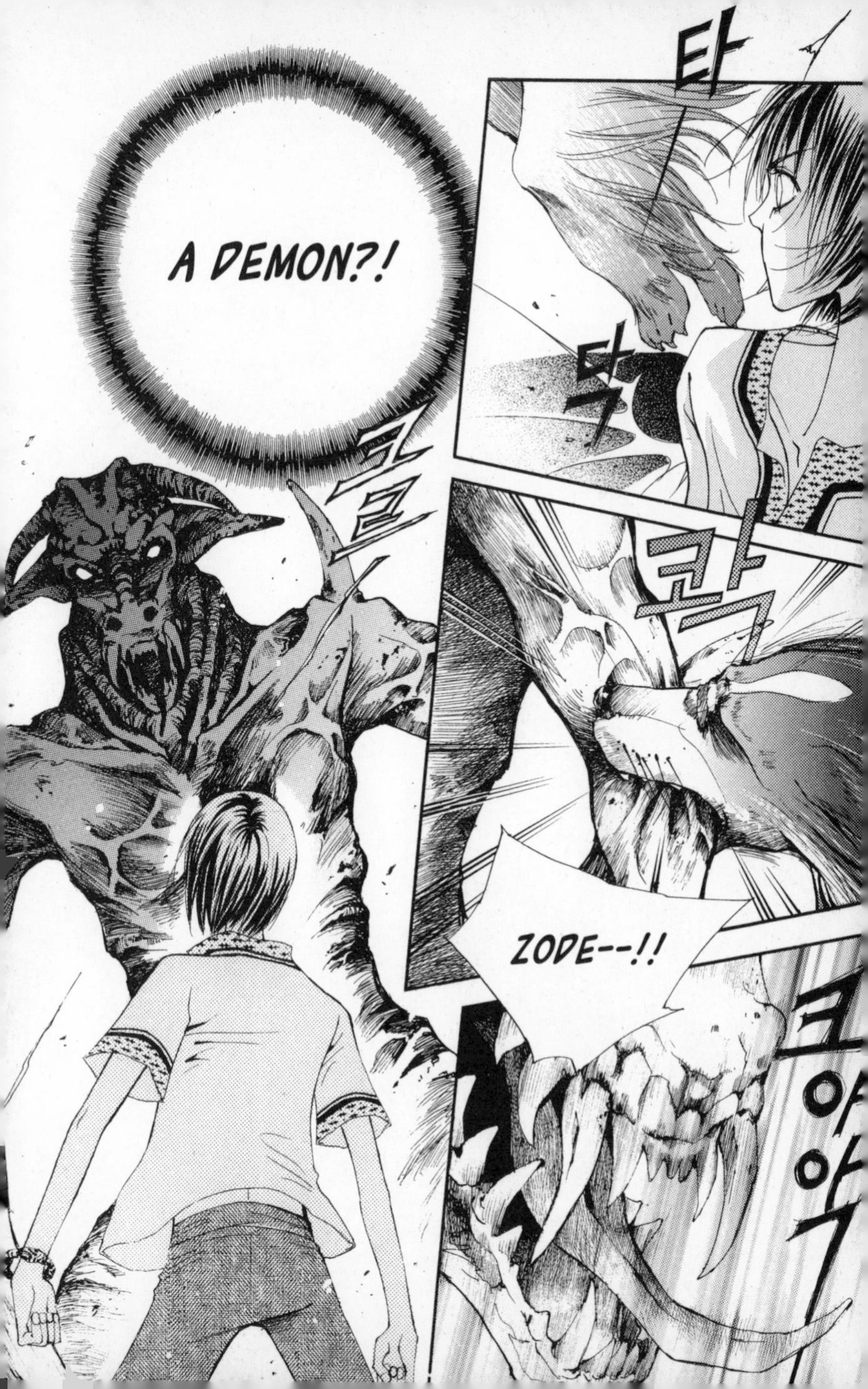
A DEMON?!
타
닥
콱
ZODE--!!
크아아악

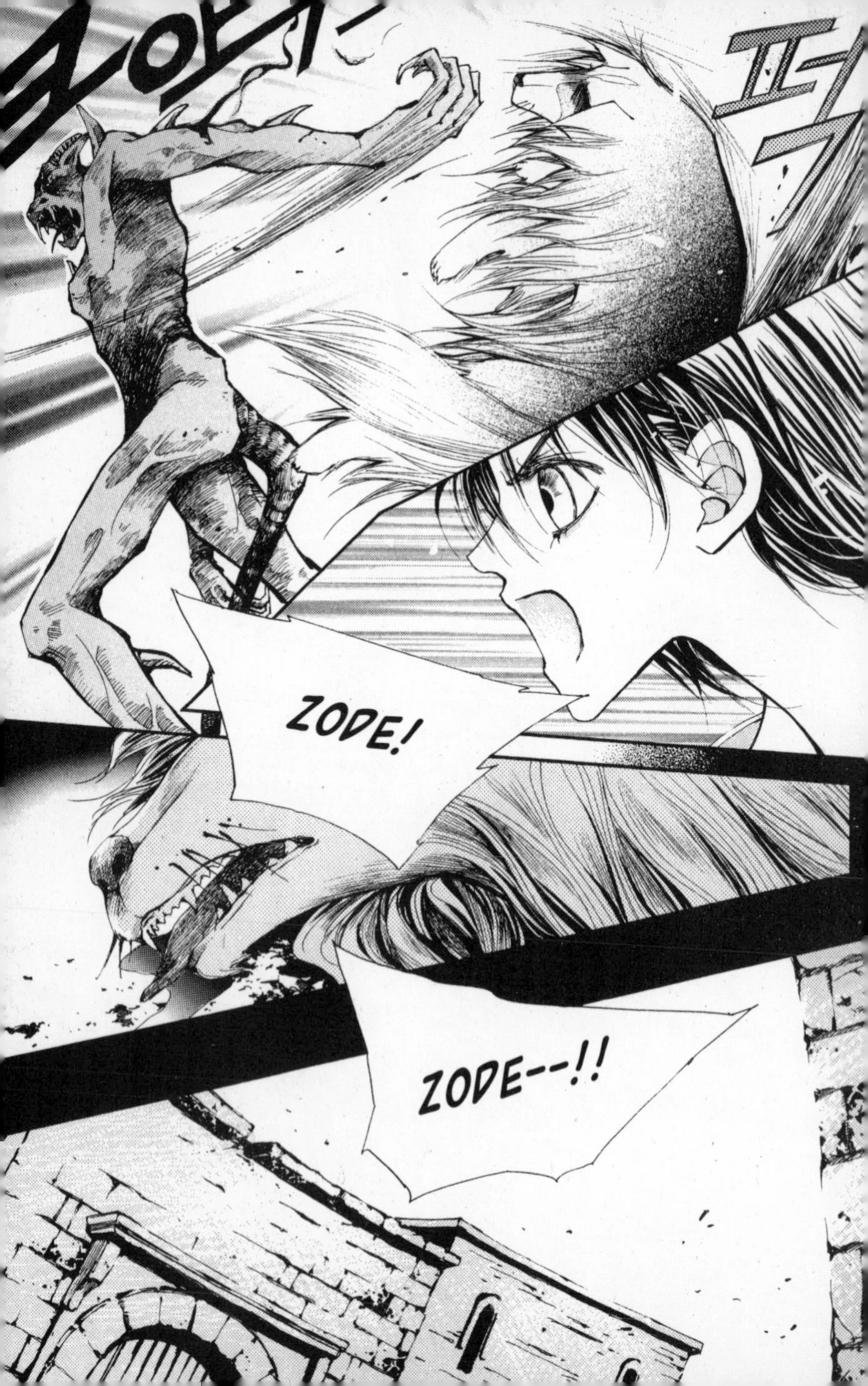
ZODE!
ZODE--!!

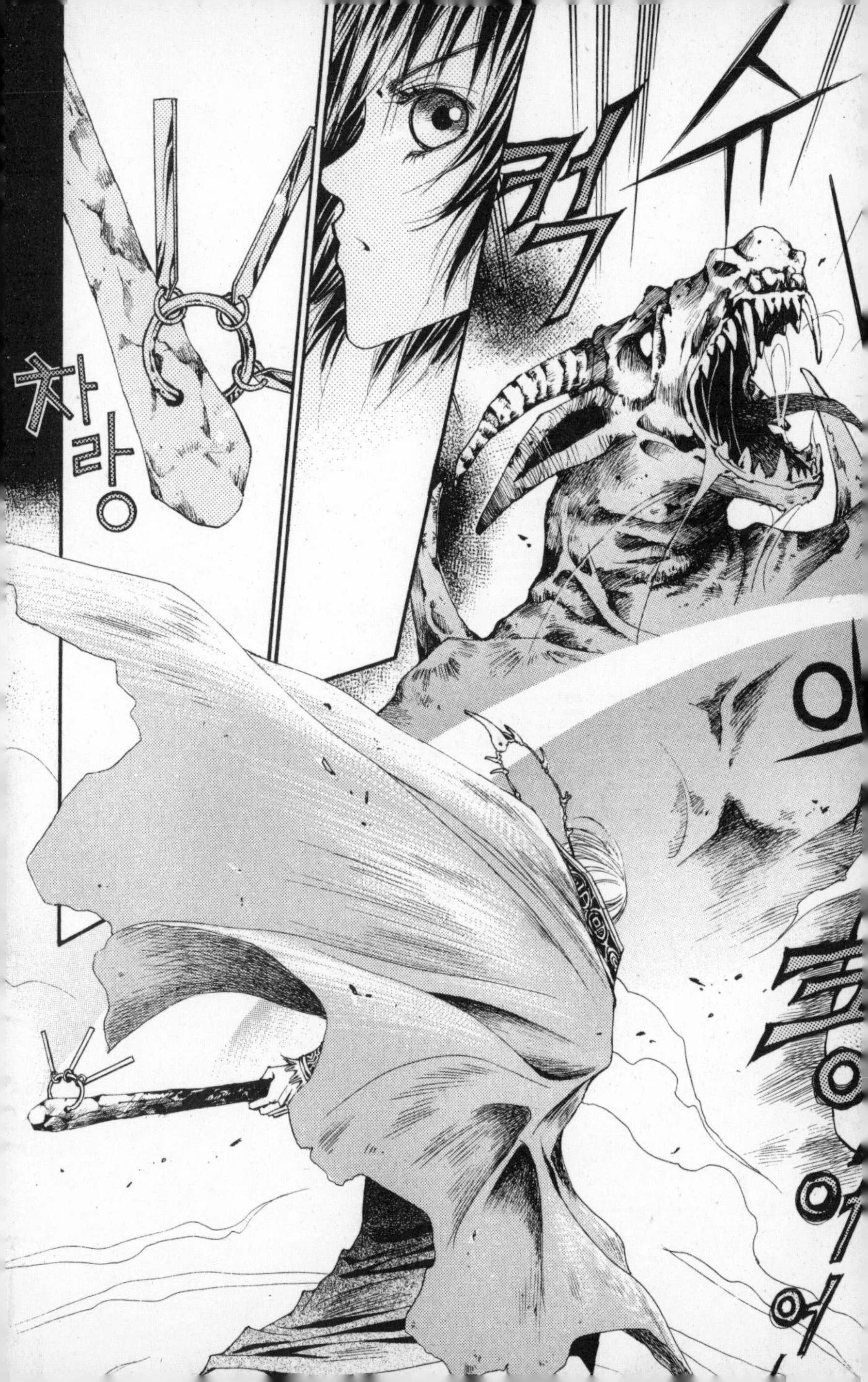
차랑

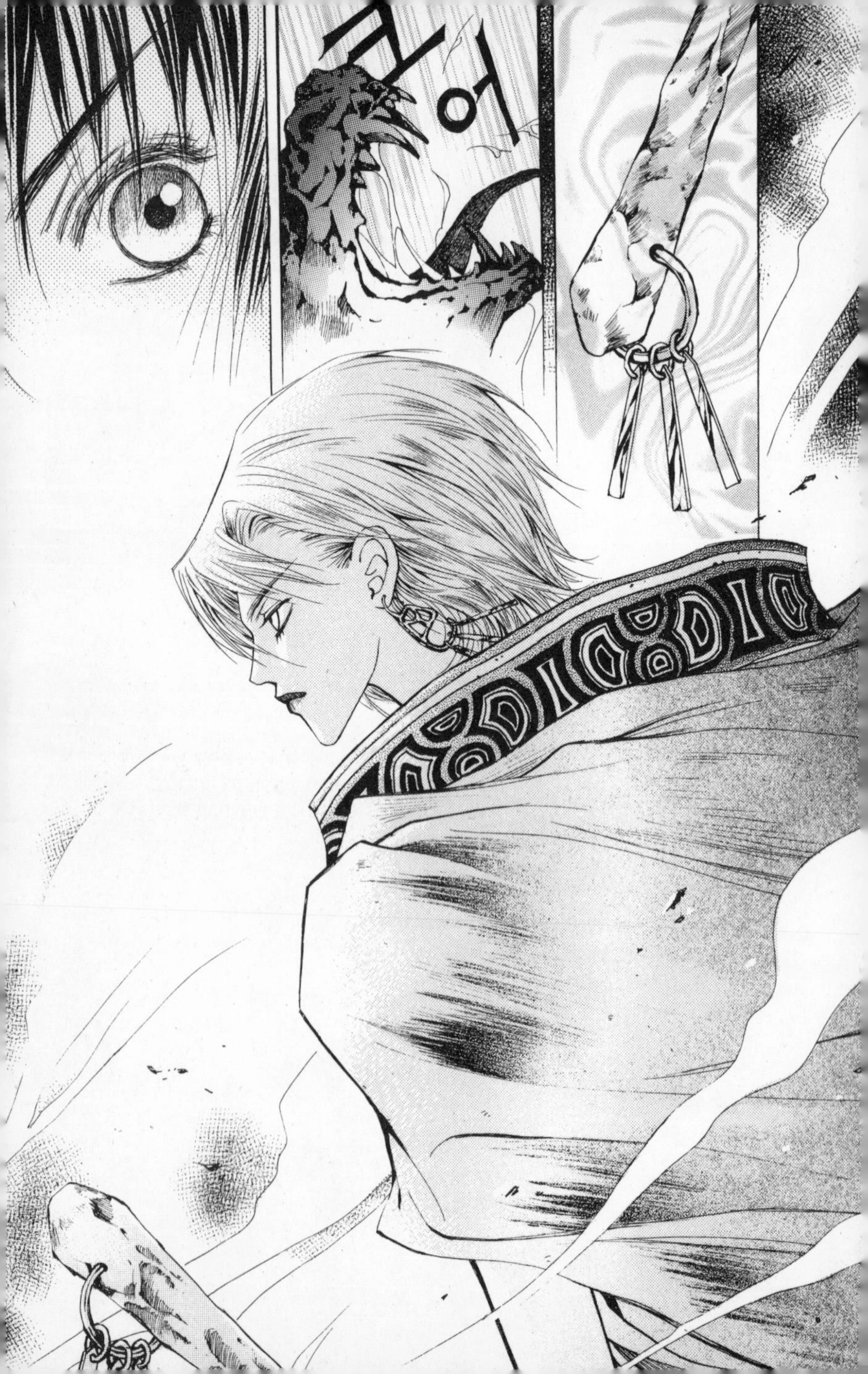
크아

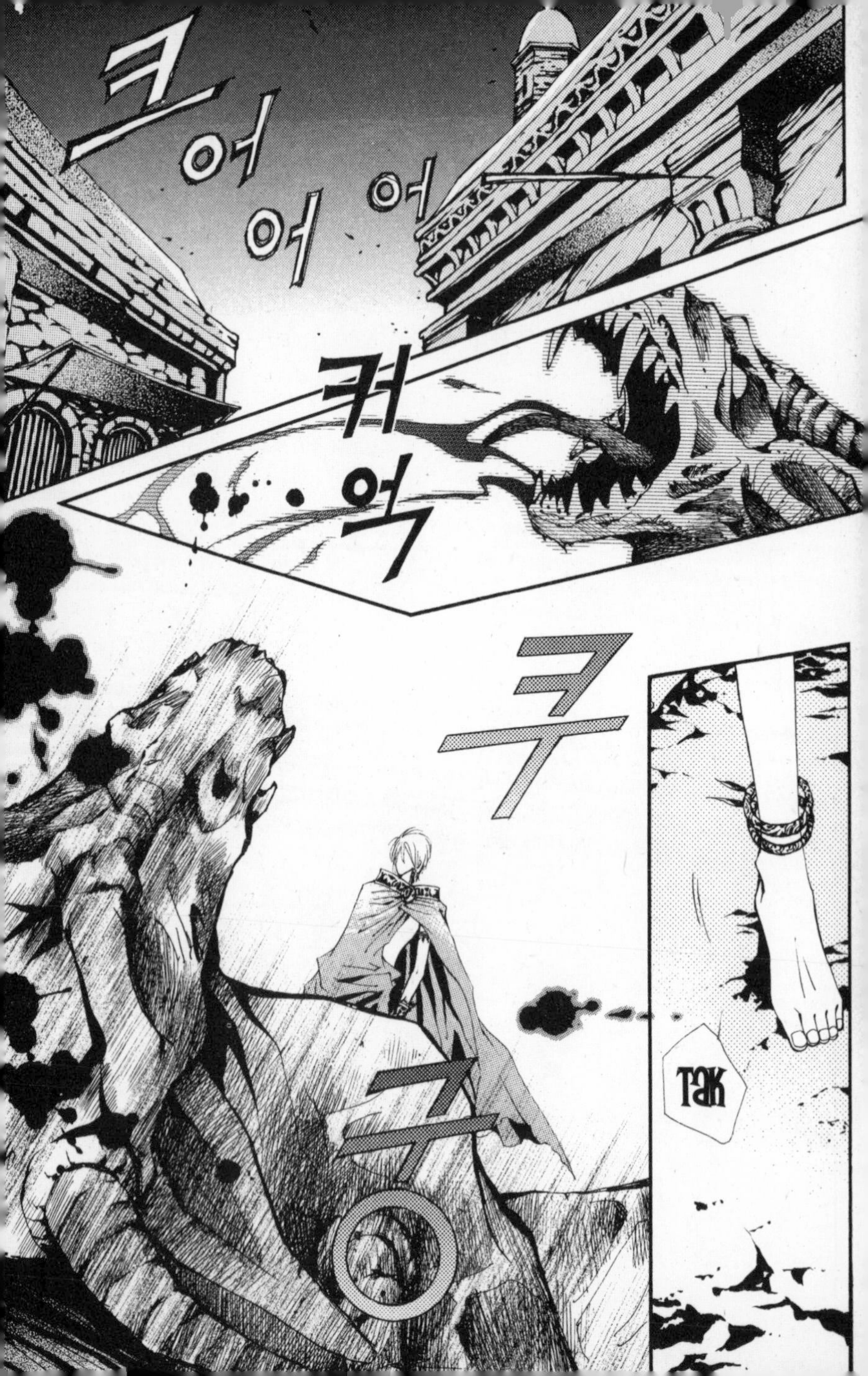
크어어어
커억
쿠
쿵
TAK

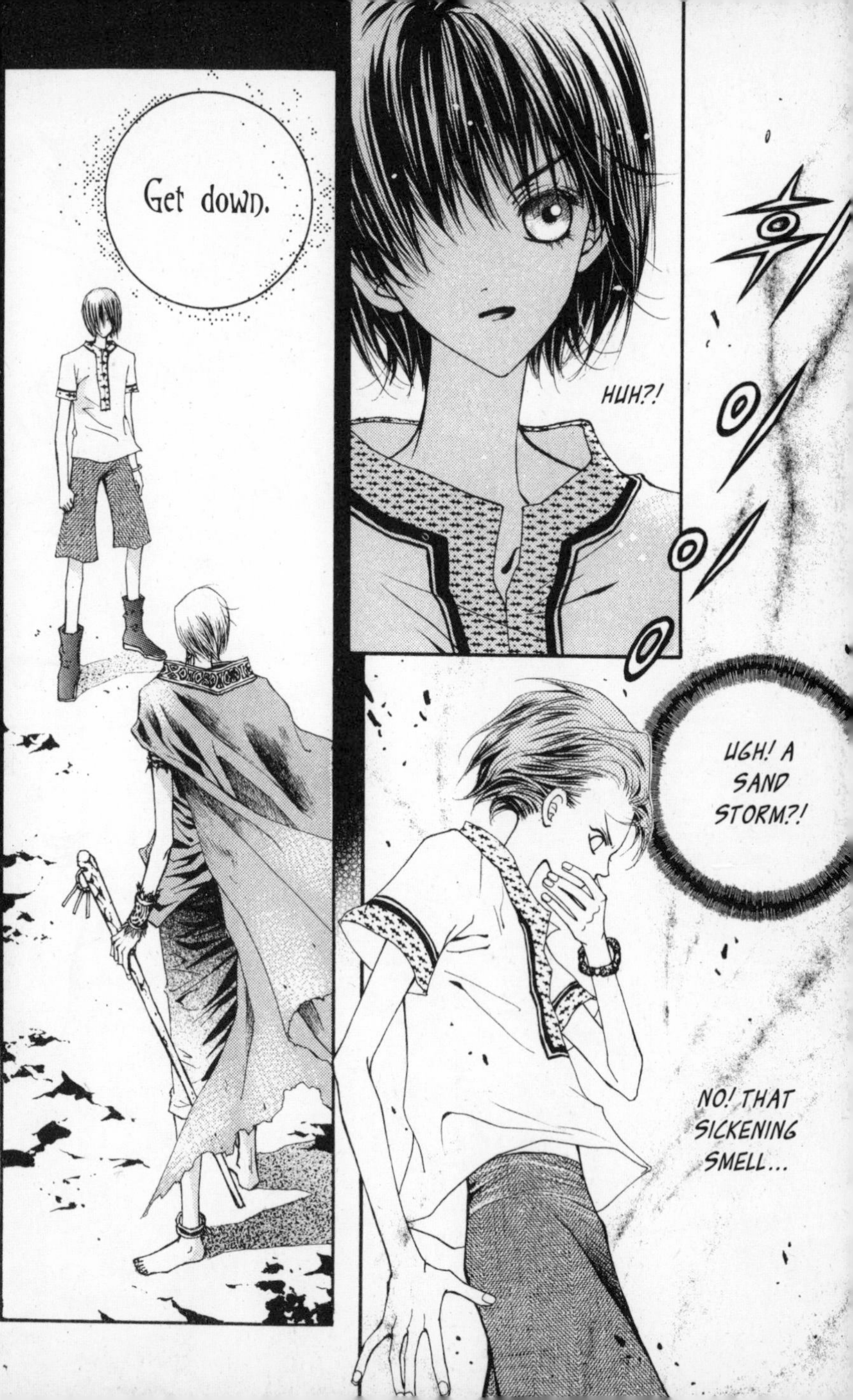
Get down.
HUH?!
UGH! A SAND STORM?!
NO! THAT SICKENING SMELL...

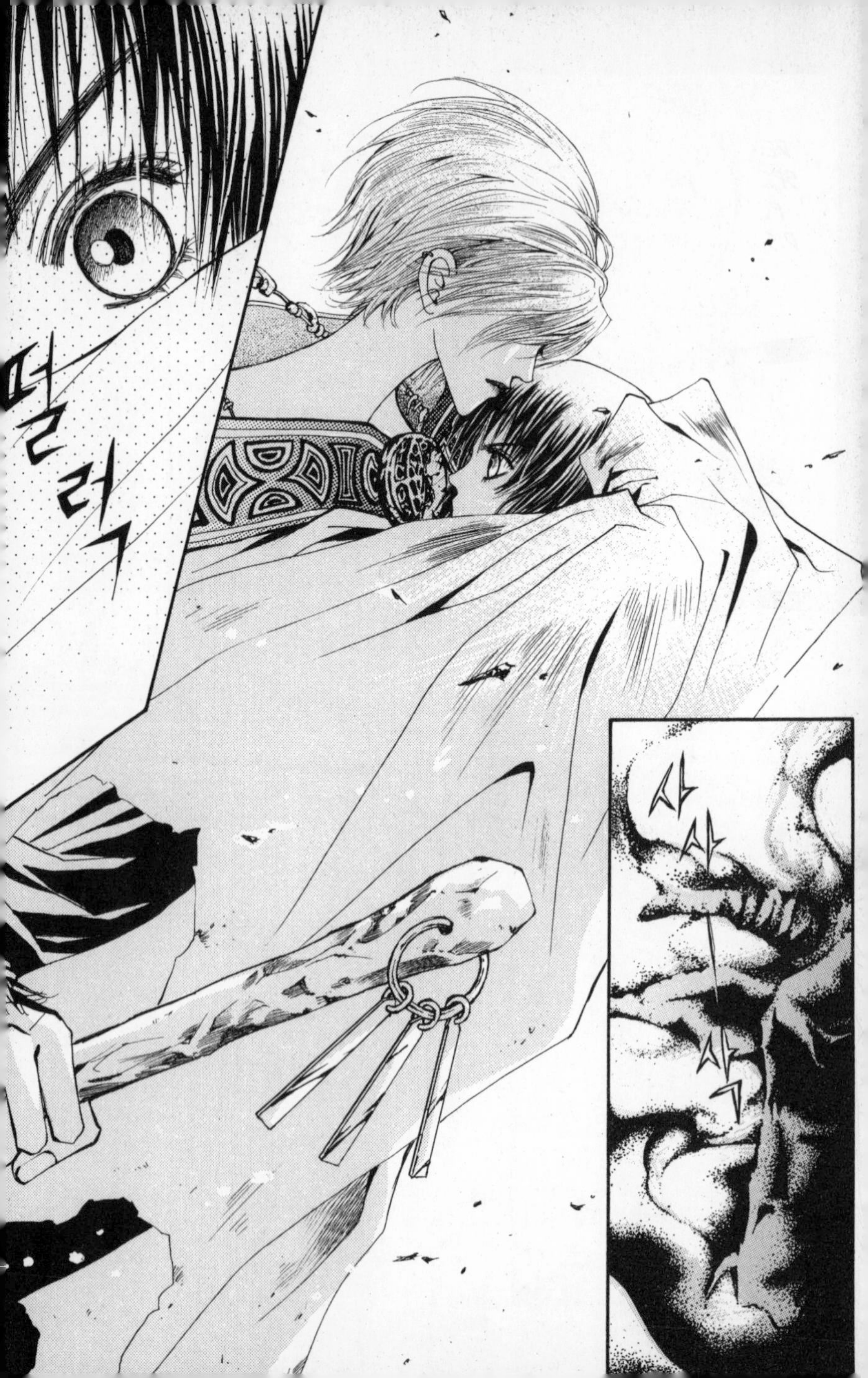
펄럭
사사삭

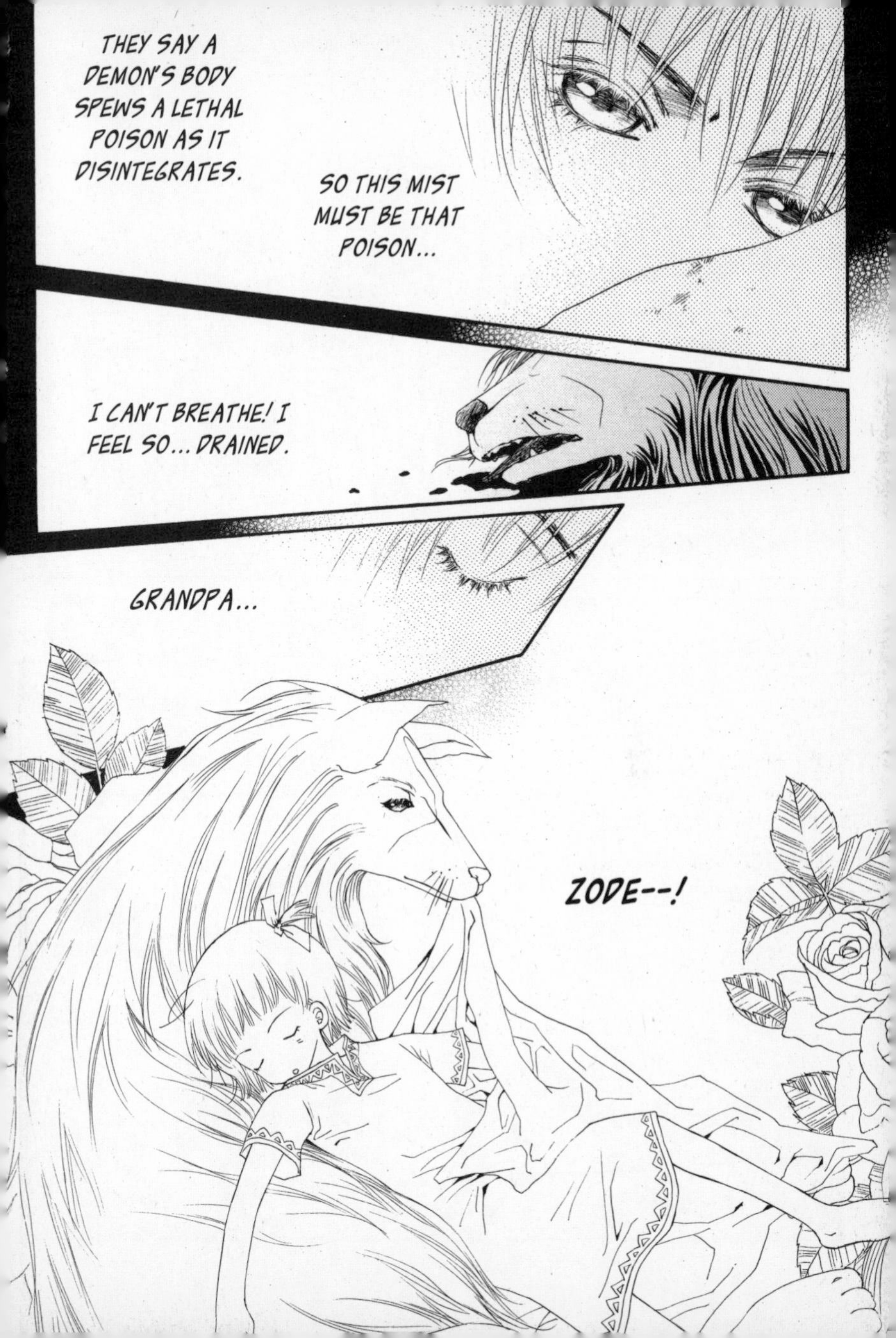
THEY SAY A DEMON'S BODY SPEWS A LETHAL POISON AS IT DISINTEGRATES.
SO THIS MIST MUST BE THAT POISON...
I CAN'T BREATHE! I FEEL SO... DRAINED.
GRANDPA...
ZODE--!

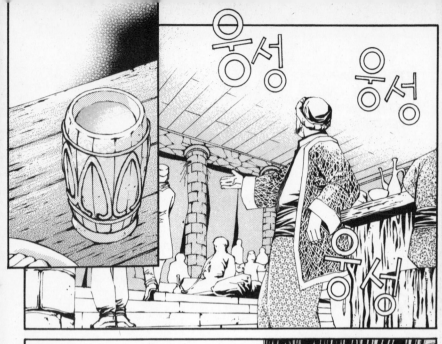

WHAT A RUCKUS.

THE TOWN'S IN AN UPROAR BECAUSE A DEMON HAS APPEARED.

DEMON?

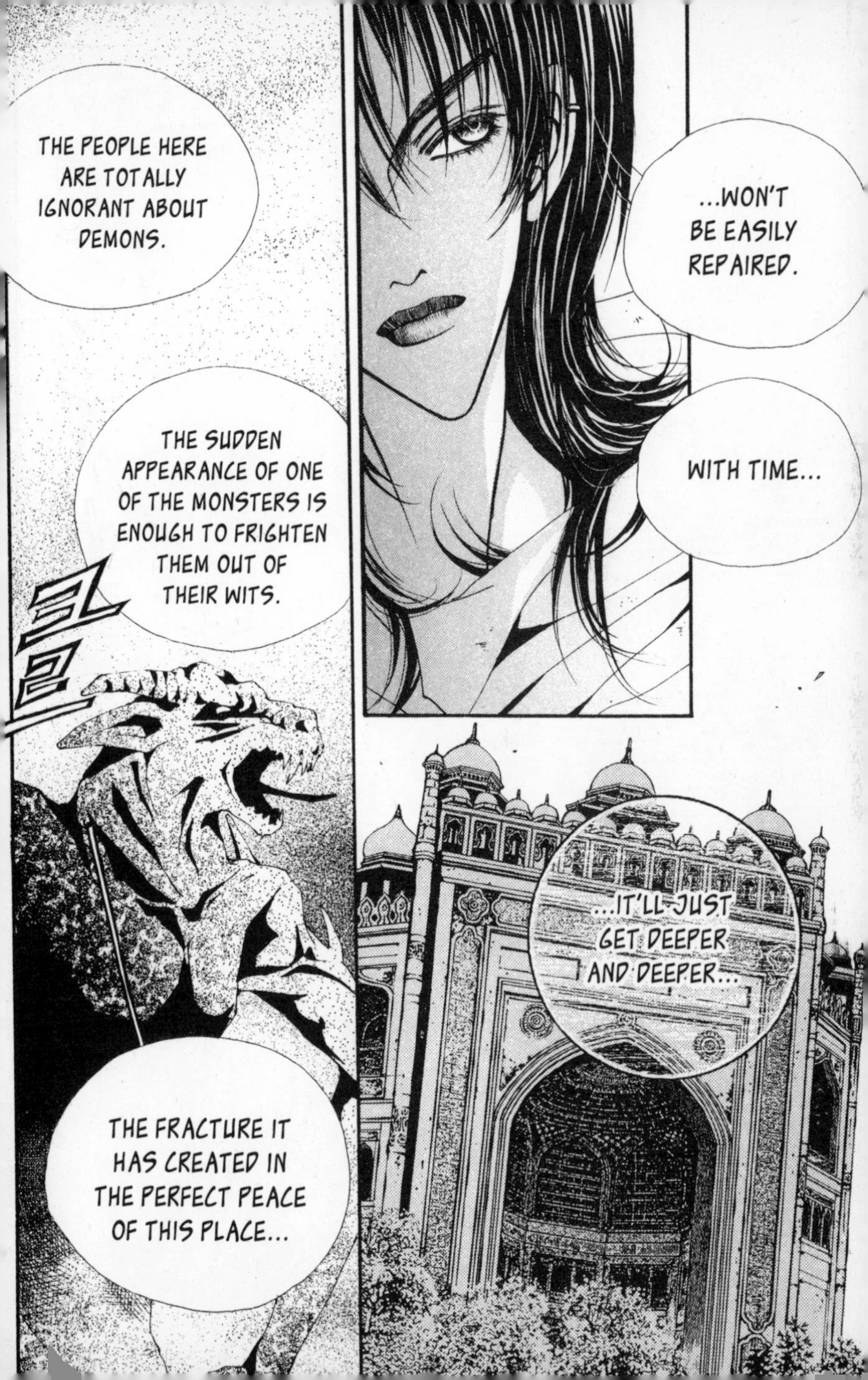
THE PEOPLE HERE ARE TOTALLY IGNORANT ABOUT DEMONS.
THE SUDDEN APPEARANCE OF ONE OF THE MONSTERS IS ENOUGH TO FRIGHTEN THEM OUT OF THEIR WITS.
크르
THE FRACTURE IT HAS CREATED IN THE PERFECT PEACE OF THIS PLACE...
...WON'T BE EASILY REPAIRED.
WITH TIME...
...IT'LL JUST GET DEEPER AND DEEPER...

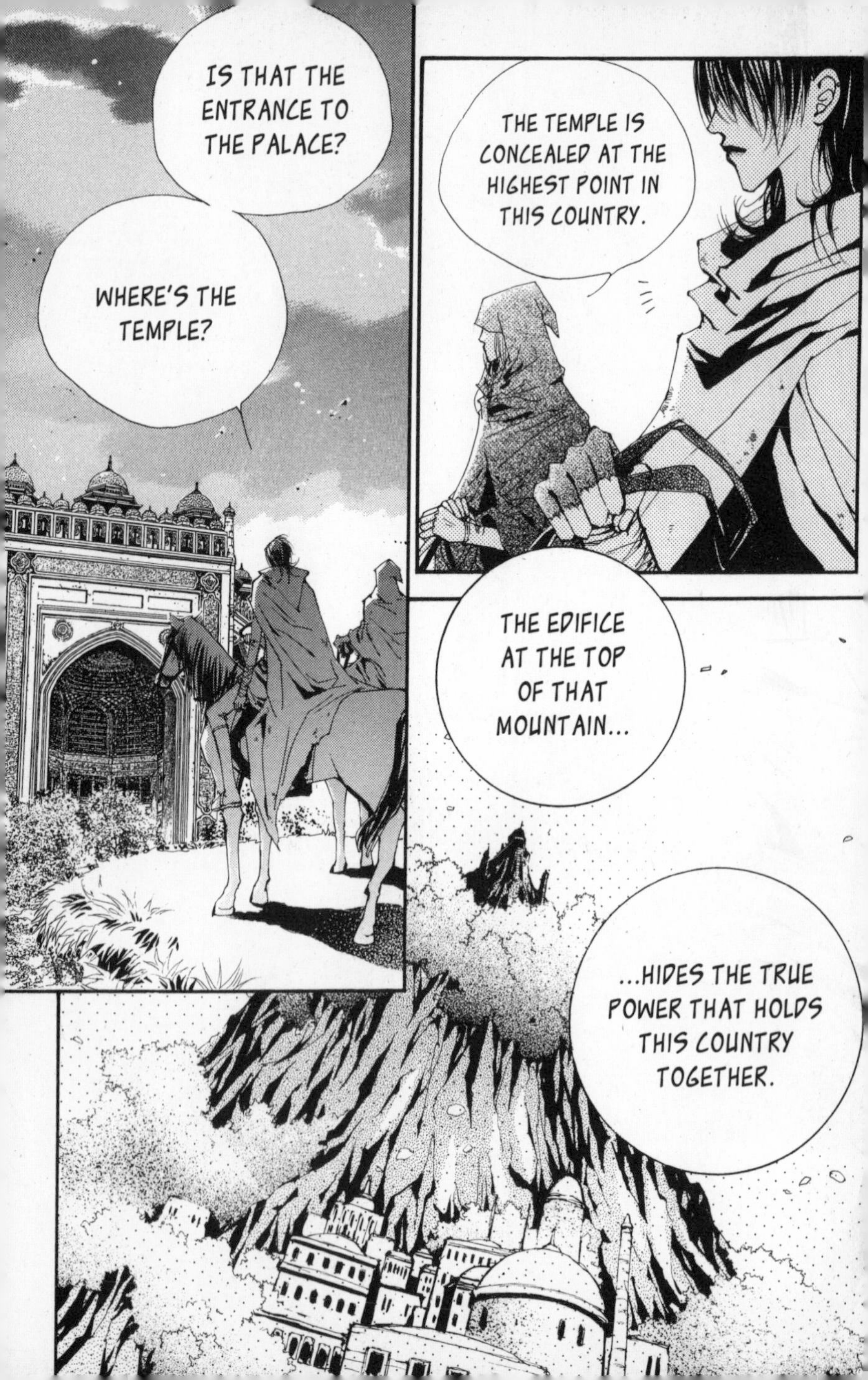
IS THAT THE ENTRANCE TO THE PALACE?
WHERE'S THE TEMPLE?
THE TEMPLE IS CONCEALED AT THE HIGHEST POINT IN THIS COUNTRY.
THE EDIFICE AT THE TOP OF THAT MOUNTAIN...
...HIDES THE TRUE POWER THAT HOLDS THIS COUNTRY TOGETHER.

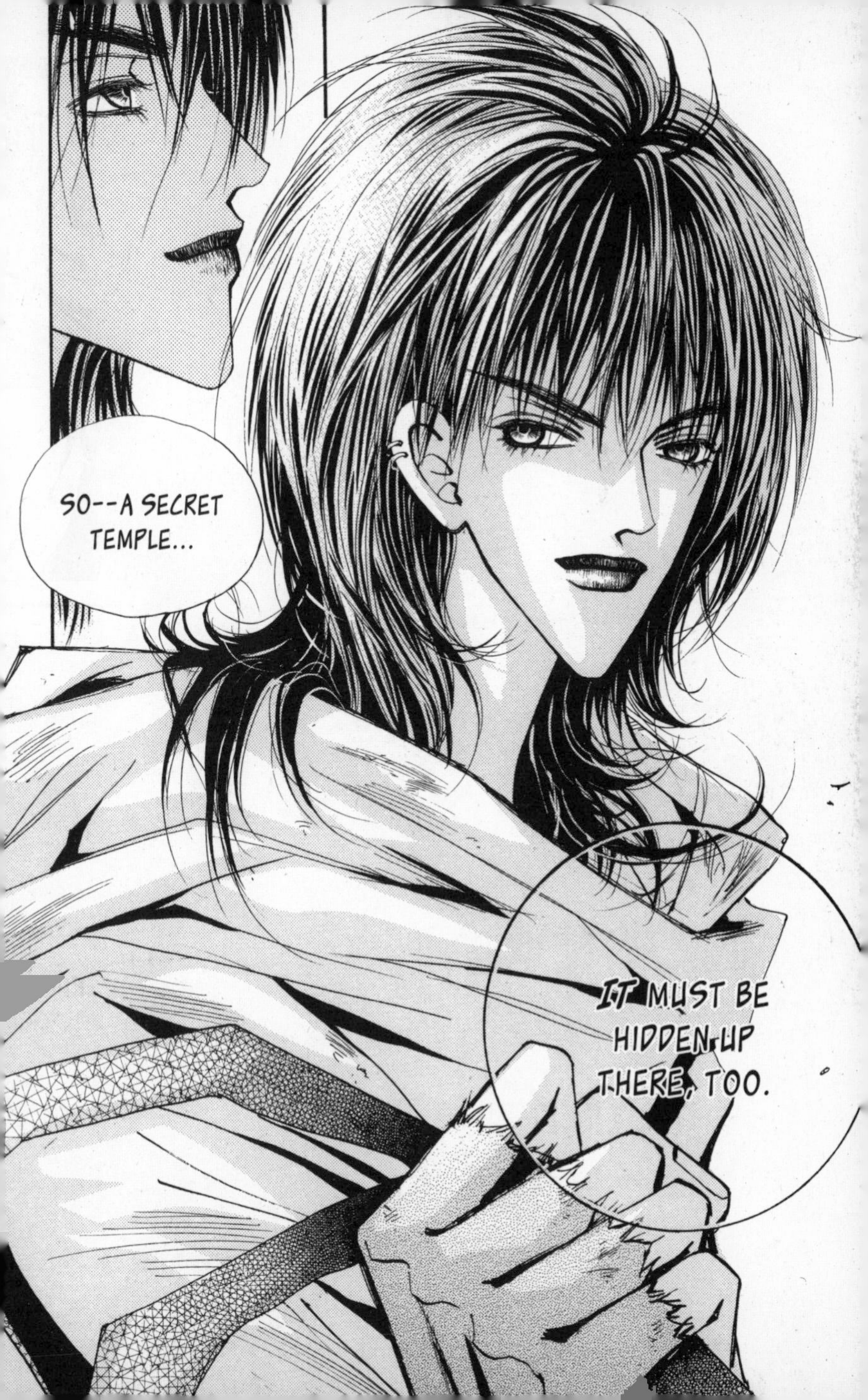
SO--A SECRET TEMPLE...
IT MUST BE HIDDEN UP THERE, TOO.

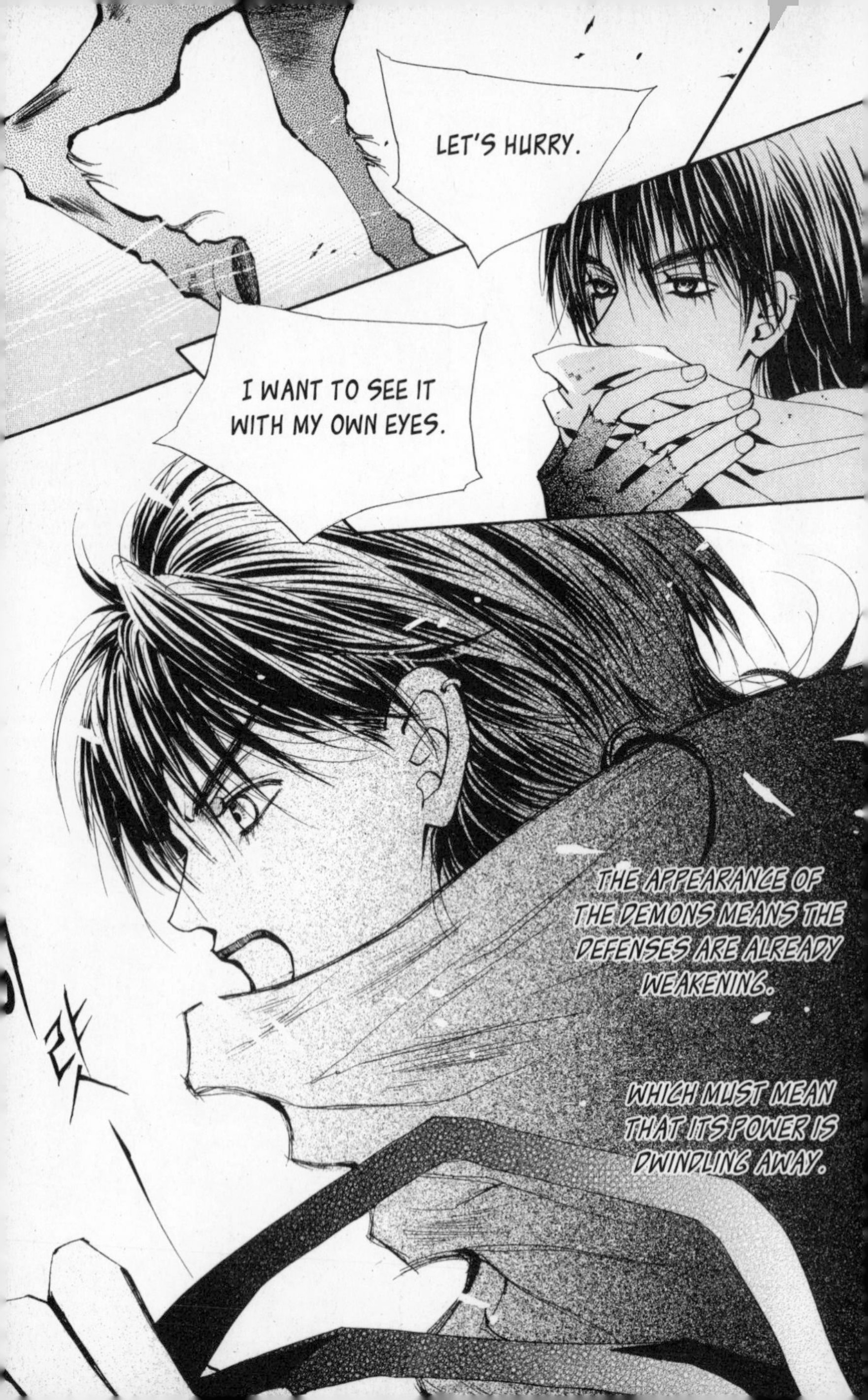
LET'S HURRY.
I WANT TO SEE IT WITH MY OWN EYES.
THE APPEARANCE OF THE DEMONS MEANS THE DEFENSES ARE ALREADY WEAKENING.
WHICH MUST MEAN THAT ITS POWER IS DWINDLING AWAY.

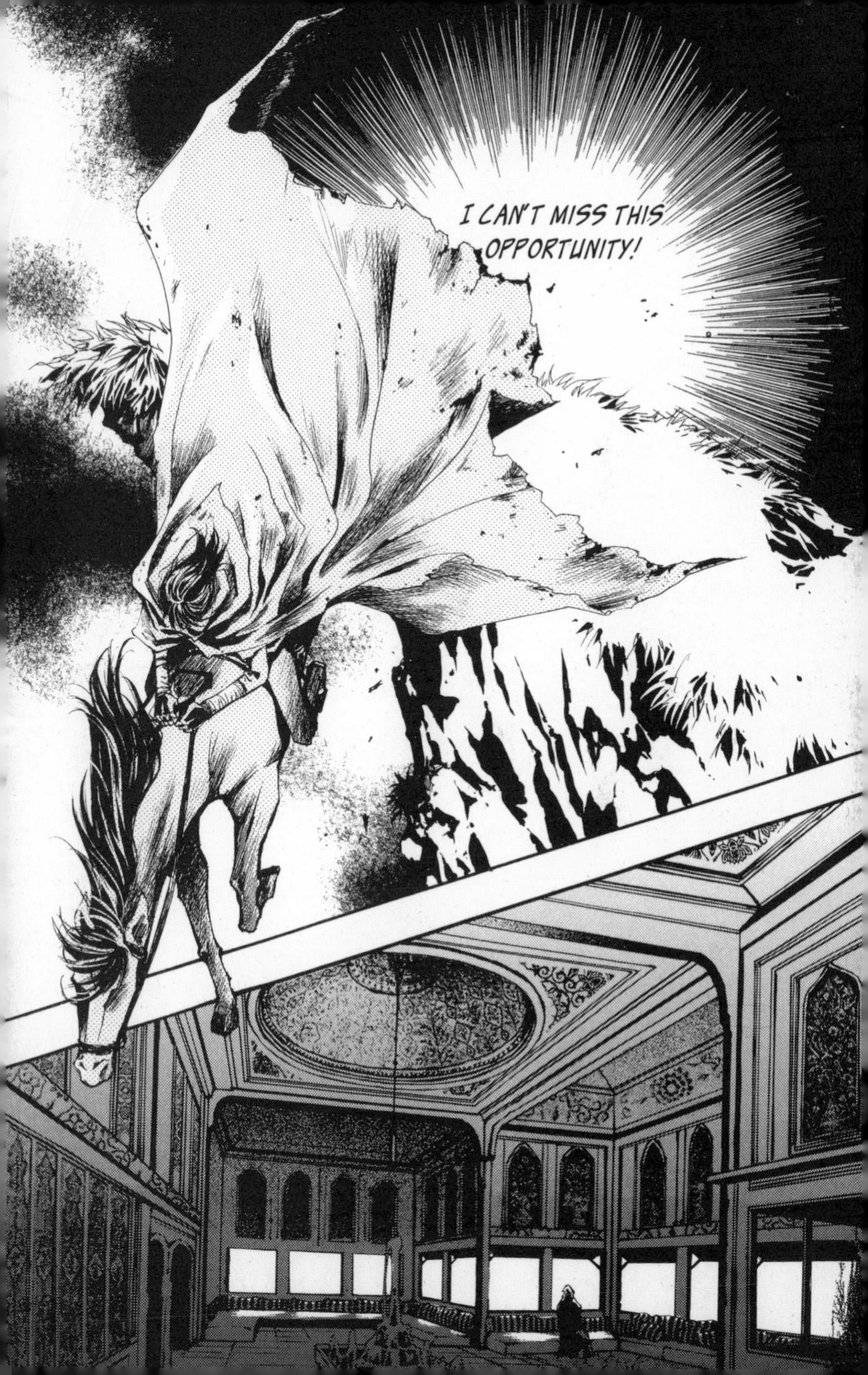
I CAN'T MISS THIS OPPORTUNITY!

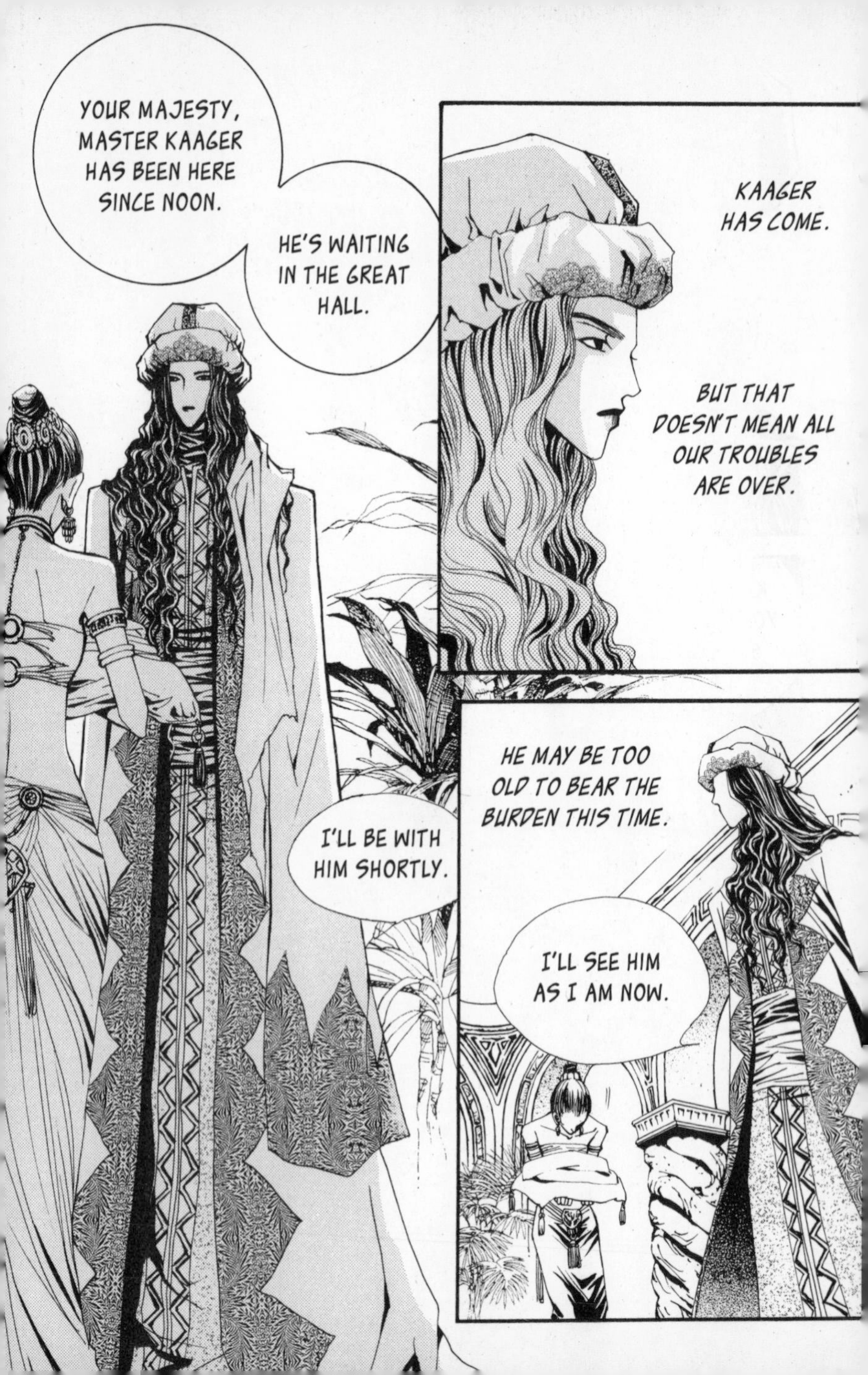
YOUR MAJESTY, MASTER KAAGER HAS BEEN HERE SINCE NOON.
HE'S WAITING IN THE GREAT HALL.
I'LL BE WITH HIM SHORTLY.
KAAGER HAS COME.
BUT THAT DOESN'T MEAN ALL OUR TROUBLES ARE OVER.
HE MAY BE TOO OLD TO BEAR THE BURDEN THIS TIME.
I'LL SEE HIM AS I AM NOW.

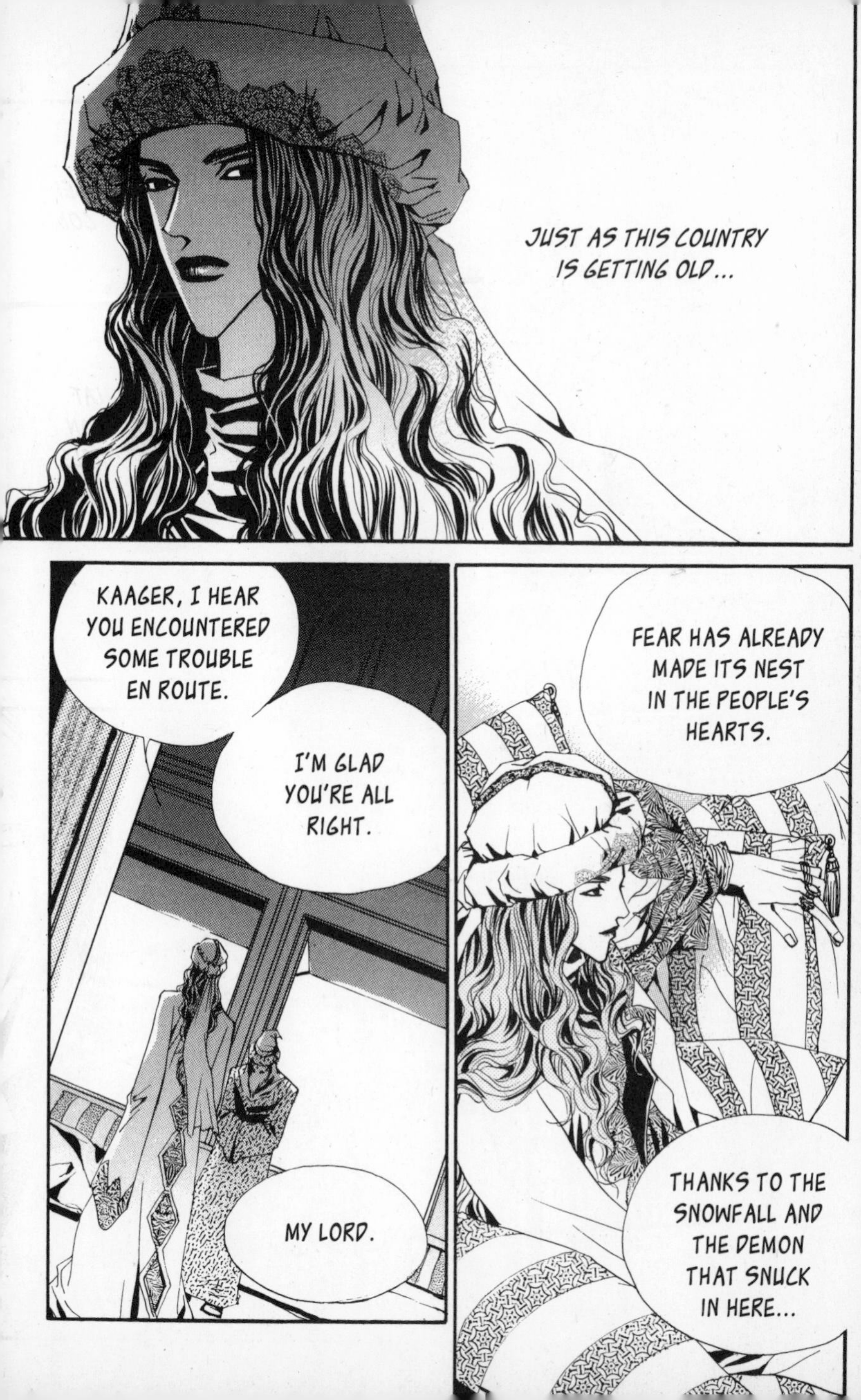
JUST AS THIS COUNTRY IS GETTING OLD...
KAAGER, I HEAR YOU ENCOUNTERED SOME TROUBLE EN ROUTE.
I'M GLAD YOU'RE ALL RIGHT.
MY LORD.
FEAR HAS ALREADY MADE ITS NEST IN THE PEOPLE'S HEARTS.
THANKS TO THE SNOWFALL AND THE DEMON THAT SNUCK IN HERE...

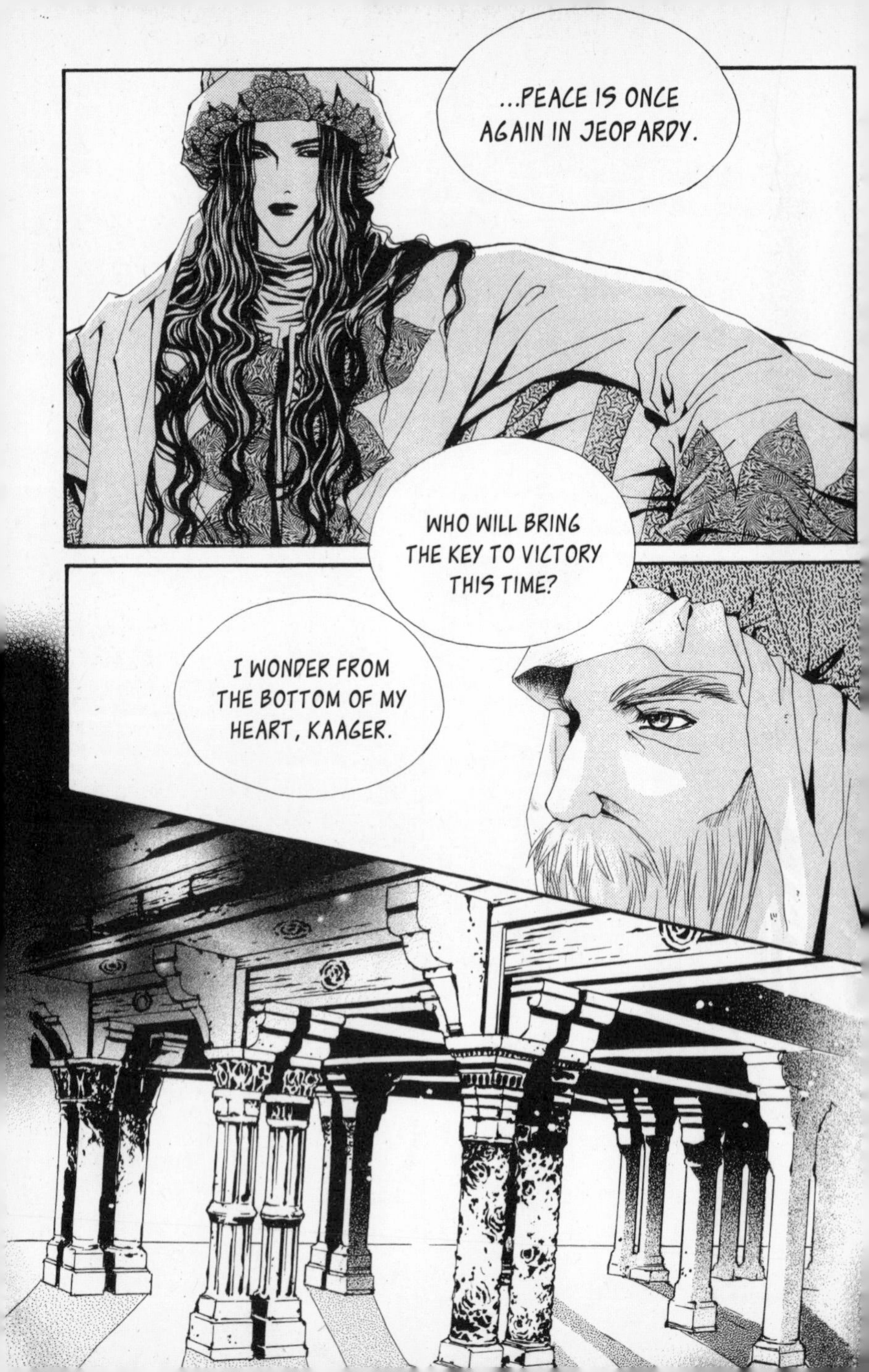
...PEACE IS ONCE AGAIN IN JEOPARDY.
WHO WILL BRING THE KEY TO VICTORY THIS TIME?
I WONDER FROM THE BOTTOM OF MY HEART, KAAGER.

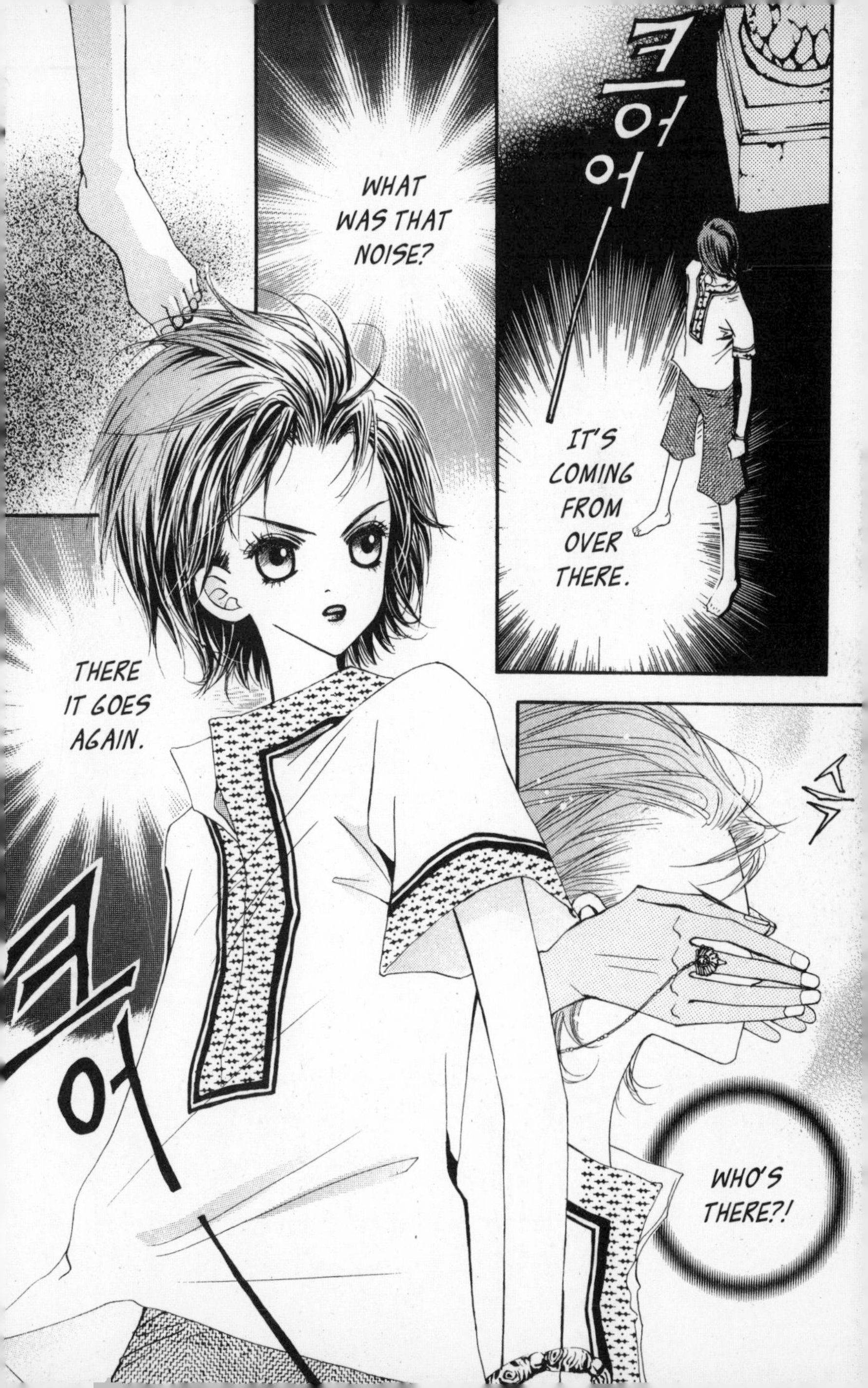
WHAT WAS THAT NOISE?
크어어
IT'S COMING FROM OVER THERE.
THERE IT GOES AGAIN.
WHO'S THERE?!

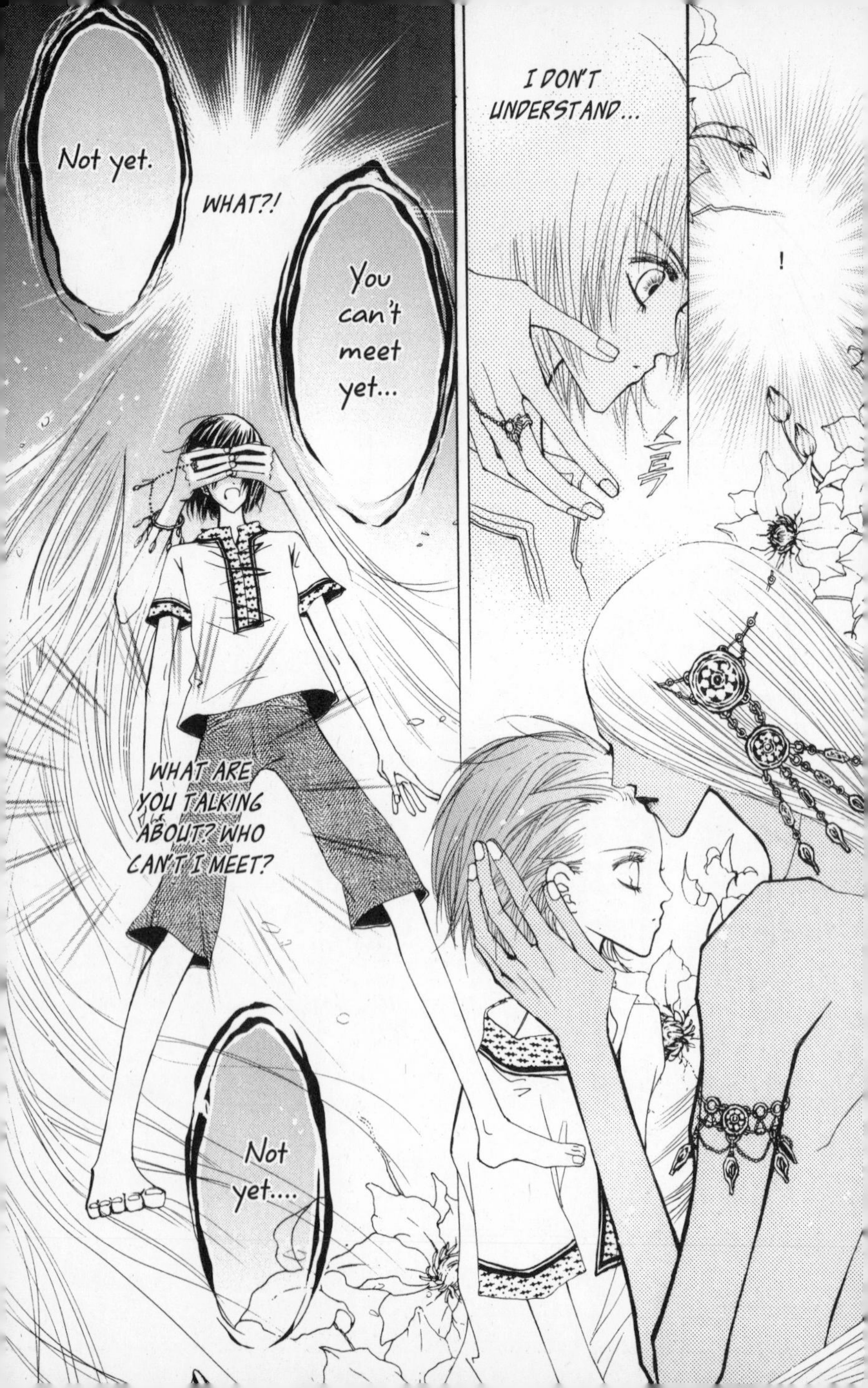
Not yet.
WHAT?!
You can't meet yet...
WHAT ARE YOU TALKING ABOUT? WHO CAN'T I MEET?
Not yet....
I DON'T UNDERSTAND...
!

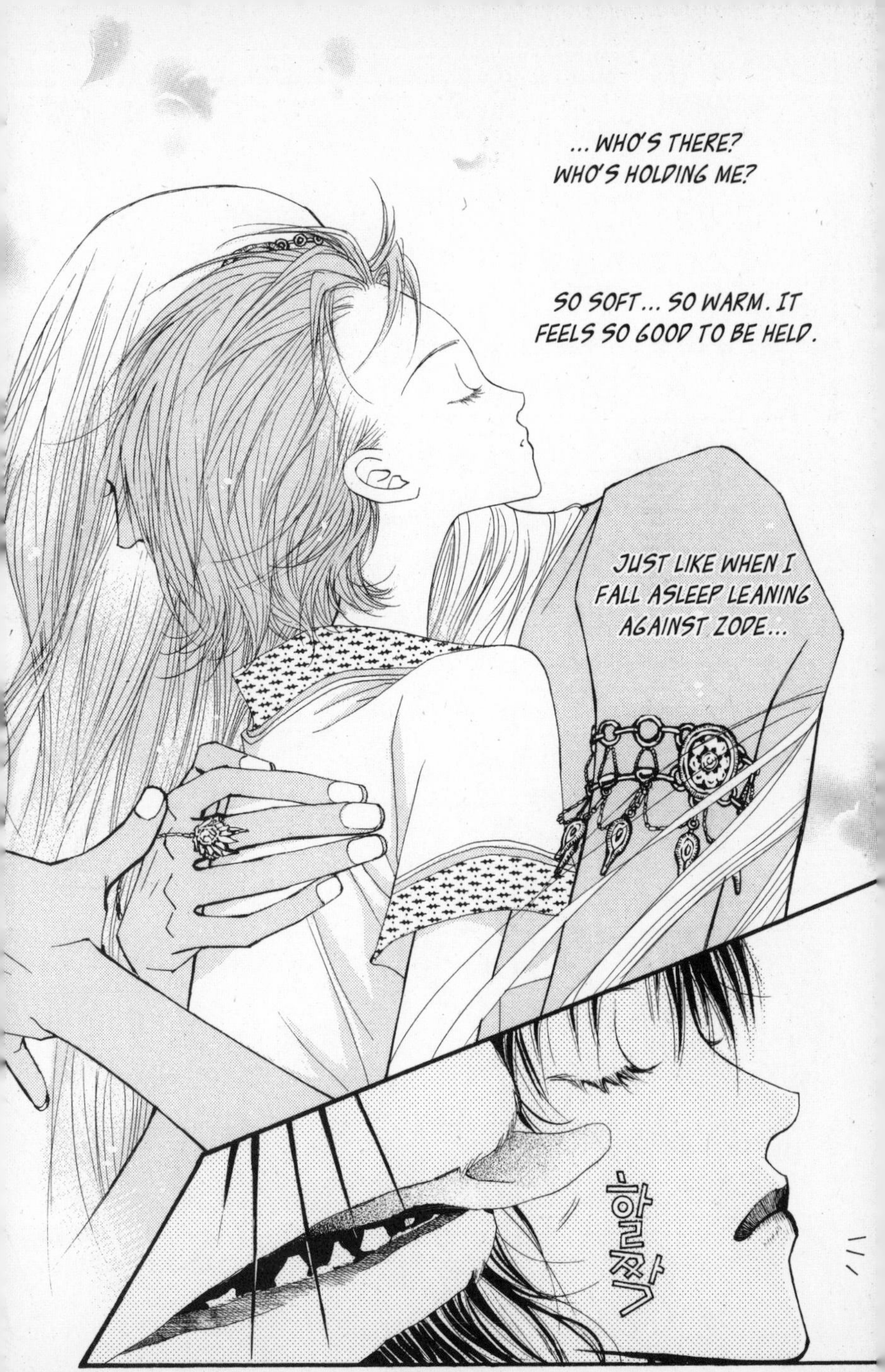
...WHO'S THERE?
WHO'S HOLDING ME?
SO SOFT... SO WARM. IT
FEELS SO GOOD TO BE HELD.
JUST LIKE WHEN I
FALL ASLEEP LEANING
AGAINST ZODE...
할짝

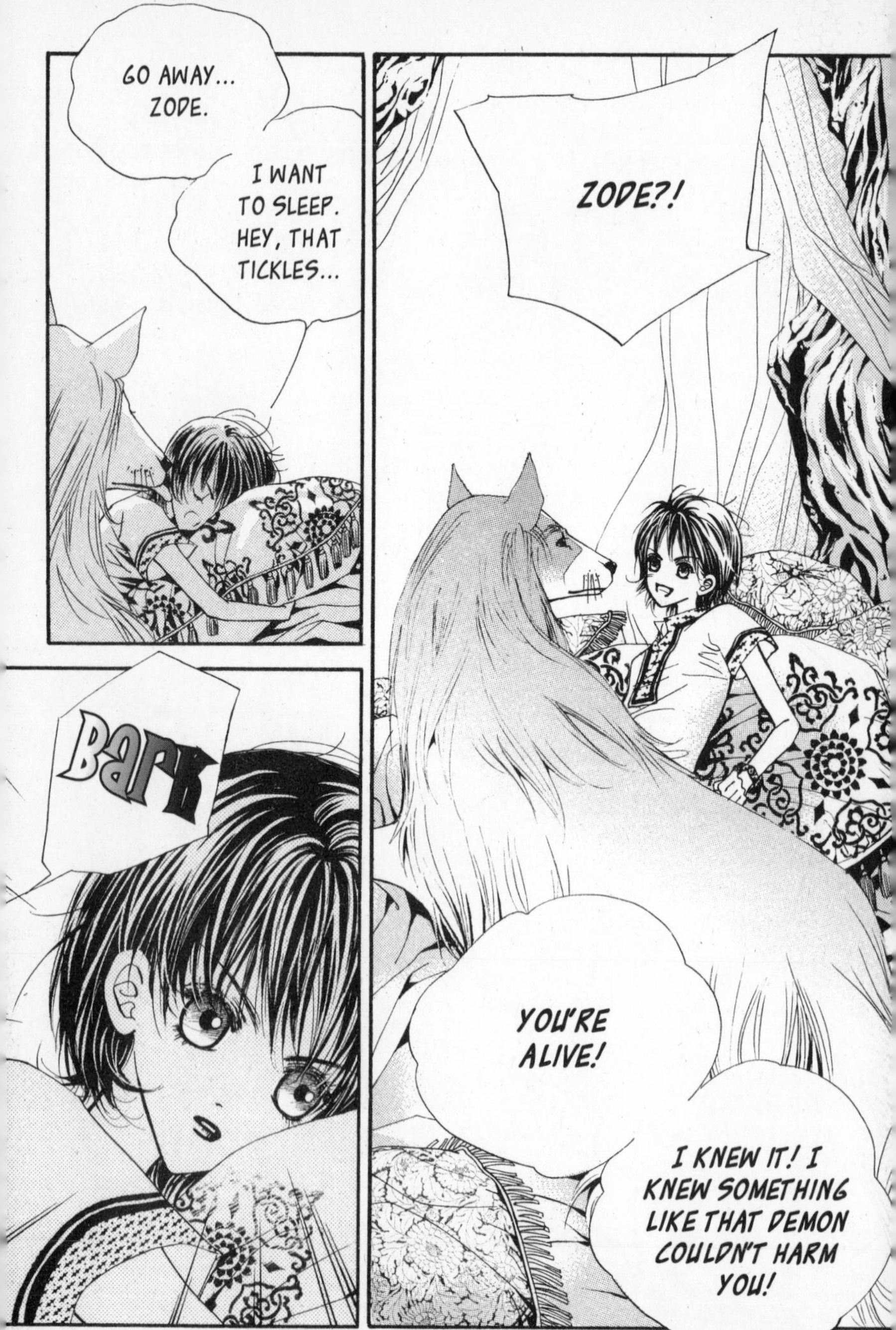
GO AWAY... ZODE.
I WANT TO SLEEP. HEY, THAT TICKLES...
BARK
ZODE?!
YOU'RE ALIVE!
I KNEW IT! I KNEW SOMETHING LIKE THAT DEMON COULDN'T HARM YOU!

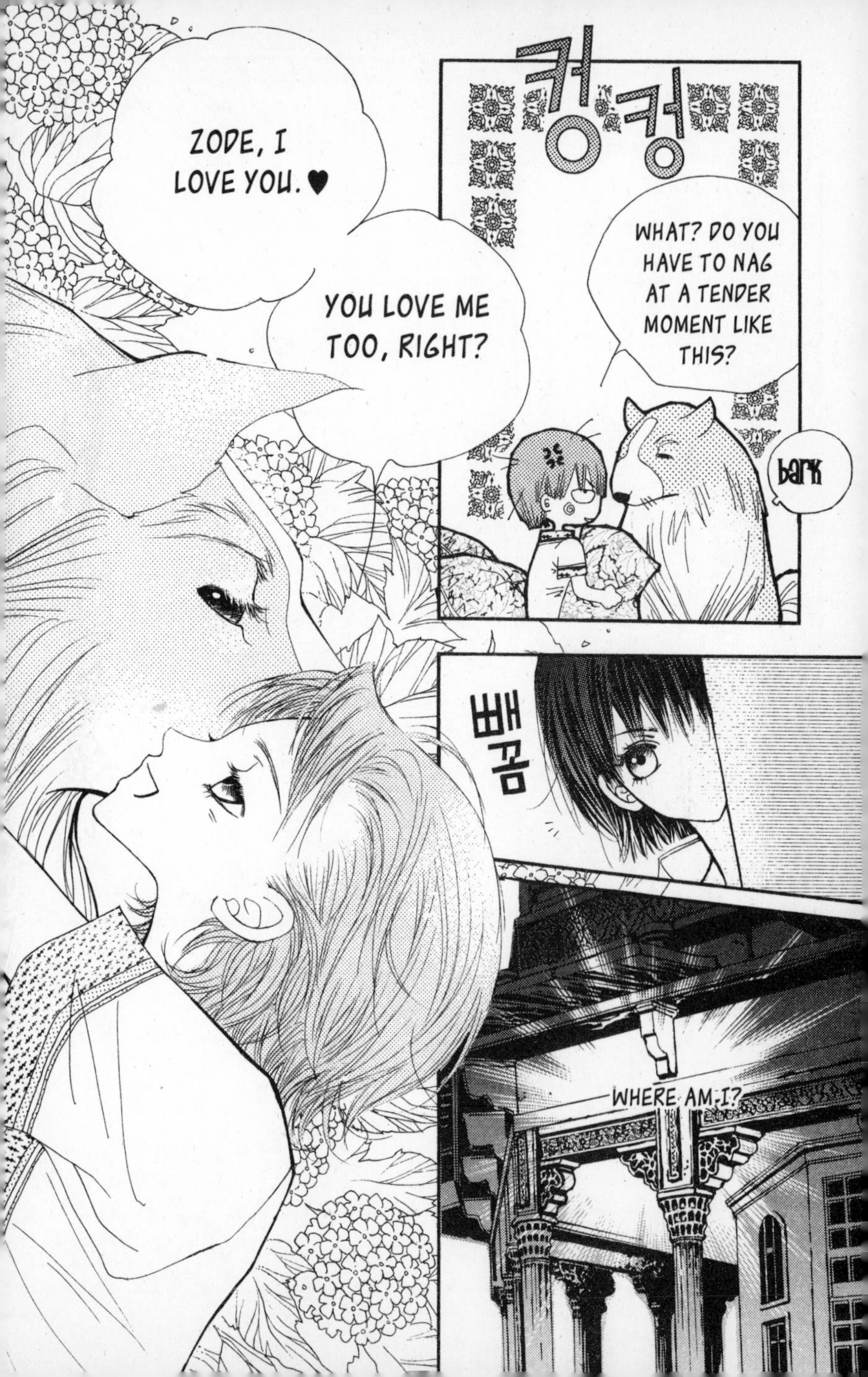
ZODE, I LOVE YOU. ♥
YOU LOVE ME TOO, RIGHT?
컹컹
WHAT? DO YOU HAVE TO NAG AT A TENDER MOMENT LIKE THIS?
bark
빼꼼
WHERE AM I?

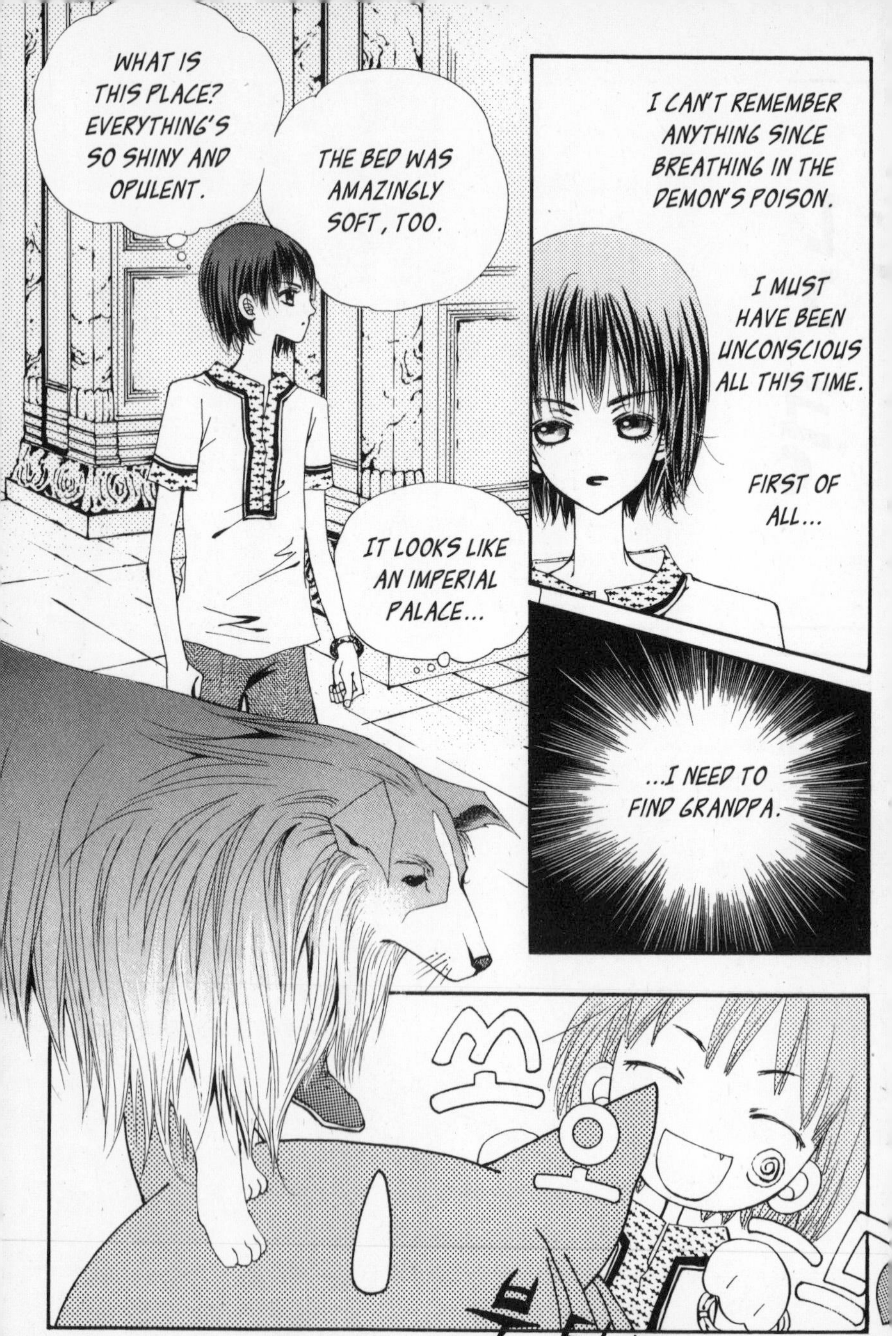
WHAT IS THIS PLACE? EVERYTHING'S SO SHINY AND OPULENT.
THE BED WAS AMAZINGLY SOFT, TOO.
IT LOOKS LIKE AN IMPERIAL PALACE...
I CAN'T REMEMBER ANYTHING SINCE BREATHING IN THE DEMON'S POISON.
I MUST HAVE BEEN UNCONSCIOUS ALL THIS TIME.
FIRST OF ALL...
...I NEED TO FIND GRANDPA.

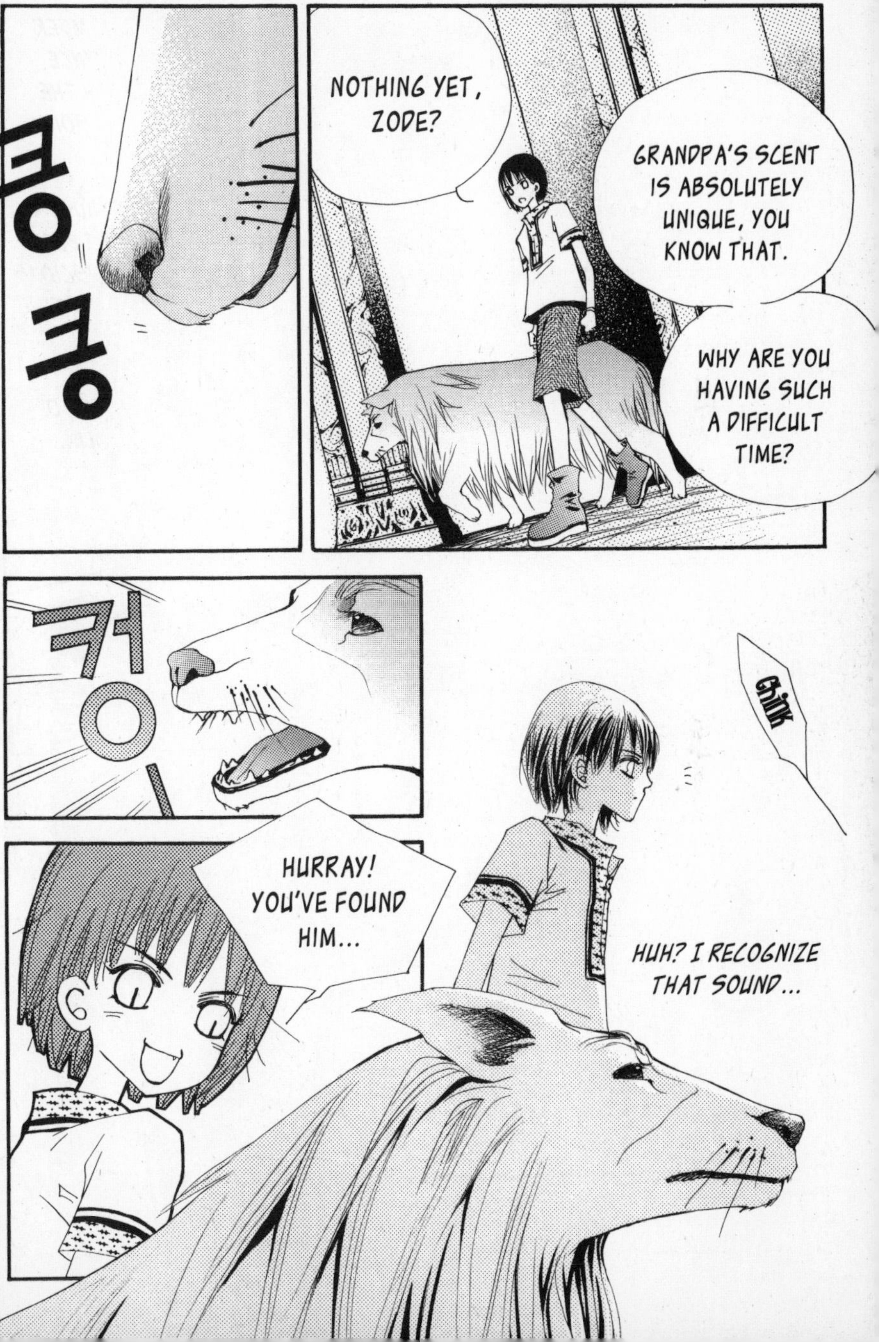
쿵 쿵
NOTHING YET, ZODE?
GRANDPA'S SCENT IS ABSOLUTELY UNIQUE, YOU KNOW THAT.
WHY ARE YOU HAVING SUCH A DIFFICULT TIME?
컹
HURRAY! YOU'VE FOUND HIM...
Chink
HUH? I RECOGNIZE THAT SOUND...

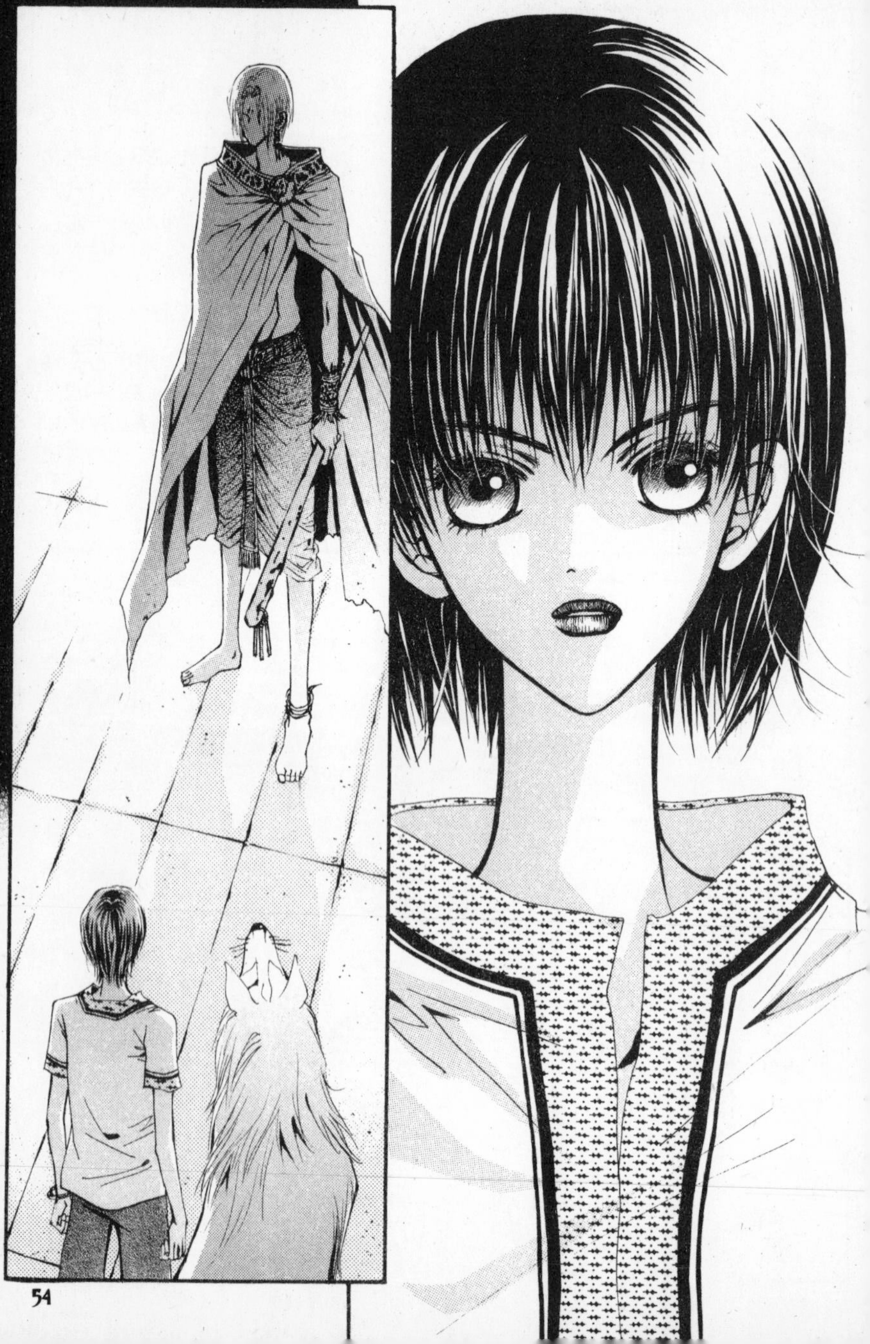

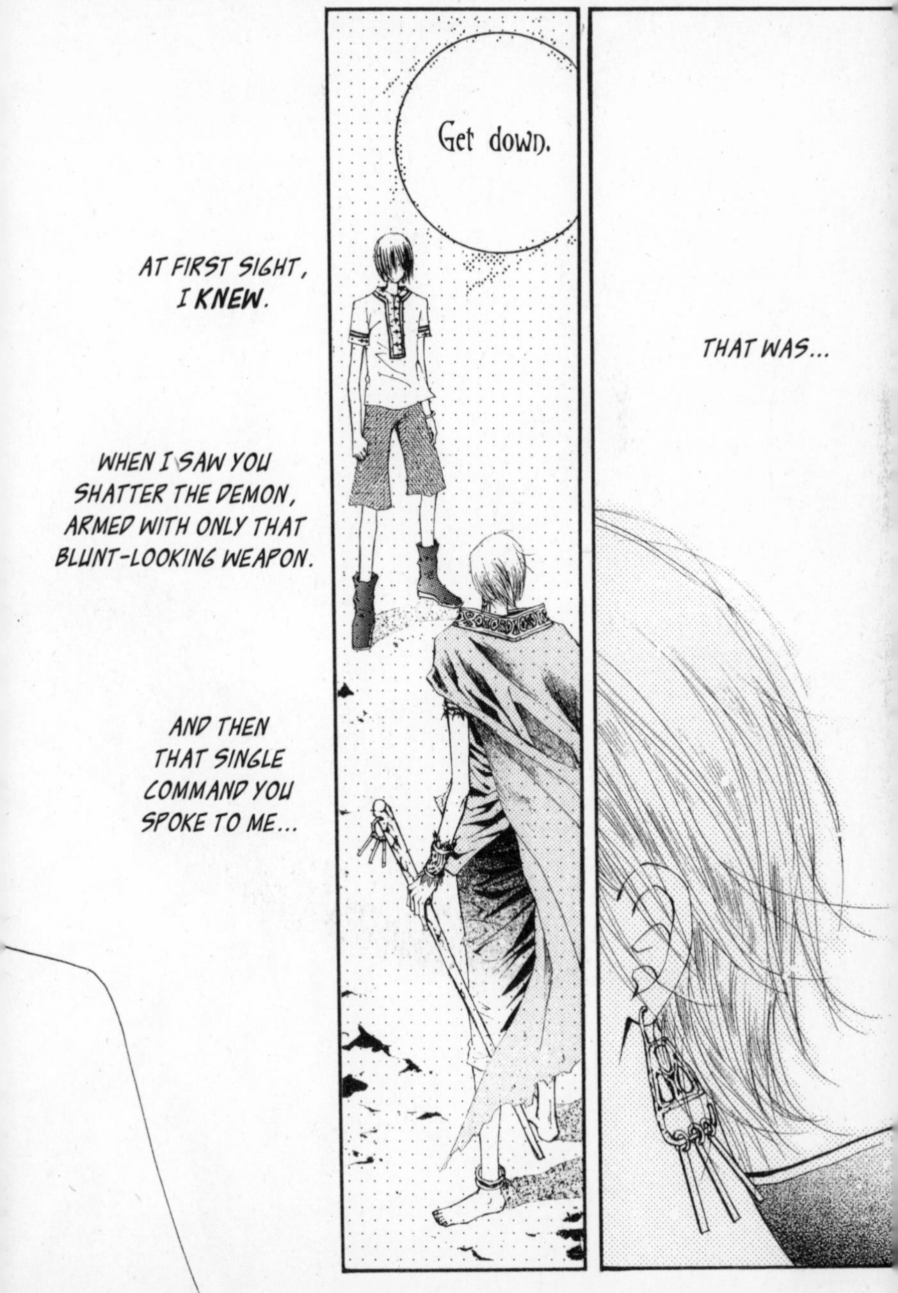
AT FIRST SIGHT, I KNEW.
WHEN I SAW YOU SHATTER THE DEMON, ARMED WITH ONLY THAT BLUNT-LOOKING WEAPON.
AND THEN THAT SINGLE COMMAND YOU SPOKE TO ME...
Get down.
THAT WAS...

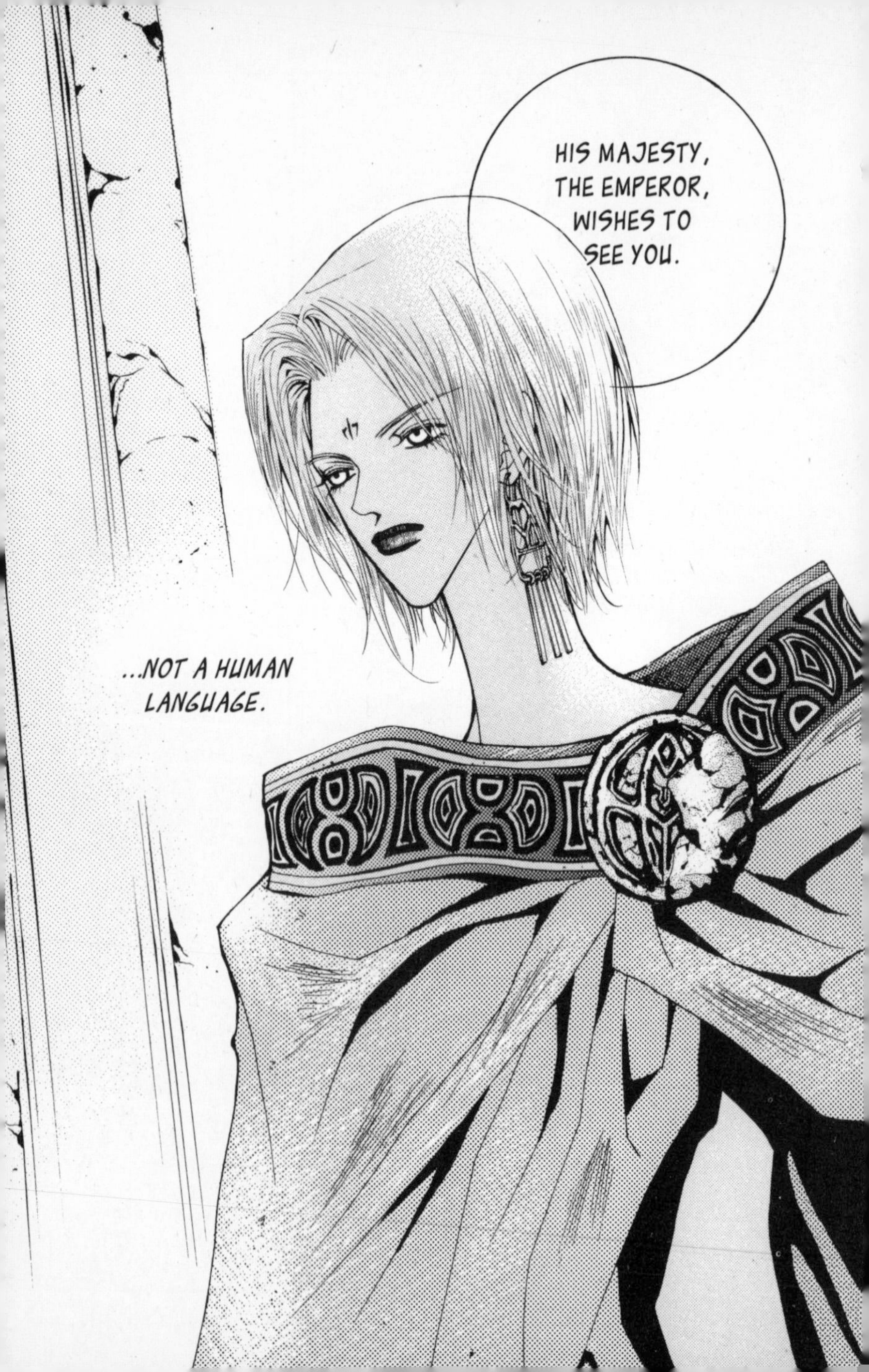
HIS MAJESTY, THE EMPEROR, WISHES TO SEE YOU.
...NOT A HUMAN LANGUAGE.

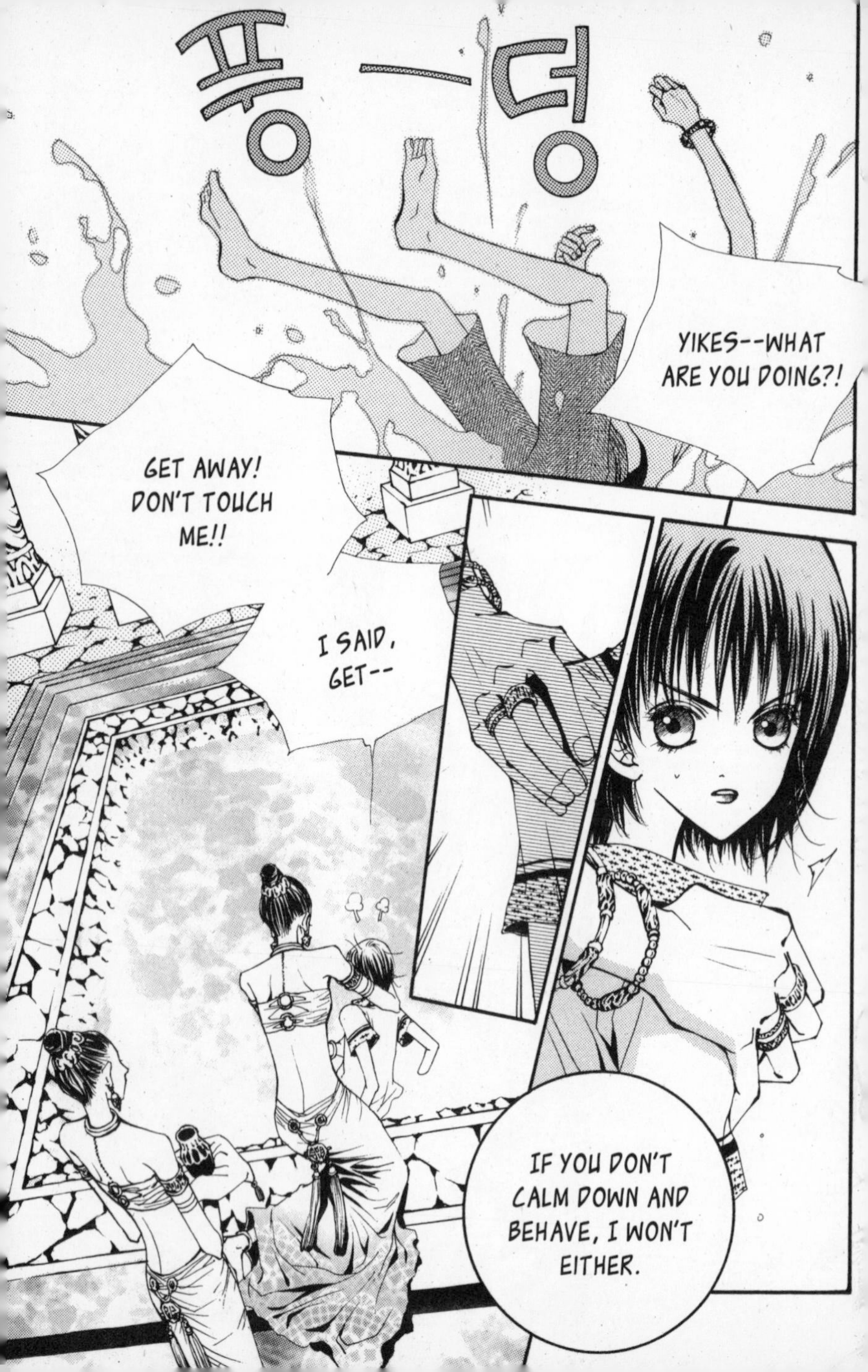
풍—덩
YIKES--WHAT ARE YOU DOING?!
GET AWAY! DON'T TOUCH ME!!
I SAID, GET--
IF YOU DON'T CALM DOWN AND BEHAVE, I WON'T EITHER.

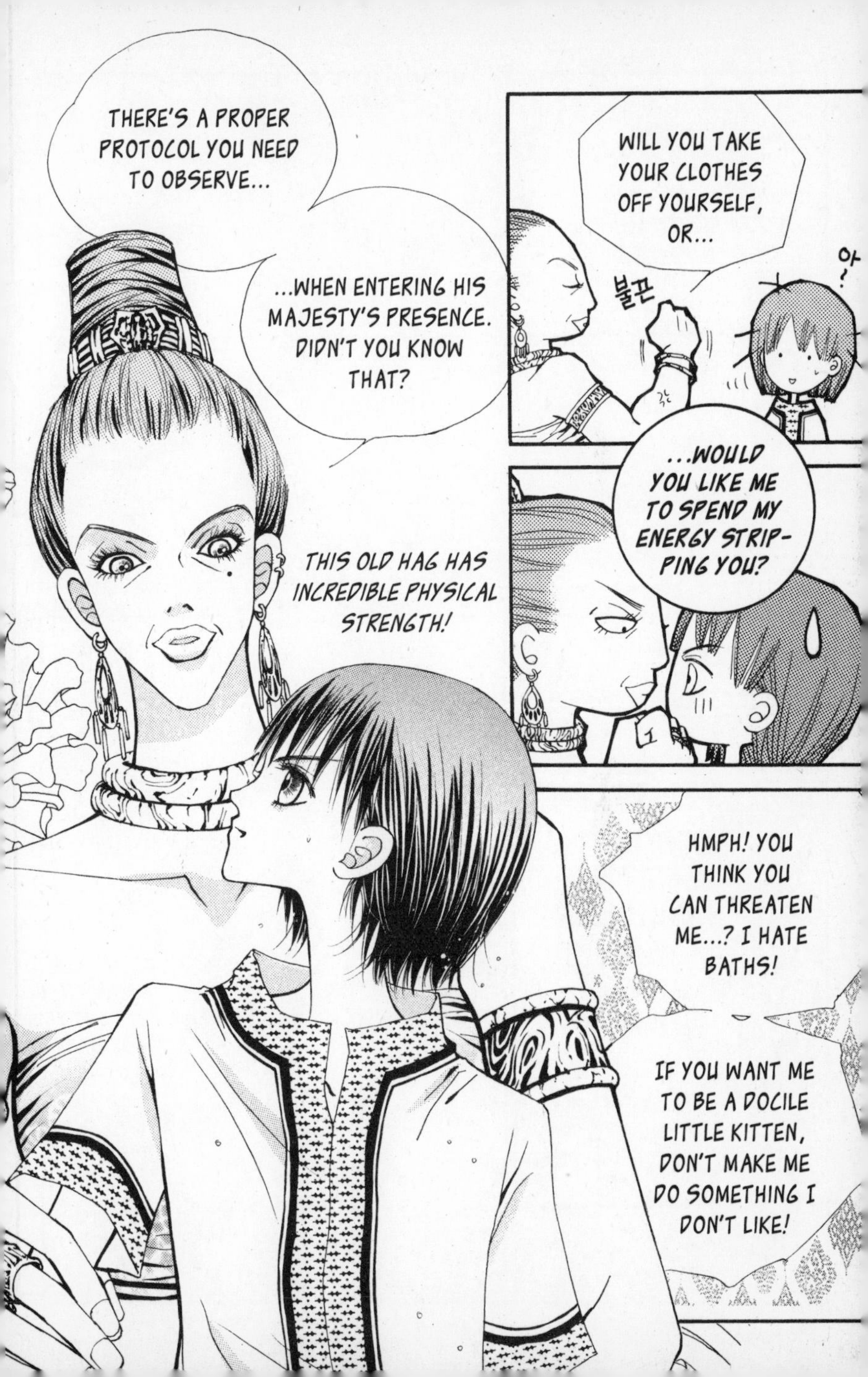
THERE'S A PROPER PROTOCOL YOU NEED TO OBSERVE...
...WHEN ENTERING HIS MAJESTY'S PRESENCE. DIDN'T YOU KNOW THAT?
THIS OLD HAG HAS INCREDIBLE PHYSICAL STRENGTH!
WILL YOU TAKE YOUR CLOTHES OFF YOURSELF, OR...
불끈
아?
...WOULD YOU LIKE ME TO SPEND MY ENERGY STRIP-PING YOU?
HMPH! YOU THINK YOU CAN THREATEN ME...? I HATE BATHS!
IF YOU WANT ME TO BE A DOCILE LITTLE KITTEN, DON'T MAKE ME DO SOMETHING I DON'T LIKE!

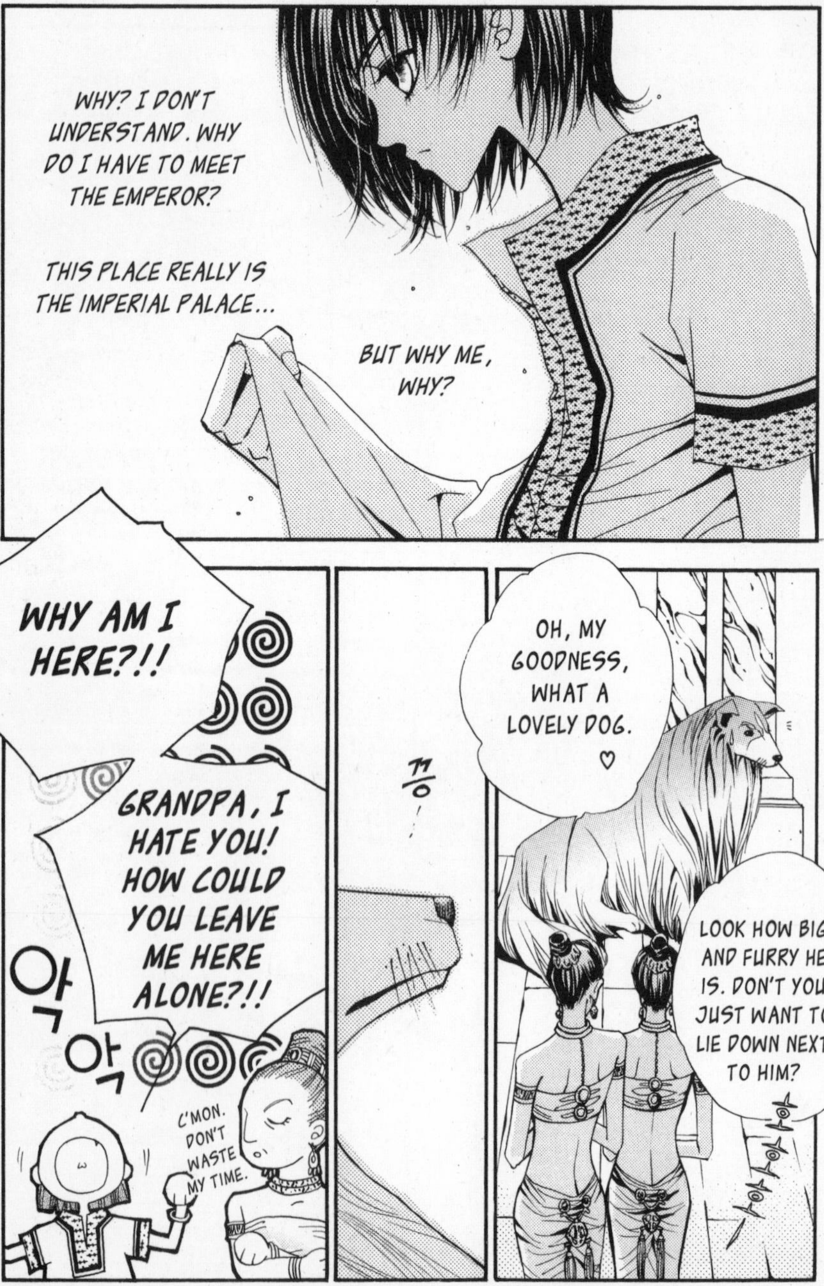

WHY? I DON'T UNDERSTAND. WHY DO I HAVE TO MEET THE EMPEROR?
THIS PLACE REALLY IS THE IMPERIAL PALACE...
BUT WHY ME, WHY?
WHY AM I HERE?!!
GRANDPA, I HATE YOU! HOW COULD YOU LEAVE ME HERE ALONE?!!
악 악
C'MON. DON'T WASTE MY TIME.
OH, MY GOODNESS, WHAT A LOVELY DOG. ♡
LOOK HOW BIG AND FURRY HE IS. DON'T YOU JUST WANT TO LIE DOWN NEXT TO HIM?

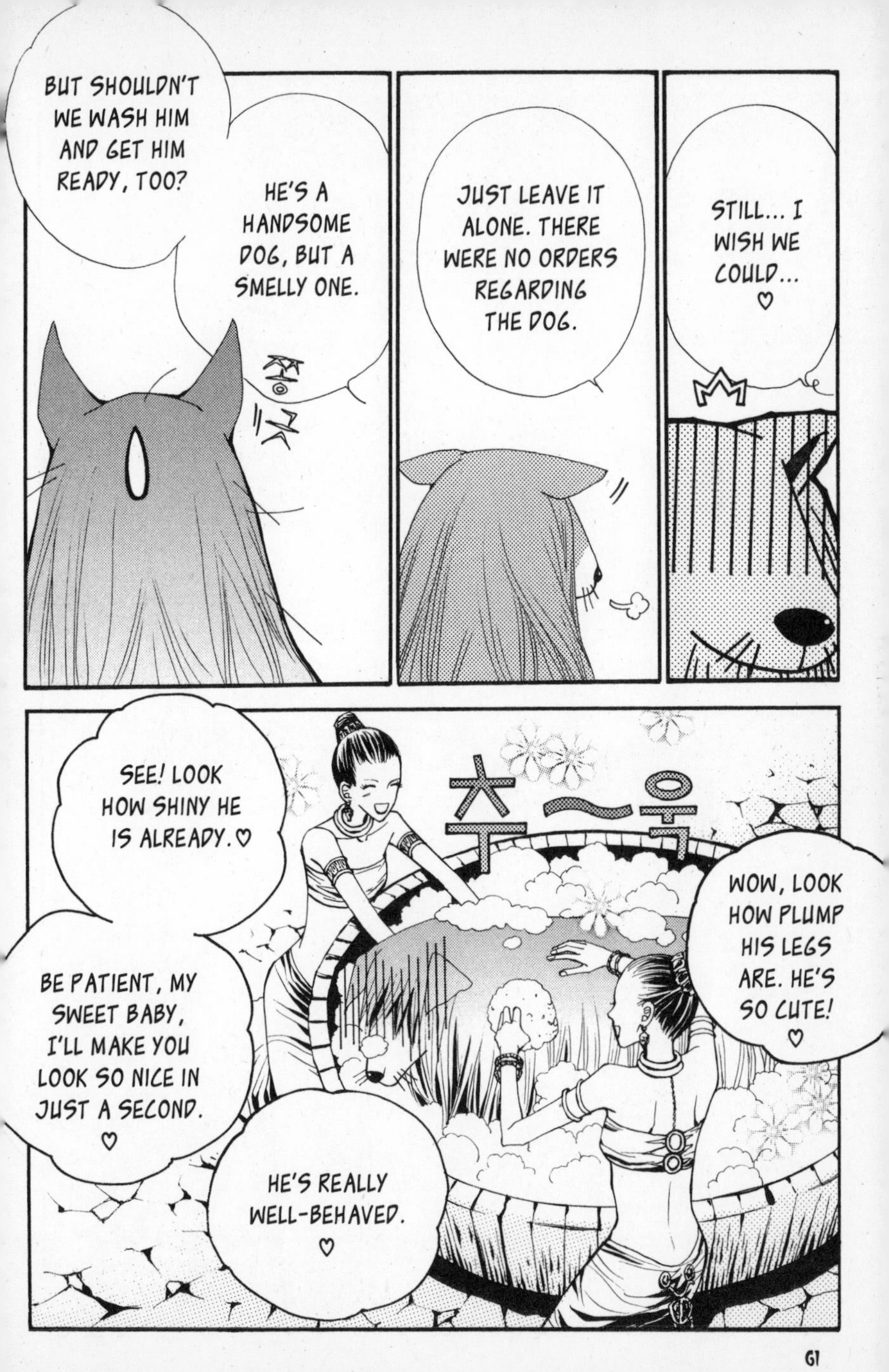
BUT SHOULDN'T WE WASH HIM AND GET HIM READY, TOO?
HE'S A HANDSOME DOG, BUT A SMELLY ONE.
JUST LEAVE IT ALONE. THERE WERE NO ORDERS REGARDING THE DOG.
STILL... I WISH WE COULD... ♡
SEE! LOOK HOW SHINY HE IS ALREADY. ♡
추~욱
BE PATIENT, MY SWEET BABY, I'LL MAKE YOU LOOK SO NICE IN JUST A SECOND. ♡
HE'S REALLY WELL-BEHAVED. ♡
WOW, LOOK HOW PLUMP HIS LEGS ARE. HE'S SO CUTE! ♡

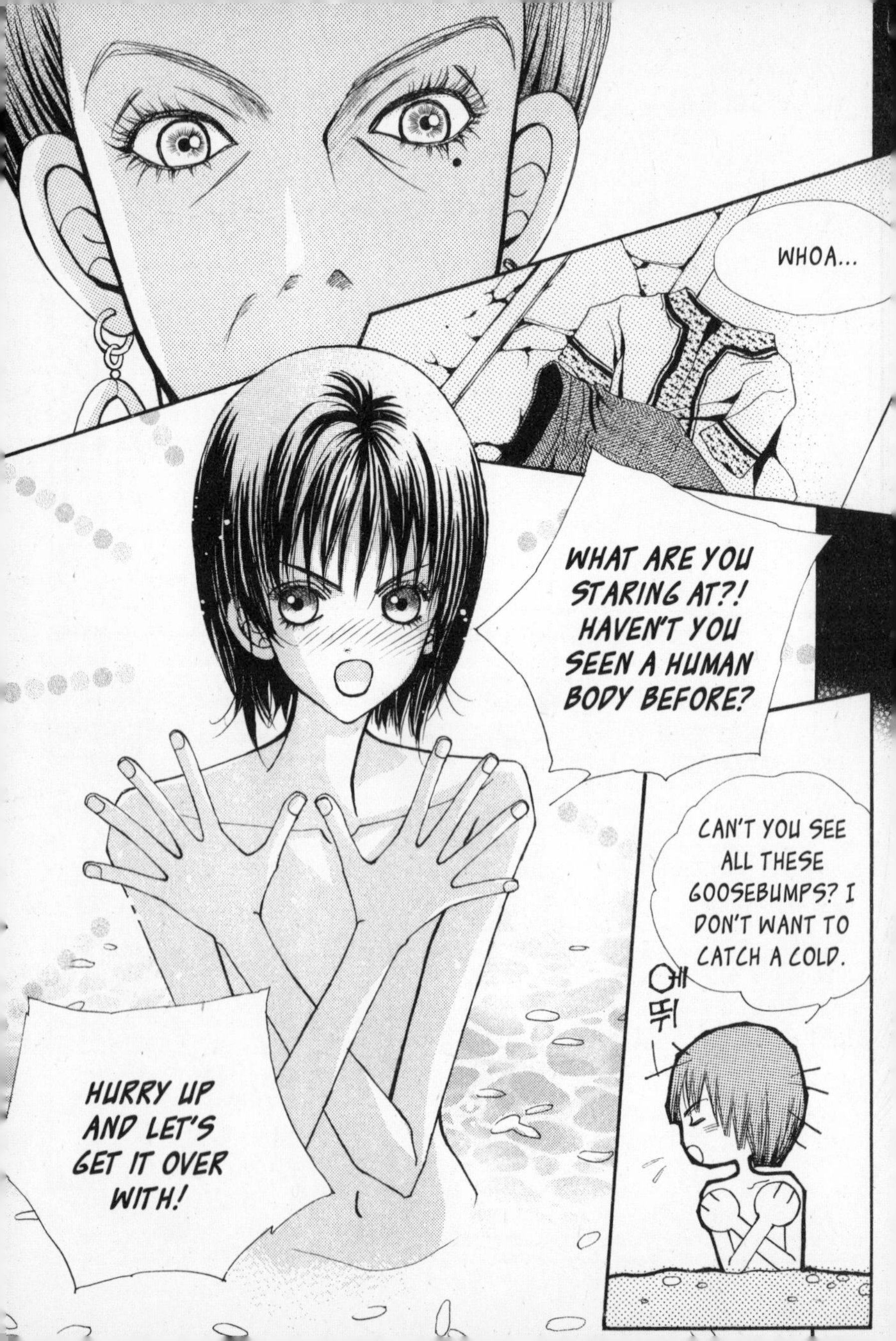
WHOA...
WHAT ARE YOU STARING AT?! HAVEN'T YOU SEEN A HUMAN BODY BEFORE?
HURRY UP AND LET'S GET IT OVER WITH!
CAN'T YOU SEE ALL THESE GOOSEBUMPS? I DON'T WANT TO CATCH A COLD.
에뛰

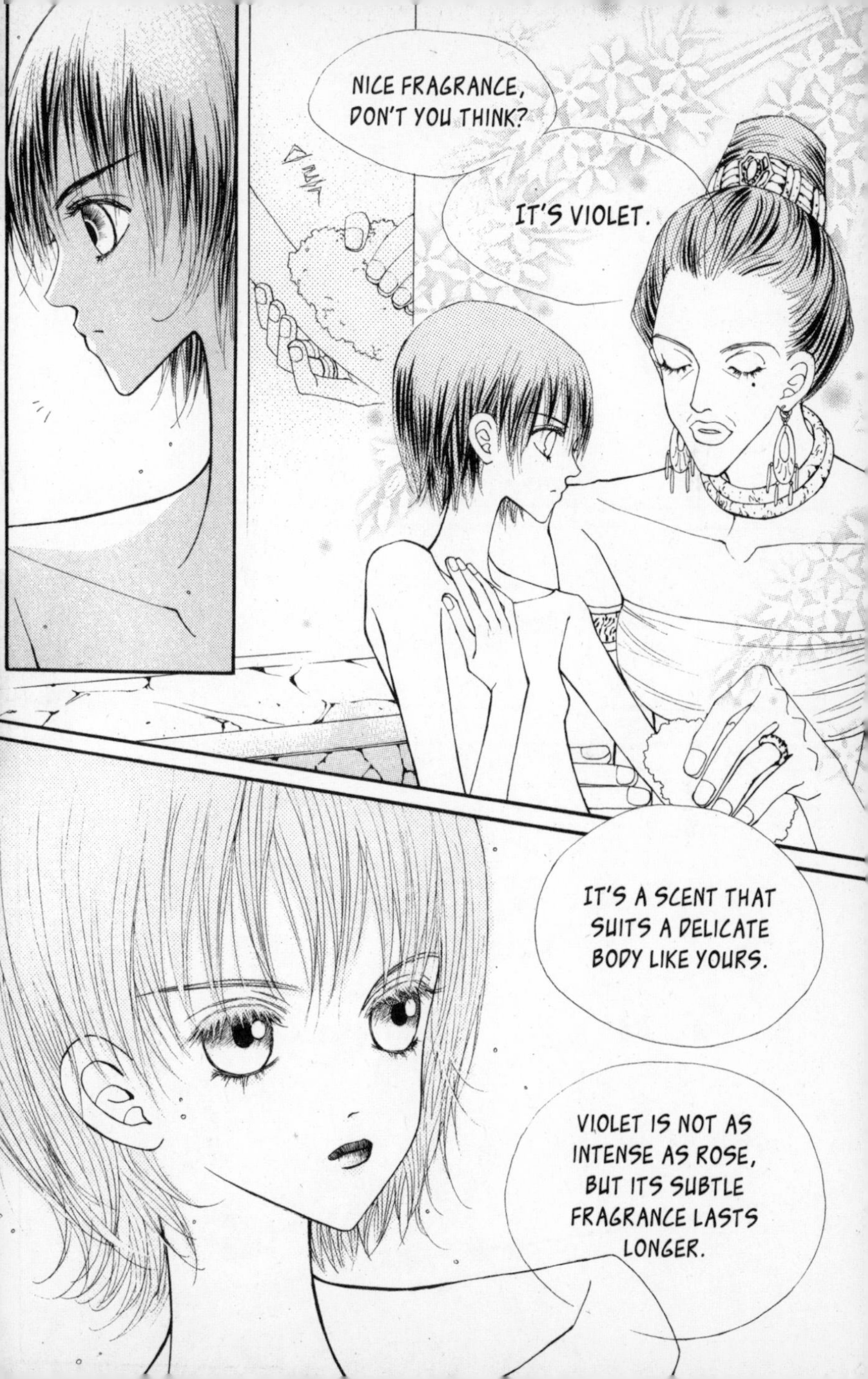
NICE FRAGRANCE, DON'T YOU THINK?
IT'S VIOLET.
IT'S A SCENT THAT SUITS A DELICATE BODY LIKE YOURS.
VIOLET IS NOT AS INTENSE AS ROSE, BUT ITS SUBTLE FRAGRANCE LASTS LONGER.

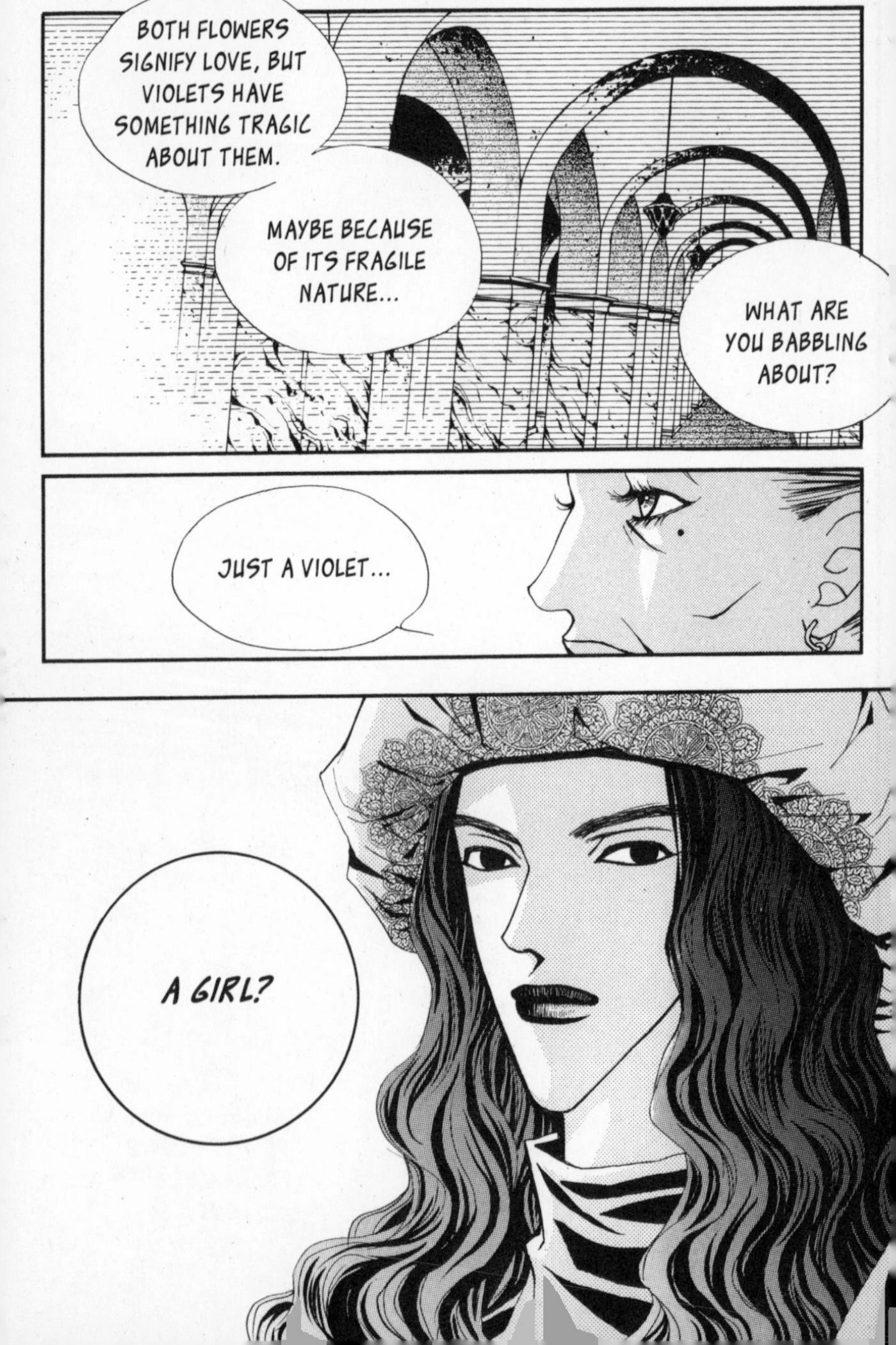
BOTH FLOWERS SIGNIFY LOVE, BUT VIOLETS HAVE SOMETHING TRAGIC ABOUT THEM.
MAYBE BECAUSE OF ITS FRAGILE NATURE...
WHAT ARE YOU BABBLING ABOUT?
JUST A VIOLET...
A GIRL?

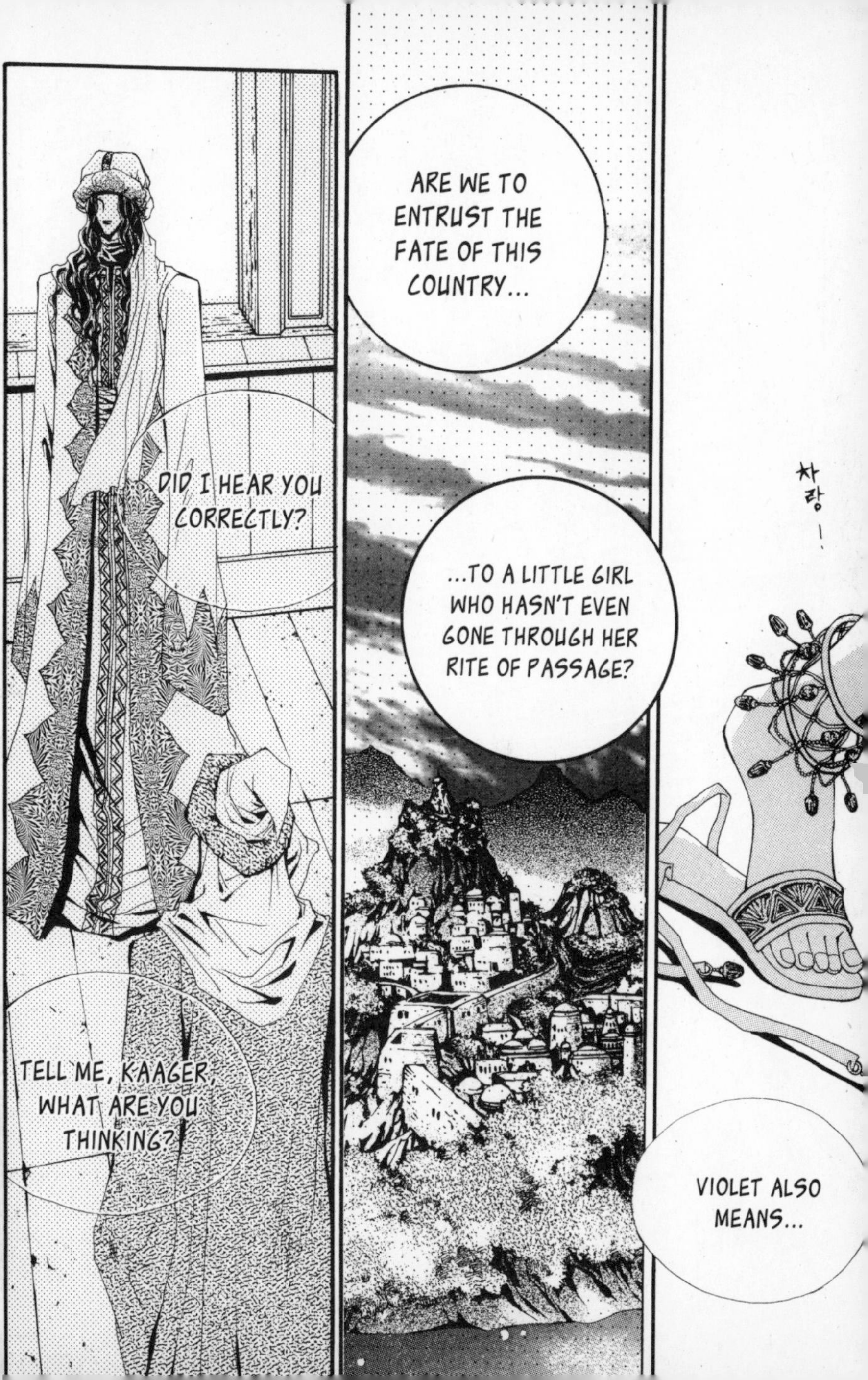
DID I HEAR YOU CORRECTLY?
TELL ME, KAAGER, WHAT ARE YOU THINKING?
ARE WE TO ENTRUST THE FATE OF THIS COUNTRY...
...TO A LITTLE GIRL WHO HASN'T EVEN GONE THROUGH HER RITE OF PASSAGE?
사랑-
VIOLET ALSO MEANS...

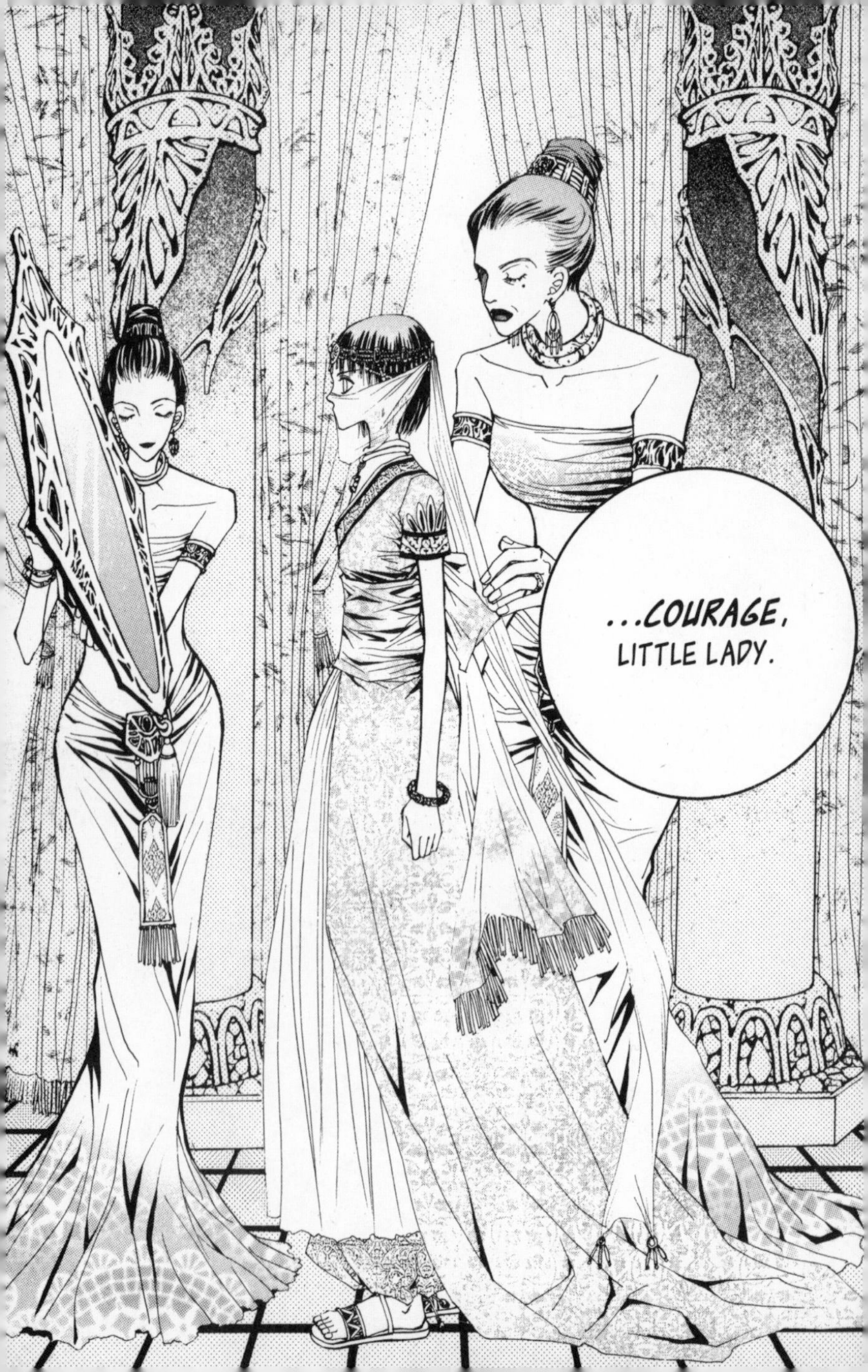
...COURAGE, LITTLE LADY.

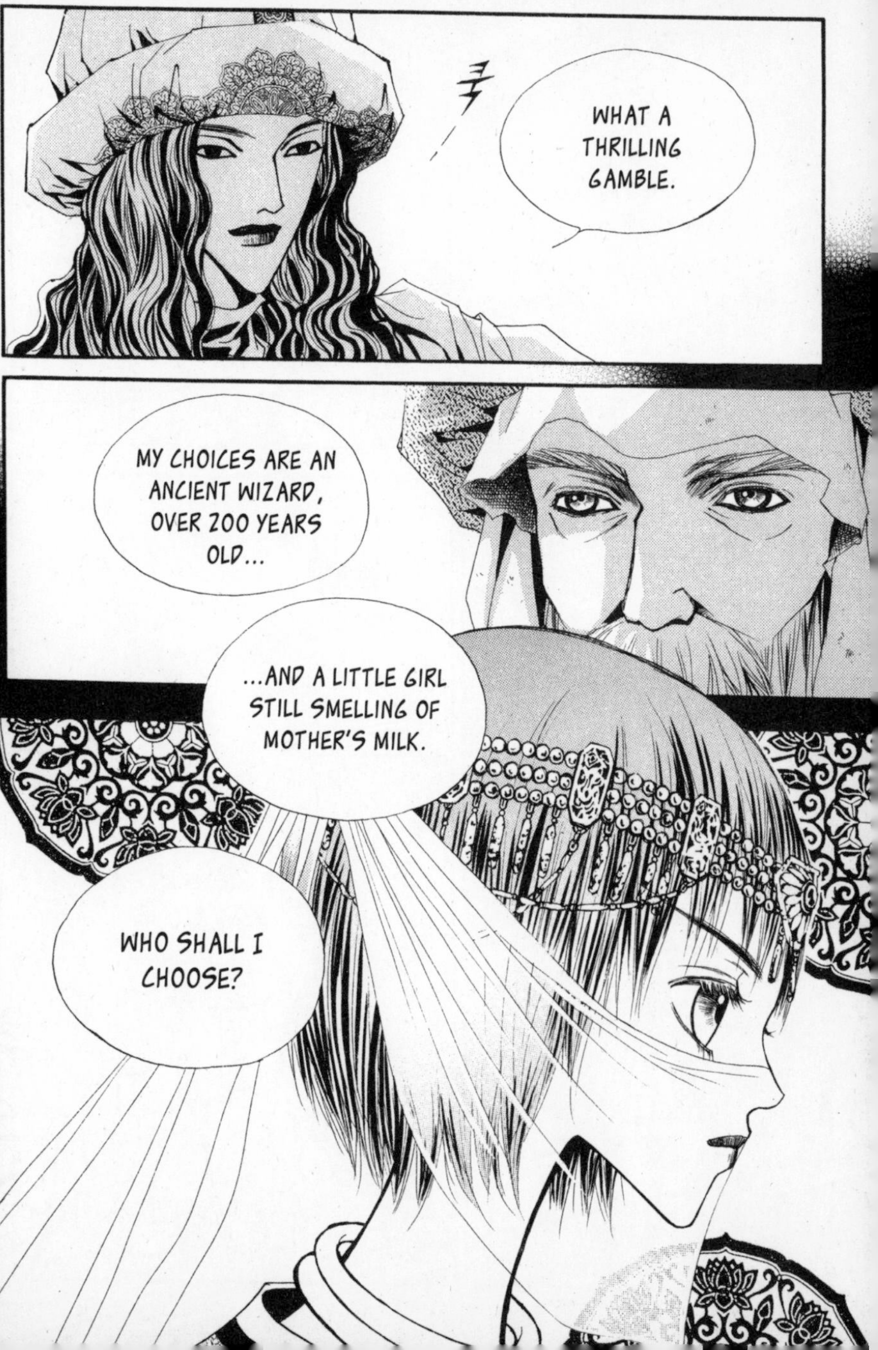
WHAT A THRILLING GAMBLE.
MY CHOICES ARE AN ANCIENT WIZARD, OVER 200 YEARS OLD...
...AND A LITTLE GIRL STILL SMELLING OF MOTHER'S MILK.
WHO SHALL I CHOOSE?

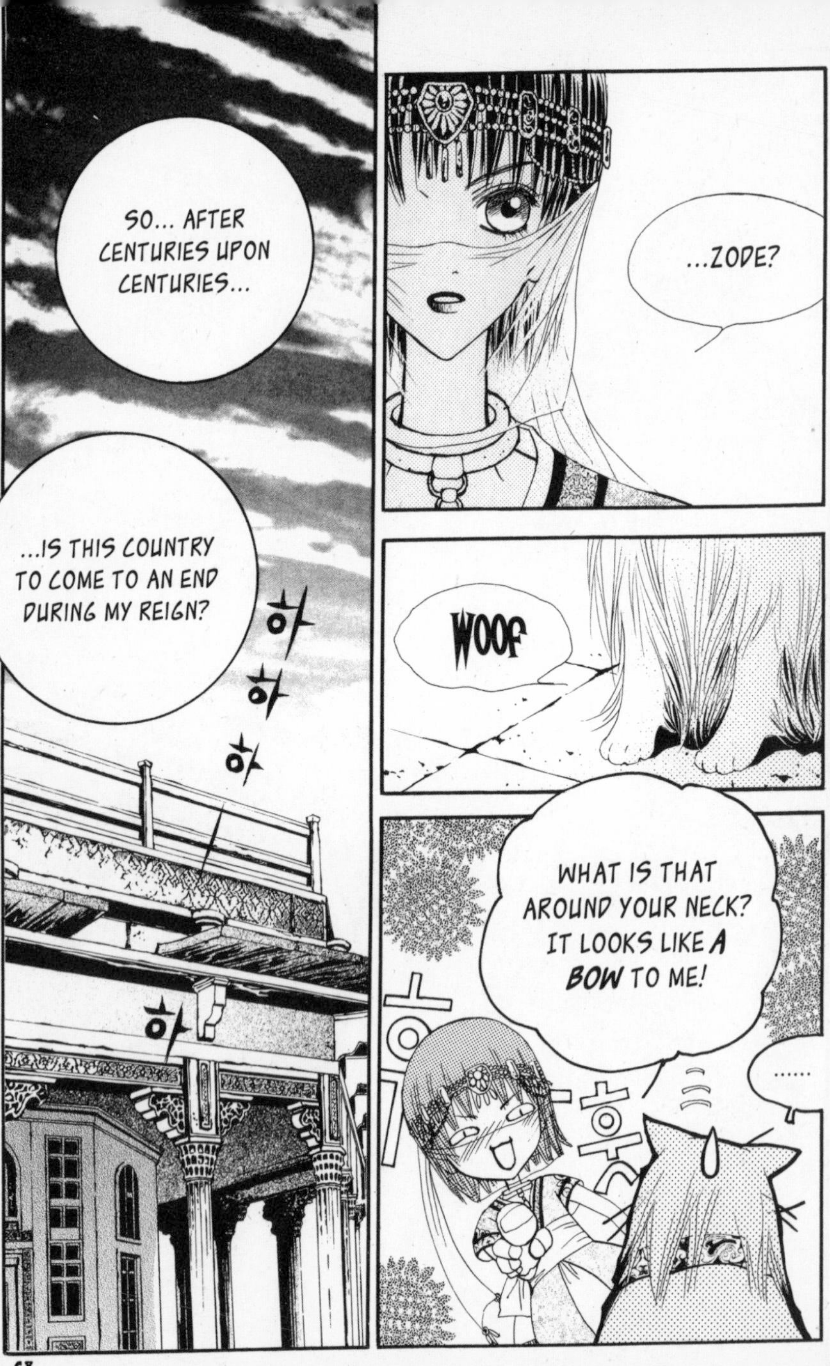
SO... AFTER CENTURIES UPON CENTURIES...
...IS THIS COUNTRY TO COME TO AN END DURING MY REIGN?
하
하
하
하
...ZODE?
WOOF
WHAT IS THAT AROUND YOUR NECK? IT LOOKS LIKE A BOW TO ME!
......

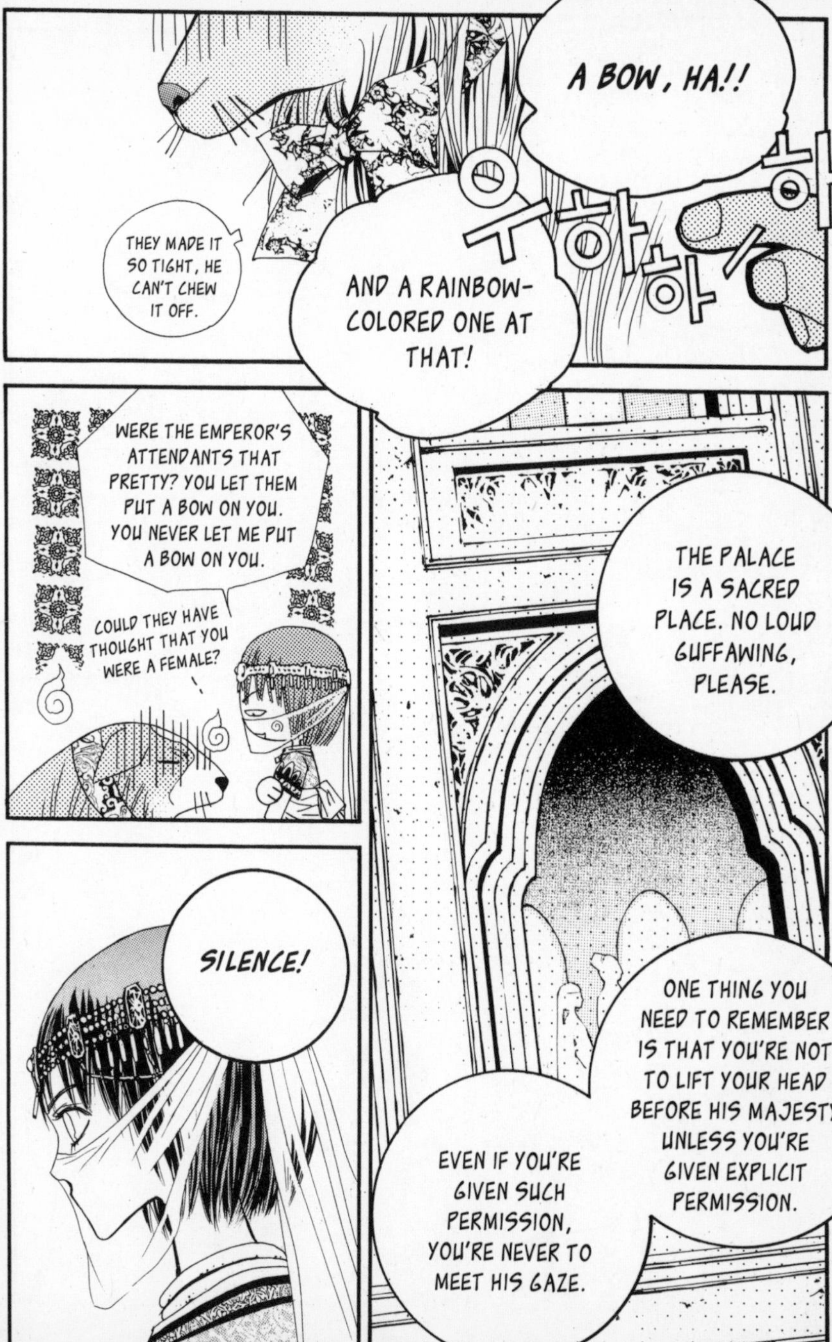
A BOW, HA!!
우하하하
THEY MADE IT SO TIGHT, HE CAN'T CHEW IT OFF.
AND A RAINBOW-COLORED ONE AT THAT!
WERE THE EMPEROR'S ATTENDANTS THAT PRETTY? YOU LET THEM PUT A BOW ON YOU. YOU NEVER LET ME PUT A BOW ON YOU.
COULD THEY HAVE THOUGHT THAT YOU WERE A FEMALE?
SILENCE!
THE PALACE IS A SACRED PLACE. NO LOUD GUFFAWING, PLEASE.
ONE THING YOU NEED TO REMEMBER IS THAT YOU'RE NOT TO LIFT YOUR HEAD BEFORE HIS MAJESTY UNLESS YOU'RE GIVEN EXPLICIT PERMISSION.
EVEN IF YOU'RE GIVEN SUCH PERMISSION, YOU'RE NEVER TO MEET HIS GAZE.

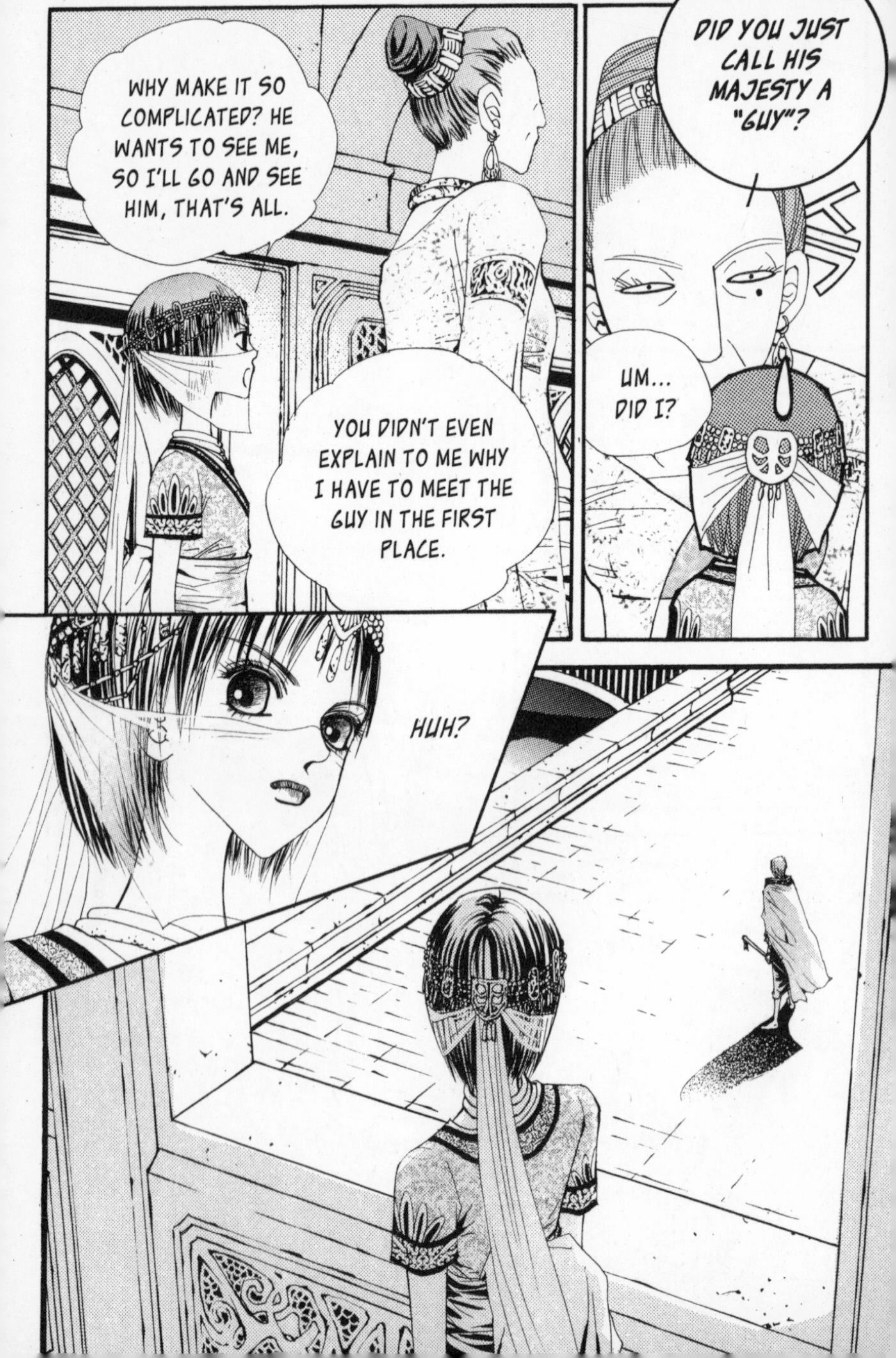
WHY MAKE IT SO COMPLICATED? HE WANTS TO SEE ME, SO I'LL GO AND SEE HIM, THAT'S ALL.
YOU DIDN'T EVEN EXPLAIN TO ME WHY I HAVE TO MEET THE GUY IN THE FIRST PLACE.
DID YOU JUST CALL HIS MAJESTY A "GUY"?
KIK
UM... DID I?
HUH?

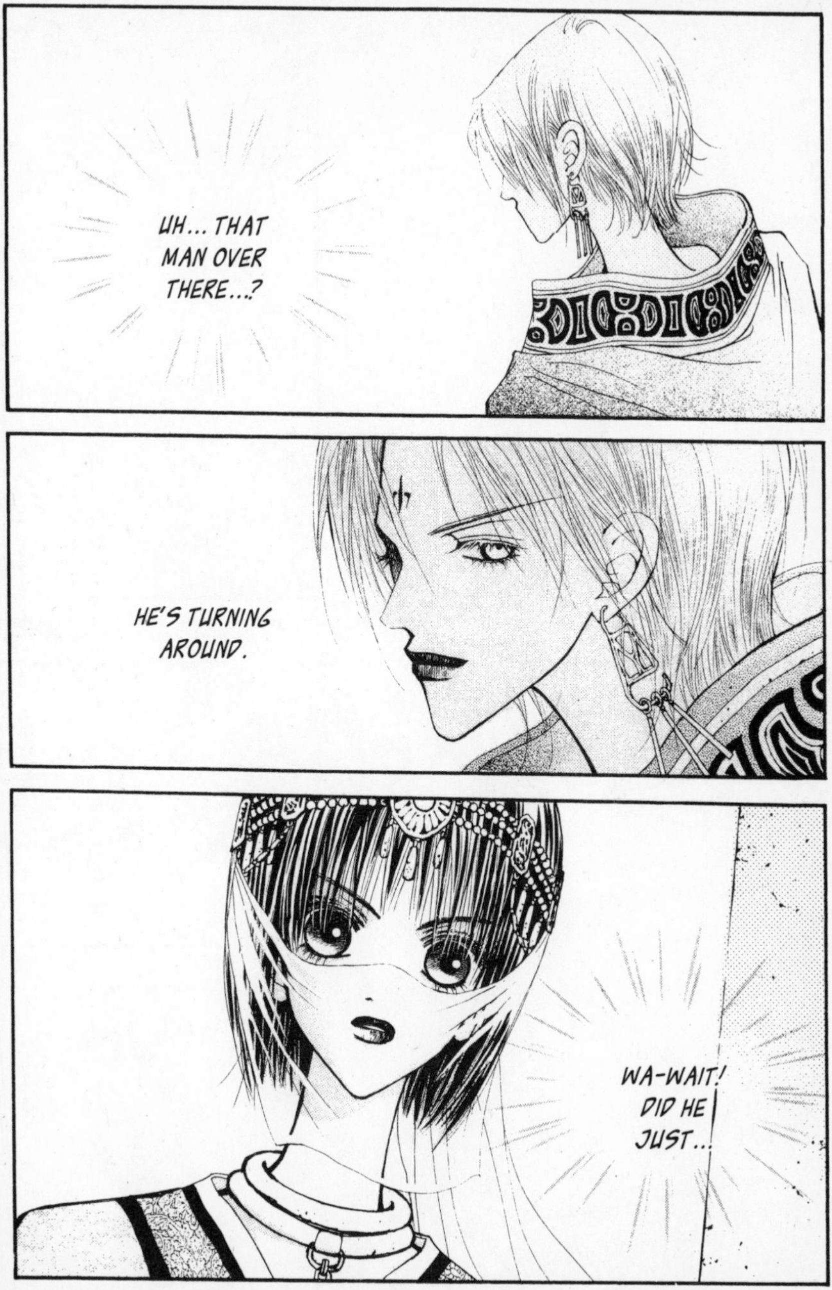
UH... THAT MAN OVER THERE...?
HE'S TURNING AROUND.
WA-WAIT! DID HE JUST...

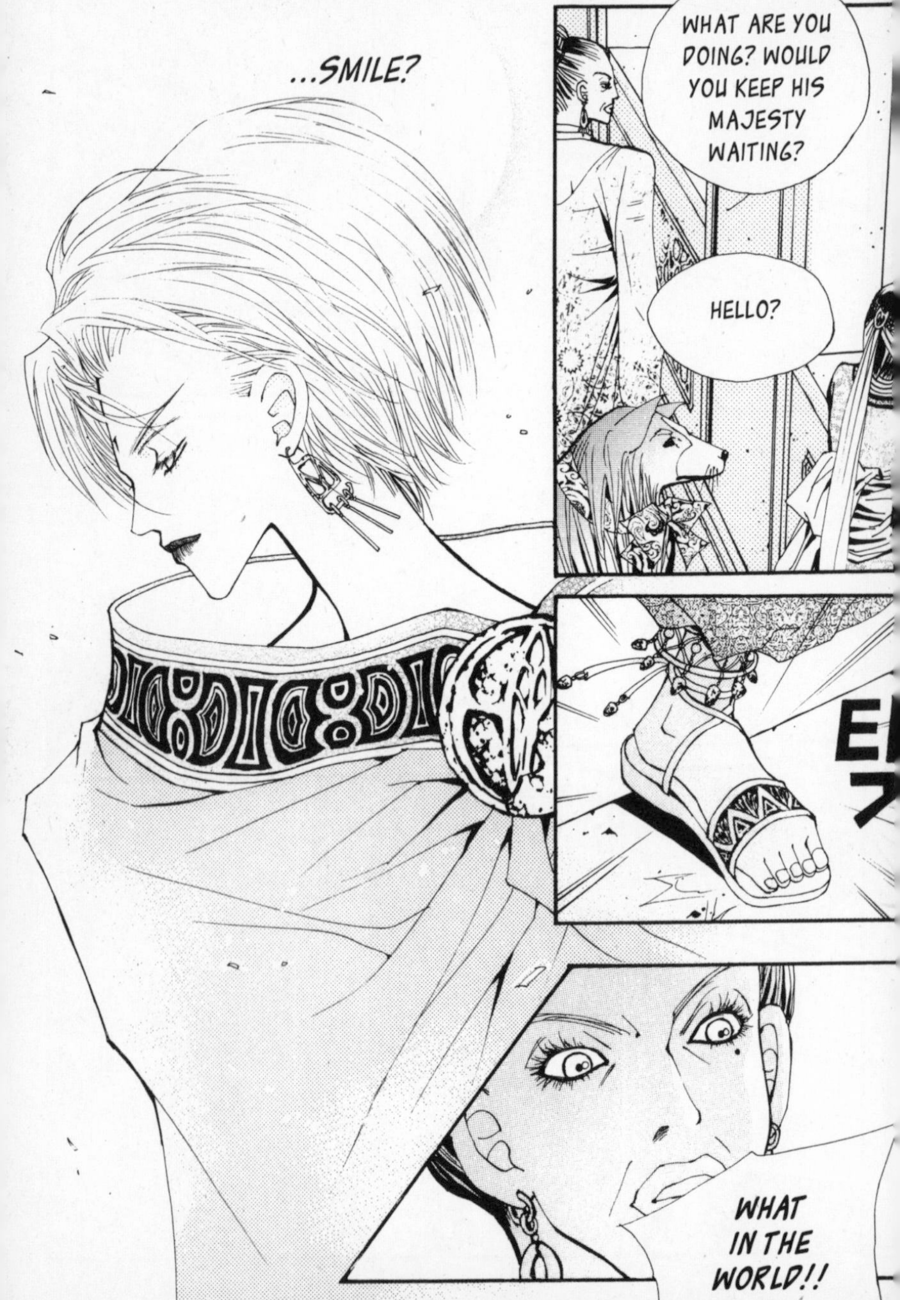
...SMILE?
WHAT ARE YOU DOING? WOULD YOU KEEP HIS MAJESTY WAITING?
HELLO?
WHAT IN THE WORLD!!

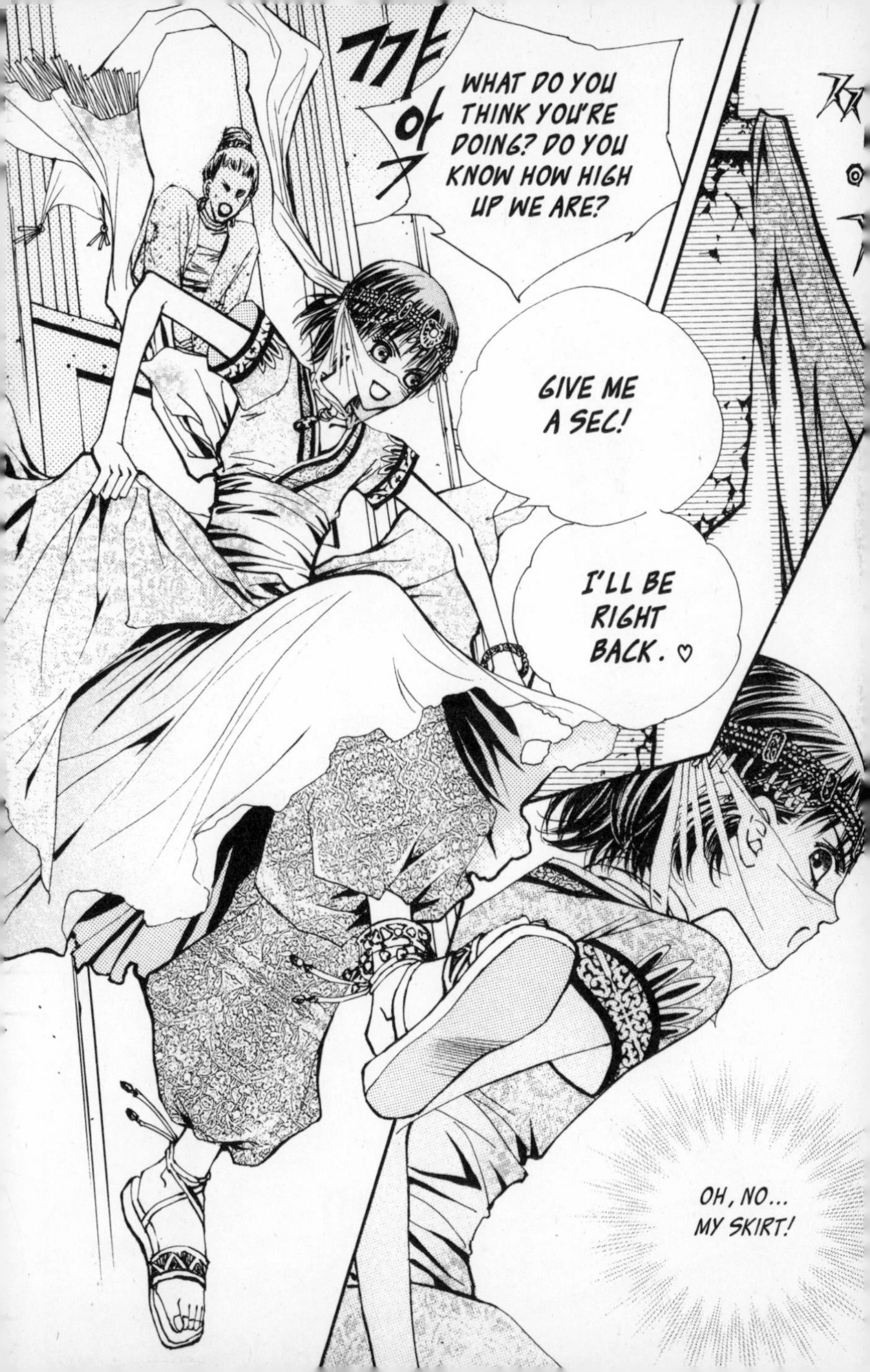
꺄아~
WHAT DO YOU THINK YOU'RE DOING? DO YOU KNOW HOW HIGH UP WE ARE?
GIVE ME A SEC!
I'LL BE RIGHT BACK. ♡
OH, NO... MY SKIRT!

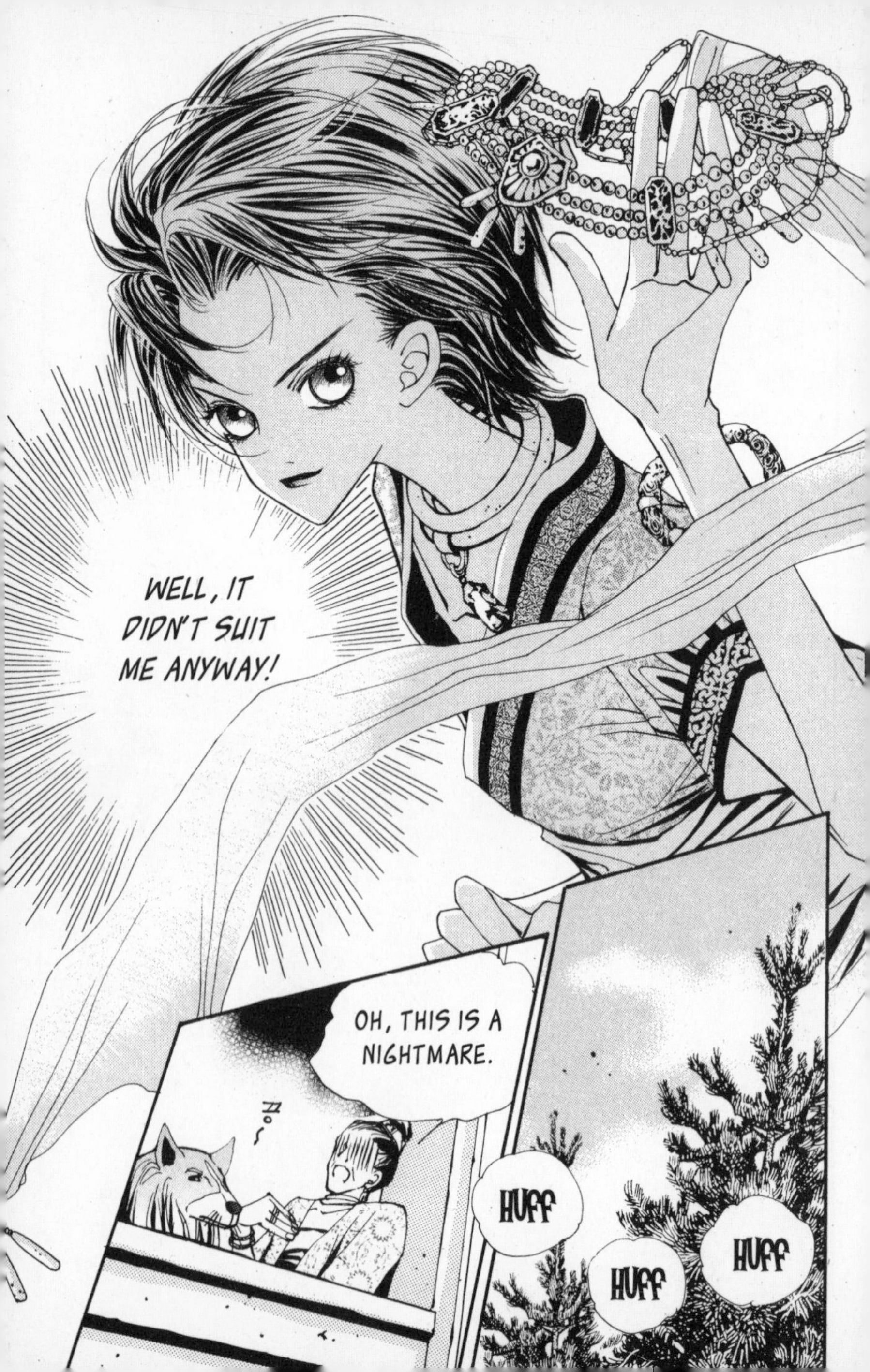
WELL, IT DIDN'T SUIT ME ANYWAY!
OH, THIS IS A NIGHTMARE.
HUFF
HUFF
HUFF

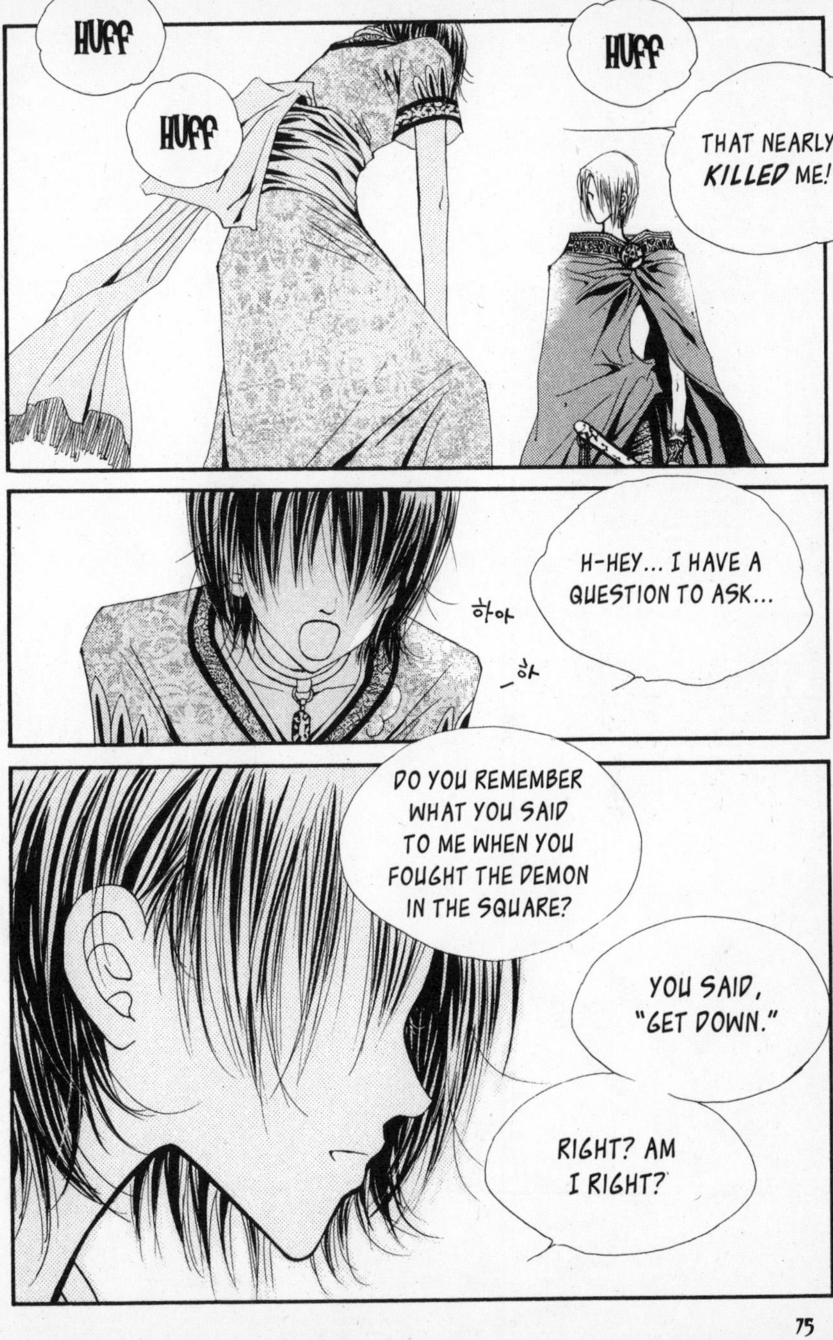
HUFF
HUFF
HUFF
THAT NEARLY KILLED ME!
하아
하
H-HEY... I HAVE A QUESTION TO ASK...
DO YOU REMEMBER WHAT YOU SAID TO ME WHEN YOU FOUGHT THE DEMON IN THE SQUARE?
YOU SAID, "GET DOWN."
RIGHT? AM I RIGHT?

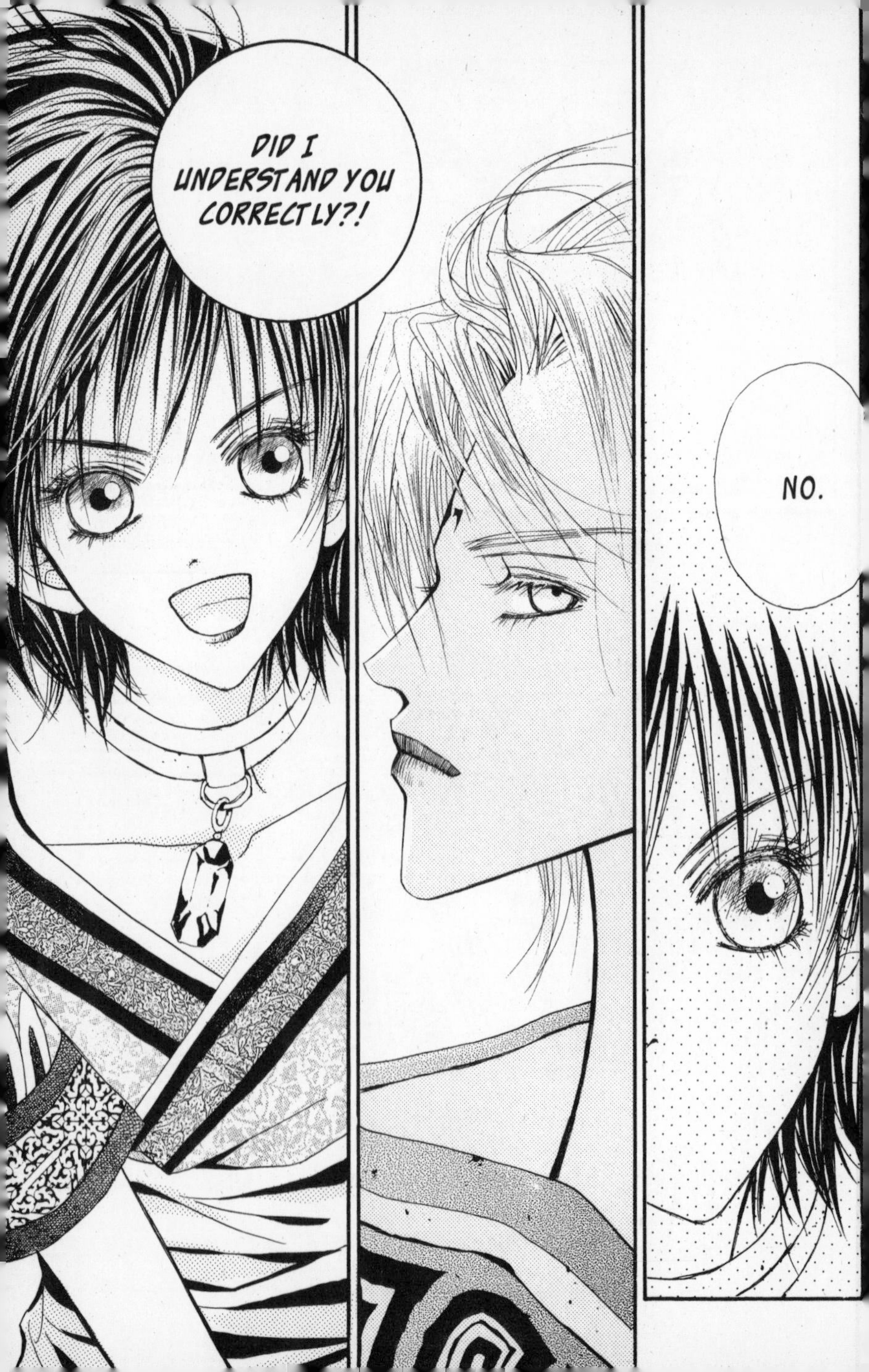
DID I UNDERSTAND YOU CORRECTLY?!
NO.

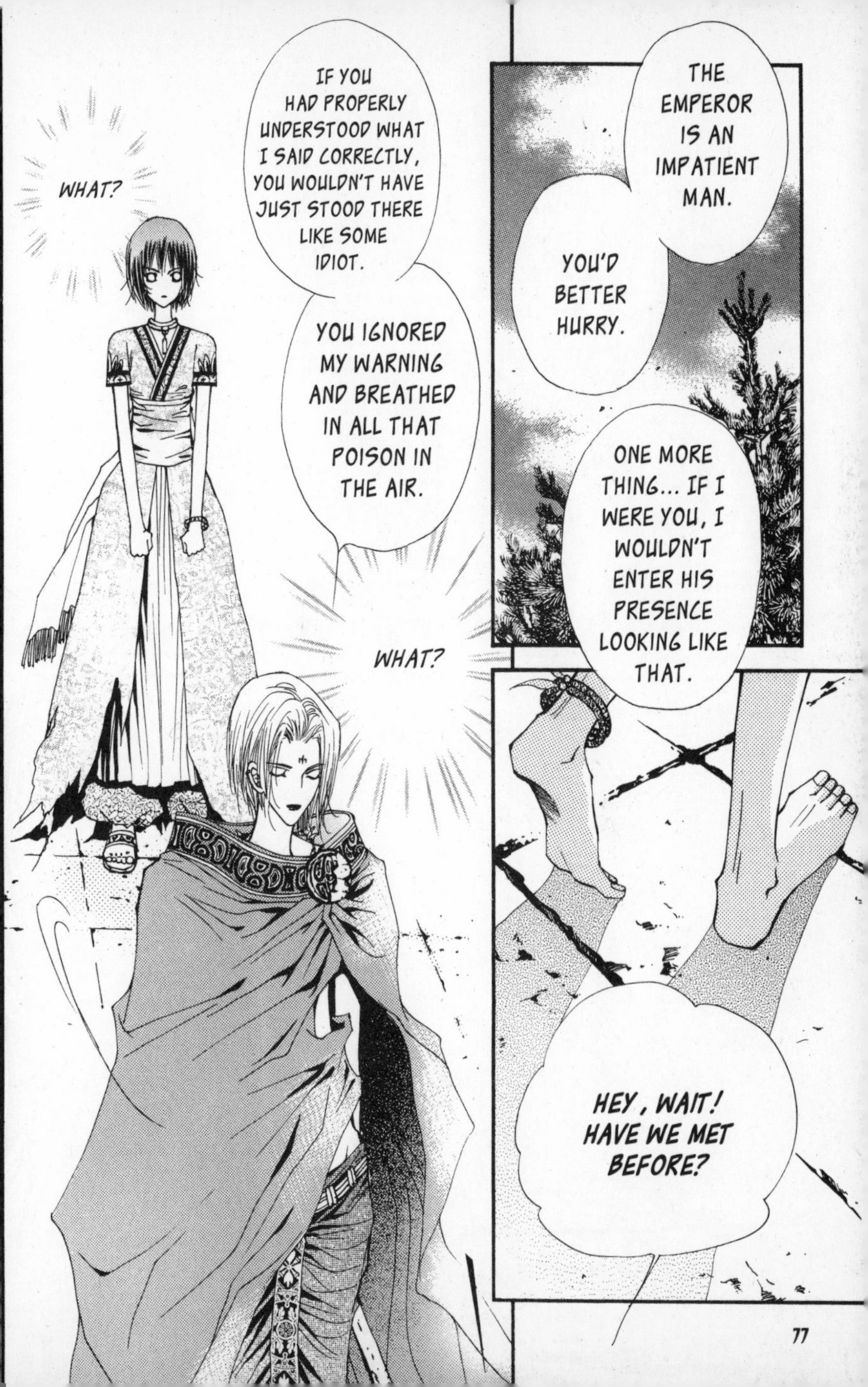

IF YOU HAD PROPERLY UNDERSTOOD WHAT I SAID CORRECTLY, YOU WOULDN'T HAVE JUST STOOD THERE LIKE SOME IDIOT.
WHAT?
YOU IGNORED MY WARNING AND BREATHED IN ALL THAT POISON IN THE AIR.
WHAT?
THE EMPEROR IS AN IMPATIENT MAN.
YOU'D BETTER HURRY.
ONE MORE THING... IF I WERE YOU, I WOULDN'T ENTER HIS PRESENCE LOOKING LIKE THAT.
HEY, WAIT! HAVE WE MET BEFORE?

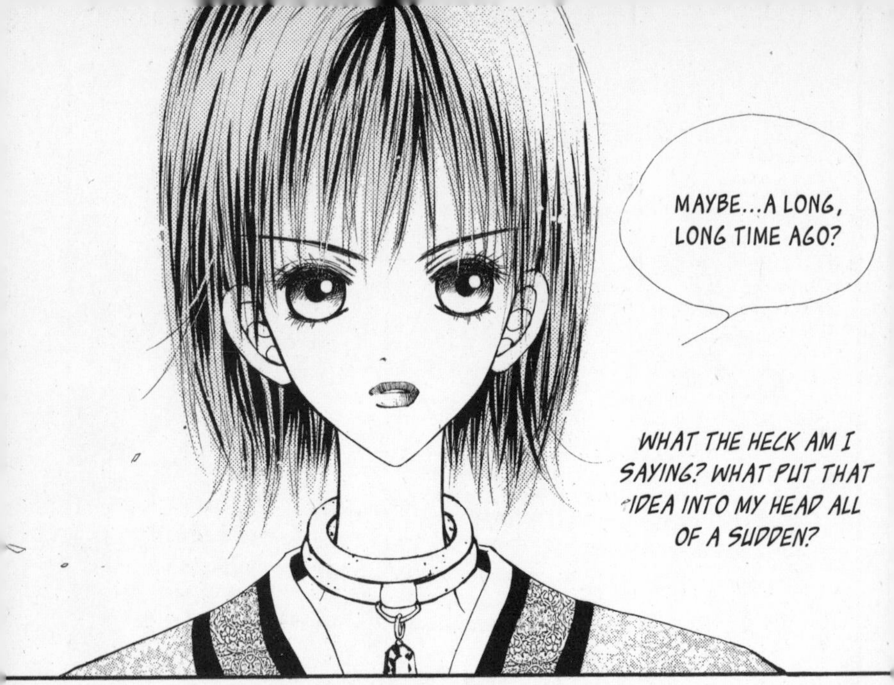
MAYBE...A LONG, LONG TIME AGO?
WHAT THE HECK AM I SAYING? WHAT PUT THAT IDEA INTO MY HEAD ALL OF A SUDDEN?
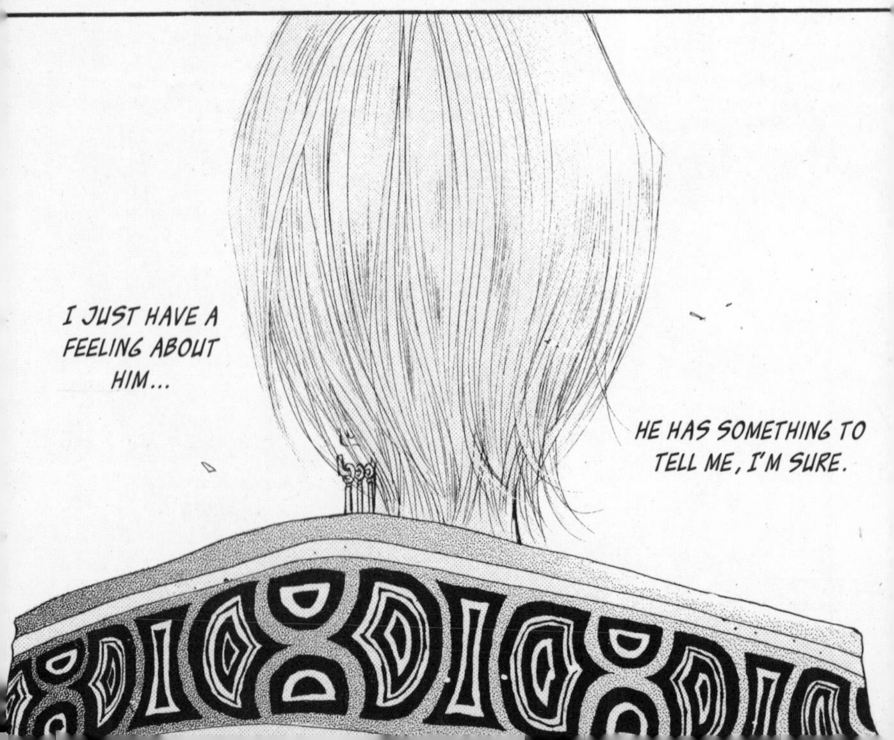
I JUST HAVE A FEELING ABOUT HIM...
HE HAS SOMETHING TO TELL ME, I'M SURE.

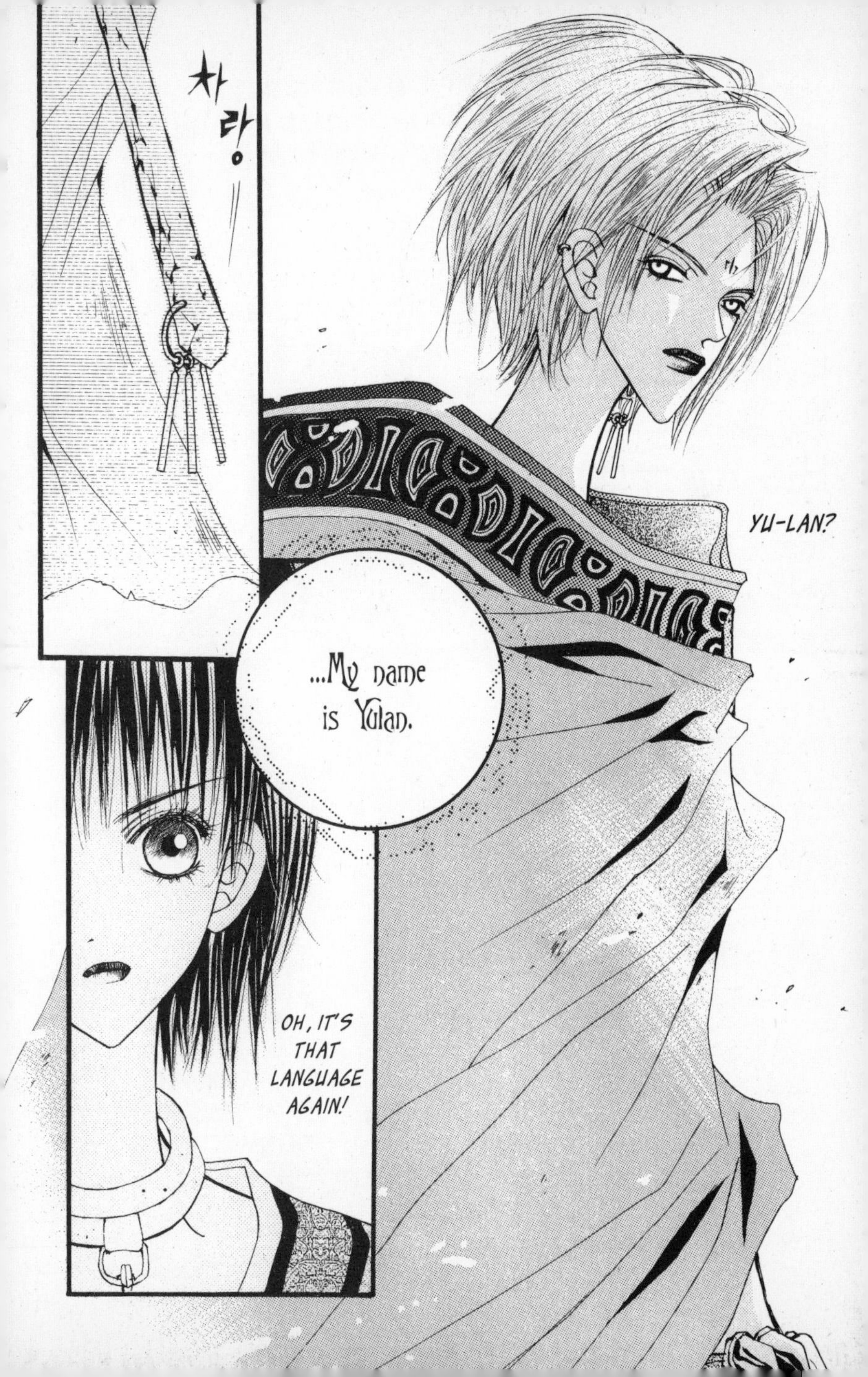
차랑
...My name is Yulan.
YU-LAN?
OH, IT'S THAT LANGUAGE AGAIN!

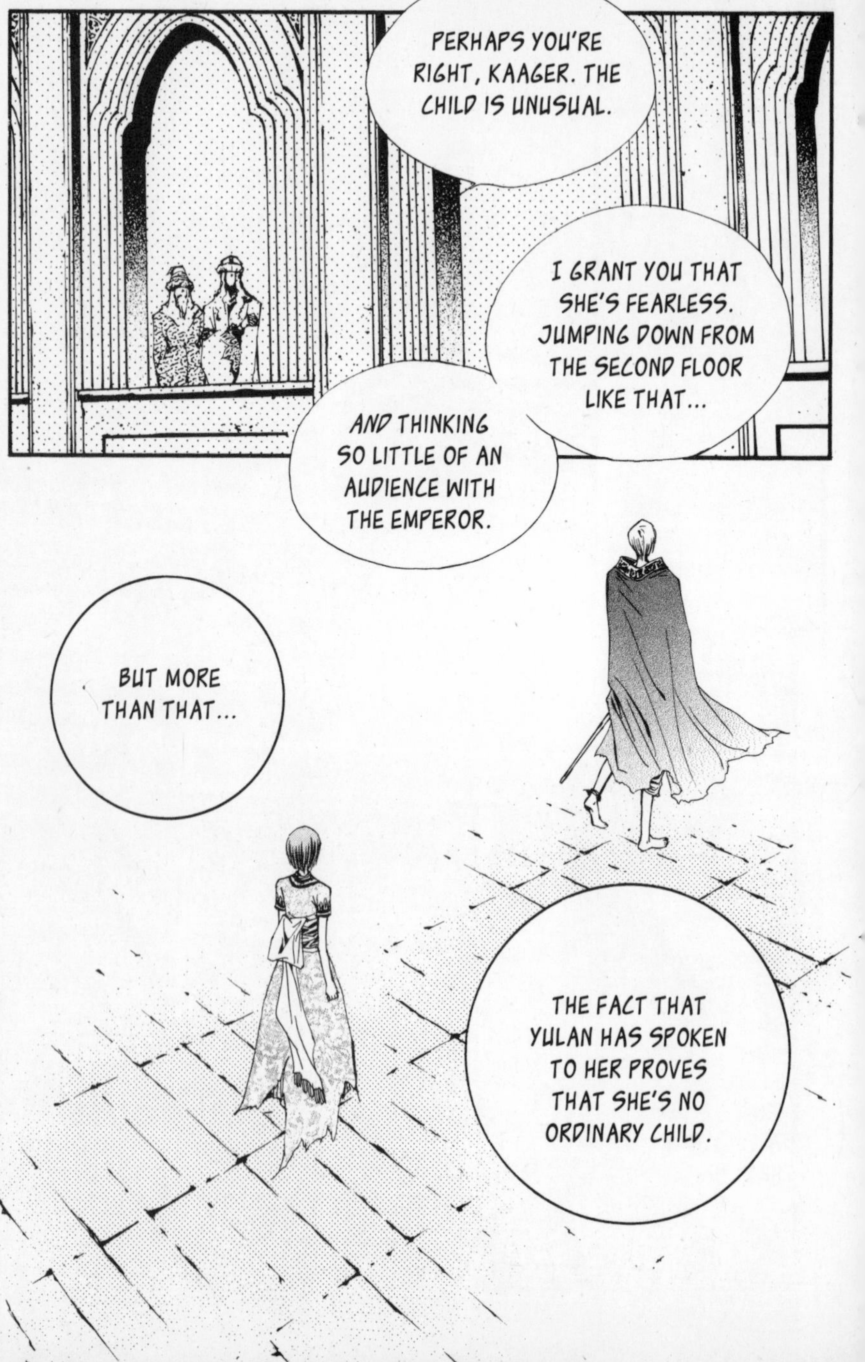
PERHAPS YOU'RE RIGHT, KAAGER. THE CHILD IS UNUSUAL.
I GRANT YOU THAT SHE'S FEARLESS. JUMPING DOWN FROM THE SECOND FLOOR LIKE THAT...
AND THINKING SO LITTLE OF AN AUDIENCE WITH THE EMPEROR.
BUT MORE THAN THAT...
THE FACT THAT YULAN HAS SPOKEN TO HER PROVES THAT SHE'S NO ORDINARY CHILD.

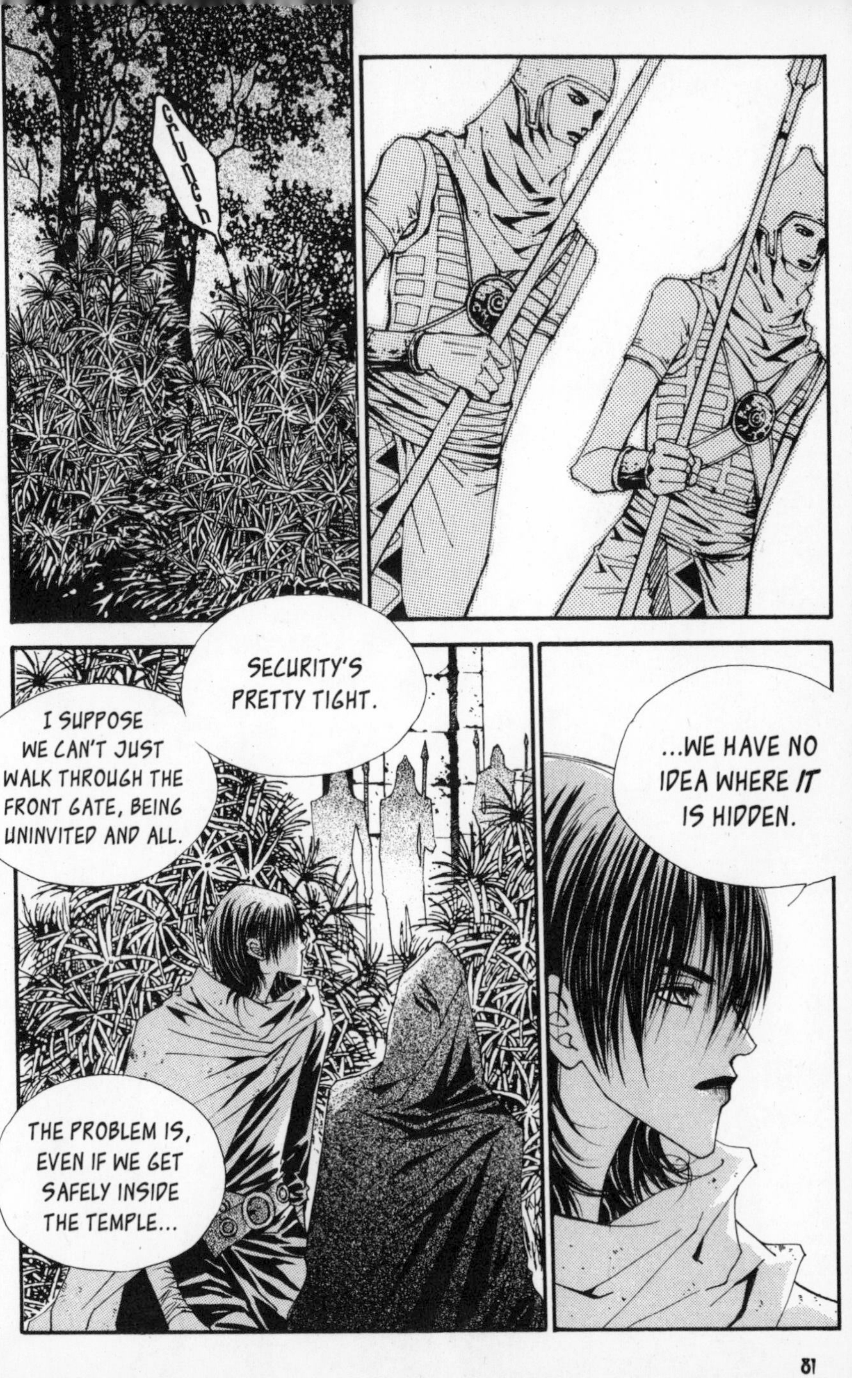
crunch
SECURITY'S PRETTY TIGHT.
I SUPPOSE WE CAN'T JUST WALK THROUGH THE FRONT GATE, BEING UNINVITED AND ALL.
THE PROBLEM IS, EVEN IF WE GET SAFELY INSIDE THE TEMPLE...
...WE HAVE NO IDEA WHERE *IT* IS HIDDEN.

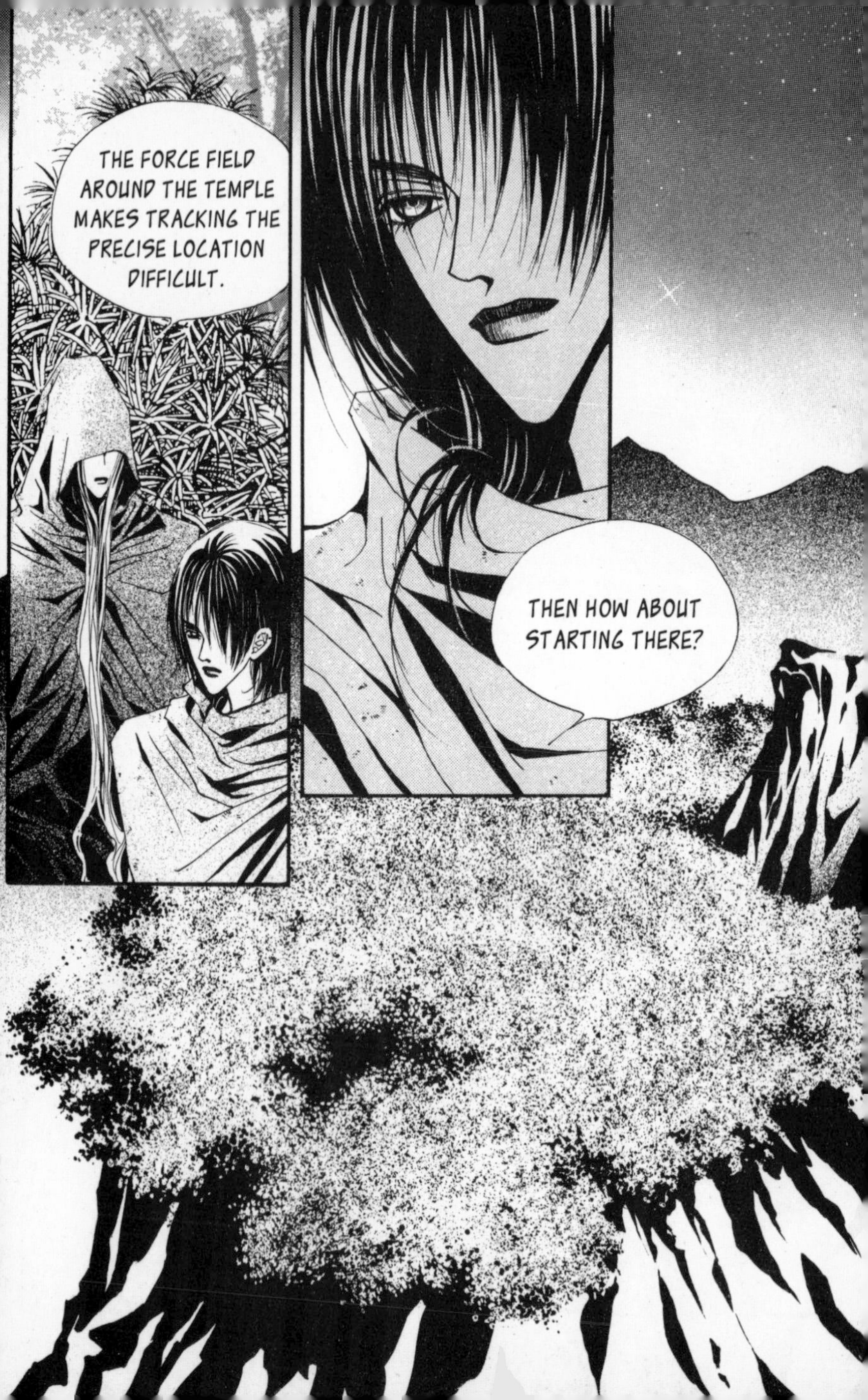
THE FORCE FIELD AROUND THE TEMPLE MAKES TRACKING THE PRECISE LOCATION DIFFICULT.
THEN HOW ABOUT STARTING THERE?

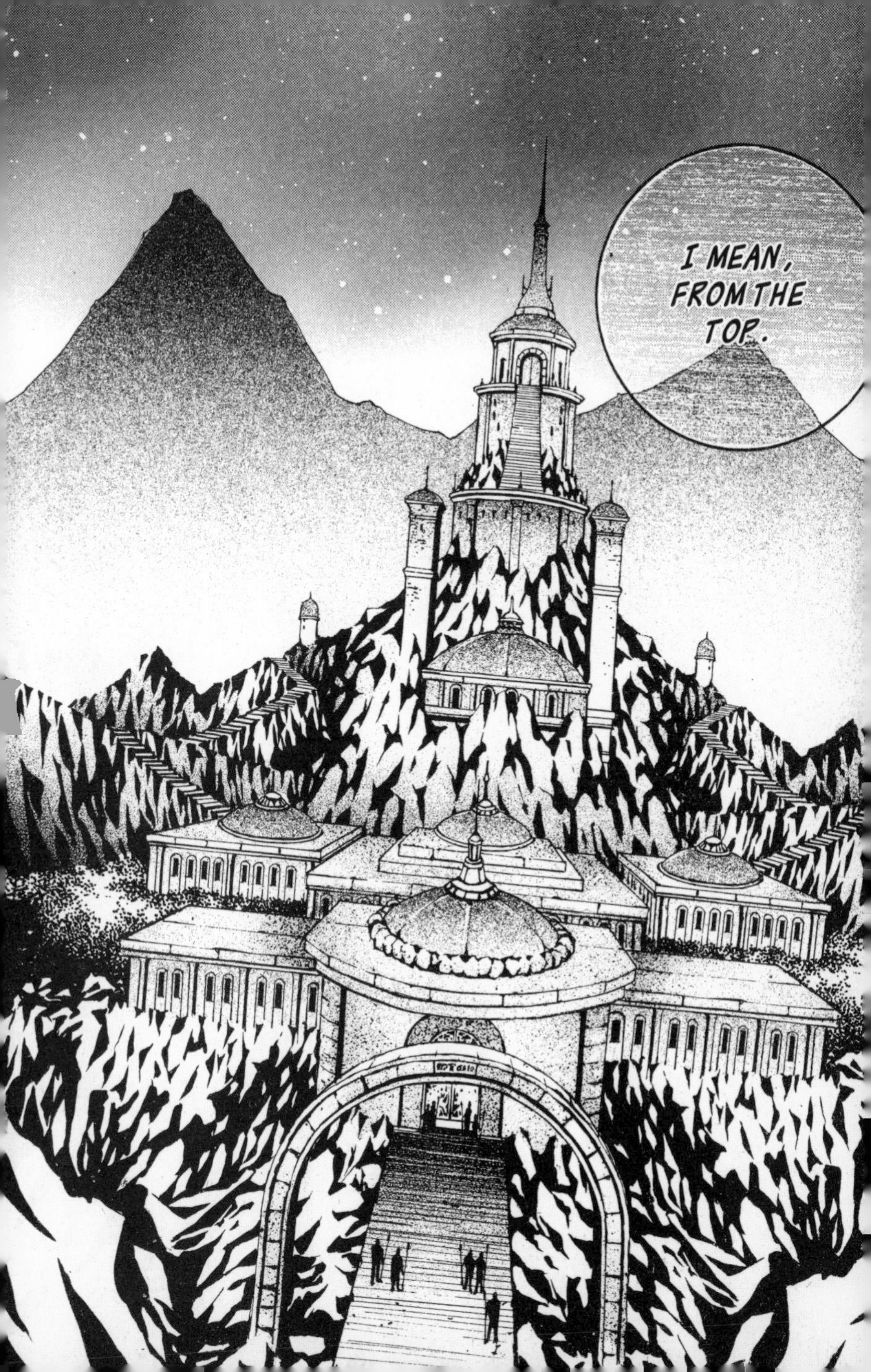
I MEAN, FROM THE TOP.

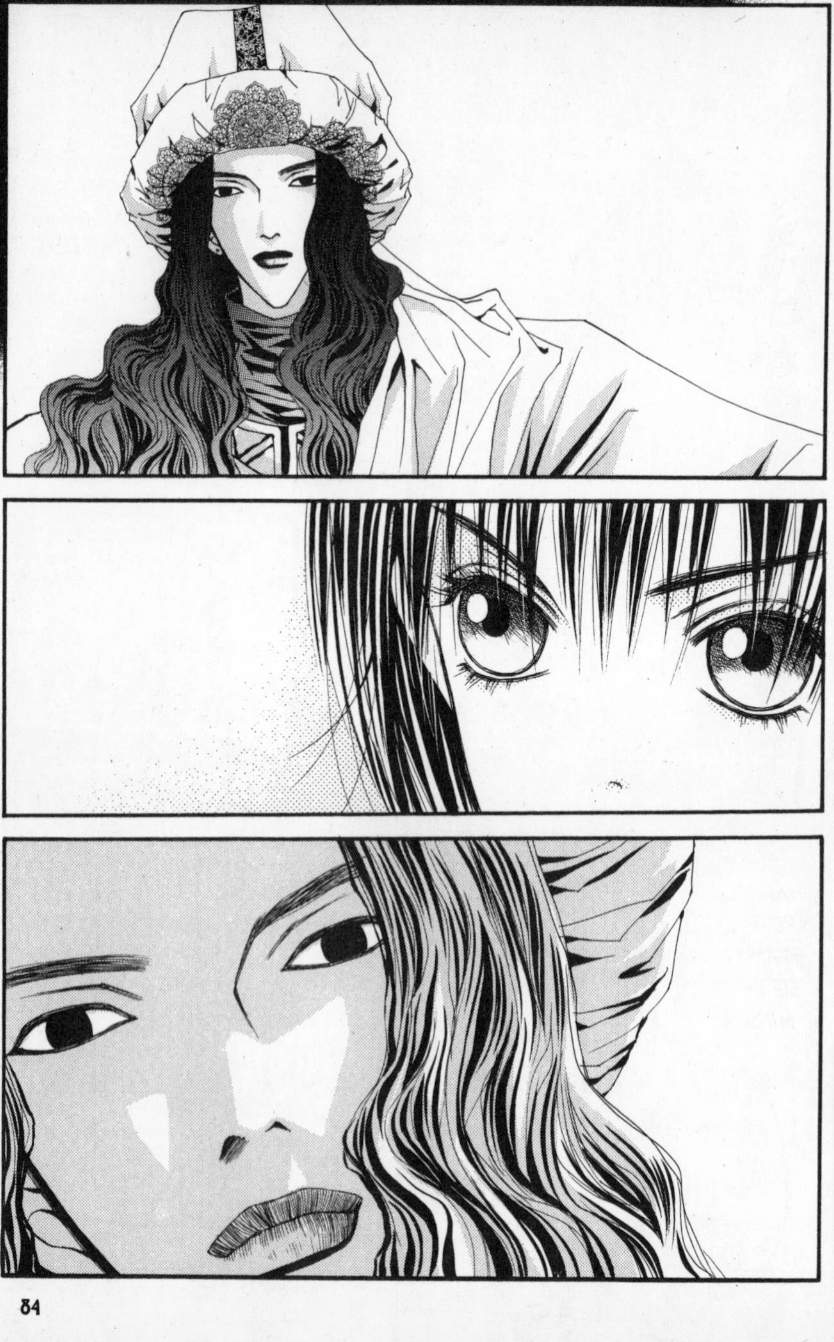

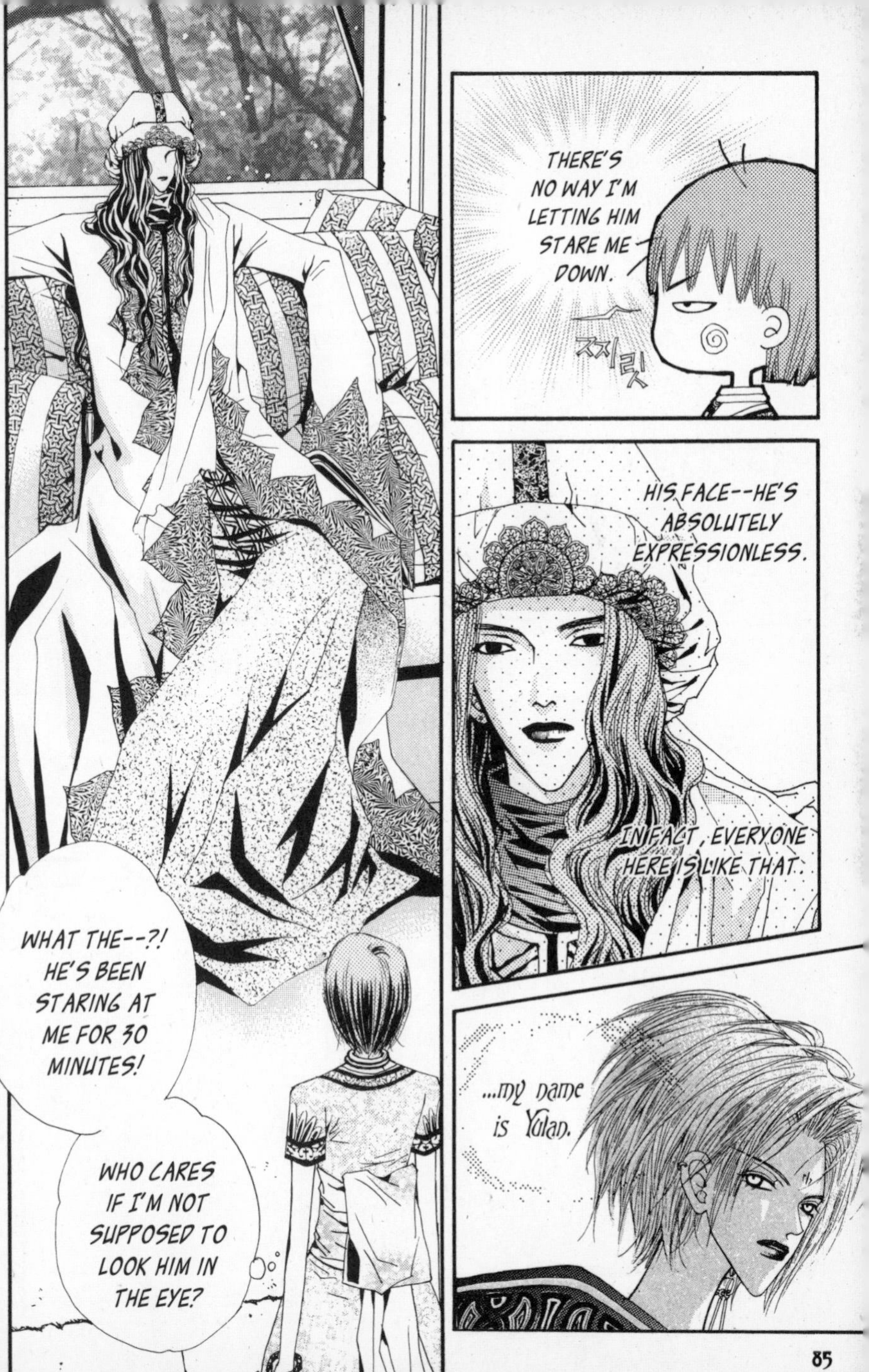
WHAT THE--?! HE'S BEEN STARING AT ME FOR 30 MINUTES!
WHO CARES IF I'M NOT SUPPOSED TO LOOK HIM IN THE EYE?
THERE'S NO WAY I'M LETTING HIM STARE ME DOWN.
즈지릿
HIS FACE--HE'S ABSOLUTELY EXPRESSIONLESS.
IN FACT, EVERYONE HERE IS LIKE THAT.
...my name is Yulan.

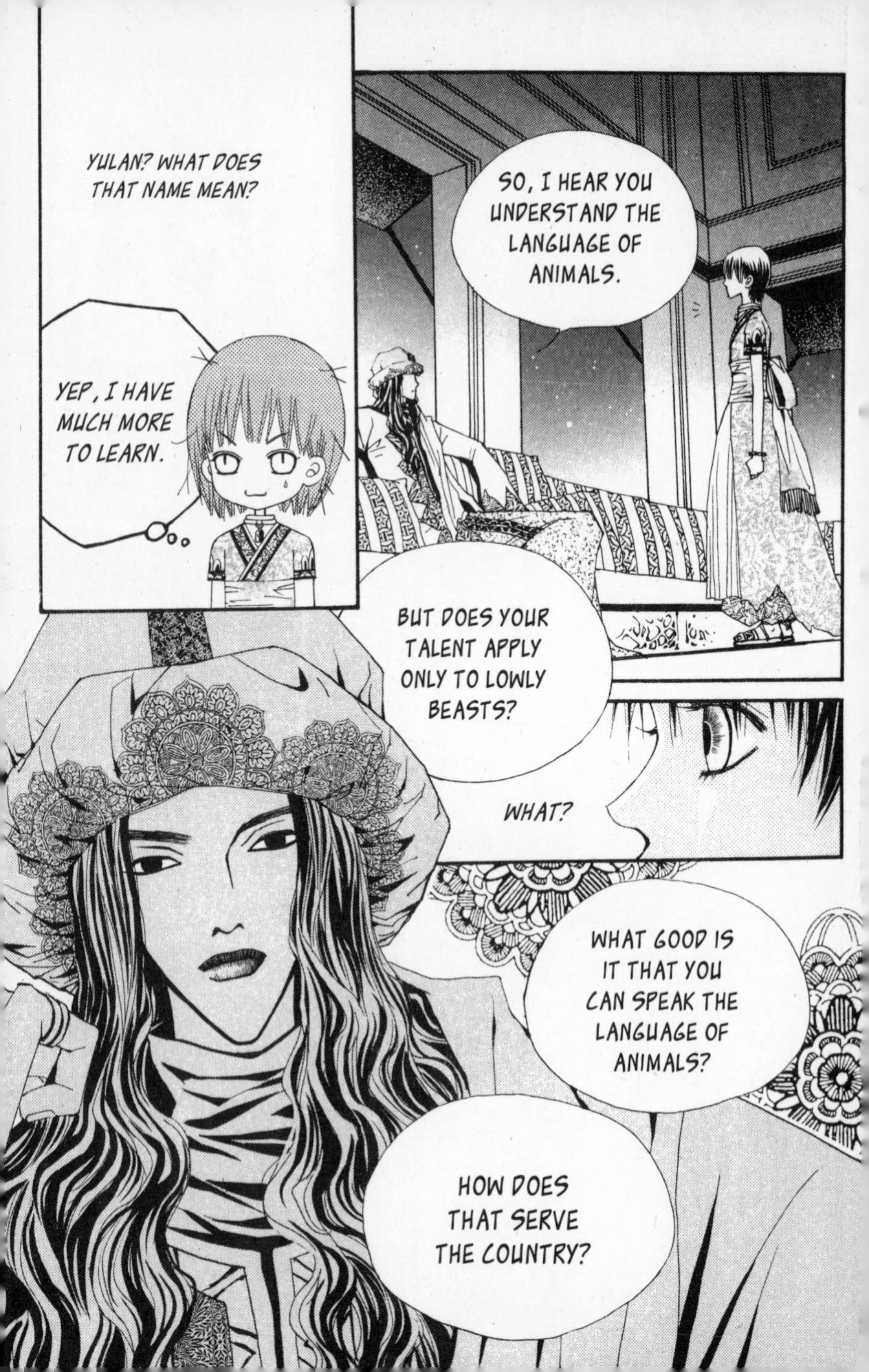
YULAN? WHAT DOES THAT NAME MEAN?
YEP, I HAVE MUCH MORE TO LEARN.
SO, I HEAR YOU UNDERSTAND THE LANGUAGE OF ANIMALS.
BUT DOES YOUR TALENT APPLY ONLY TO LOWLY BEASTS?
WHAT?
WHAT GOOD IS IT THAT YOU CAN SPEAK THE LANGUAGE OF ANIMALS?
HOW DOES THAT SERVE THE COUNTRY?

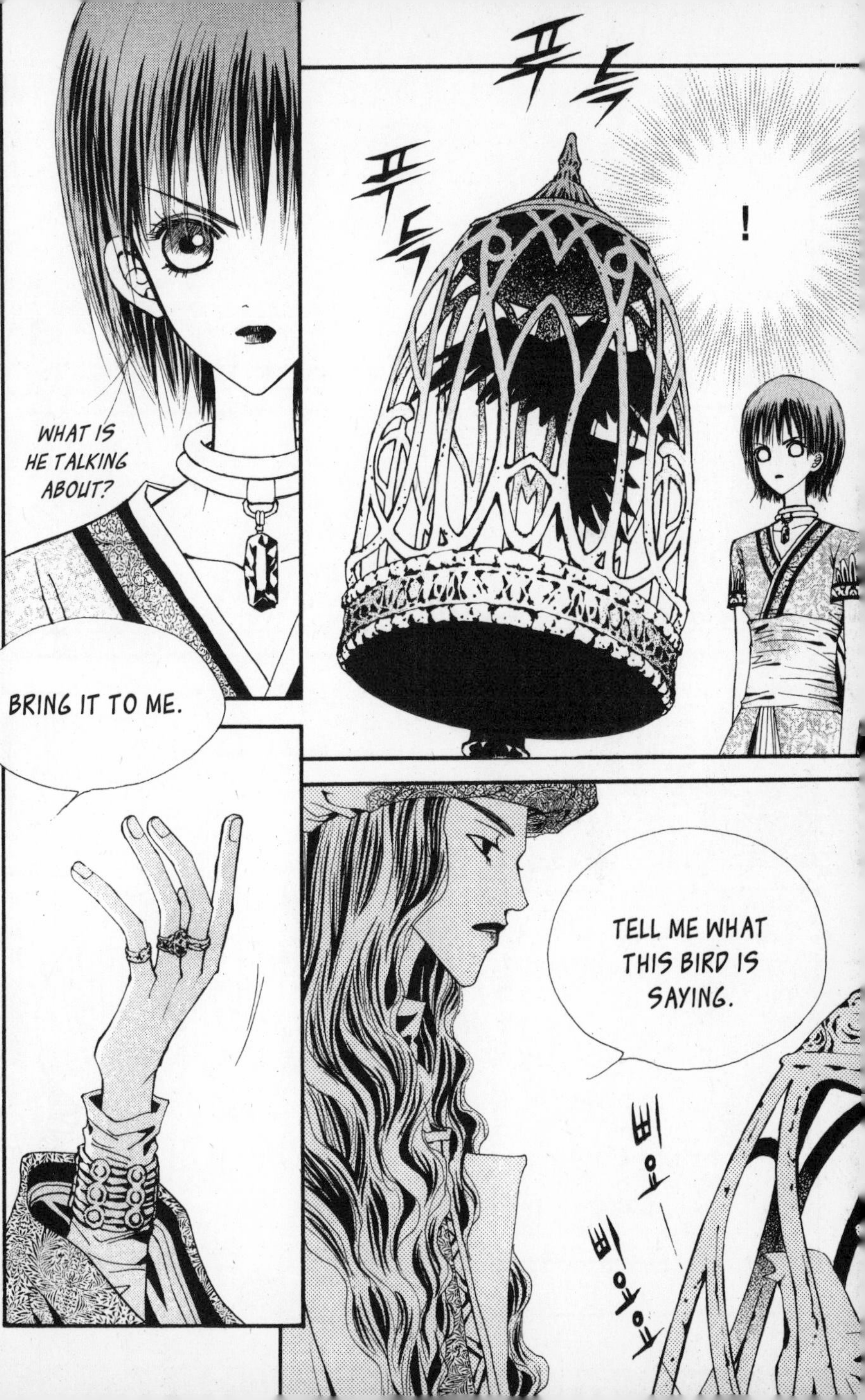
WHAT IS HE TALKING ABOUT?
푸득
푸득
!
BRING IT TO ME.
TELL ME WHAT THIS BIRD IS SAYING.
삐요—
삐요요

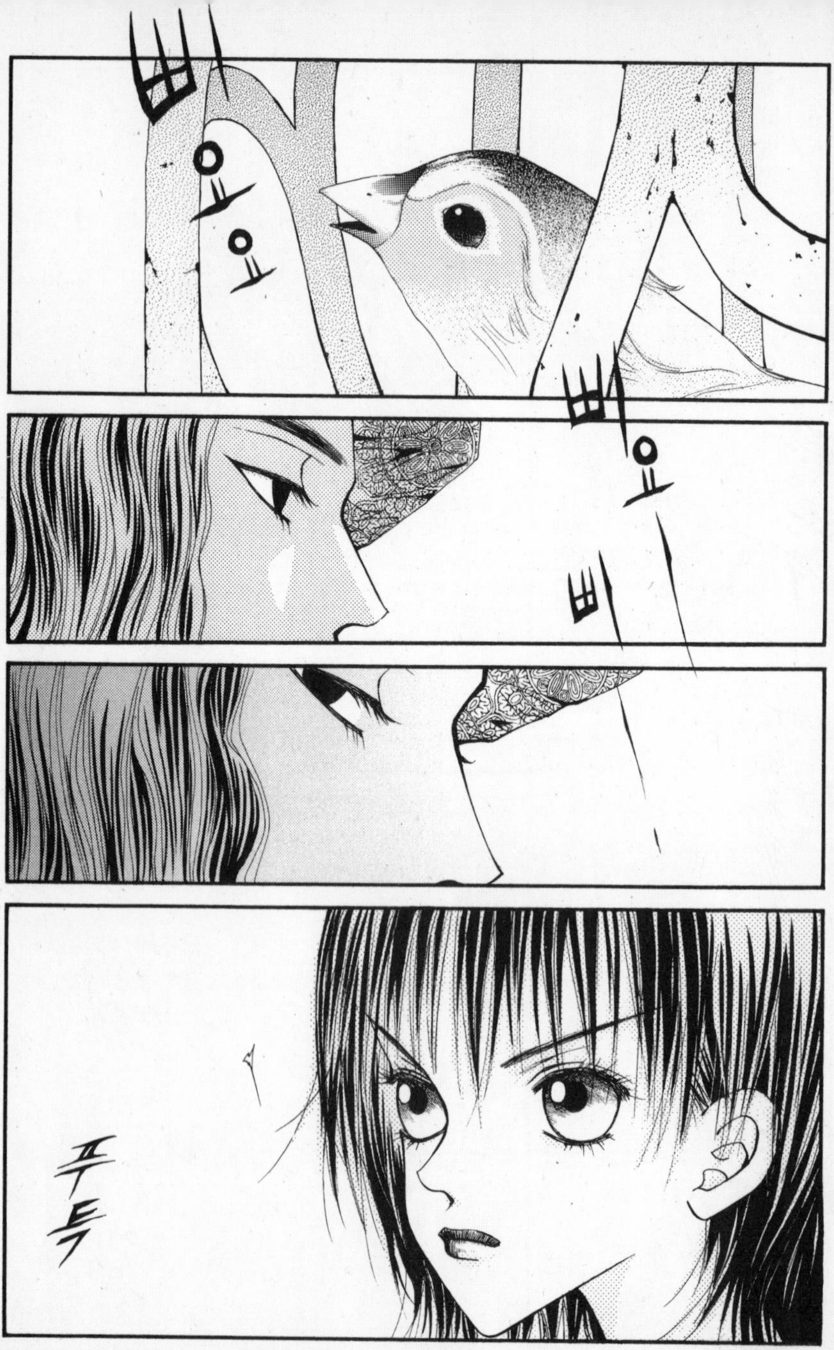
삐요요
삐요
삐
푸특

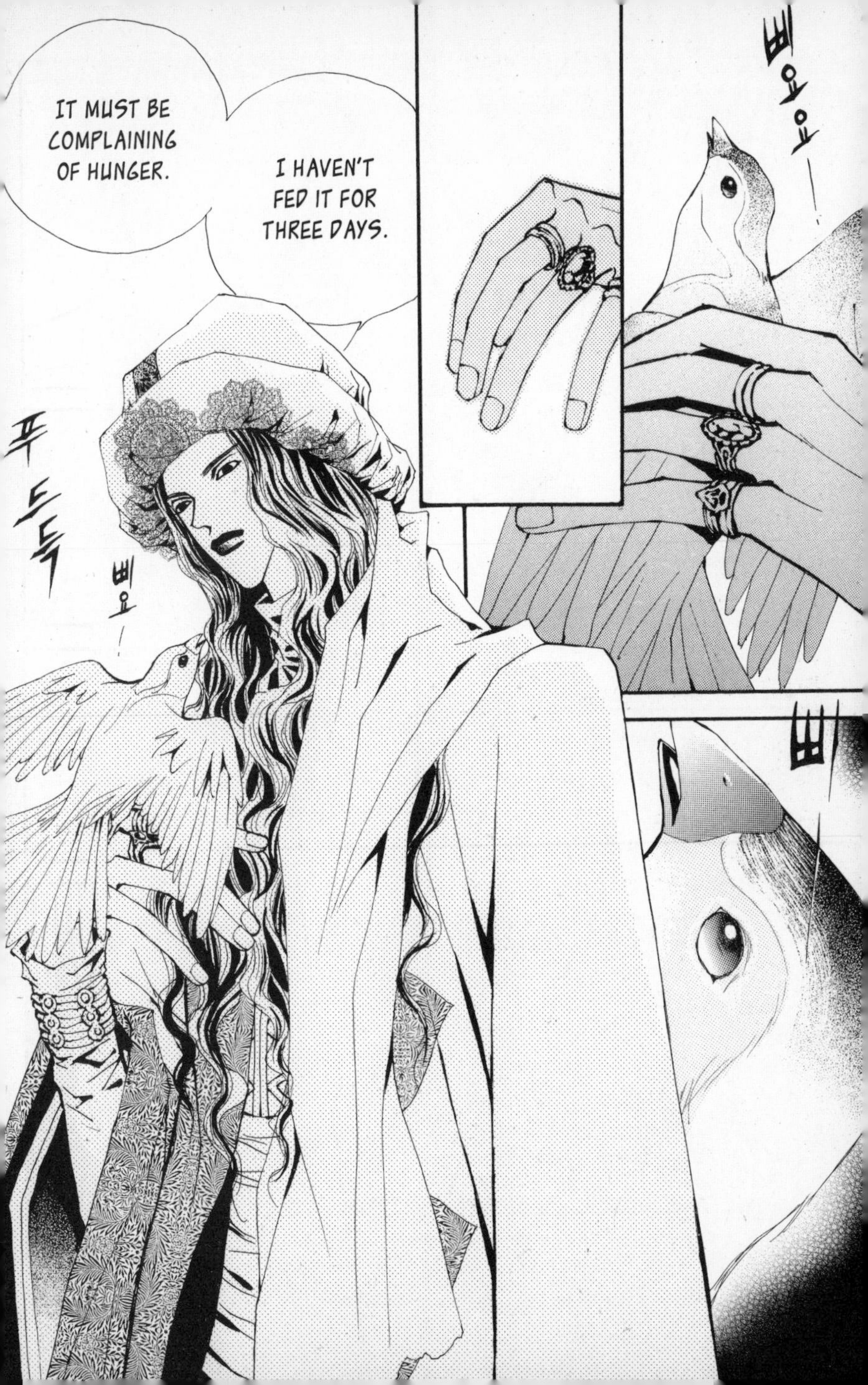
IT MUST BE COMPLAINING OF HUNGER.
I HAVEN'T FED IT FOR THREE DAYS.
푸드득
삐요—!
삐요요—!
삐

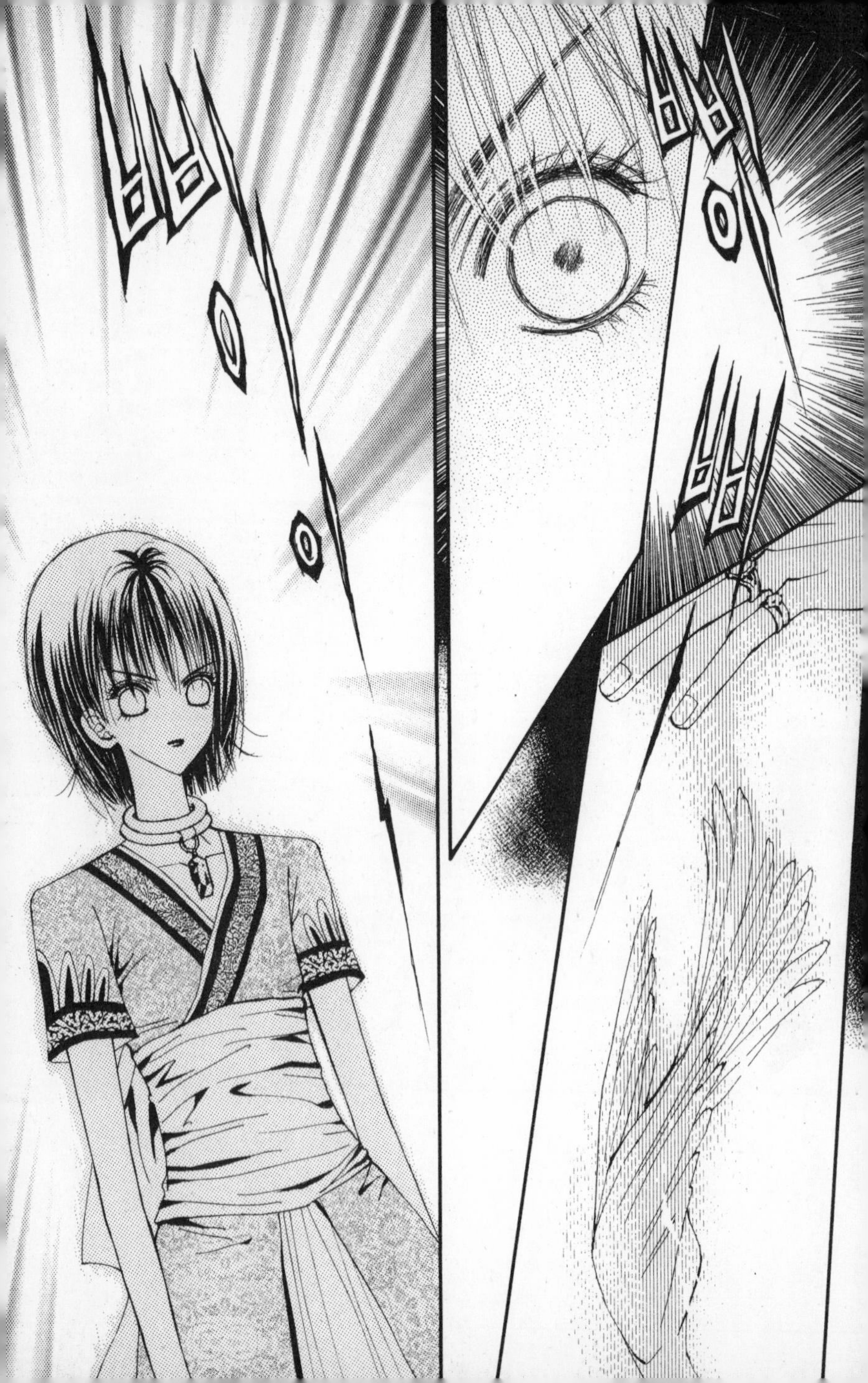

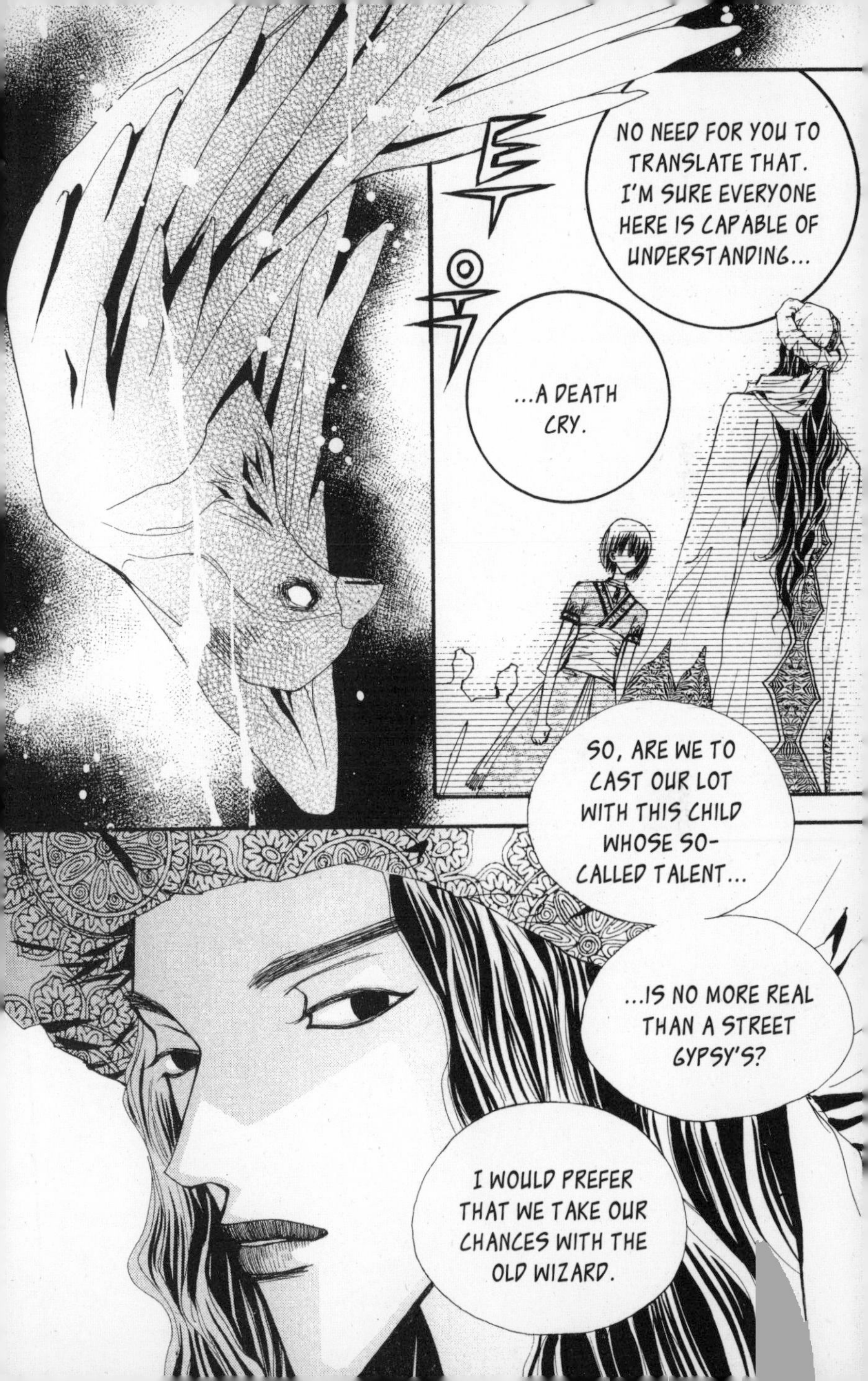
NO NEED FOR YOU TO TRANSLATE THAT. I'M SURE EVERYONE HERE IS CAPABLE OF UNDERSTANDING...
...A DEATH CRY.
SO, ARE WE TO CAST OUR LOT WITH THIS CHILD WHOSE SO-CALLED TALENT...
...IS NO MORE REAL THAN A STREET GYPSY'S?
I WOULD PREFER THAT WE TAKE OUR CHANCES WITH THE OLD WIZARD.

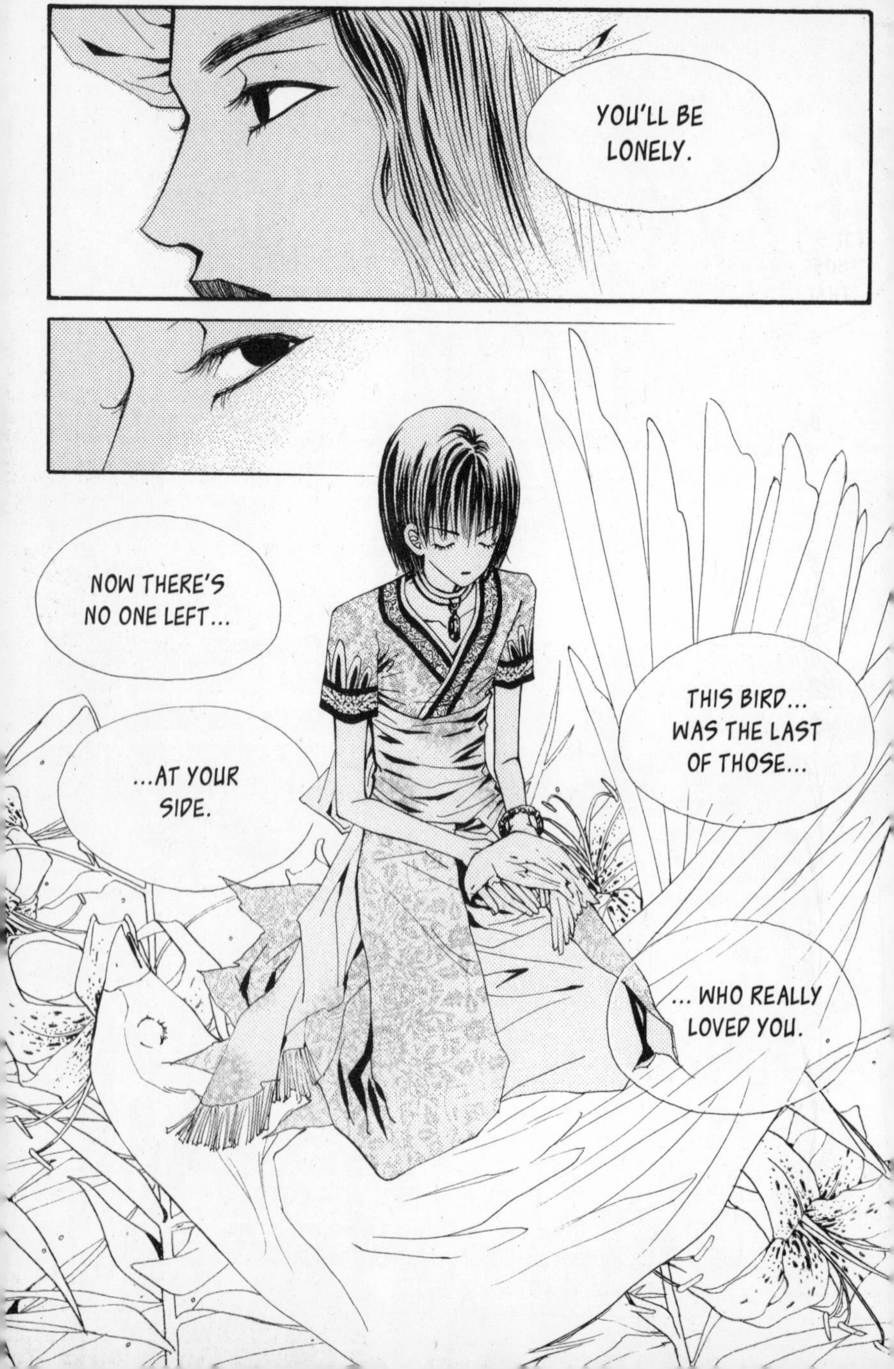
YOU'LL BE LONELY.
NOW THERE'S NO ONE LEFT...
...AT YOUR SIDE.
THIS BIRD... WAS THE LAST OF THOSE...
... WHO REALLY LOVED YOU.

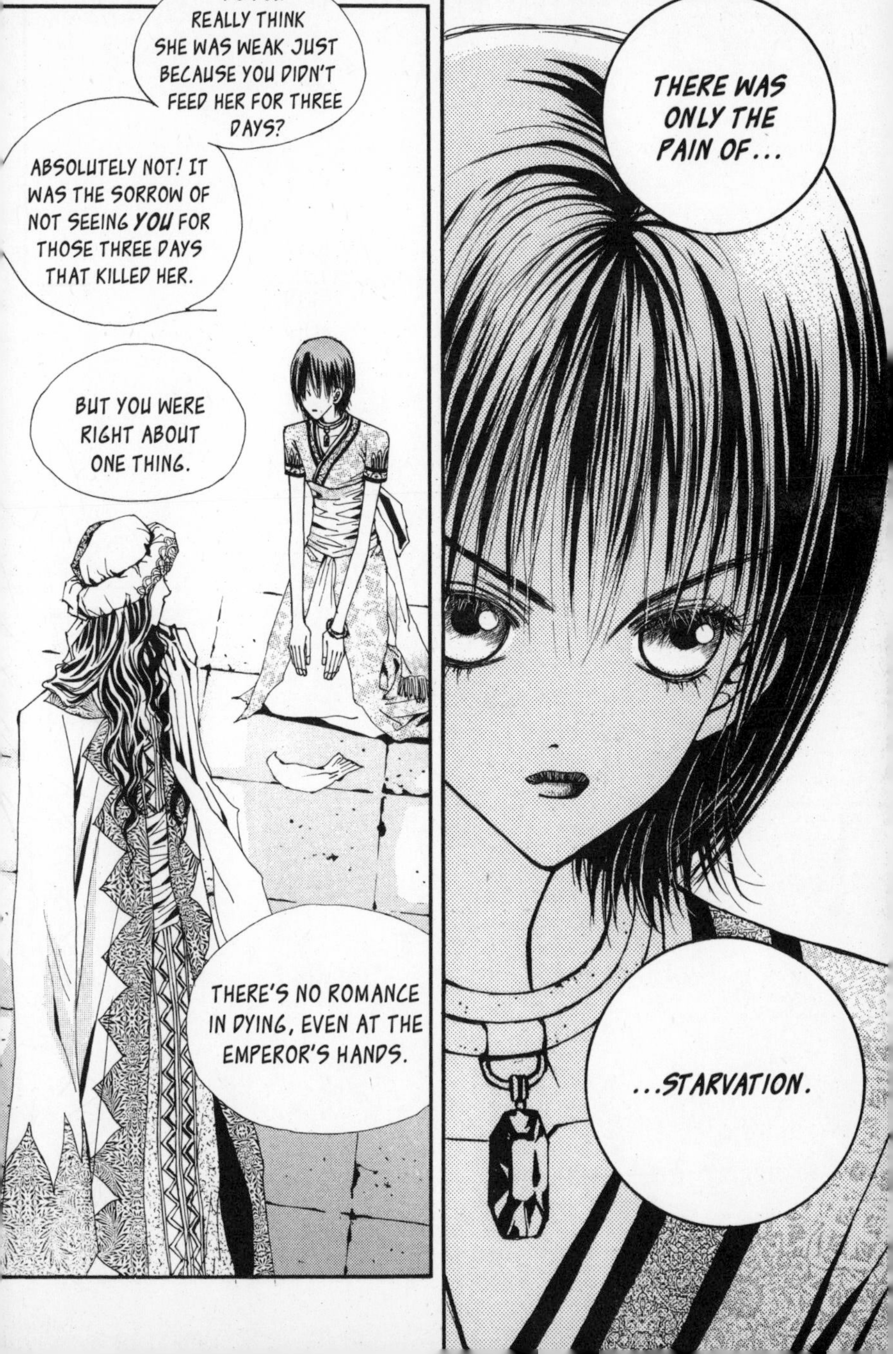
DO YOU REALLY THINK SHE WAS WEAK JUST BECAUSE YOU DIDN'T FEED HER FOR THREE DAYS?
ABSOLUTELY NOT! IT WAS THE SORROW OF NOT SEEING *YOU* FOR THOSE THREE DAYS THAT KILLED HER.
BUT YOU WERE RIGHT ABOUT ONE THING.
THERE'S NO ROMANCE IN DYING, EVEN AT THE EMPEROR'S HANDS.
THERE WAS ONLY THE PAIN OF...
...STARVATION.

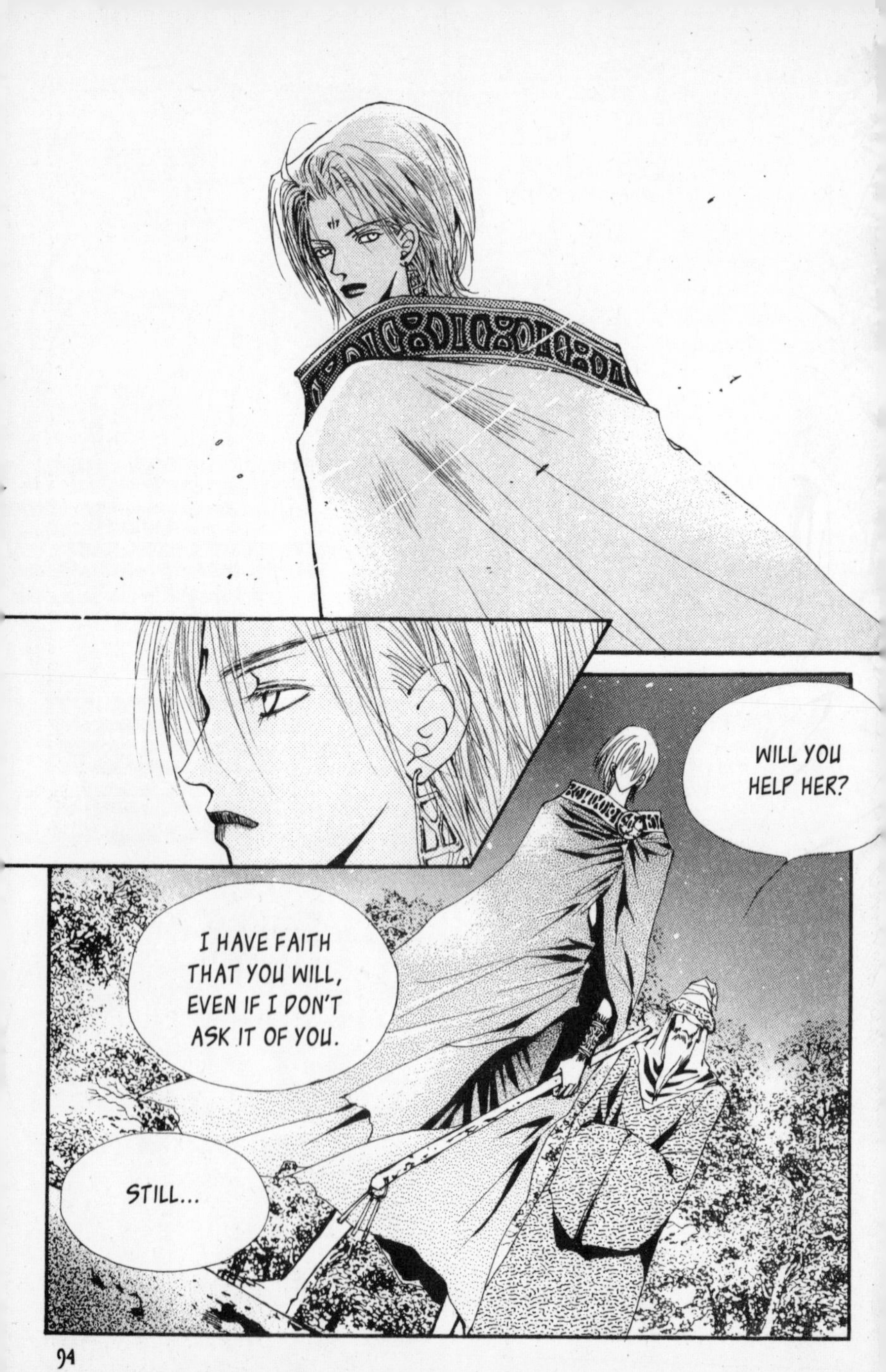
WILL YOU HELP HER?
I HAVE FAITH THAT YOU WILL, EVEN IF I DON'T ASK IT OF YOU.
STILL...

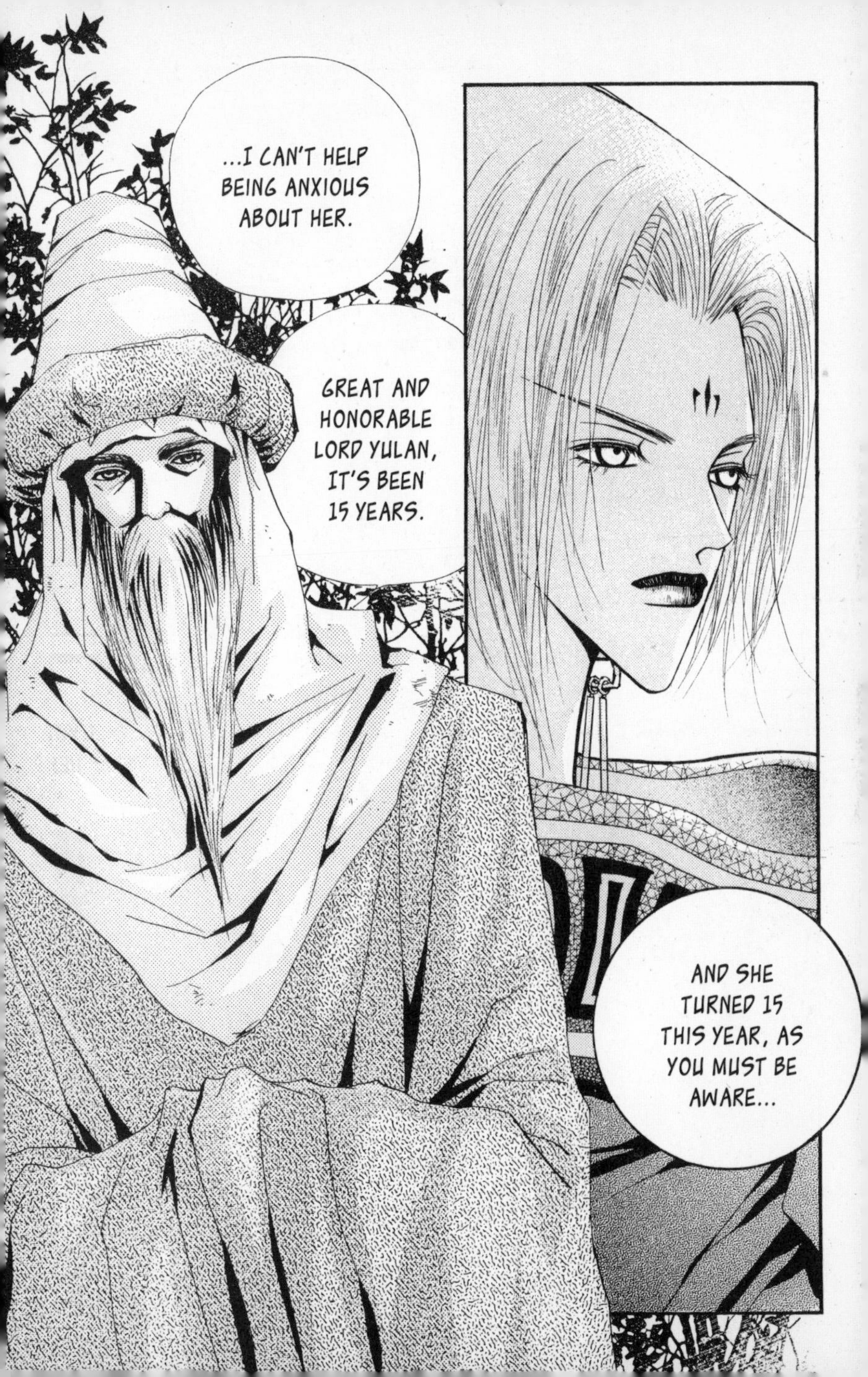
...I CAN'T HELP BEING ANXIOUS ABOUT HER.
GREAT AND HONORABLE LORD YULAN, IT'S BEEN 15 YEARS.
AND SHE TURNED 15 THIS YEAR, AS YOU MUST BE AWARE...

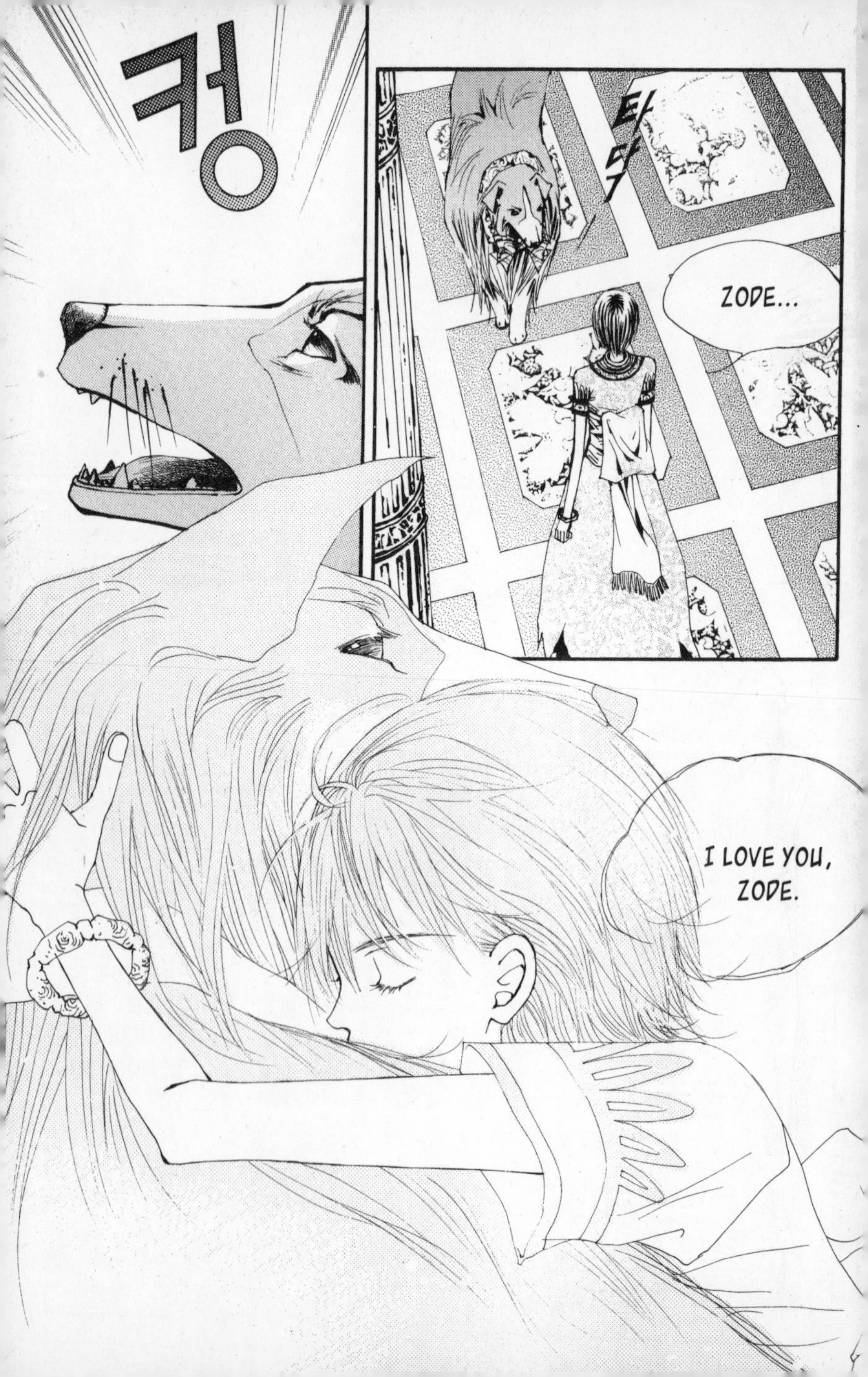
컹
타닥
ZODE...
I LOVE YOU, ZODE.

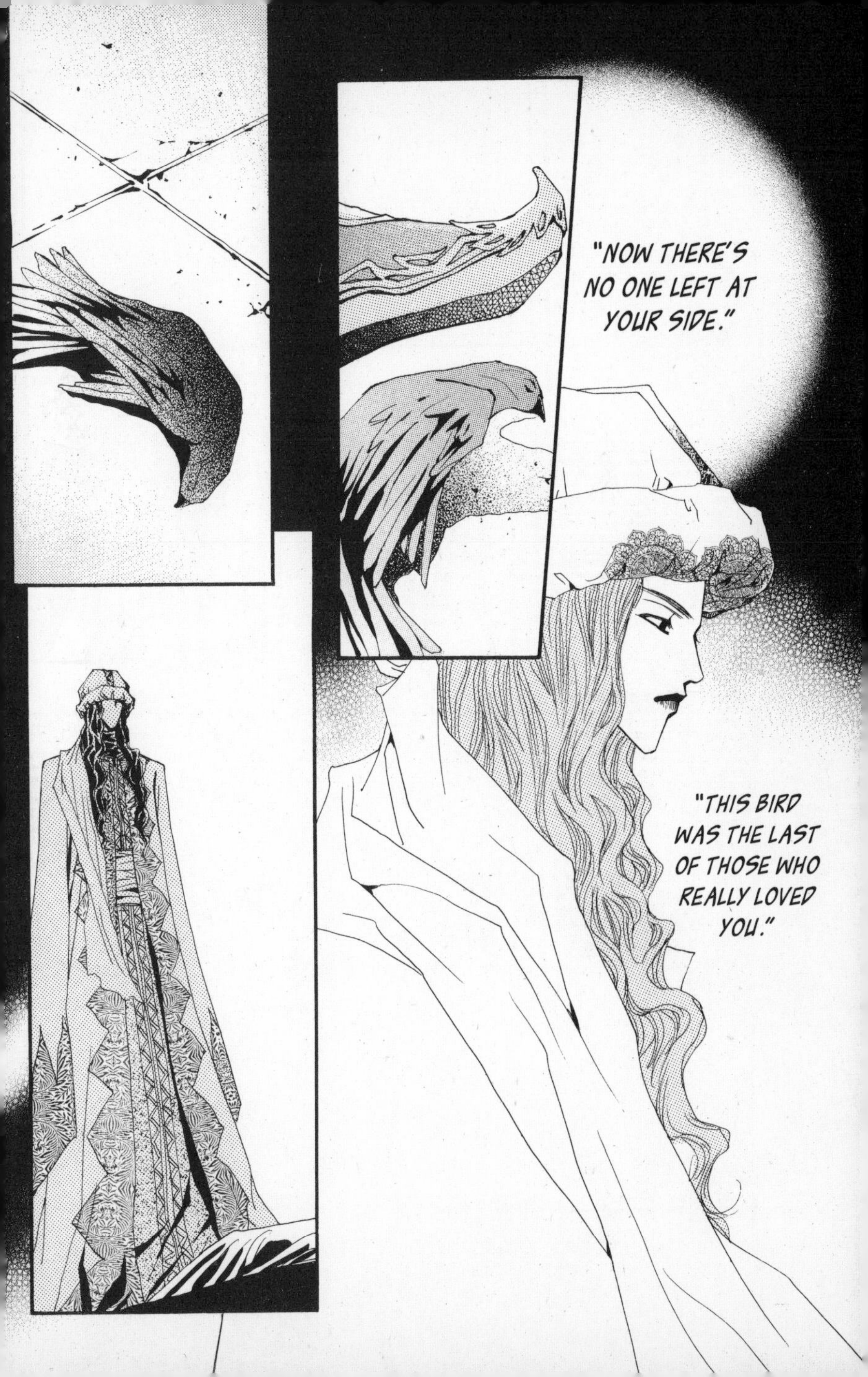
"NOW THERE'S NO ONE LEFT AT YOUR SIDE."
"THIS BIRD WAS THE LAST OF THOSE WHO REALLY LOVED YOU."

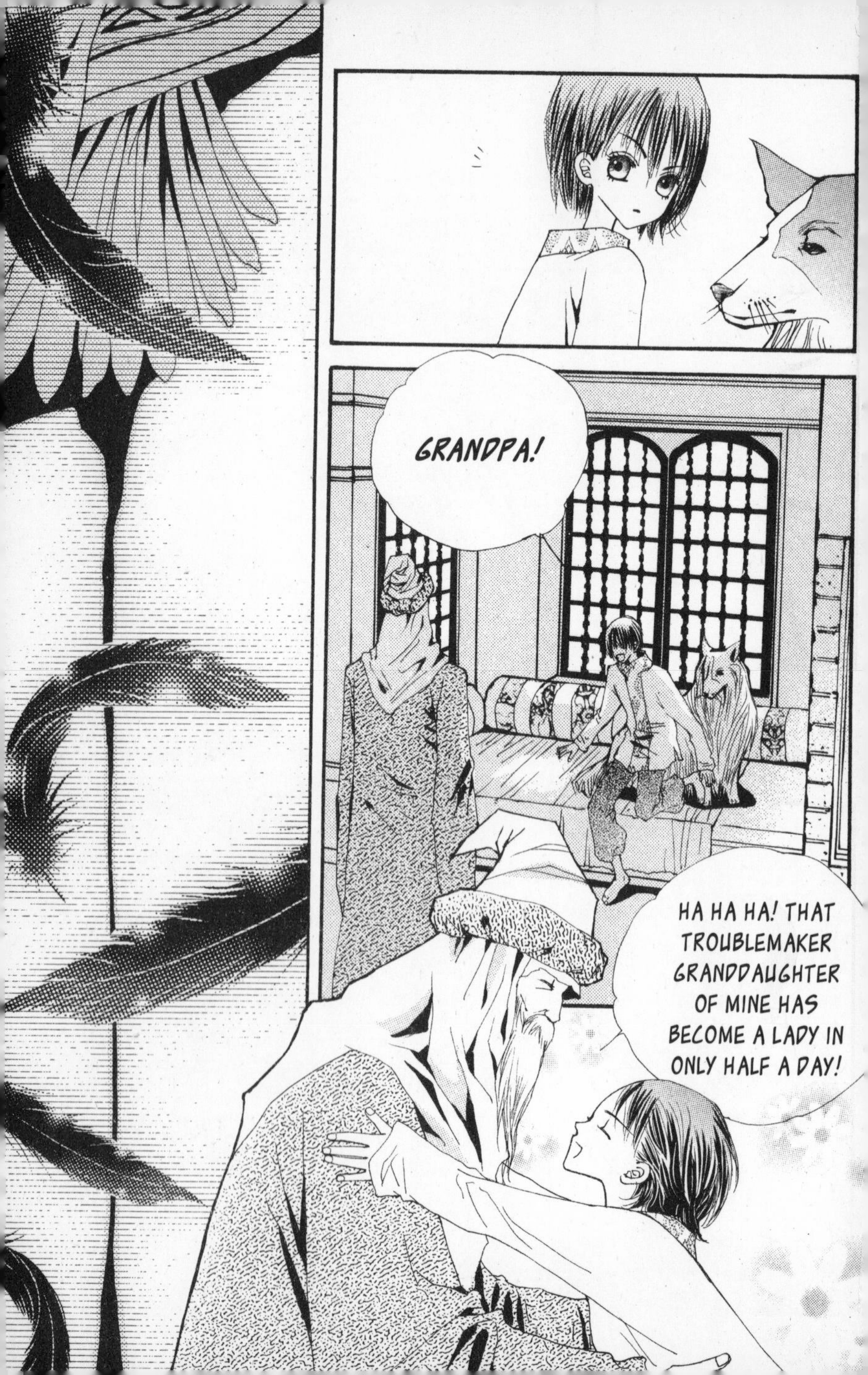
GRANDPA!
HA HA HA! THAT TROUBLEMAKER GRANDDAUGHTER OF MINE HAS BECOME A LADY IN ONLY HALF A DAY!

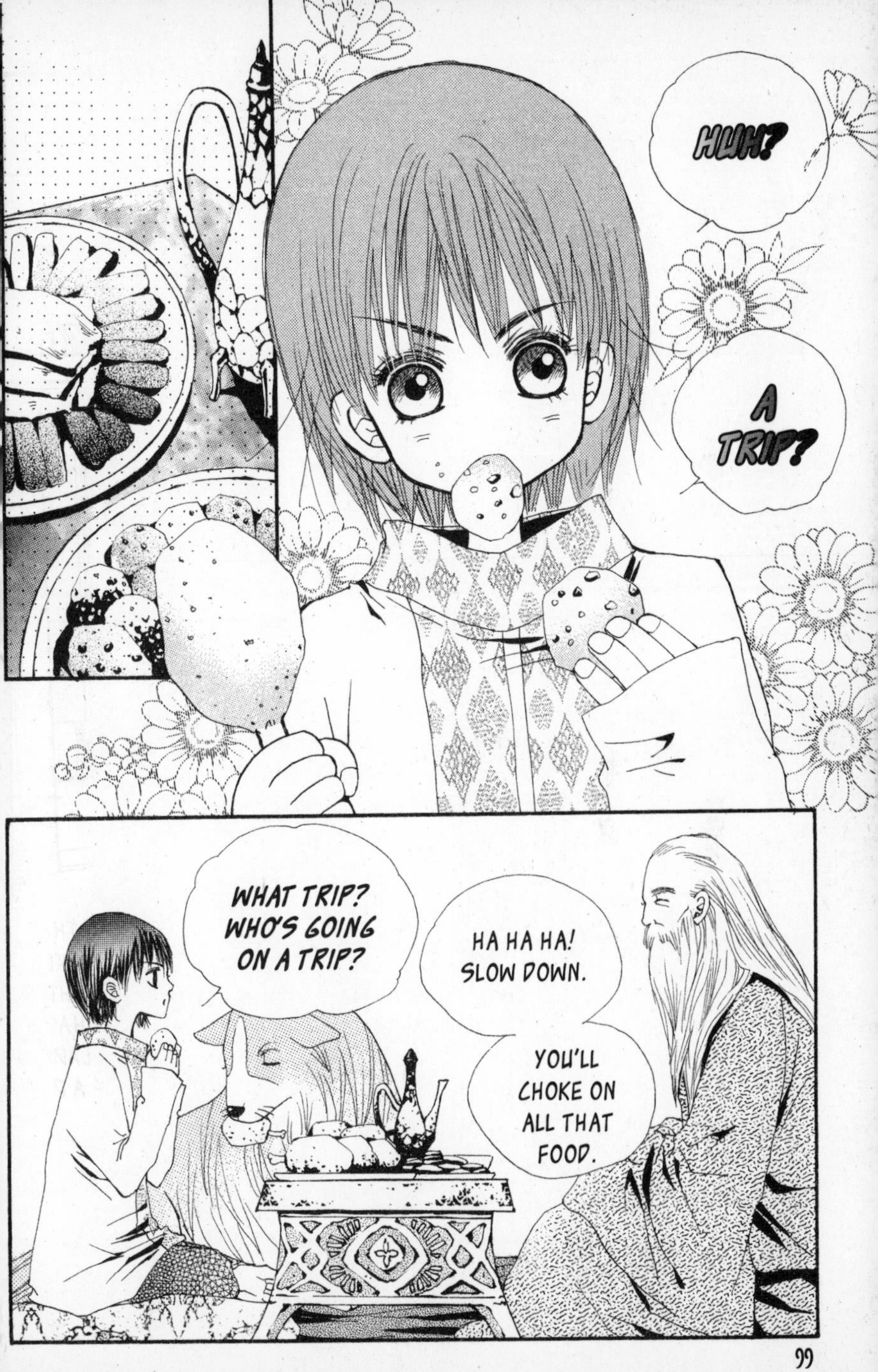

HUH?
A TRIP?
WHAT TRIP? WHO'S GOING ON A TRIP?
HA HA HA! SLOW DOWN.
YOU'LL CHOKE ON ALL THAT FOOD.

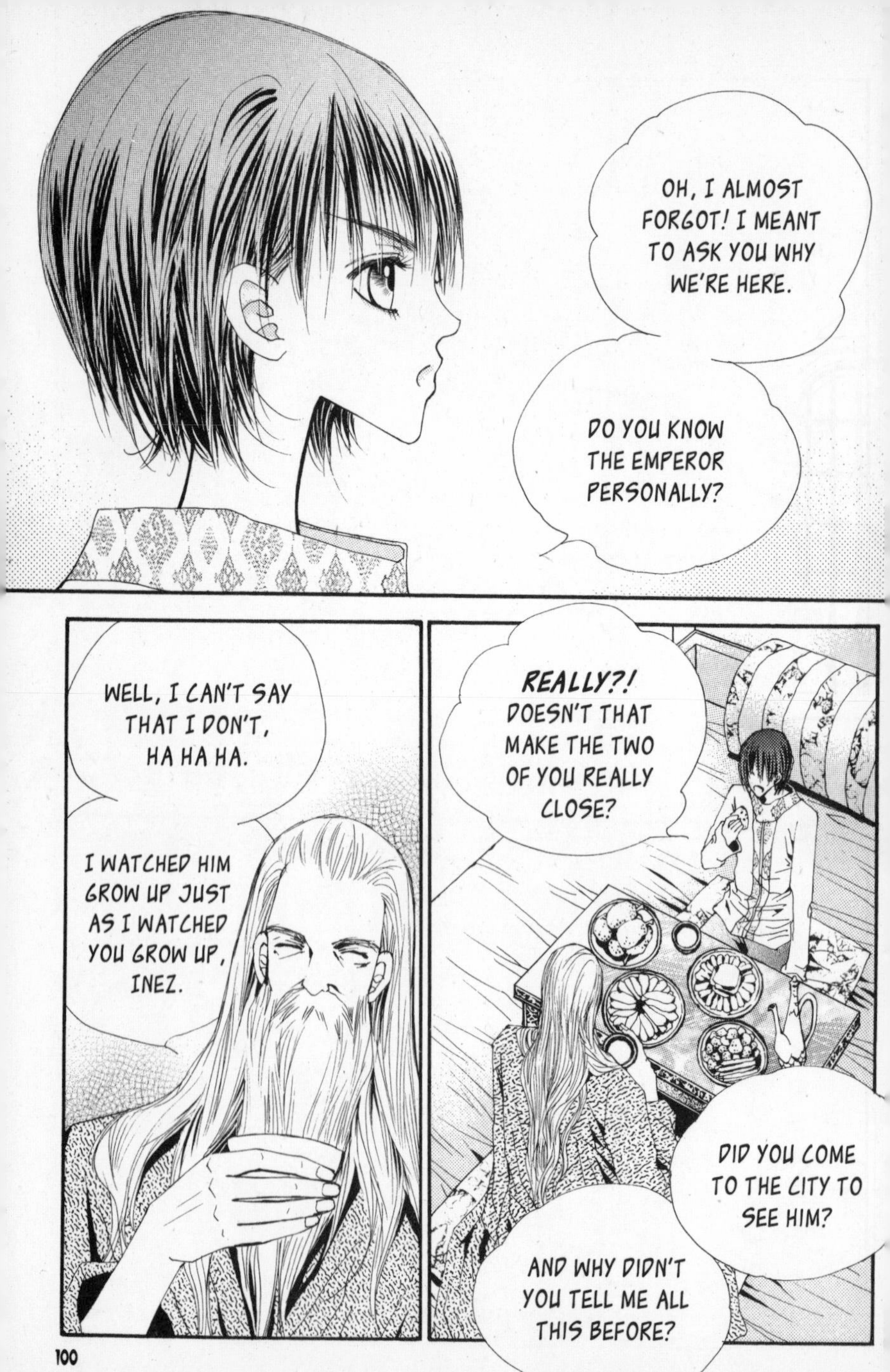
OH, I ALMOST FORGOT! I MEANT TO ASK YOU WHY WE'RE HERE.
DO YOU KNOW THE EMPEROR PERSONALLY?
WELL, I CAN'T SAY THAT I DON'T, HA HA HA.
I WATCHED HIM GROW UP JUST AS I WATCHED YOU GROW UP, INEZ.
REALLY?! DOESN'T THAT MAKE THE TWO OF YOU REALLY CLOSE?
DID YOU COME TO THE CITY TO SEE HIM?
AND WHY DIDN'T YOU TELL ME ALL THIS BEFORE?

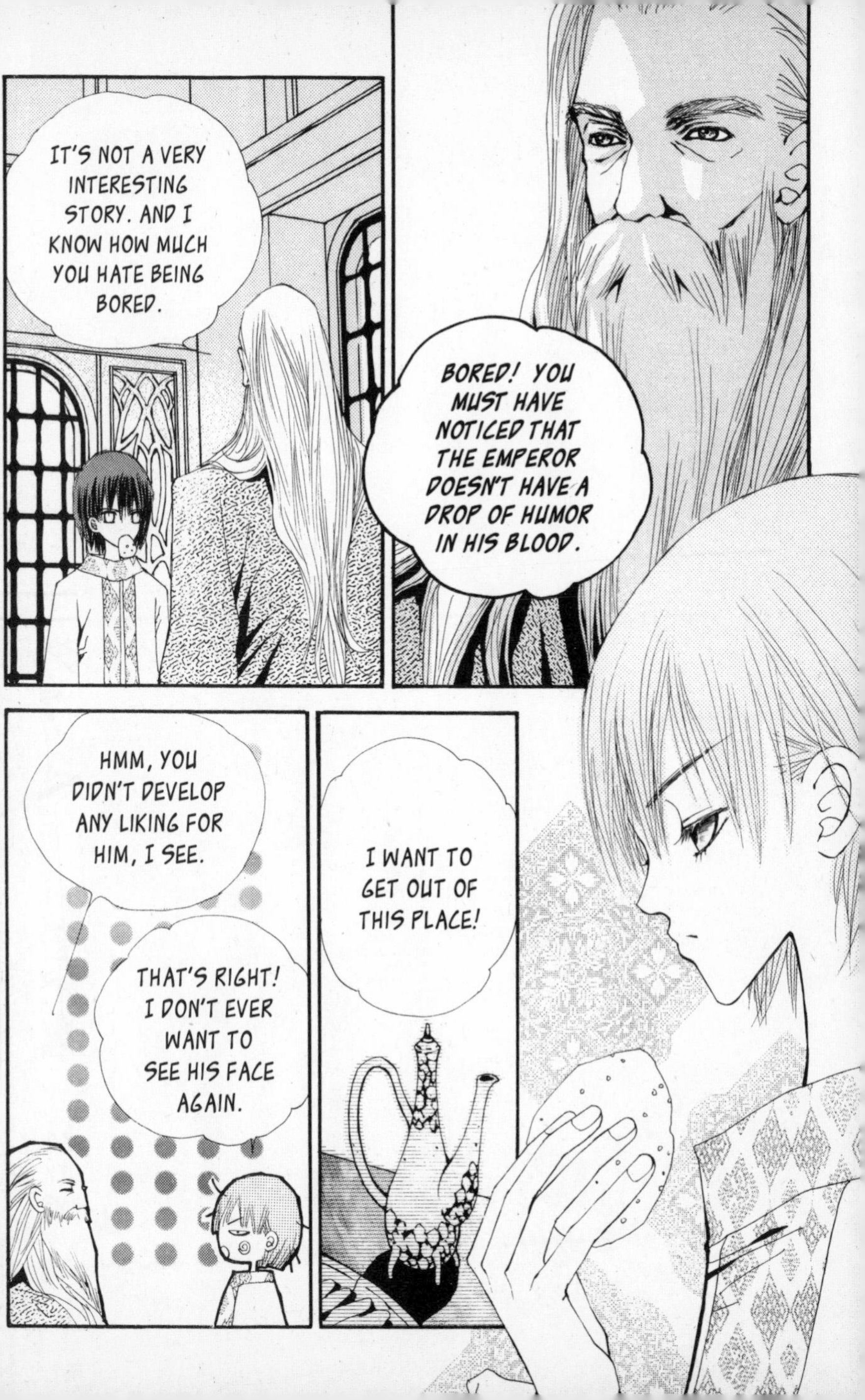
IT'S NOT A VERY INTERESTING STORY. AND I KNOW HOW MUCH YOU HATE BEING BORED.
BORED! YOU MUST HAVE NOTICED THAT THE EMPEROR DOESN'T HAVE A DROP OF HUMOR IN HIS BLOOD.
HMM, YOU DIDN'T DEVELOP ANY LIKING FOR HIM, I SEE.
THAT'S RIGHT! I DON'T EVER WANT TO SEE HIS FACE AGAIN.
I WANT TO GET OUT OF THIS PLACE!

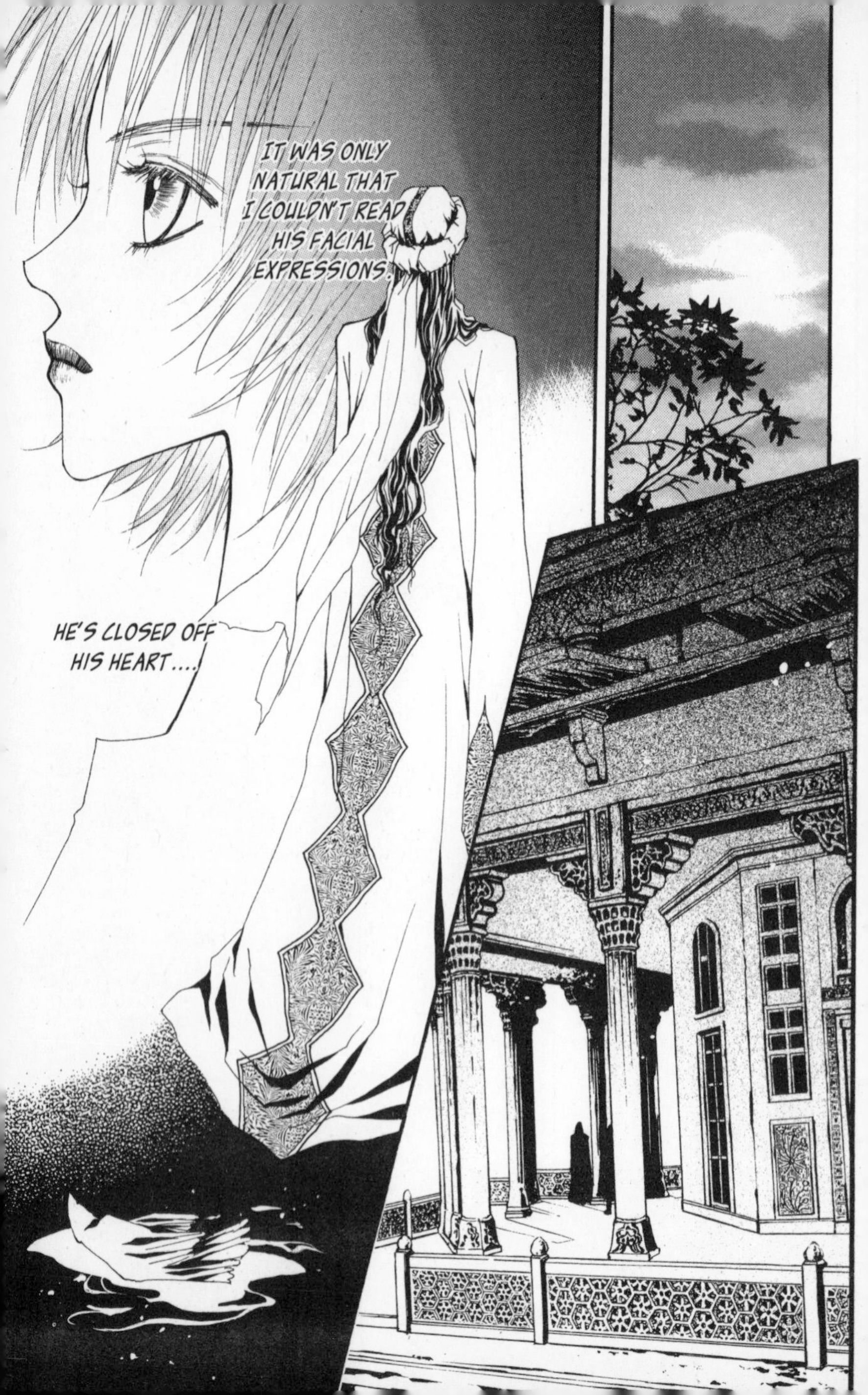
IT WAS ONLY NATURAL THAT I COULDN'T READ HIS FACIAL EXPRESSIONS.
HE'S CLOSED OFF HIS HEART....

FROM THE BEGINNING, THE EMPEROR HAD *NO* CHOICE.

FATE HAD CHOSEN HER ALREADY.

HE JUST DIDN'T WANT TO ACKNOWLEDGE THAT THE EMPEROR'S POWER MIGHT BE WEAKER THAN A LITTLE GIRL'S POWERS OF PERCEPTION.

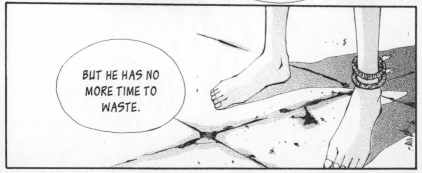

BUT HE HAS NO MORE TIME TO WASTE.

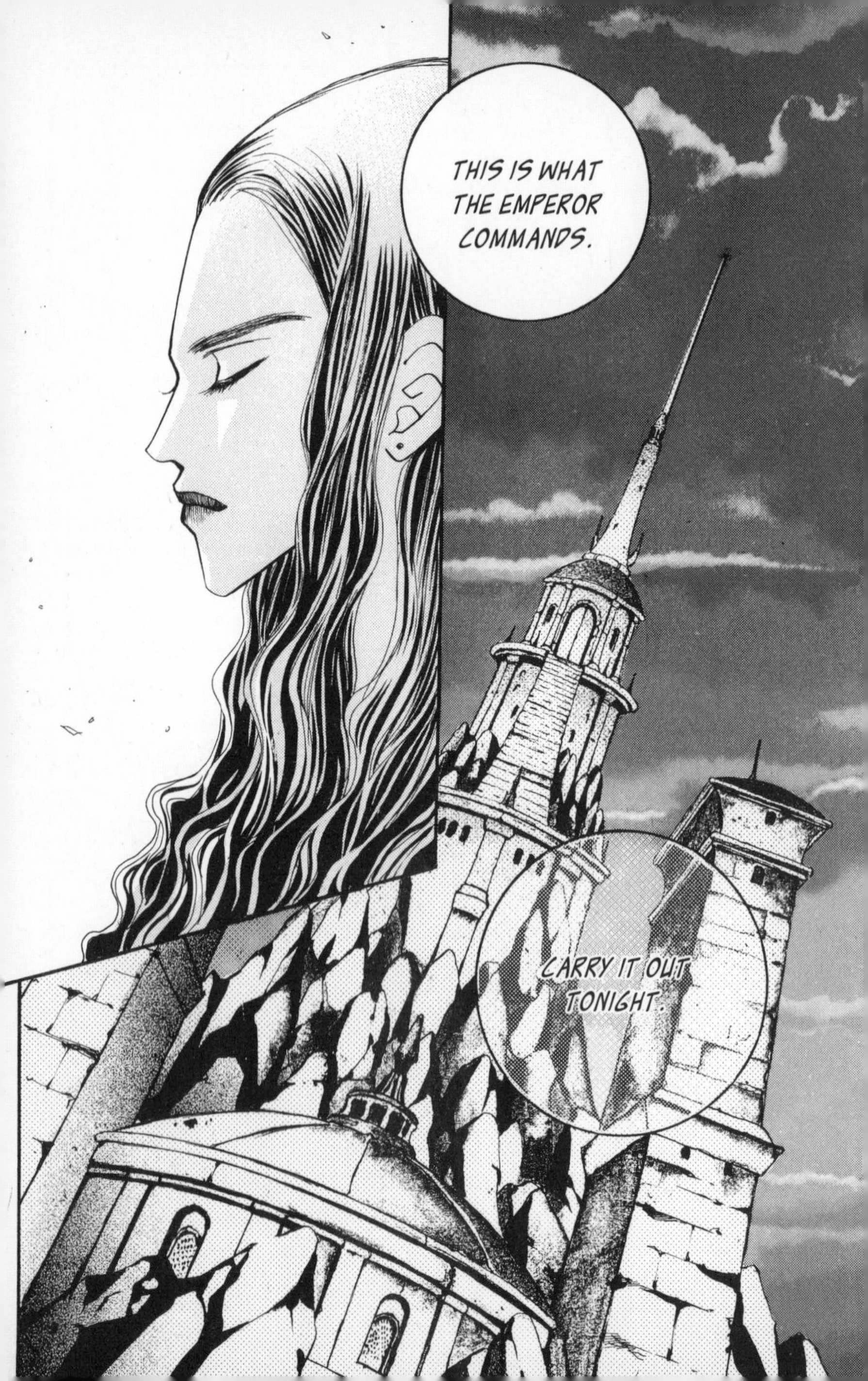
THIS IS WHAT THE EMPEROR COMMANDS.
CARRY IT OUT TONIGHT.

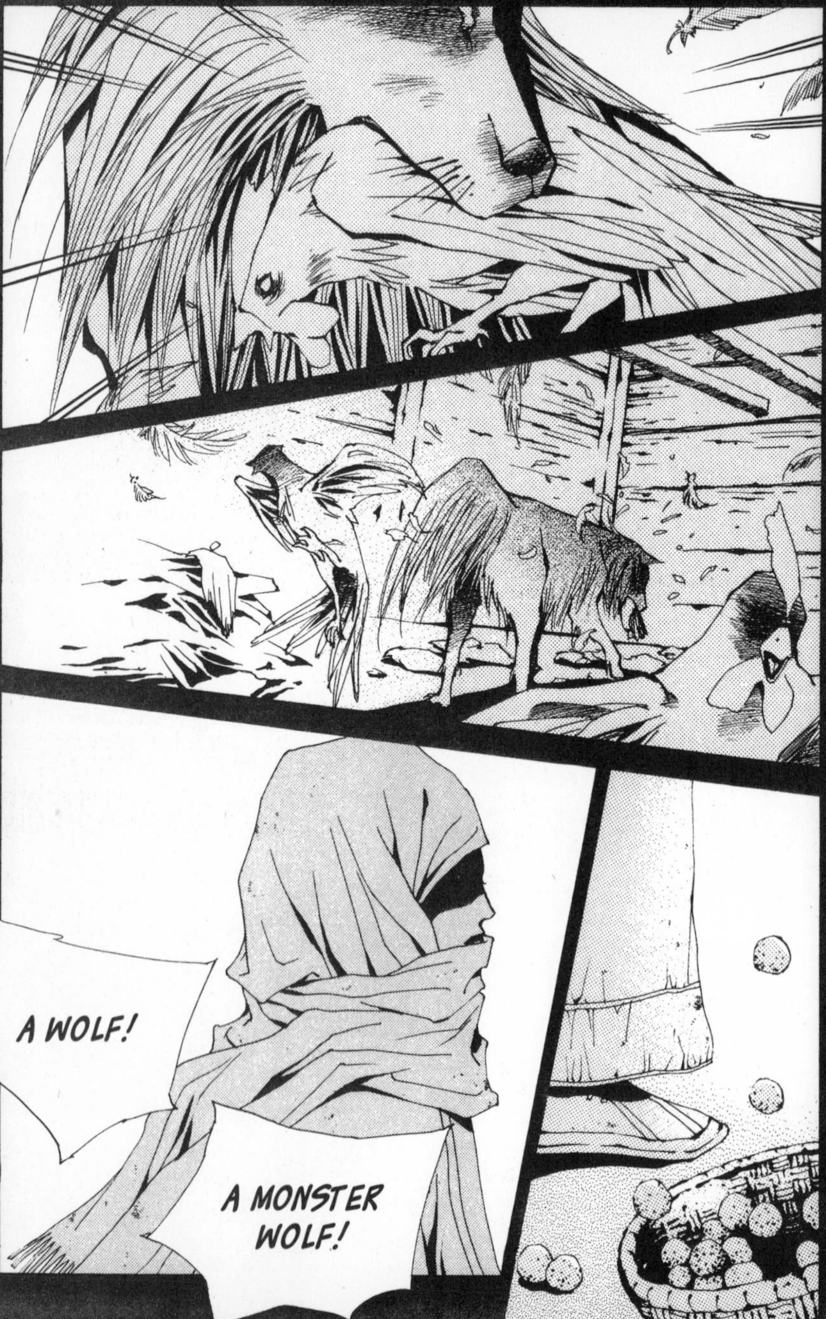
A WOLF!
A MONSTER WOLF!

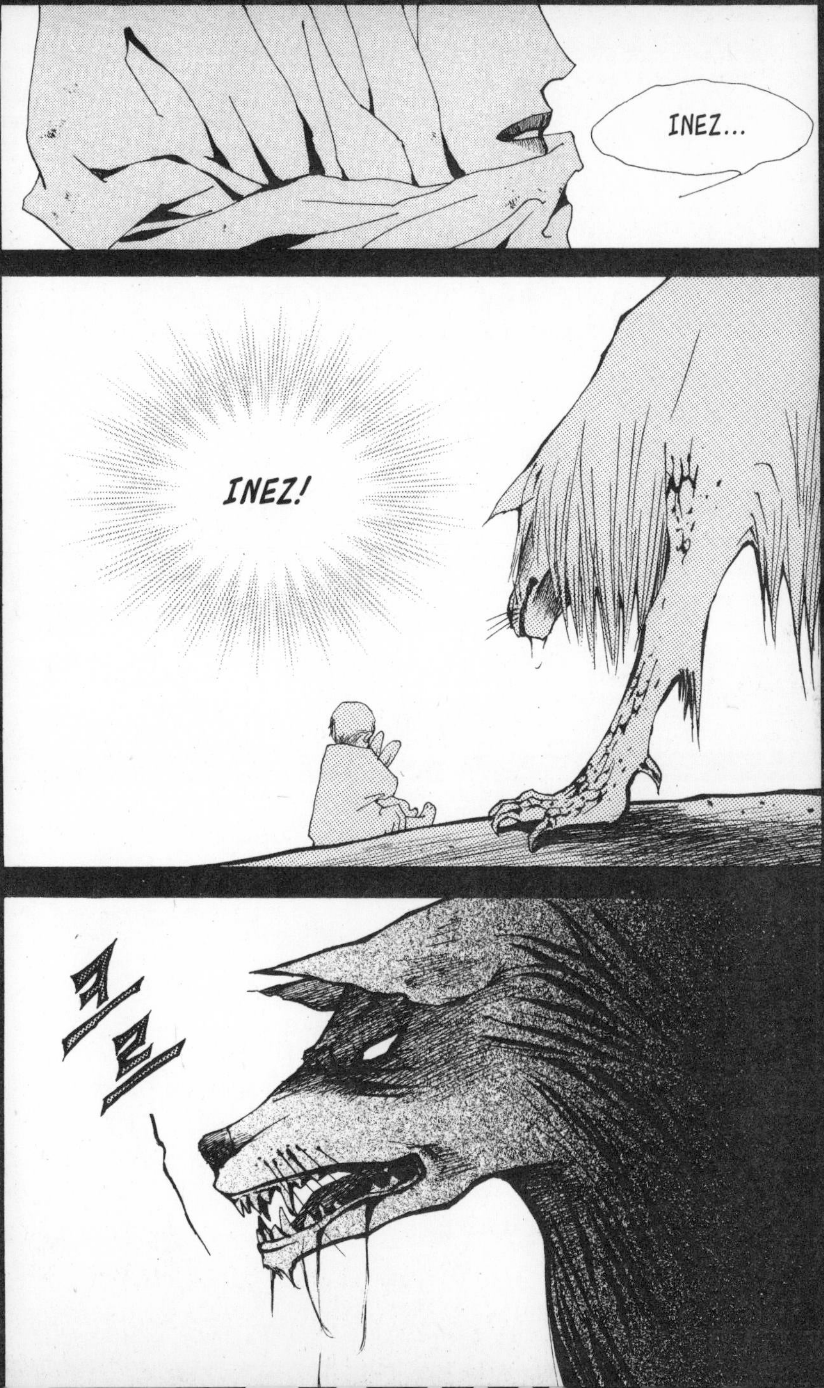
INEZ...
INEZ!
크르

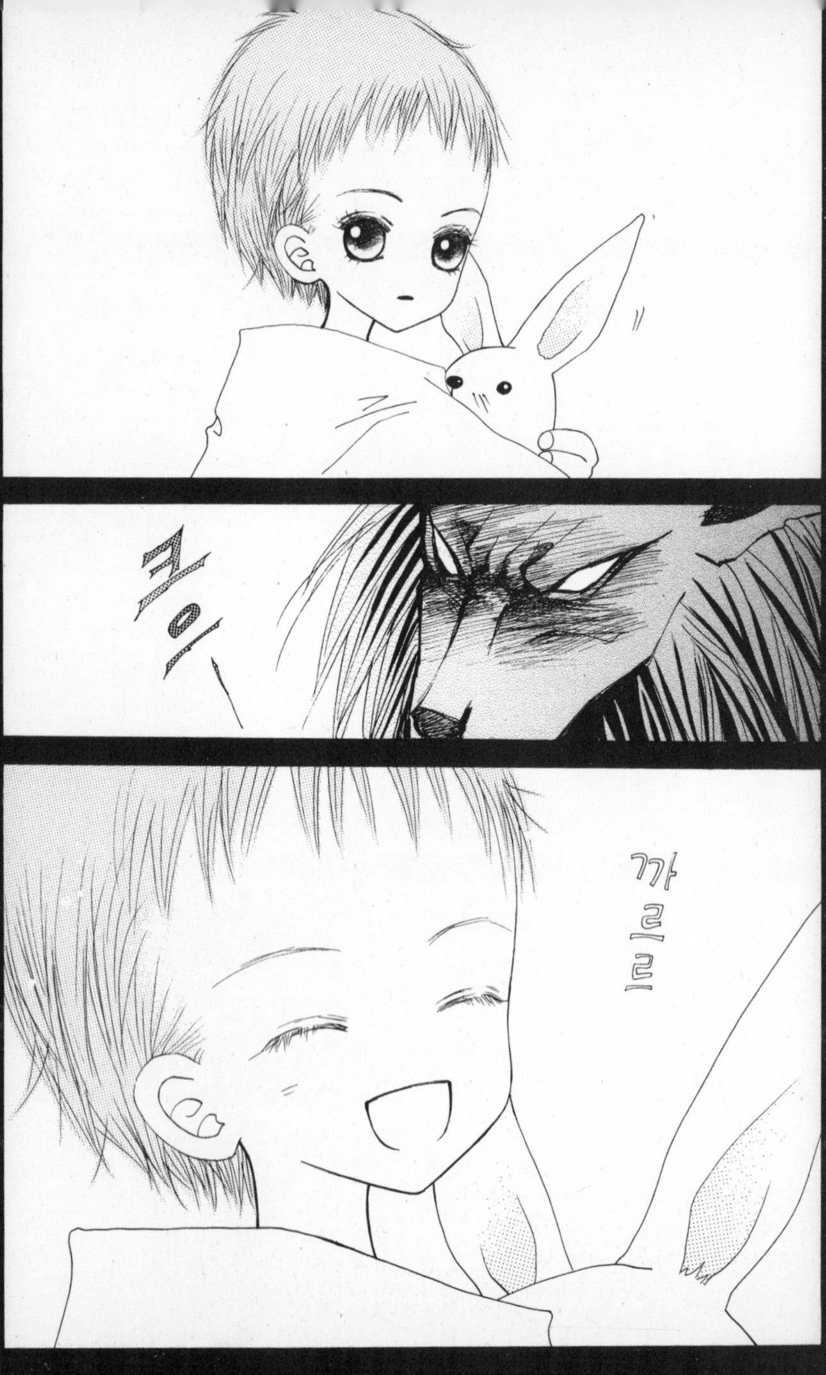
크으!
까르르

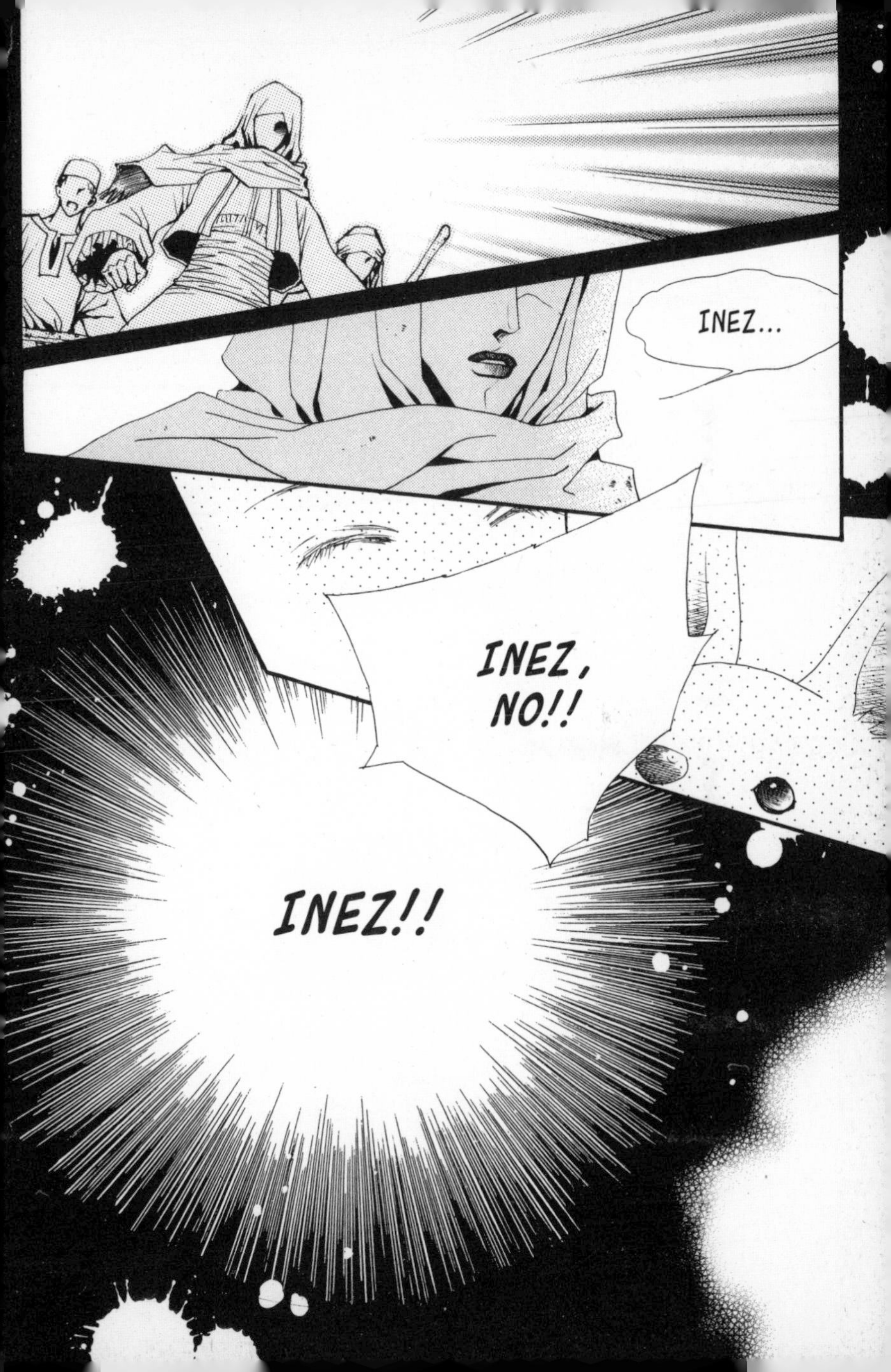
INEZ...
INEZ, NO!!
INEZ!!

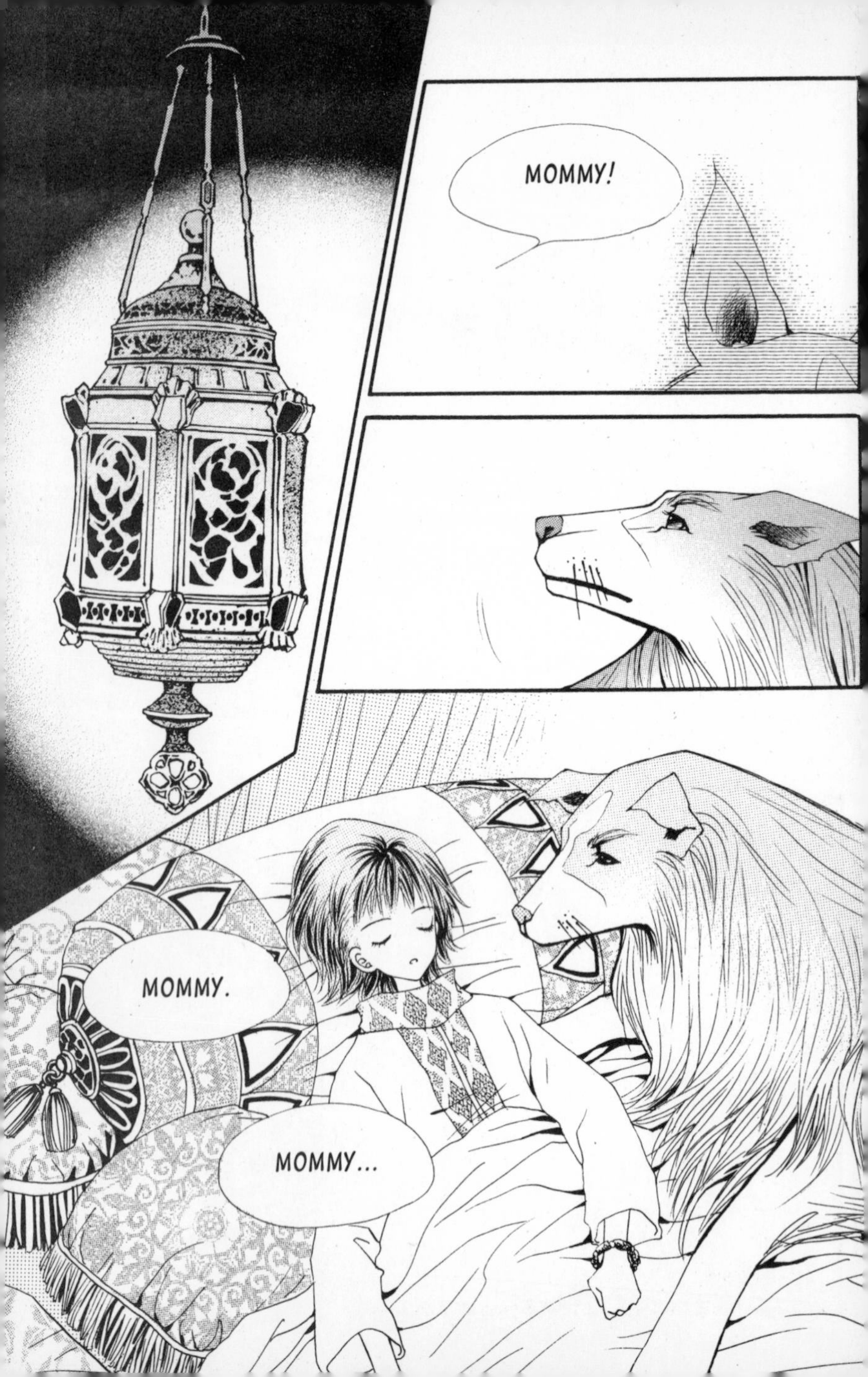
MOMMY!
MOMMY.
MOMMY...

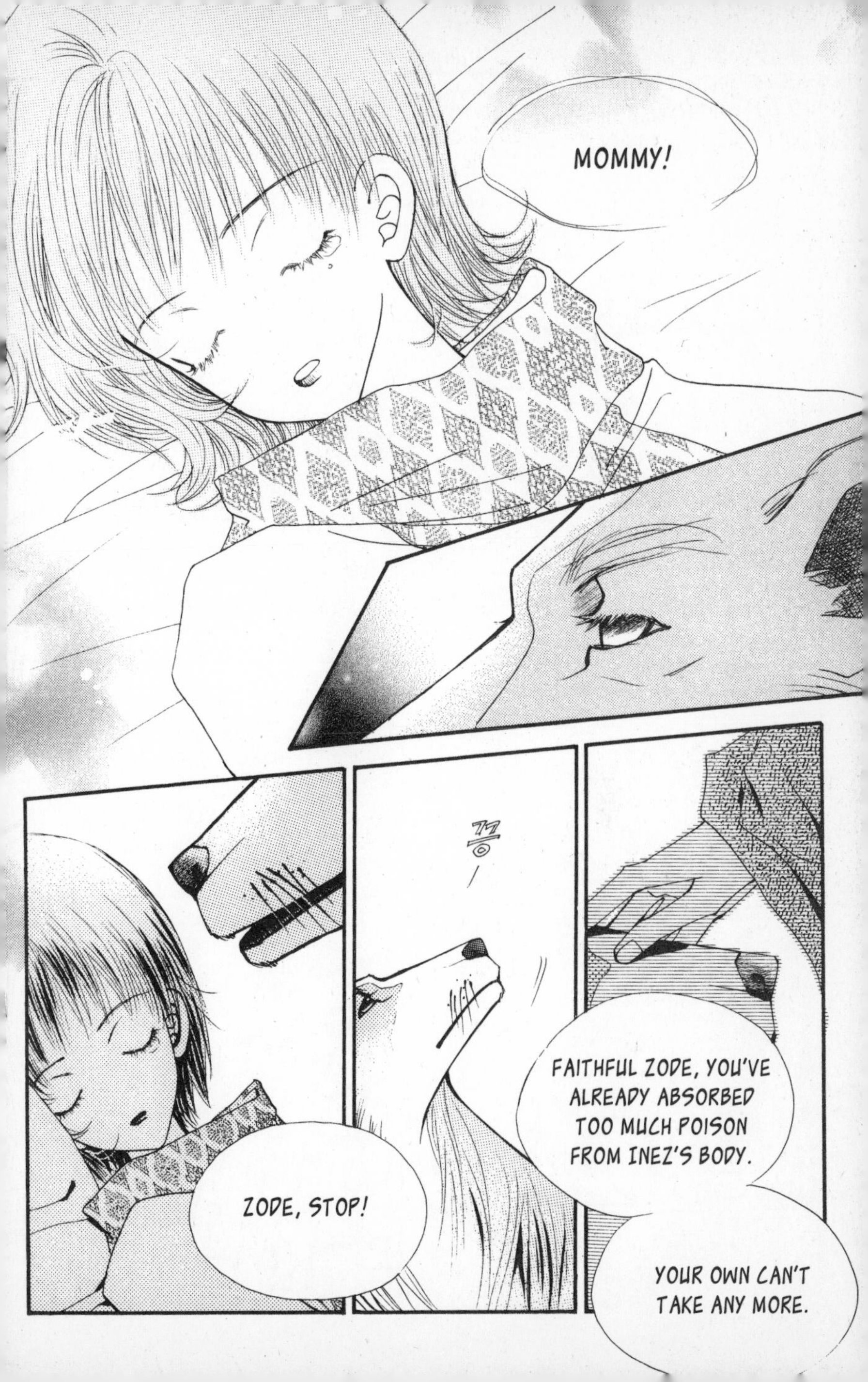
MOMMY!
ZODE, STOP!
끙
FAITHFUL ZODE, YOU'VE ALREADY ABSORBED TOO MUCH POISON FROM INEZ'S BODY.
YOUR OWN CAN'T TAKE ANY MORE.

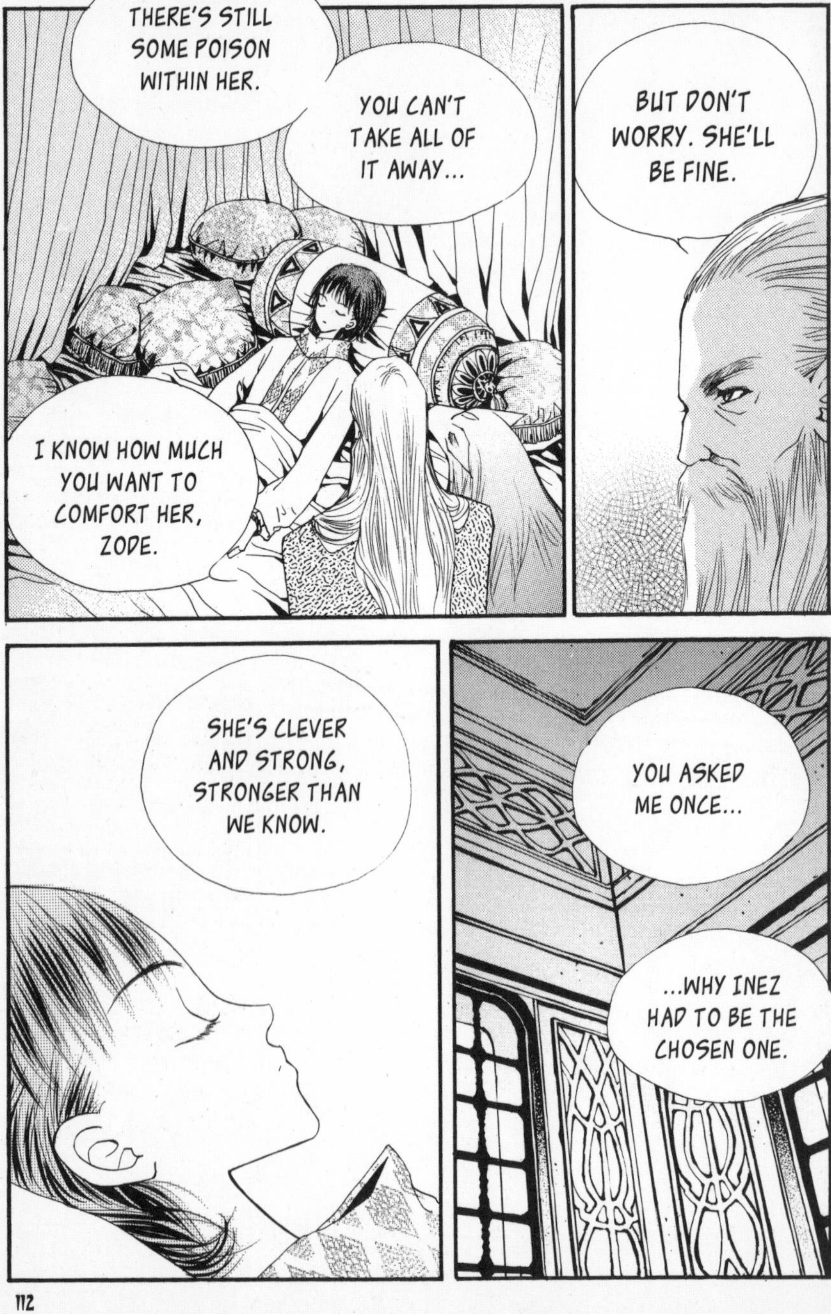
THERE'S STILL SOME POISON WITHIN HER.
YOU CAN'T TAKE ALL OF IT AWAY...
I KNOW HOW MUCH YOU WANT TO COMFORT HER, ZODE.
BUT DON'T WORRY. SHE'LL BE FINE.
SHE'S CLEVER AND STRONG, STRONGER THAN WE KNOW.
YOU ASKED ME ONCE...
...WHY INEZ HAD TO BE THE CHOSEN ONE.

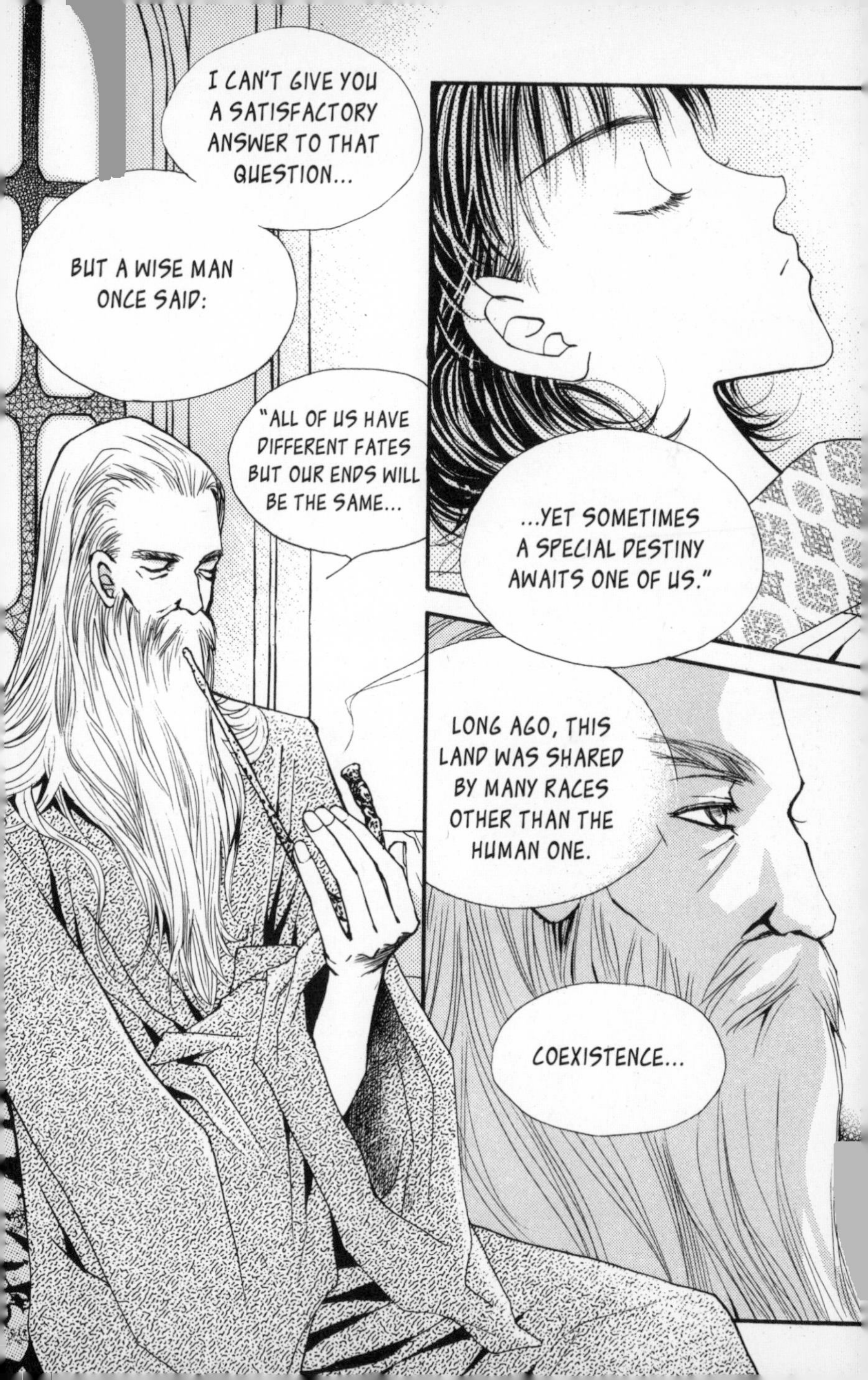
I CAN'T GIVE YOU A SATISFACTORY ANSWER TO THAT QUESTION...
BUT A WISE MAN ONCE SAID:
"ALL OF US HAVE DIFFERENT FATES BUT OUR ENDS WILL BE THE SAME...
...YET SOMETIMES A SPECIAL DESTINY AWAITS ONE OF US."
LONG AGO, THIS LAND WAS SHARED BY MANY RACES OTHER THAN THE HUMAN ONE.
COEXISTENCE...

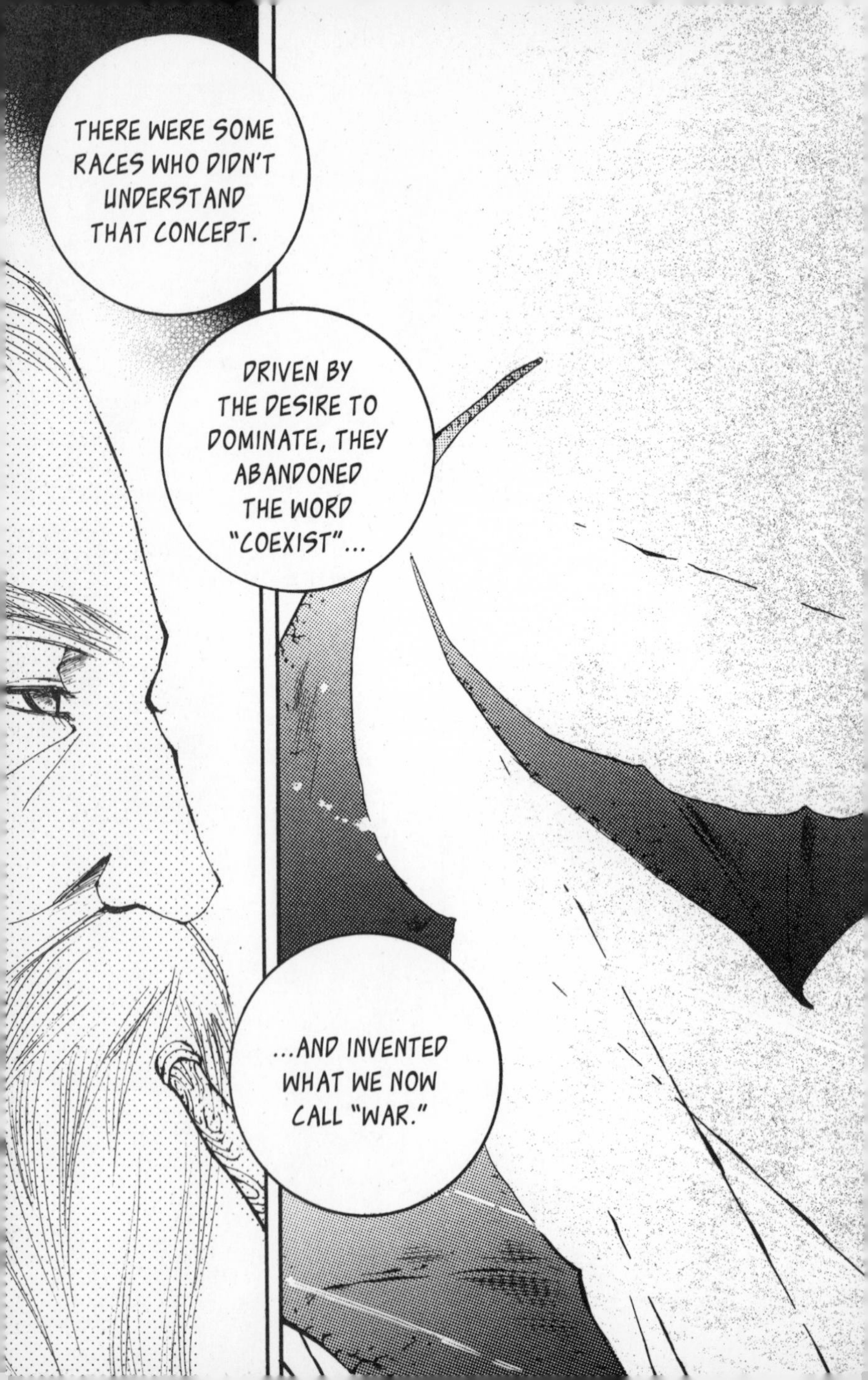
THERE WERE SOME RACES WHO DIDN'T UNDERSTAND THAT CONCEPT.
DRIVEN BY THE DESIRE TO DOMINATE, THEY ABANDONED THE WORD "COEXIST"...
...AND INVENTED WHAT WE NOW CALL "WAR."

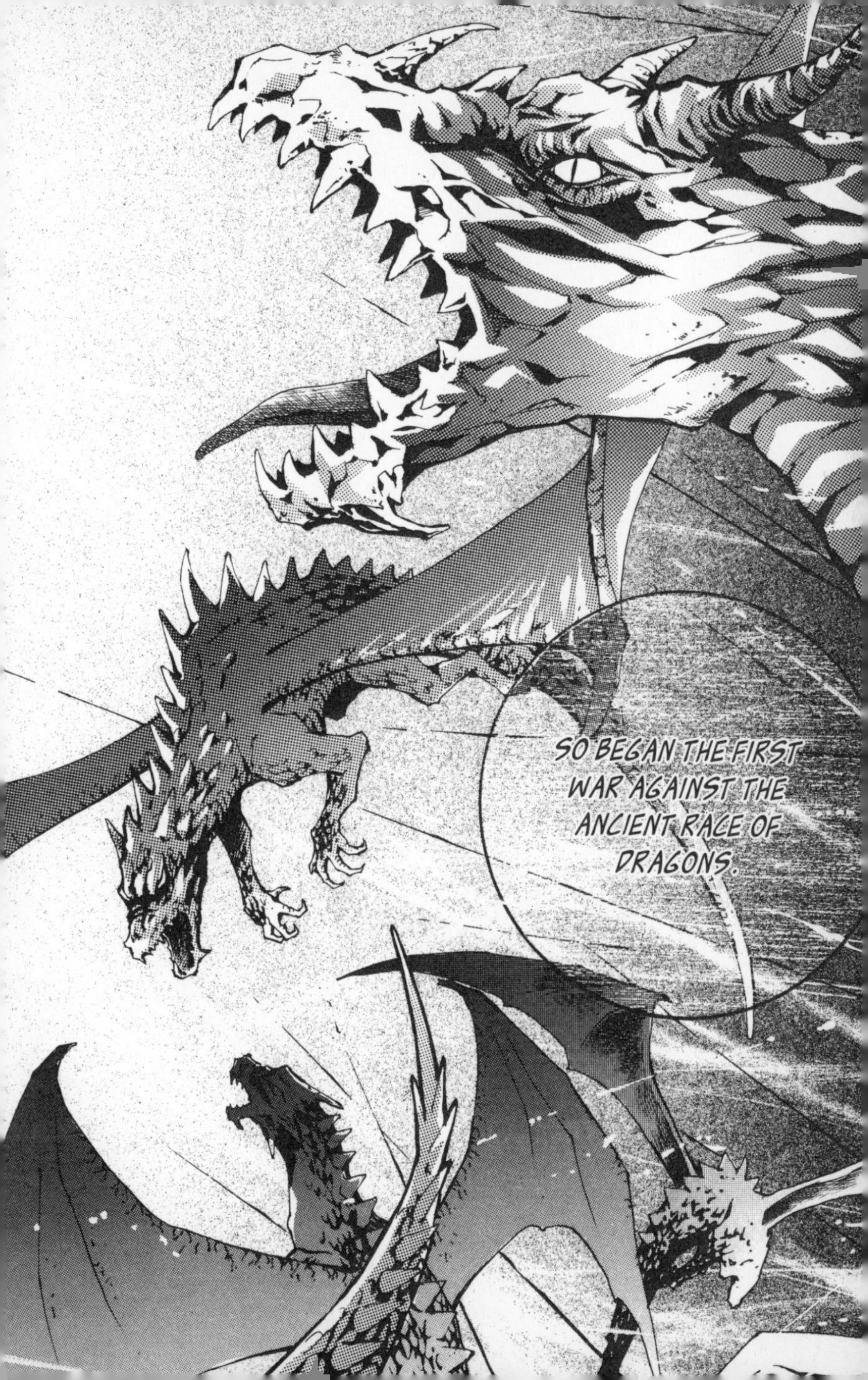
SO BEGAN THE FIRST WAR AGAINST THE ANCIENT RACE OF DRAGONS.

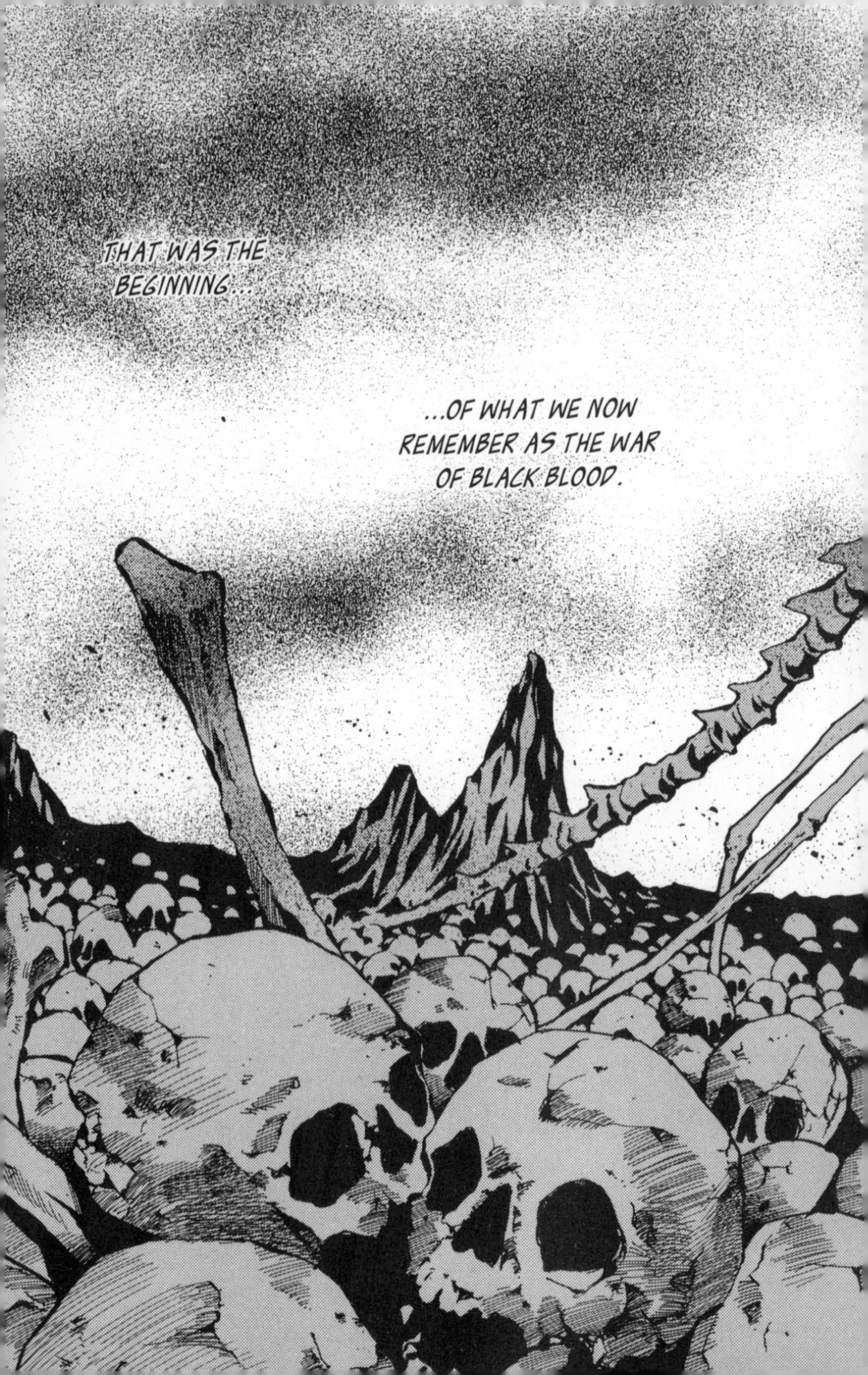

THAT WAS THE BEGINNING...
...OF WHAT WE NOW REMEMBER AS THE WAR OF BLACK BLOOD.

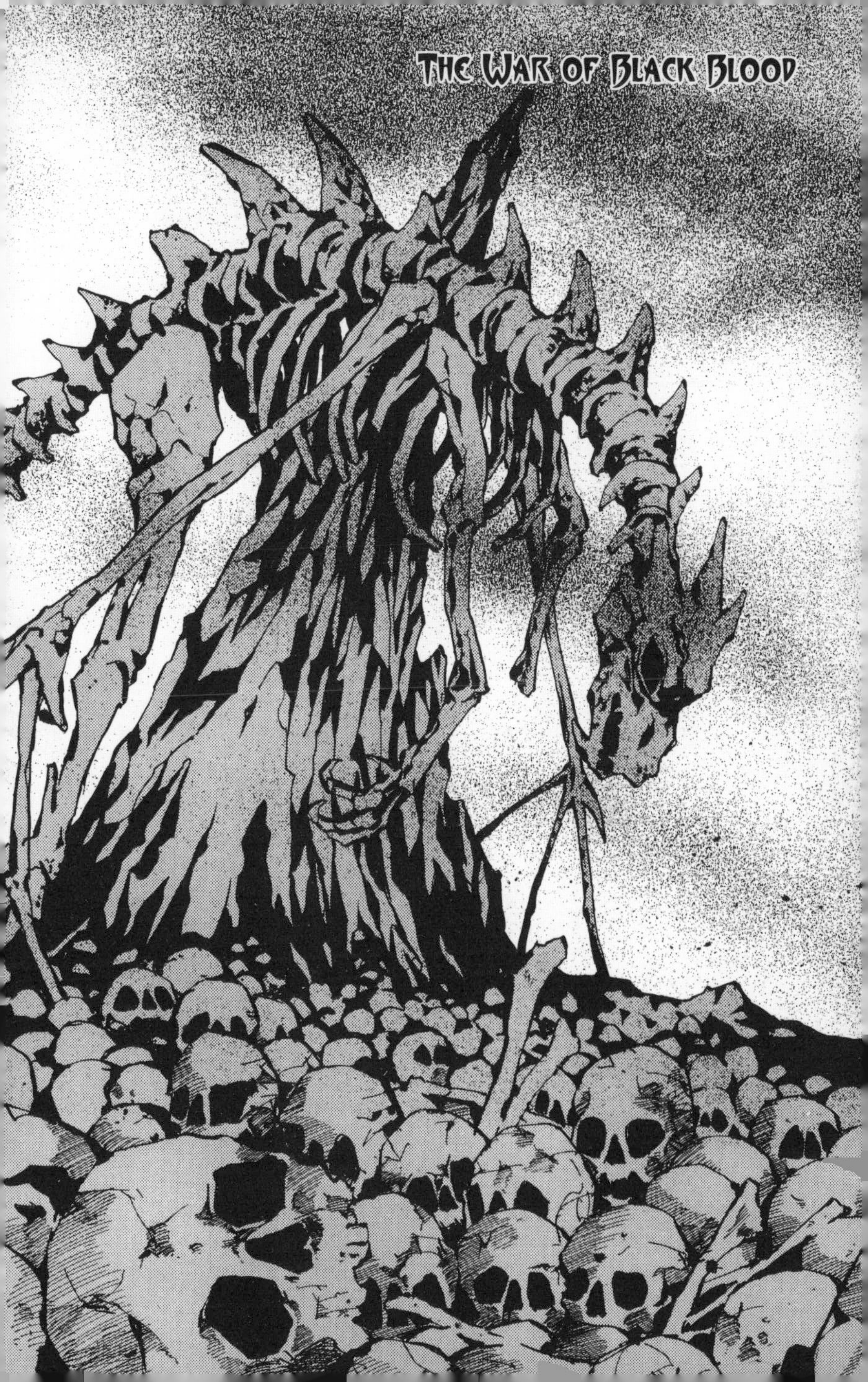
THE WAR OF BLACK BLOOD

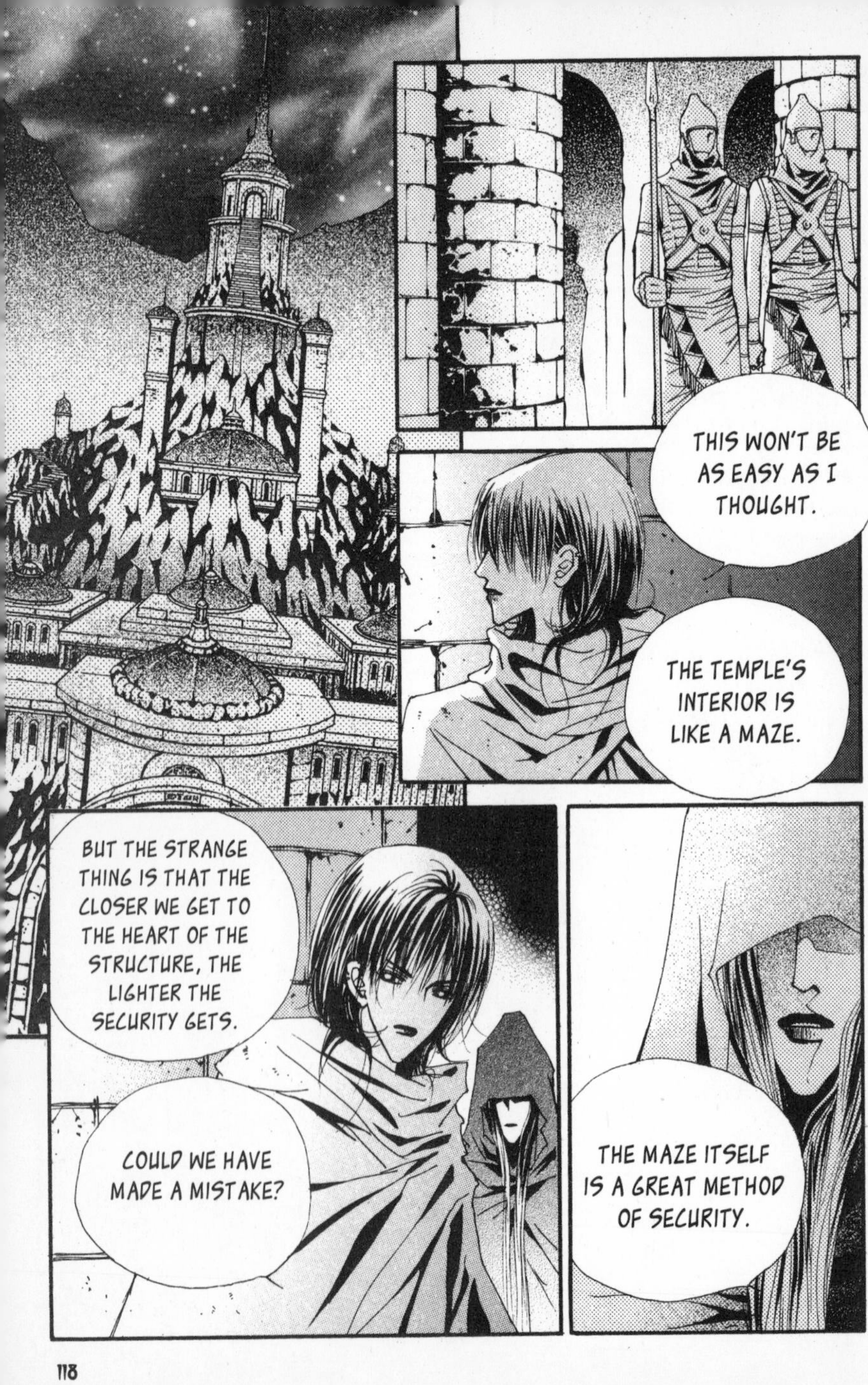

THIS WON'T BE AS EASY AS I THOUGHT.
THE TEMPLE'S INTERIOR IS LIKE A MAZE.
BUT THE STRANGE THING IS THAT THE CLOSER WE GET TO THE HEART OF THE STRUCTURE, THE LIGHTER THE SECURITY GETS.
COULD WE HAVE MADE A MISTAKE?
THE MAZE ITSELF IS A GREAT METHOD OF SECURITY.

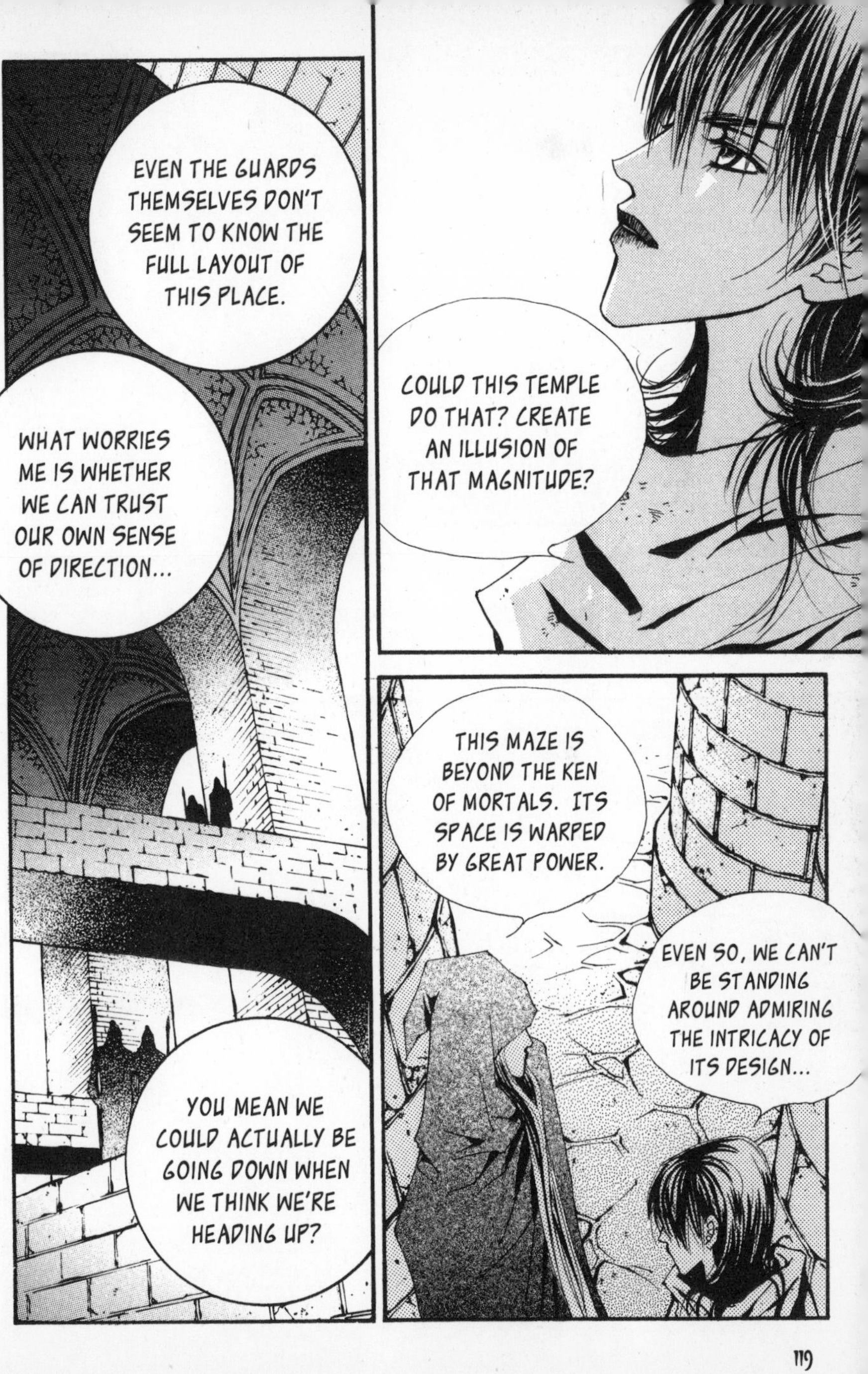
EVEN THE GUARDS THEMSELVES DON'T SEEM TO KNOW THE FULL LAYOUT OF THIS PLACE.
WHAT WORRIES ME IS WHETHER WE CAN TRUST OUR OWN SENSE OF DIRECTION...
YOU MEAN WE COULD ACTUALLY BE GOING DOWN WHEN WE THINK WE'RE HEADING UP?
COULD THIS TEMPLE DO THAT? CREATE AN ILLUSION OF THAT MAGNITUDE?
THIS MAZE IS BEYOND THE KEN OF MORTALS. ITS SPACE IS WARPED BY GREAT POWER.
EVEN SO, WE CAN'T BE STANDING AROUND ADMIRING THE INTRICACY OF ITS DESIGN...

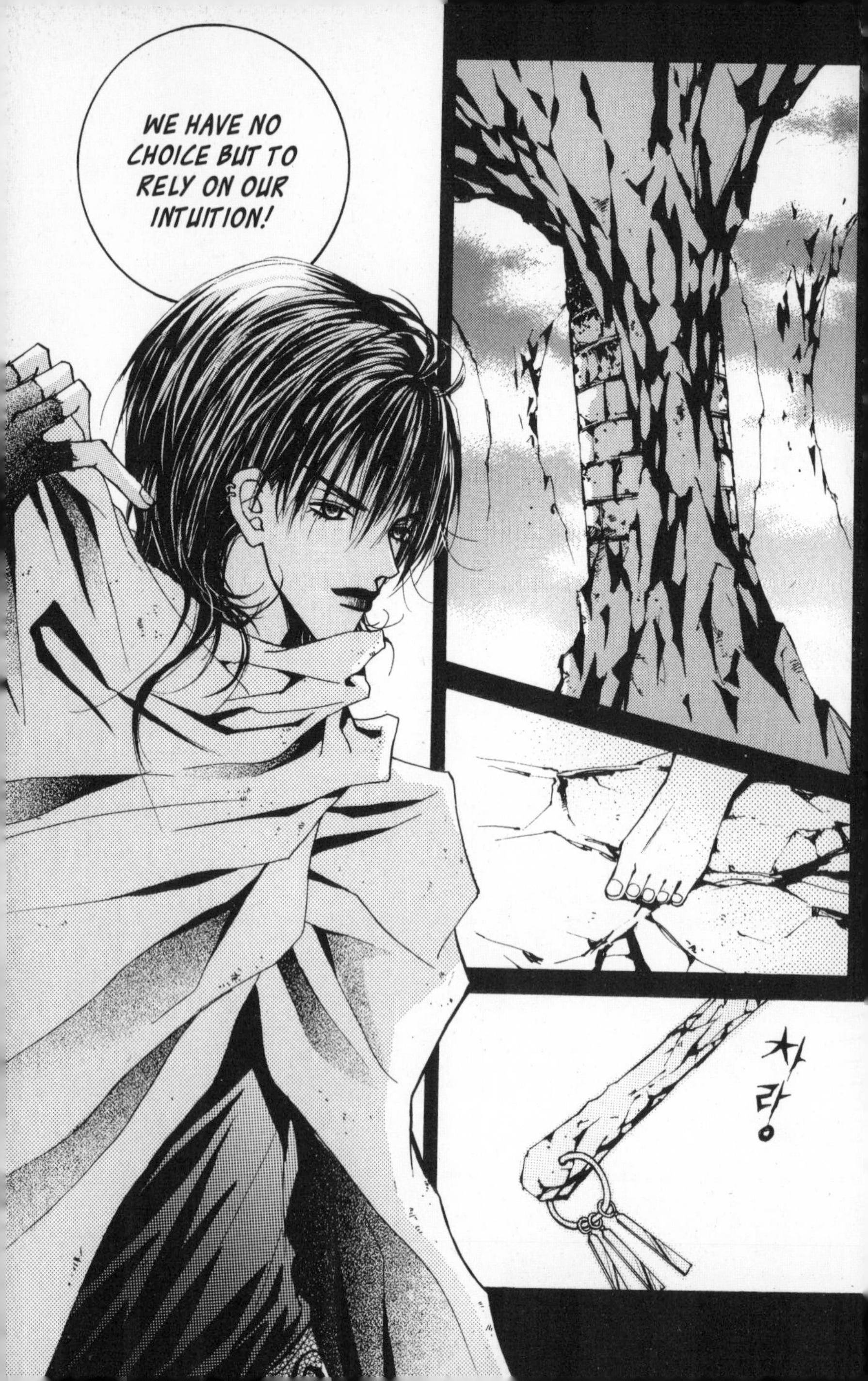
WE HAVE NO CHOICE BUT TO RELY ON OUR INTUITION!
차랑

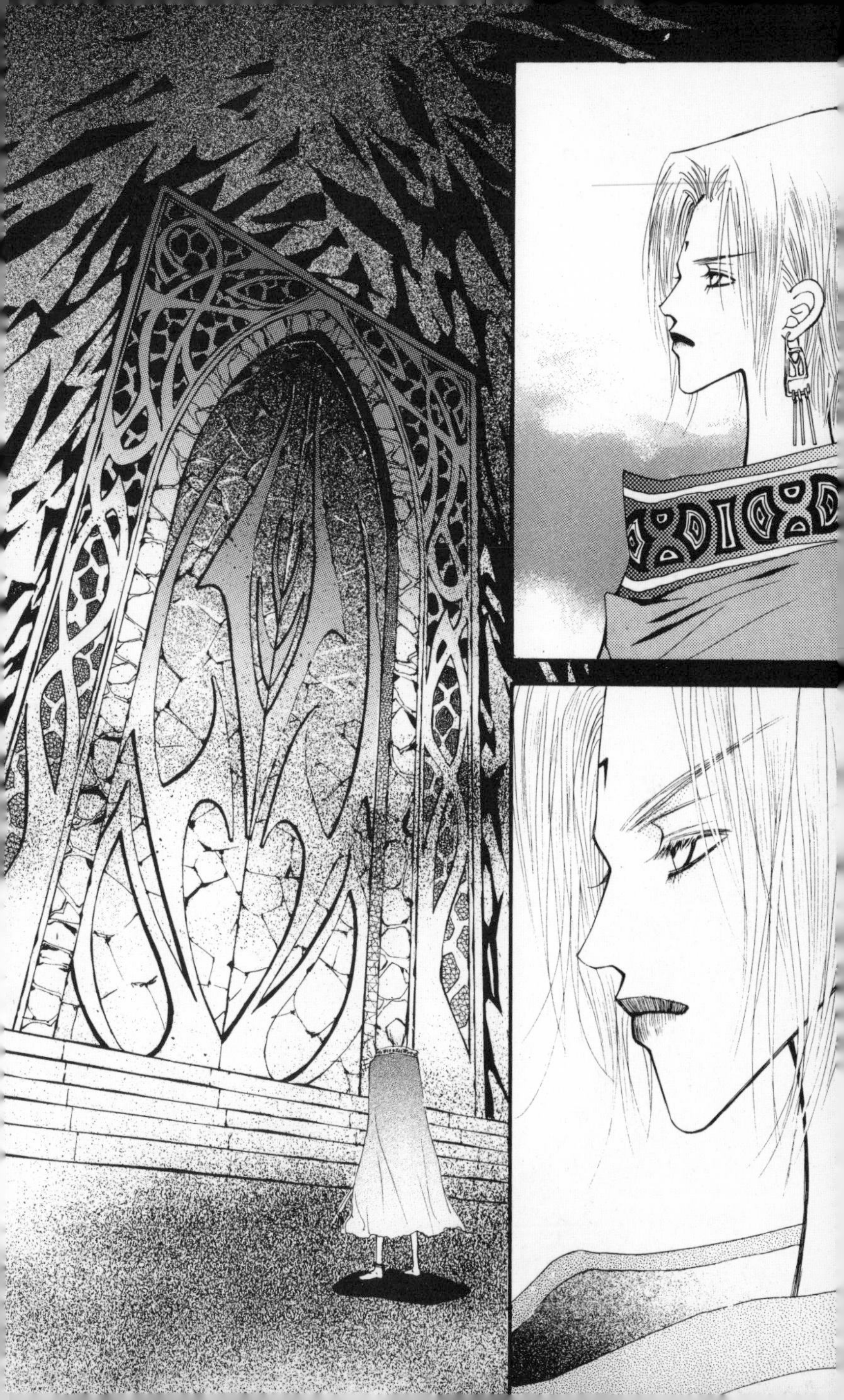

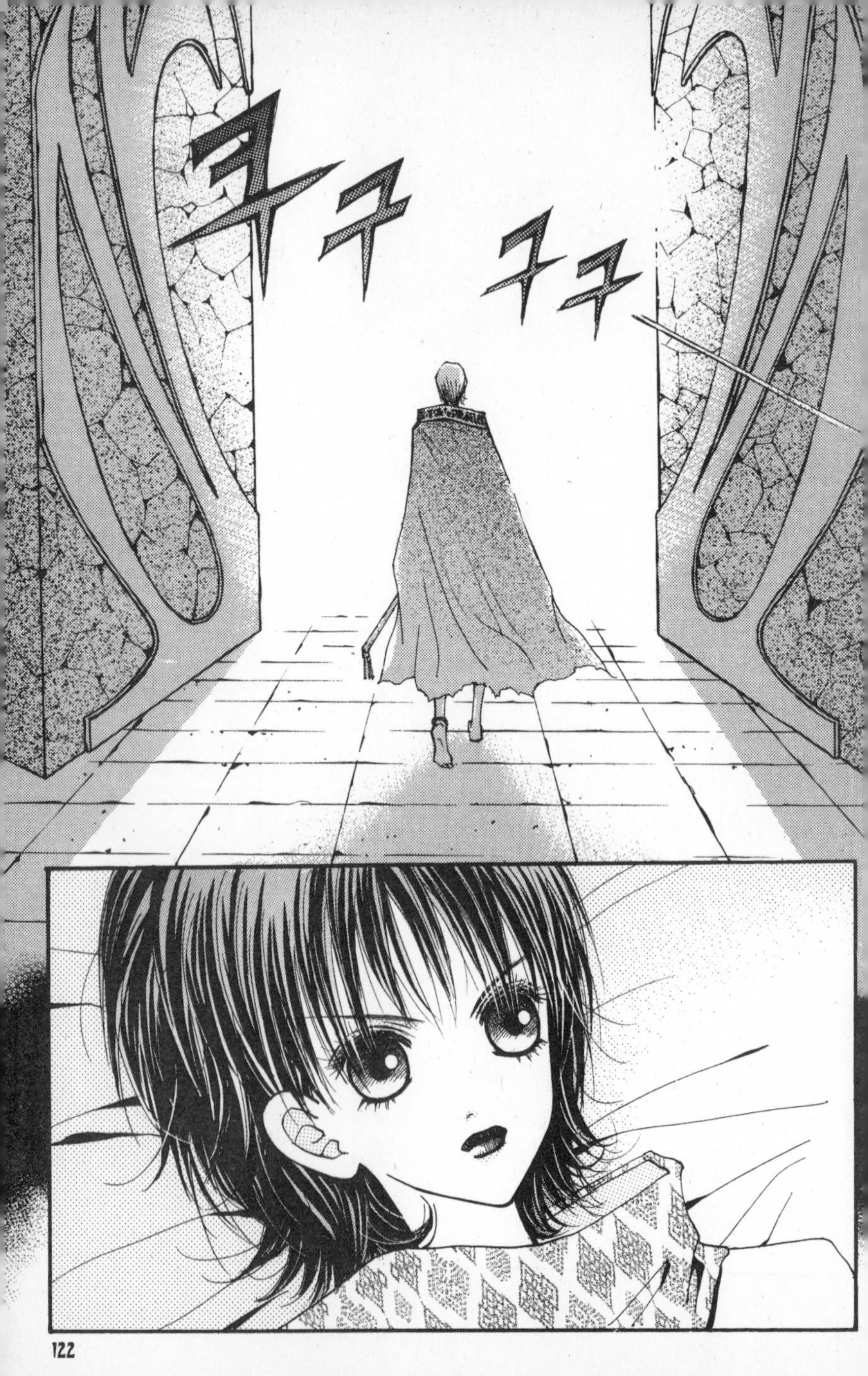

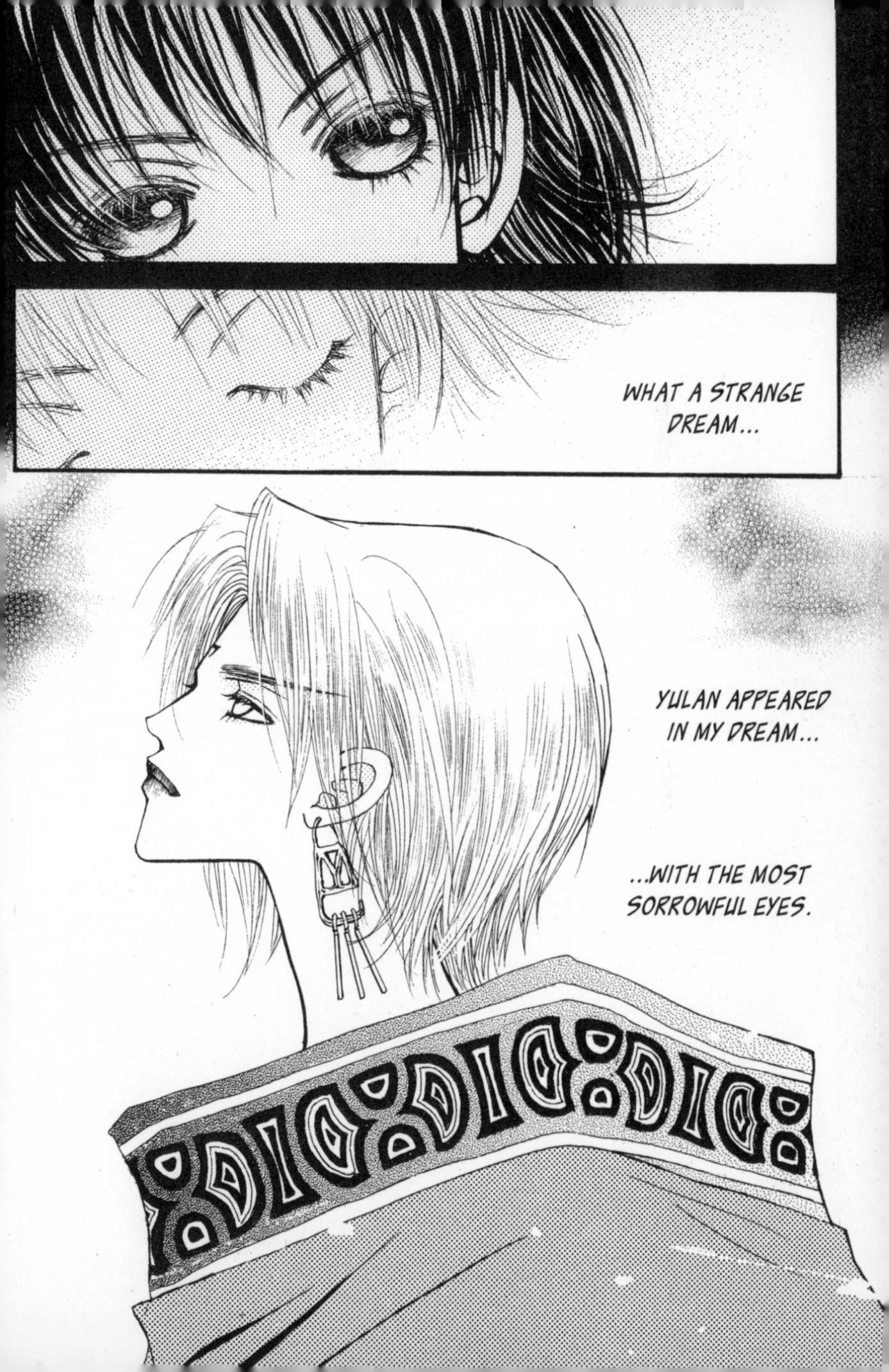
WHAT A STRANGE DREAM...
YULAN APPEARED IN MY DREAM...
...WITH THE MOST SORROWFUL EYES.

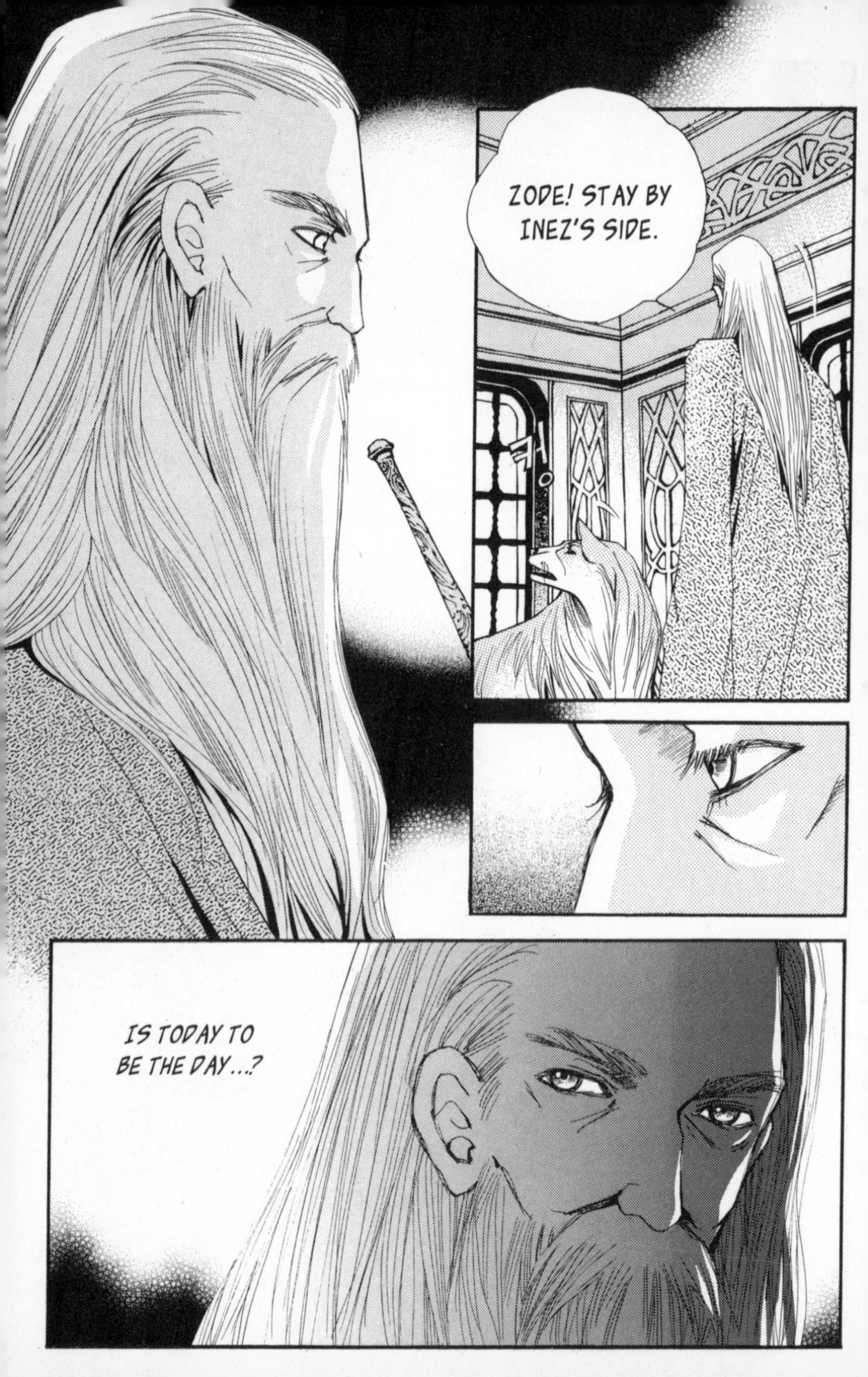
ZODE! STAY BY INEZ'S SIDE.
IS TODAY TO BE THE DAY...?

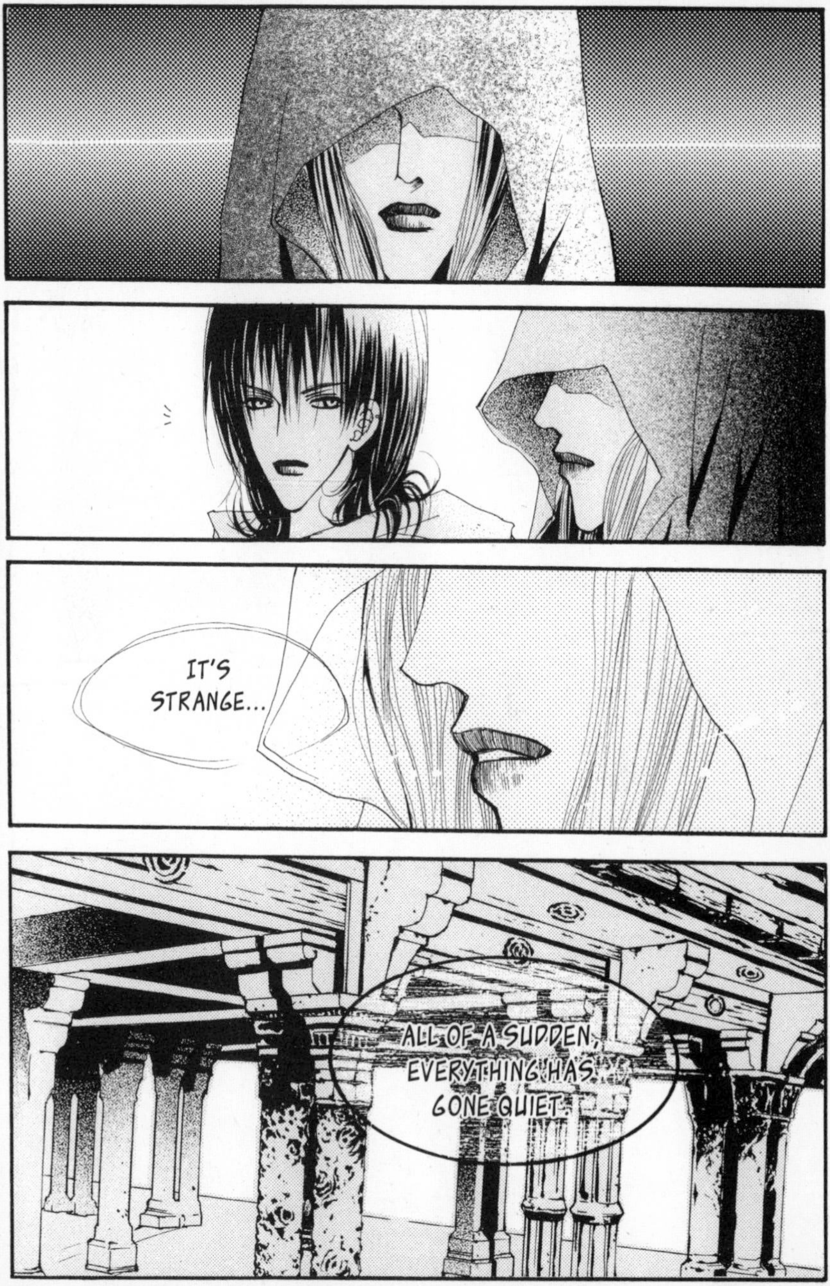
IT'S STRANGE...
ALL OF A SUDDEN, EVERYTHING HAS GONE QUIET.

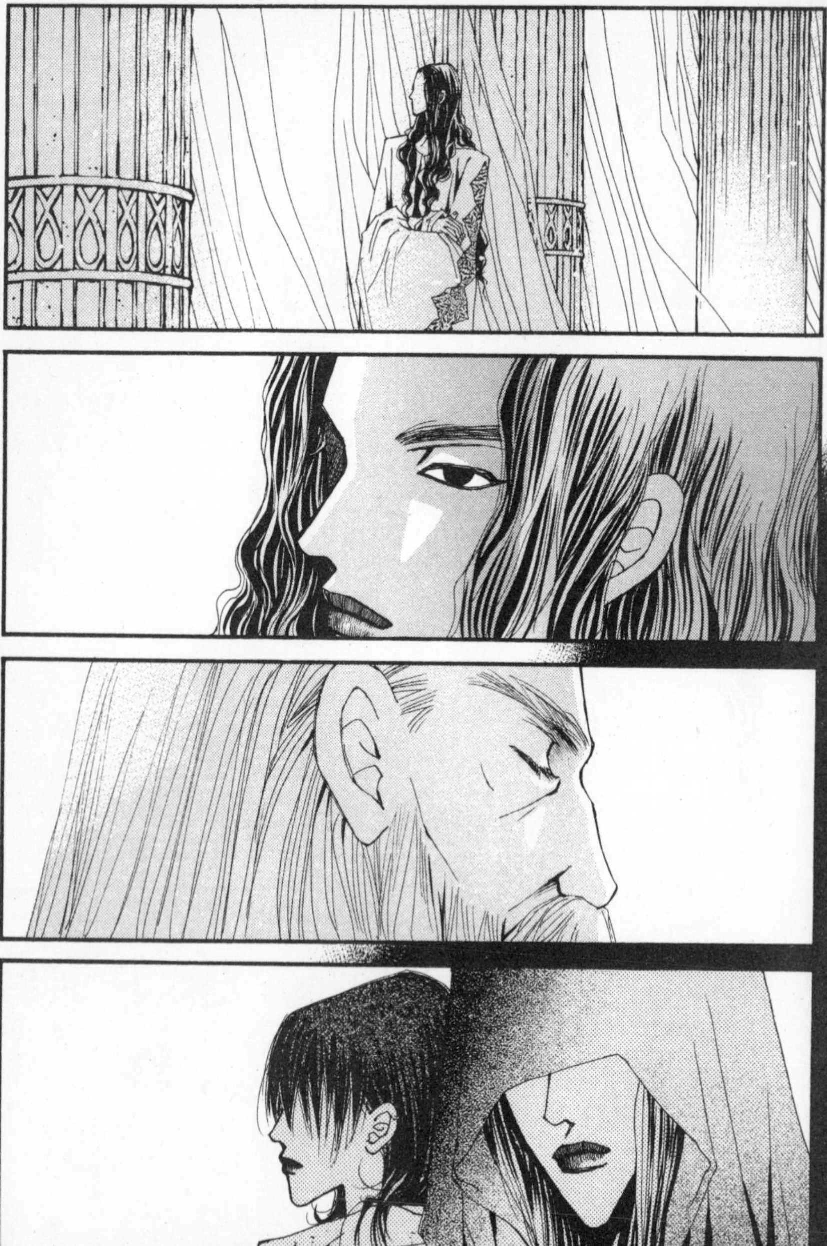

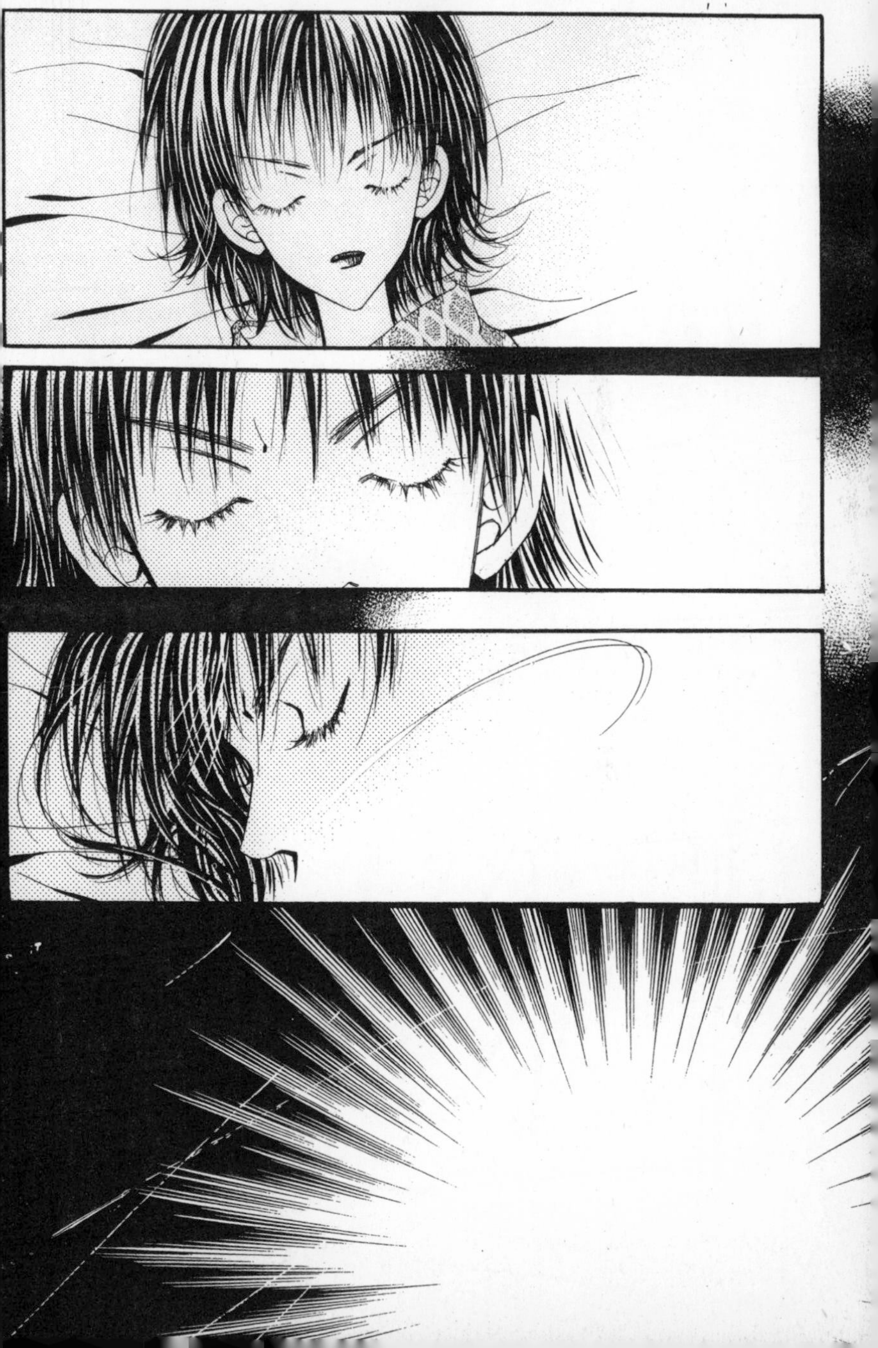

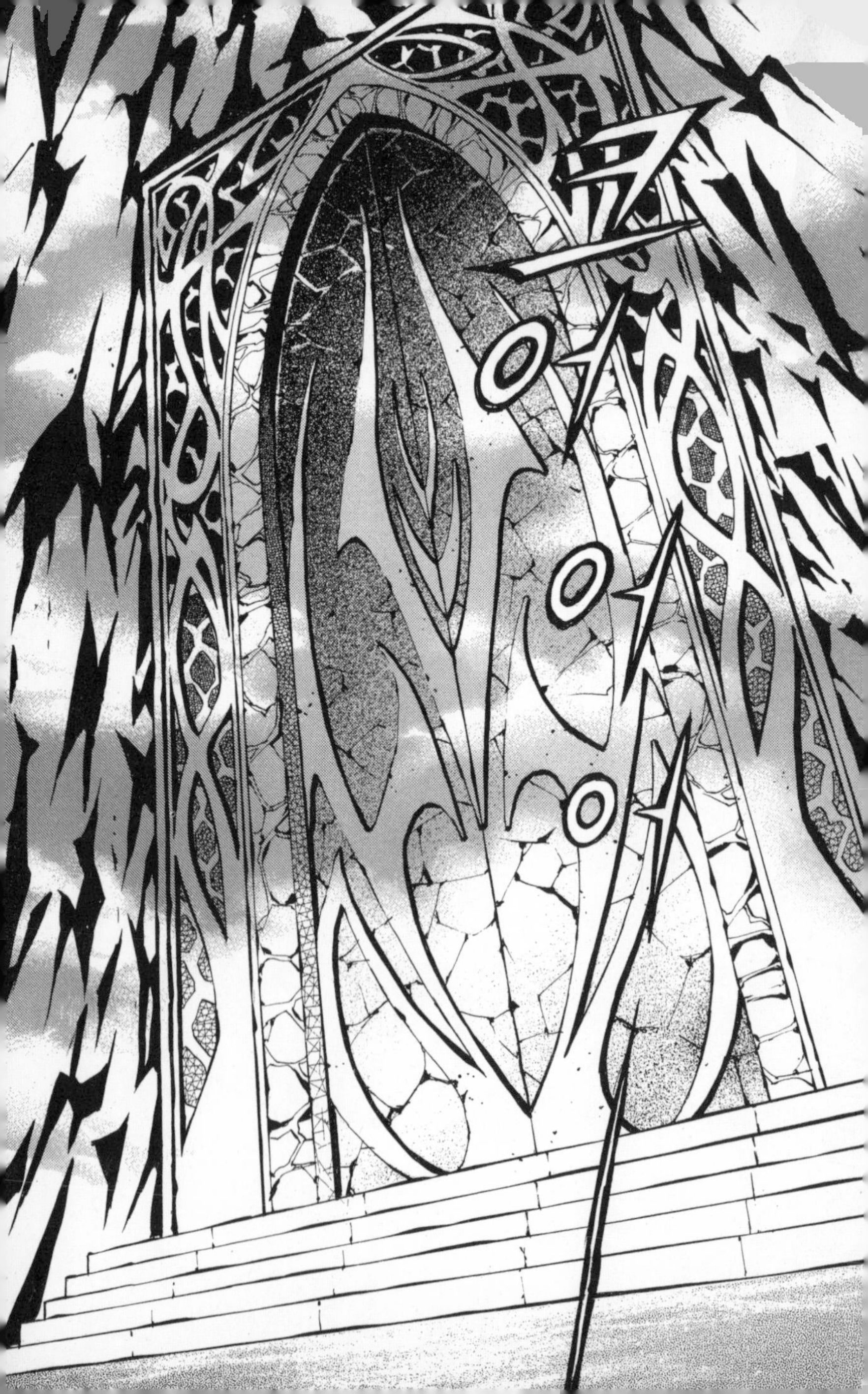
ZOOO

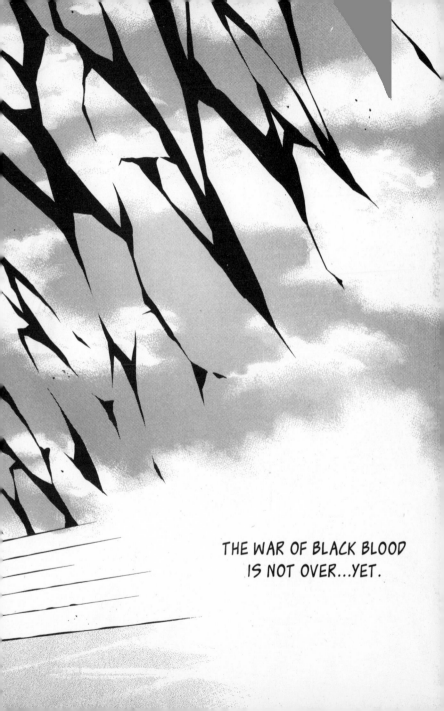

THE WAR OF BLACK BLOOD
IS NOT OVER...YET.

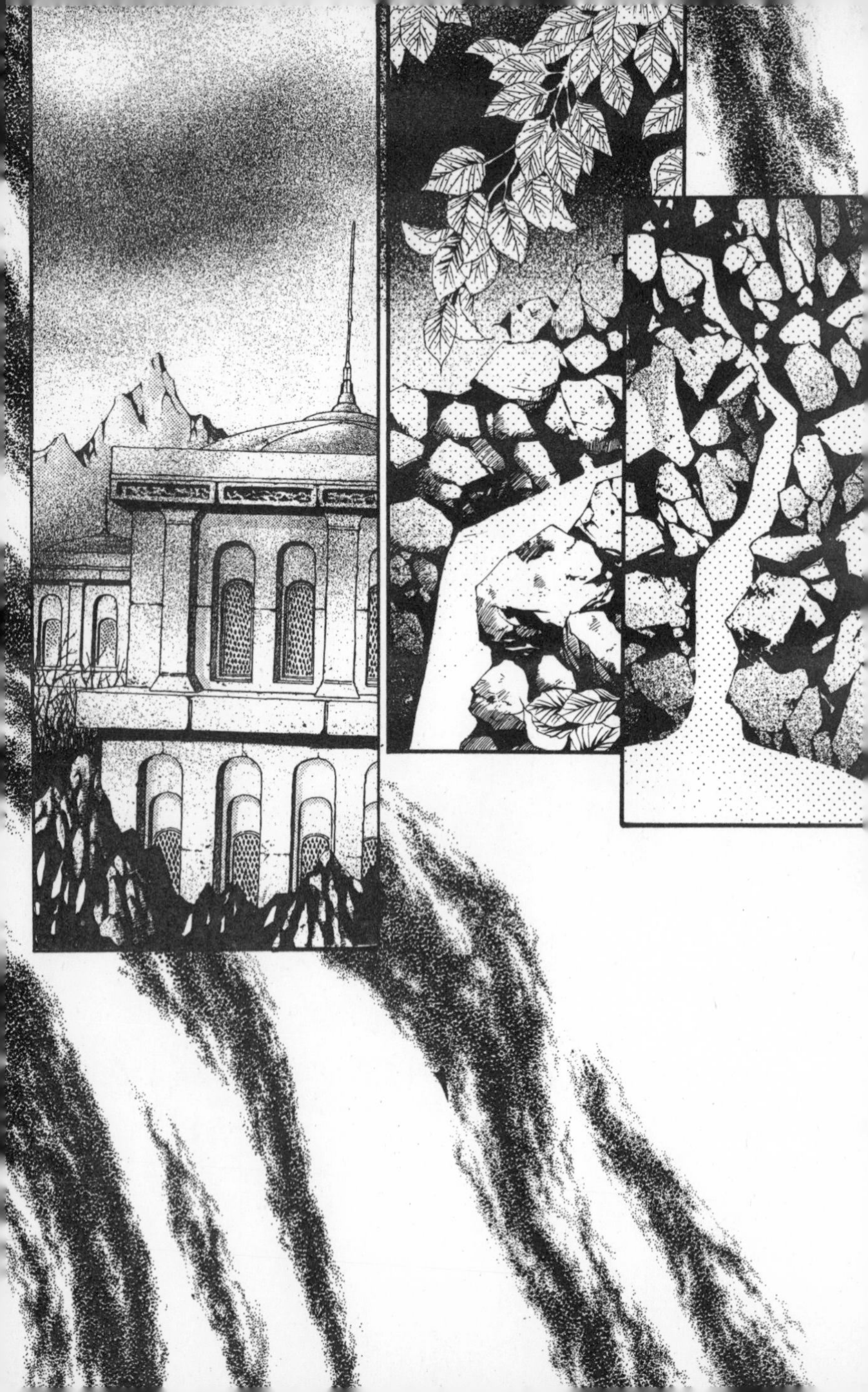

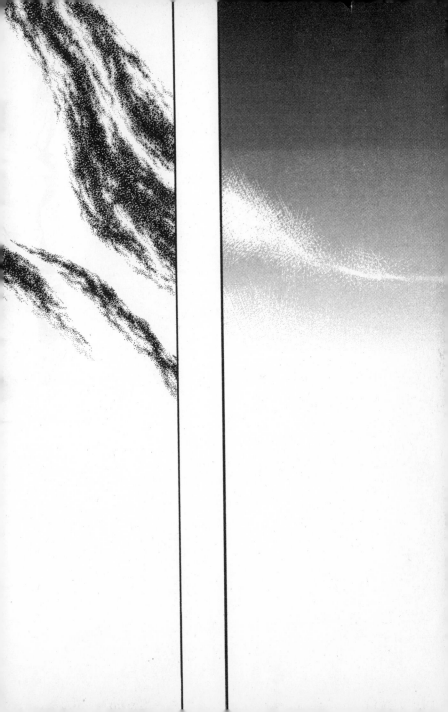

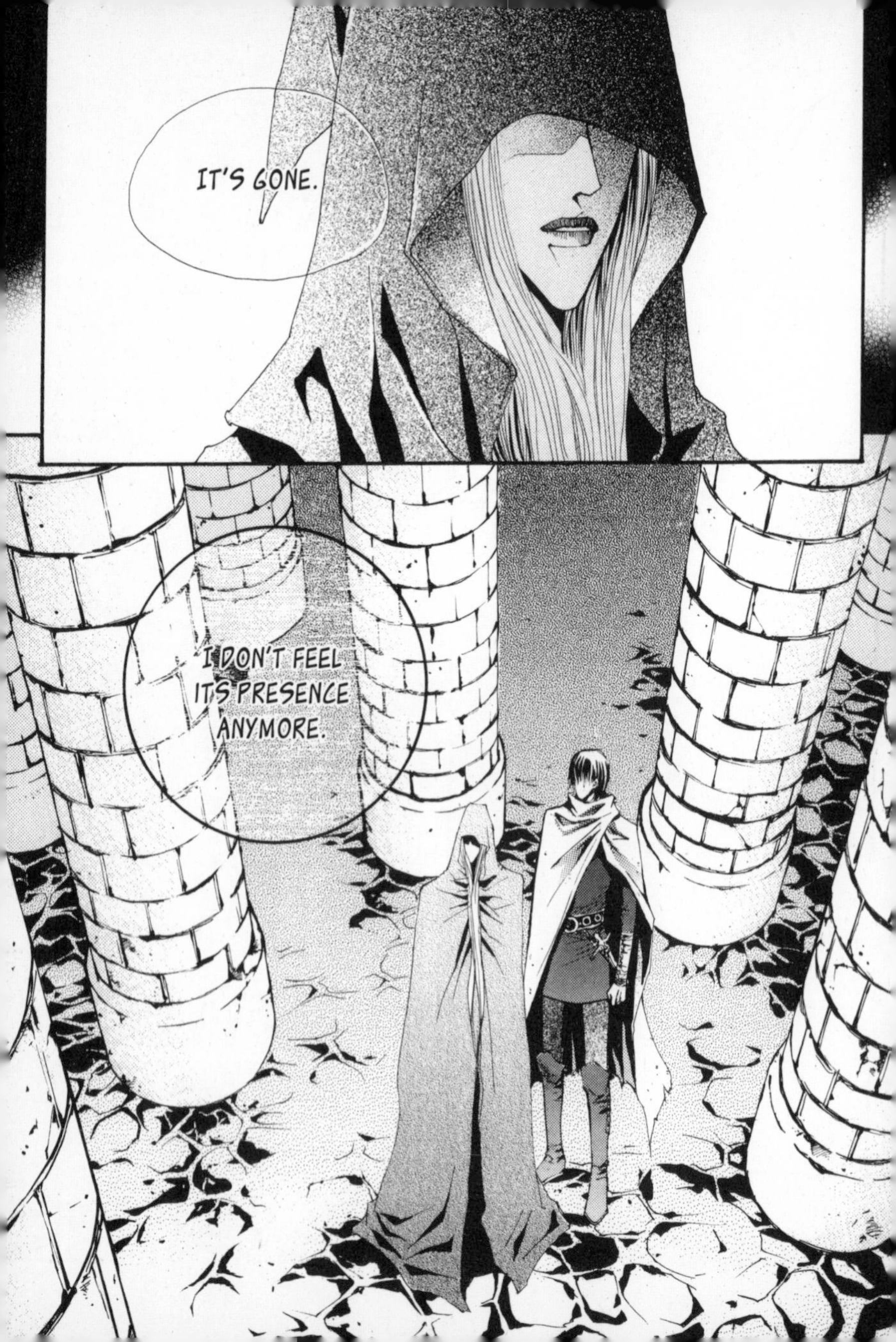
IT'S GONE.
I DON'T FEEL IT'S PRESENCE ANYMORE.

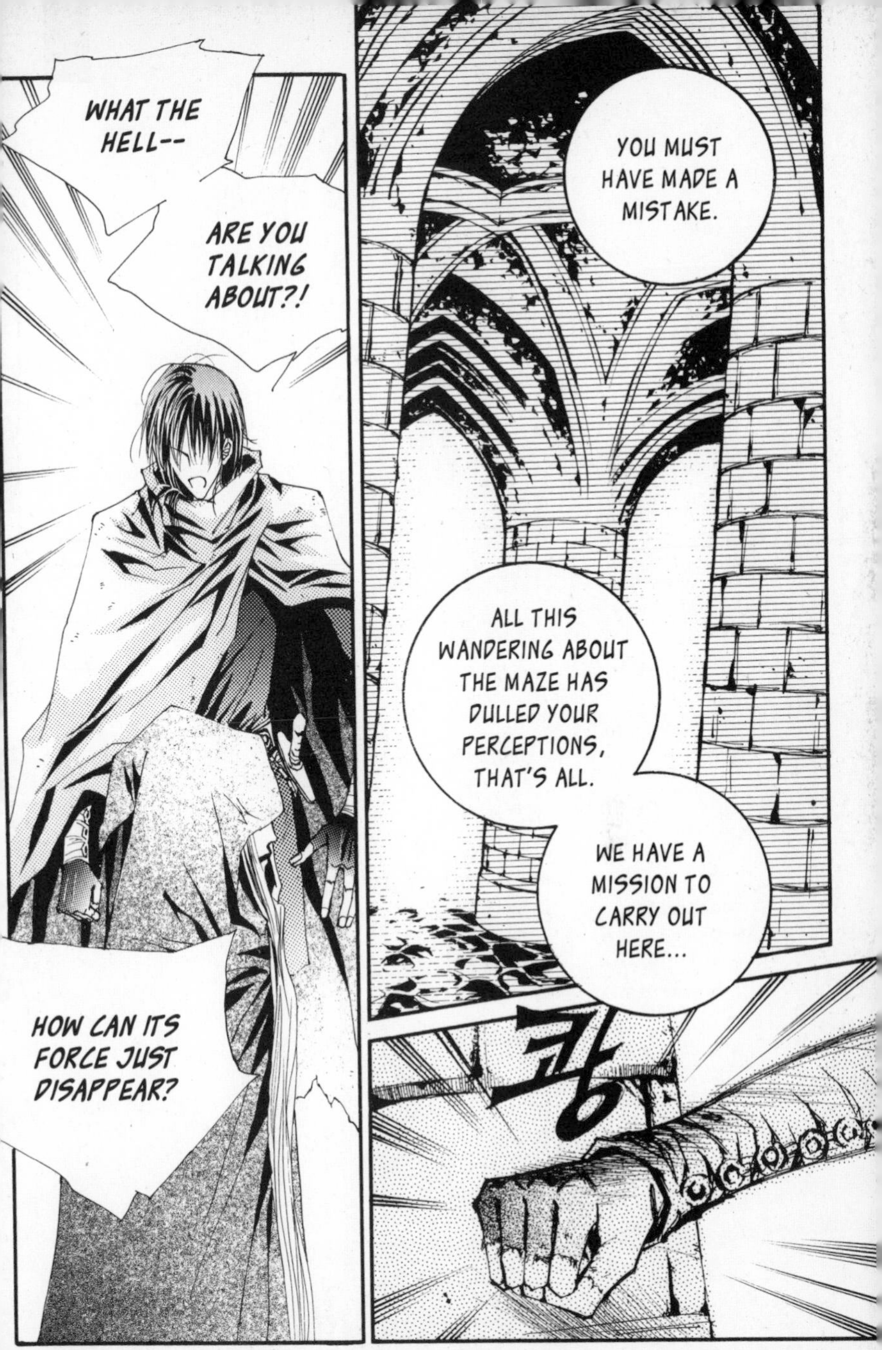
WHAT THE HELL--
ARE YOU TALKING ABOUT?!
HOW CAN ITS FORCE JUST DISAPPEAR?
YOU MUST HAVE MADE A MISTAKE.
ALL THIS WANDERING ABOUT THE MAZE HAS DULLED YOUR PERCEPTIONS, THAT'S ALL.
WE HAVE A MISSION TO CARRY OUT HERE...
쾅

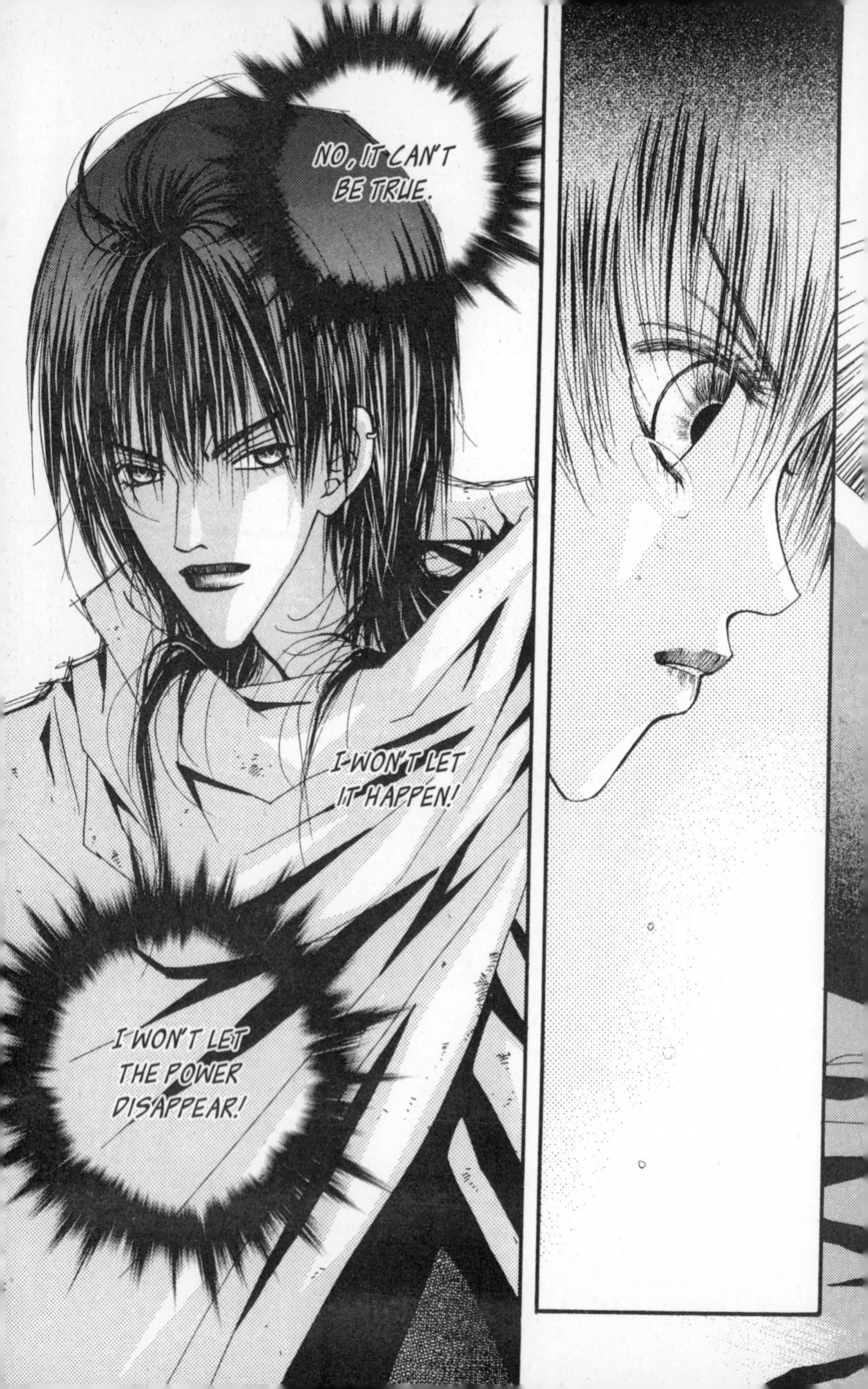
NO, IT CAN'T BE TRUE.
I WON'T LET IT HAPPEN!
I WON'T LET THE POWER DISAPPEAR!

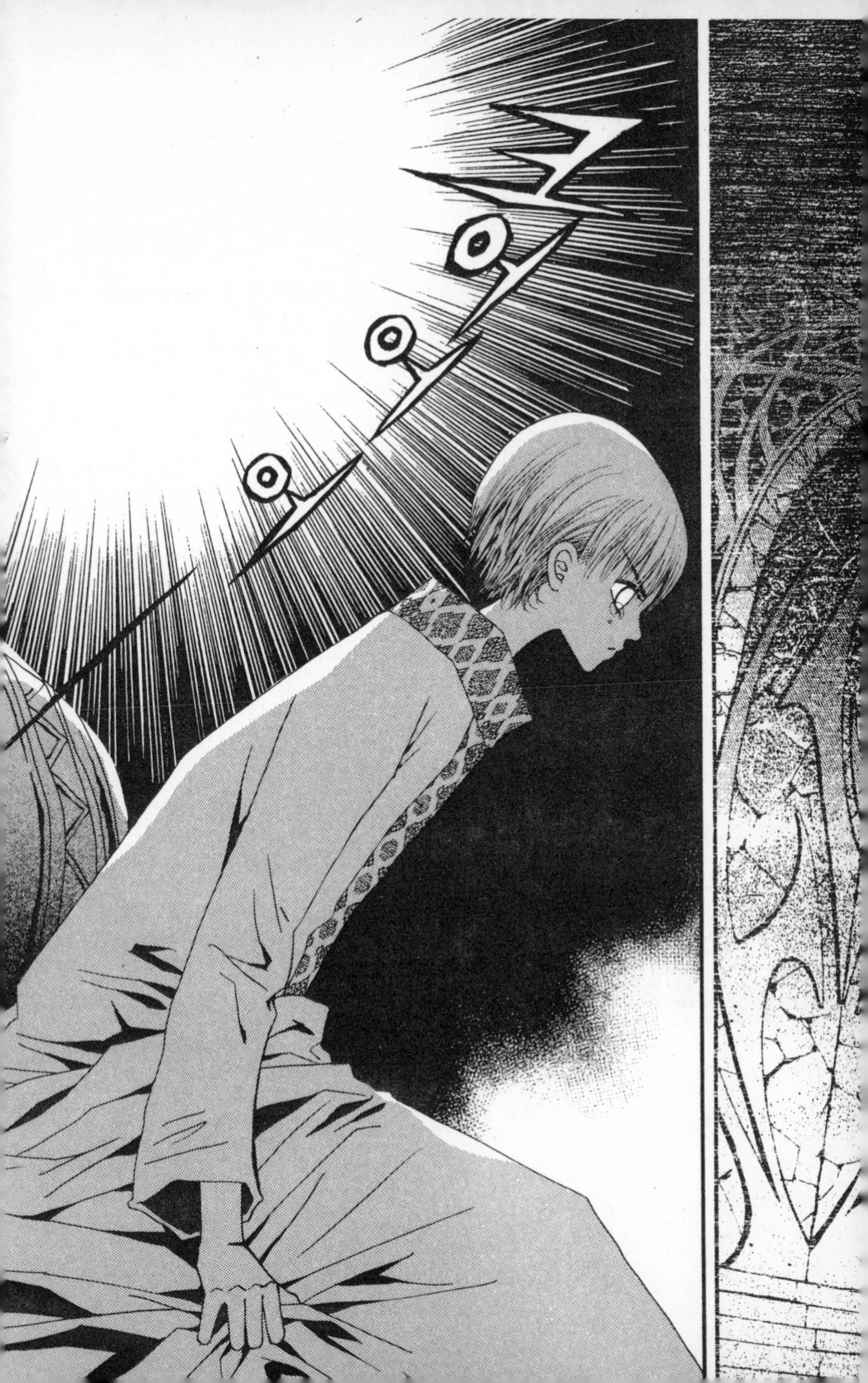

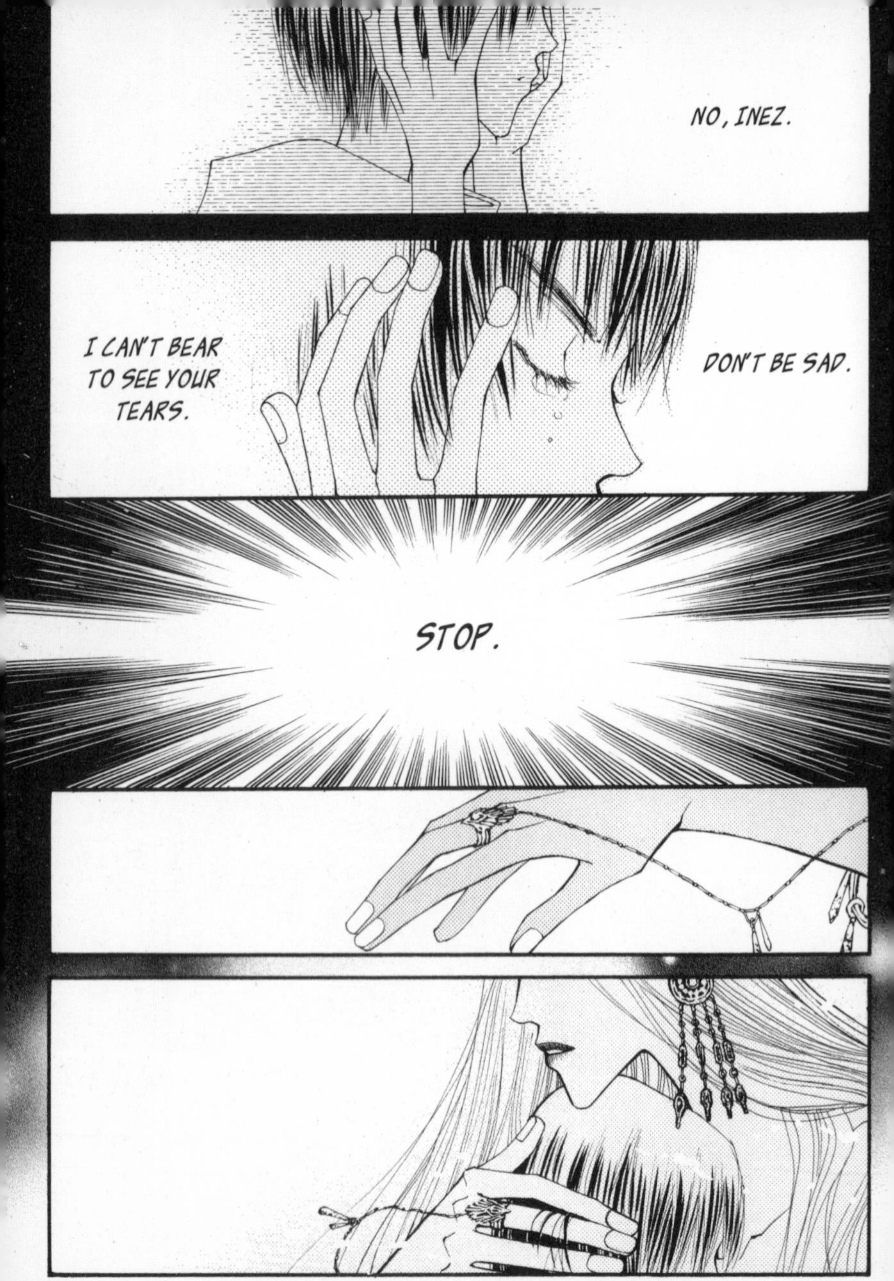
NO, INEZ.
I CAN'T BEAR TO SEE YOUR TEARS.
DON'T BE SAD.
STOP.

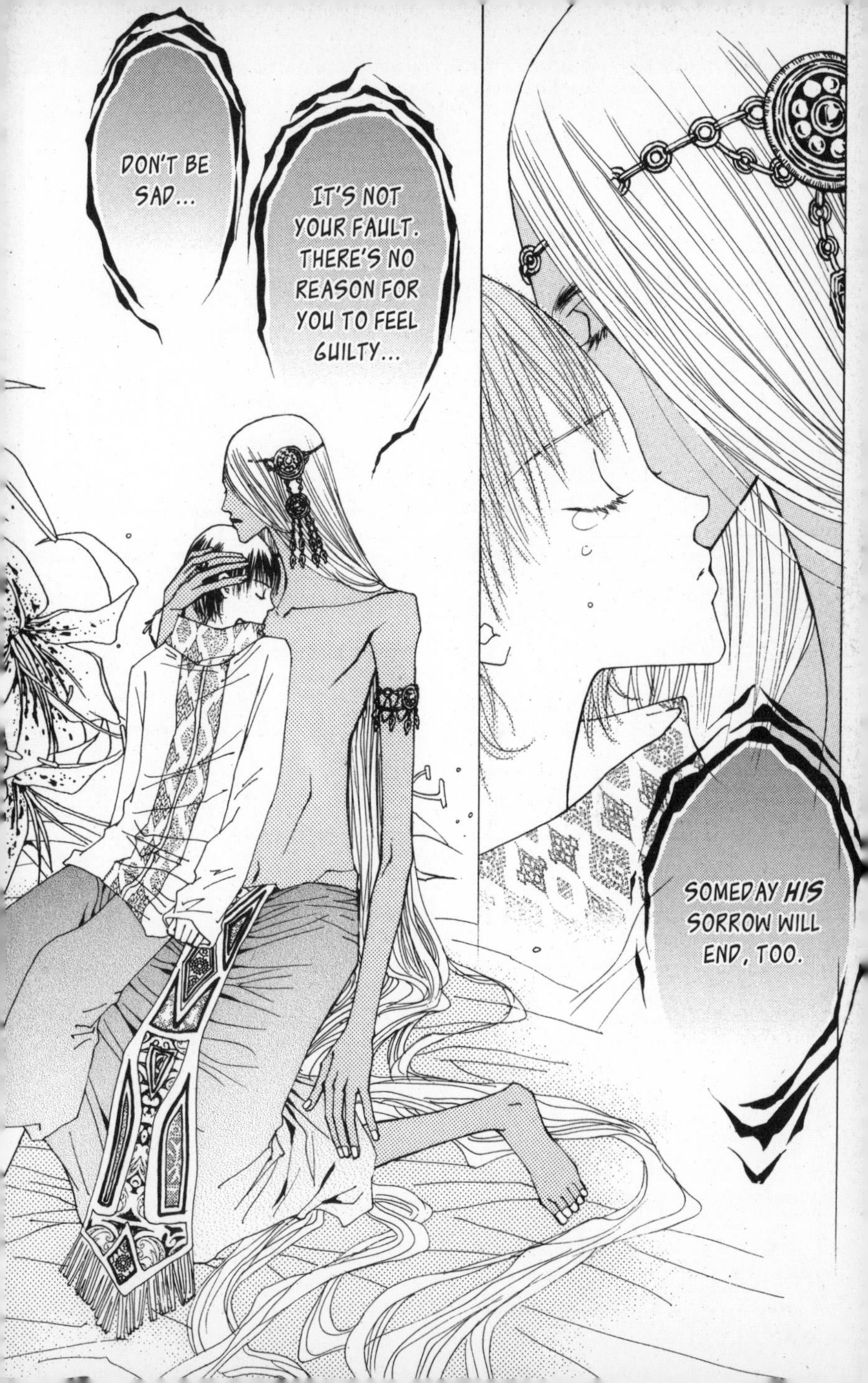
DON'T BE SAD...
IT'S NOT YOUR FAULT. THERE'S NO REASON FOR YOU TO FEEL GUILTY...
SOMEDAY *HIS* SORROW WILL END, TOO.

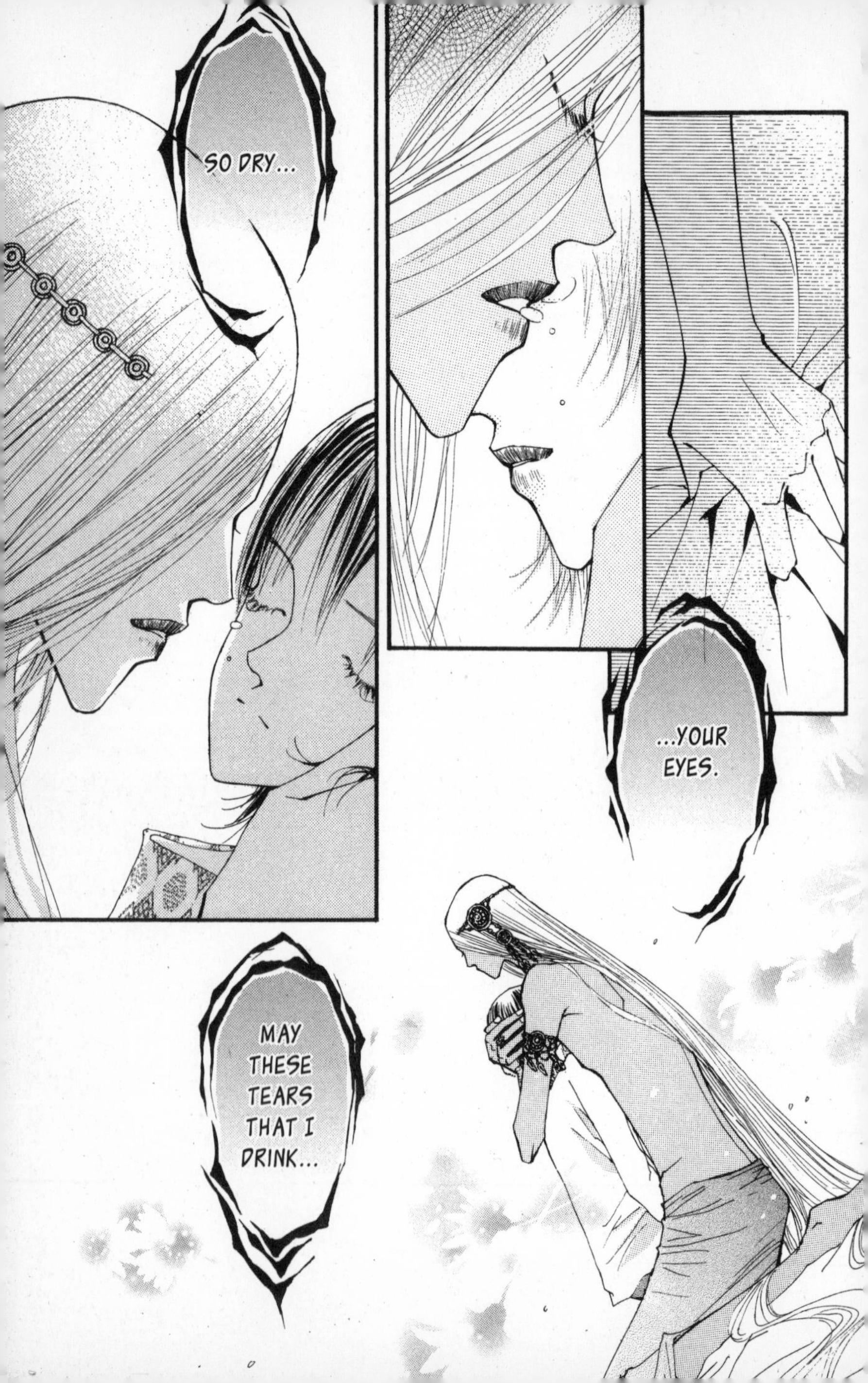
SO DRY...
...YOUR EYES.
MAY THESE TEARS THAT I DRINK...

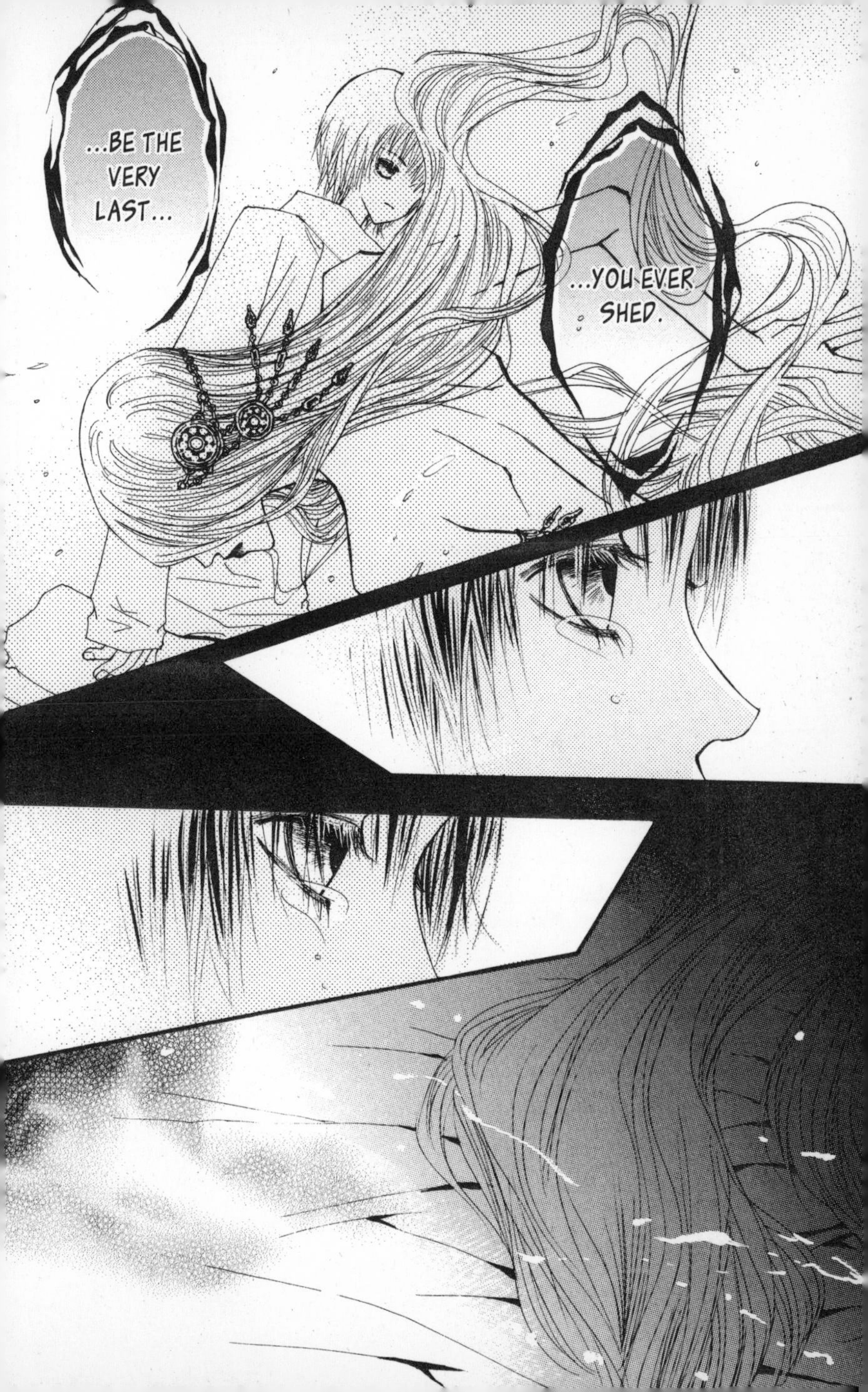
...BE THE VERY LAST...
...YOU EVER SHED.

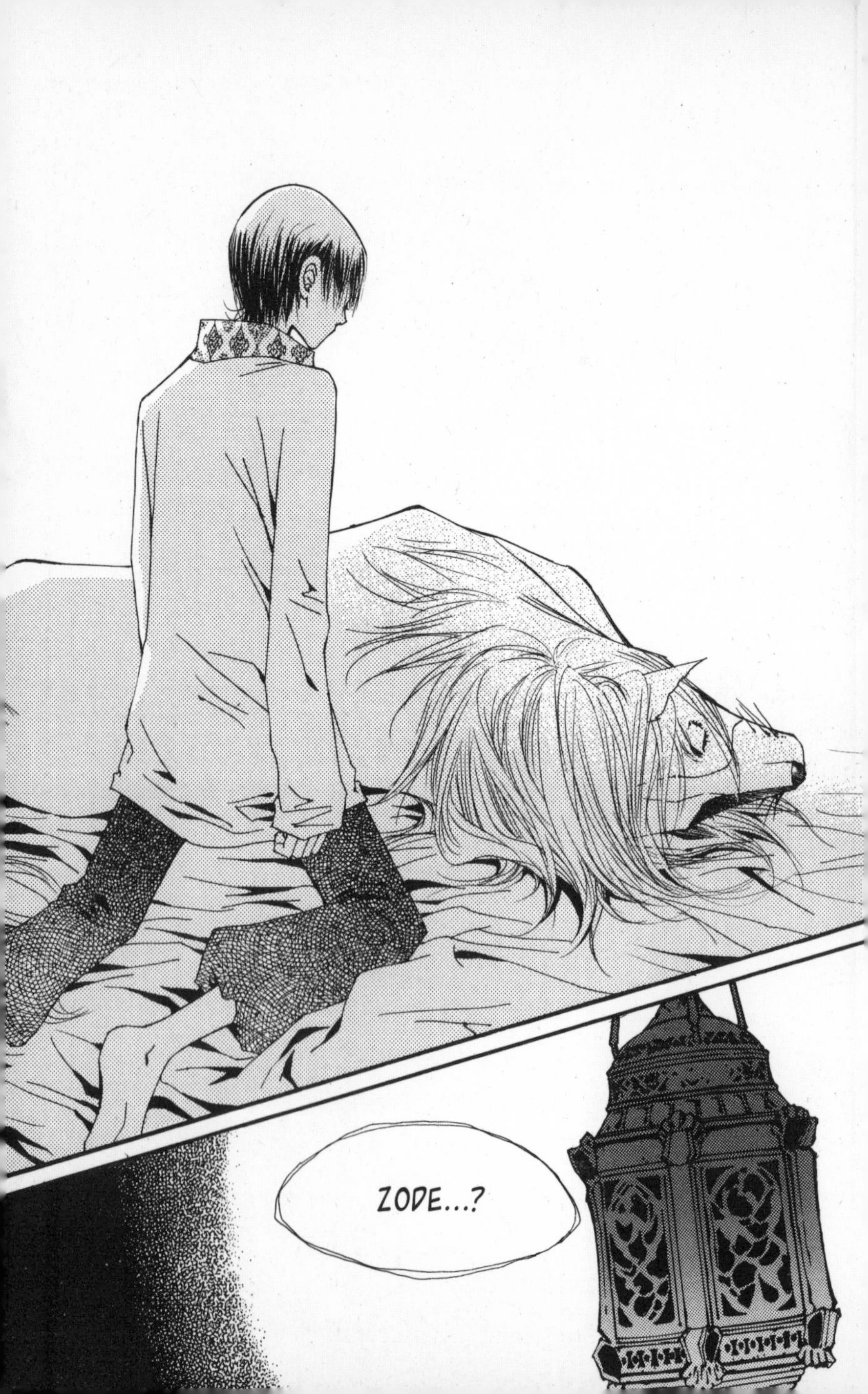
ZODE...?

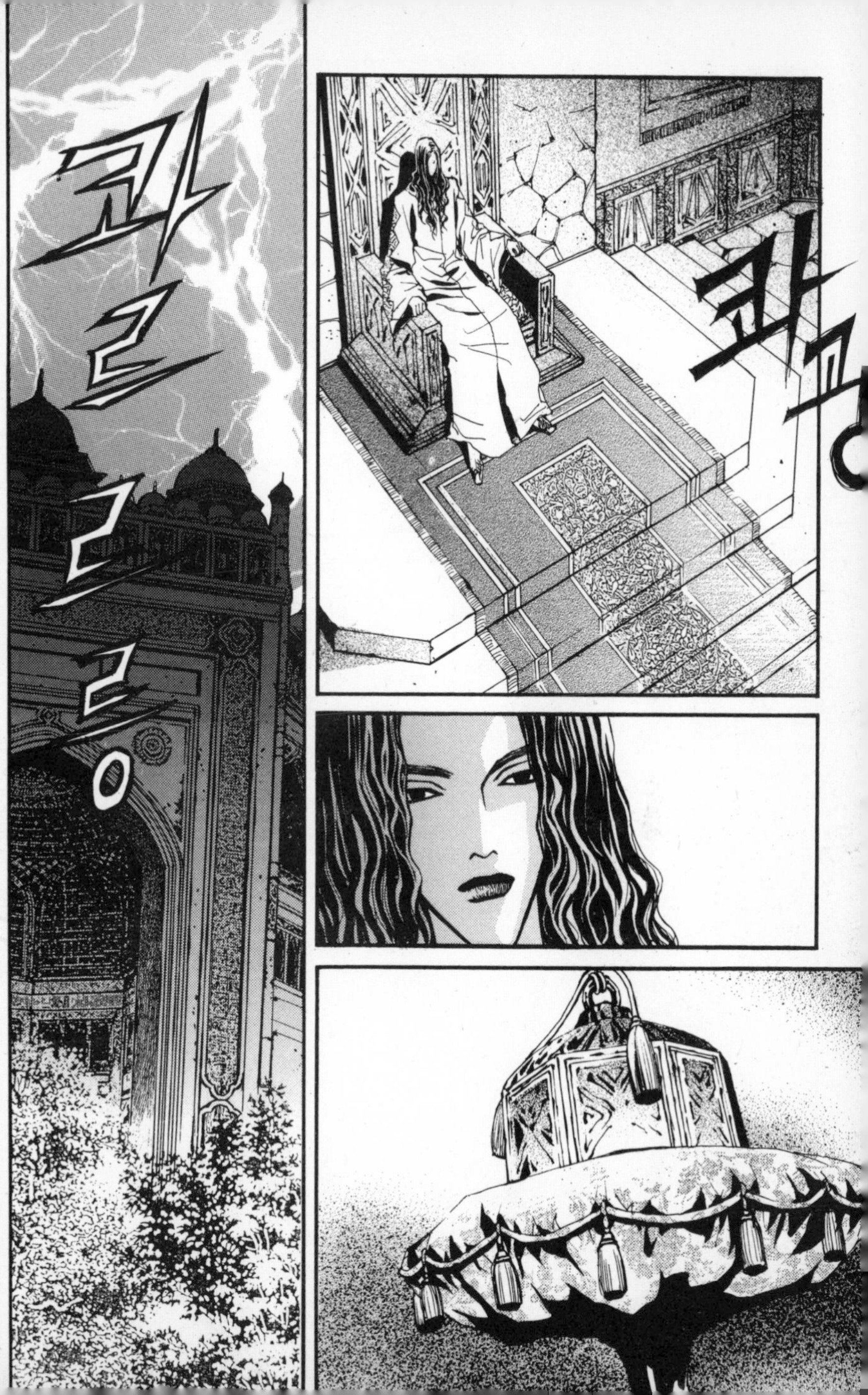
콰르르릉
콰공

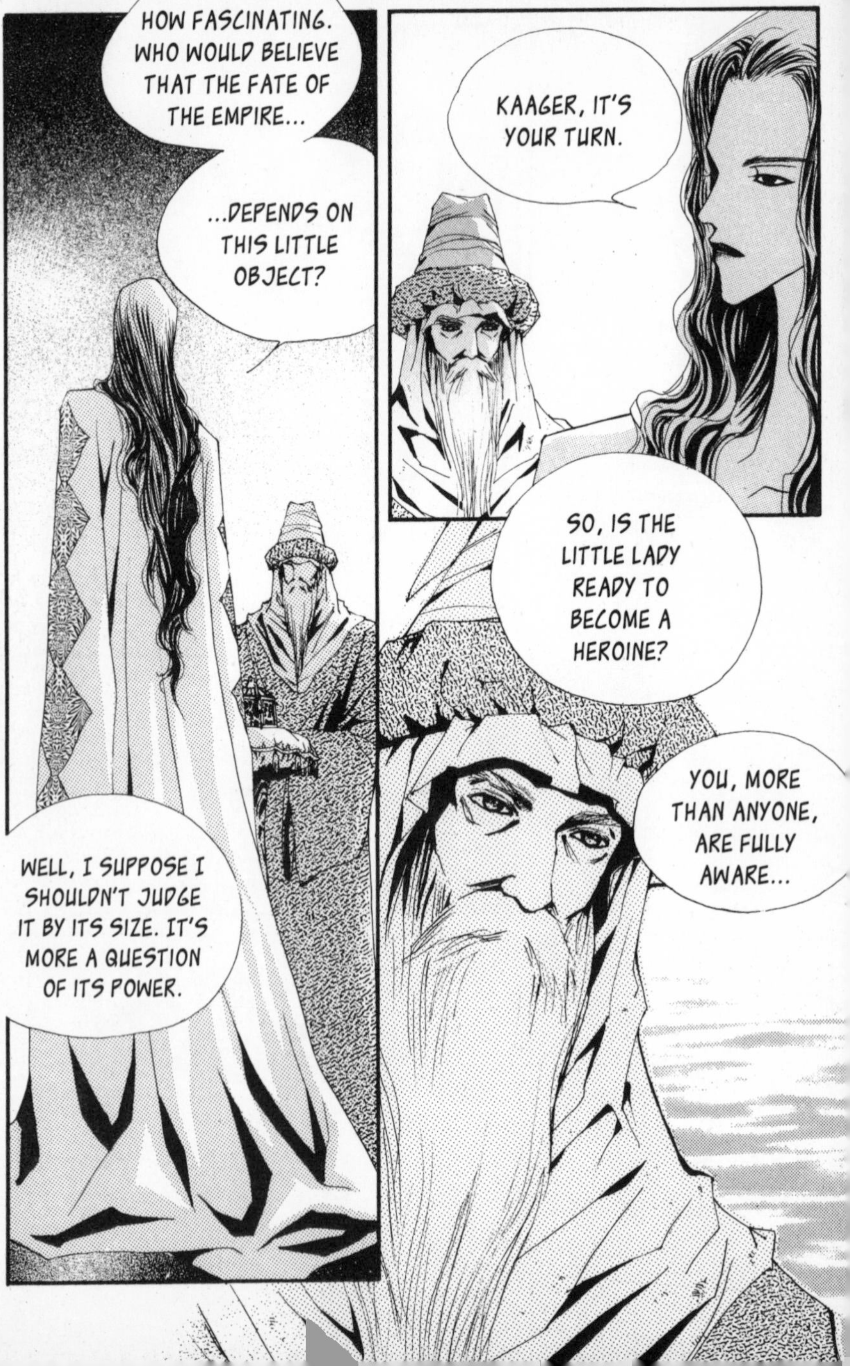
HOW FASCINATING. WHO WOULD BELIEVE THAT THE FATE OF THE EMPIRE...
...DEPENDS ON THIS LITTLE OBJECT?
WELL, I SUPPOSE I SHOULDN'T JUDGE IT BY ITS SIZE. IT'S MORE A QUESTION OF ITS POWER.
KAAGER, IT'S YOUR TURN.
SO, IS THE LITTLE LADY READY TO BECOME A HEROINE?
YOU, MORE THAN ANYONE, ARE FULLY AWARE...

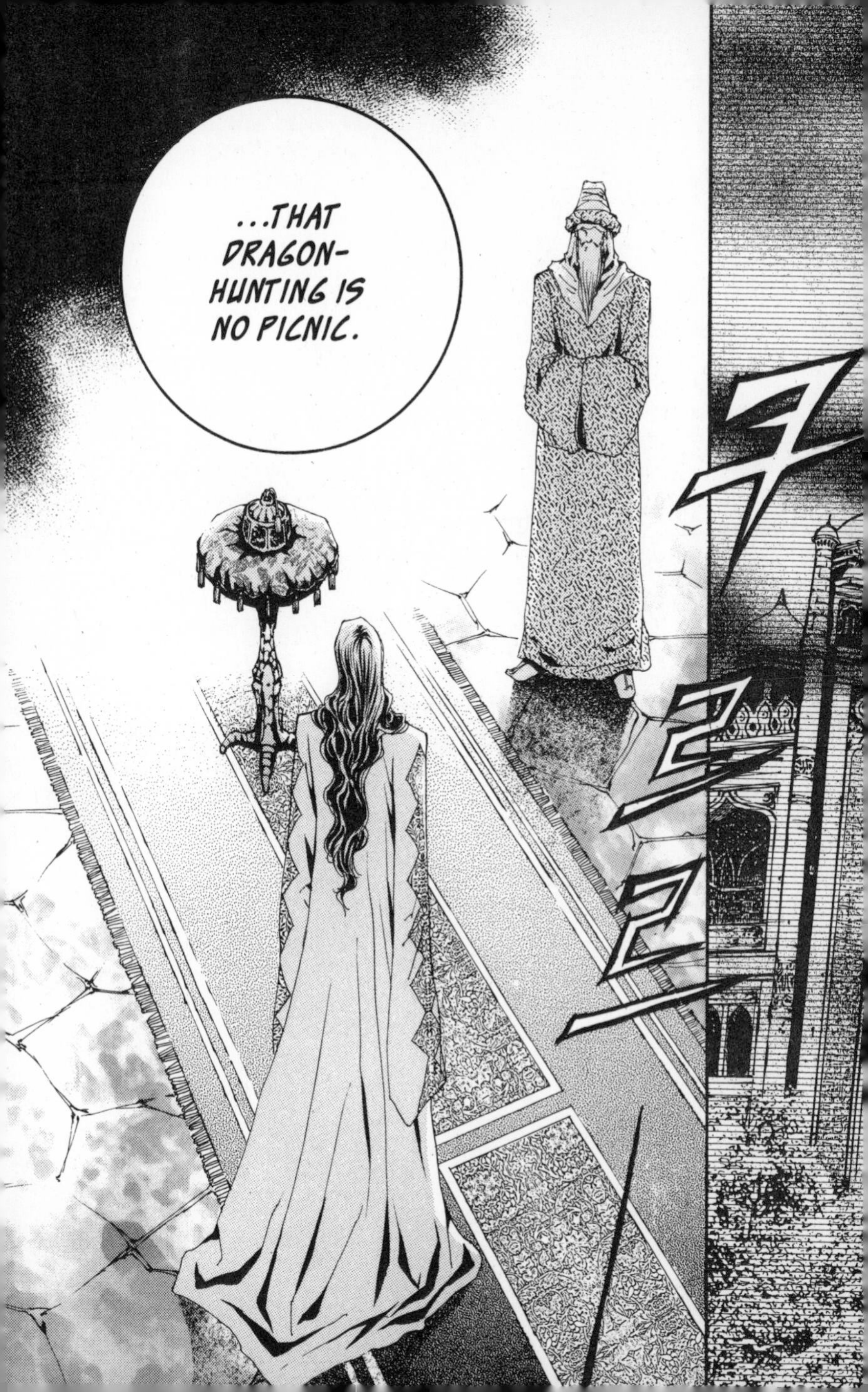
...THAT DRAGON-HUNTING IS NO PICNIC.

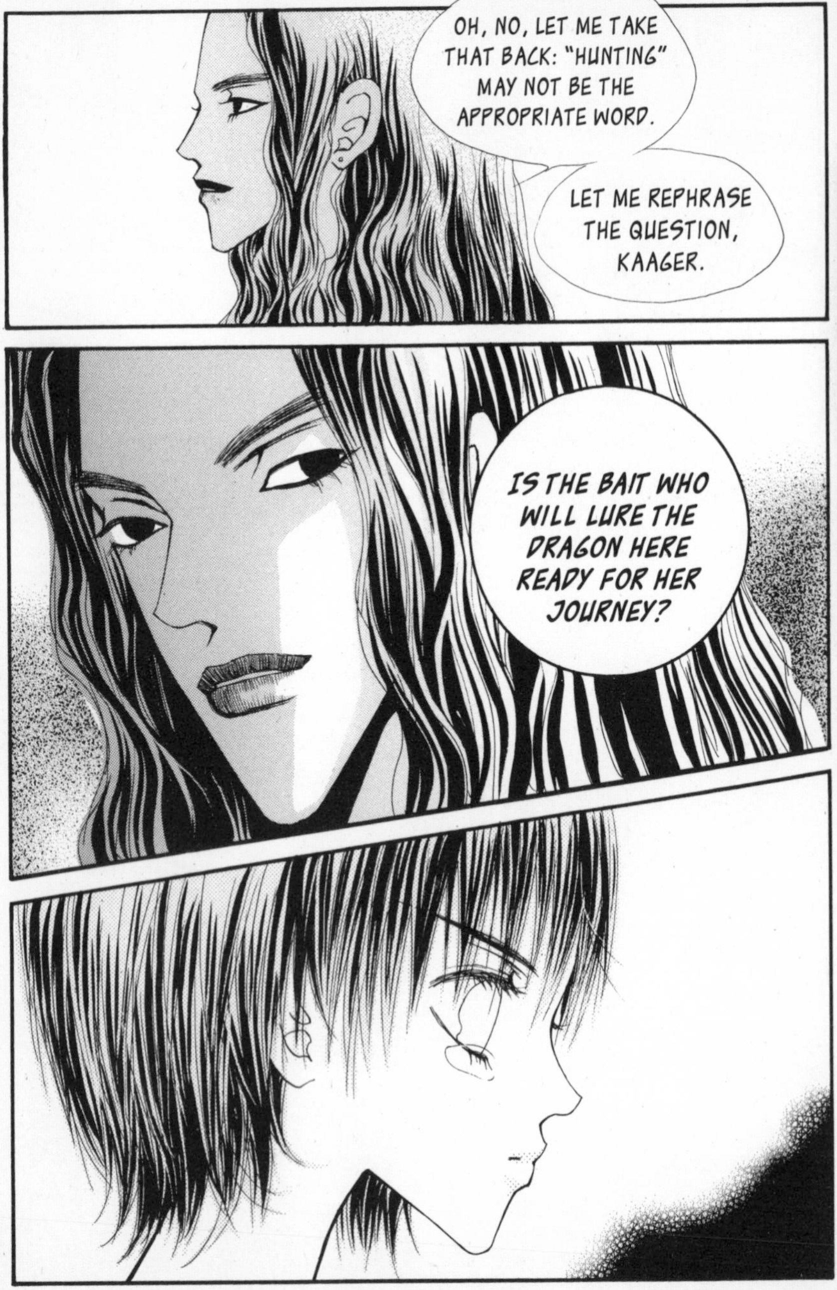
OH, NO, LET ME TAKE THAT BACK: "HUNTING" MAY NOT BE THE APPROPRIATE WORD.
LET ME REPHRASE THE QUESTION, KAAGER.
IS THE BAIT WHO WILL LURE THE DRAGON HERE READY FOR HER JOURNEY?

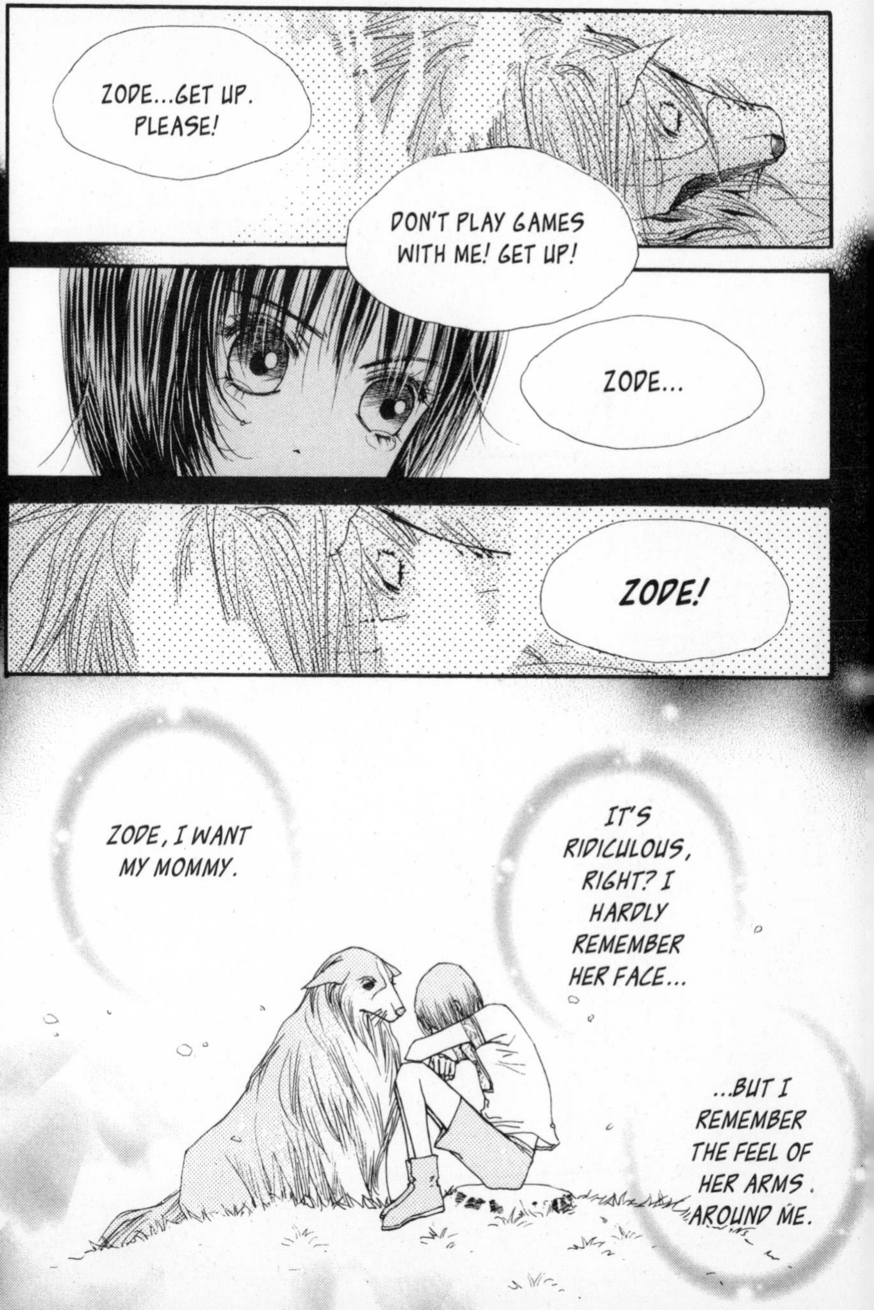
ZODE...GET UP. PLEASE!
DON'T PLAY GAMES WITH ME! GET UP!
ZODE...
ZODE!
ZODE, I WANT MY MOMMY.
IT'S RIDICULOUS, RIGHT? I HARDLY REMEMBER HER FACE...
...BUT I REMEMBER THE FEEL OF HER ARMS AROUND ME.

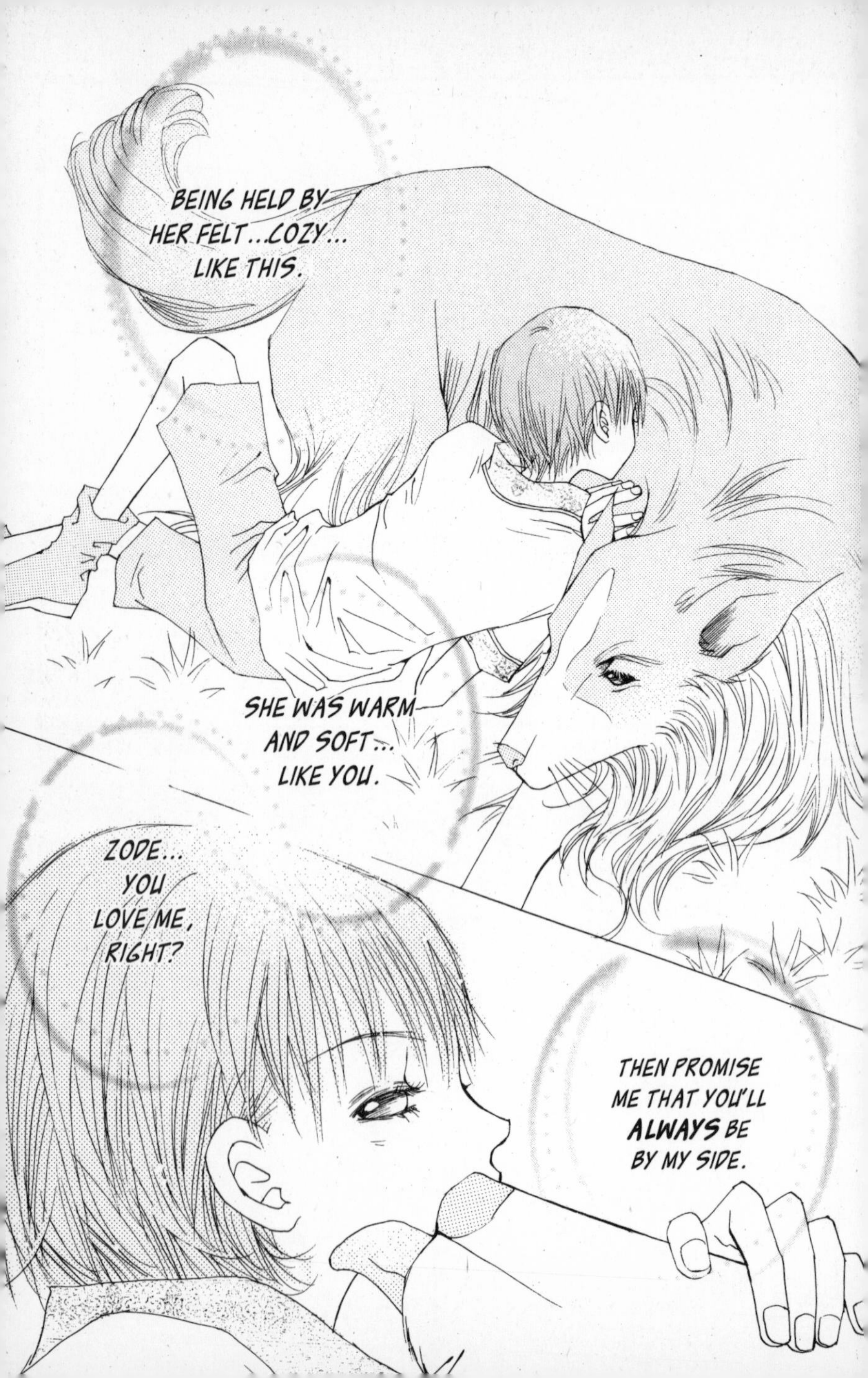
BEING HELD BY HER FELT...COZY... LIKE THIS.
SHE WAS WARM AND SOFT... LIKE YOU.
ZODE... YOU LOVE ME, RIGHT?
THEN PROMISE ME THAT YOU'LL **ALWAYS** BE BY MY SIDE.

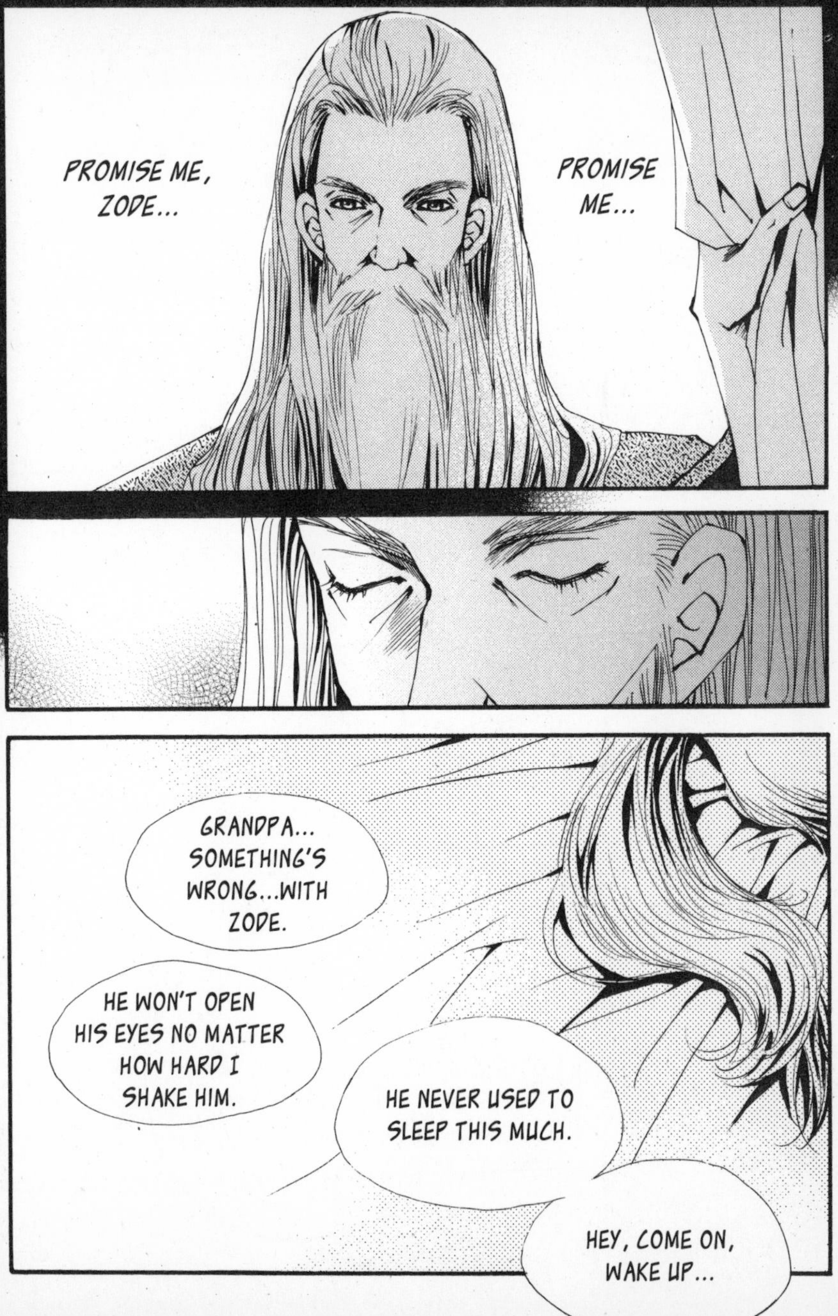
PROMISE ME, ZODE...
PROMISE ME...
GRANDPA... SOMETHING'S WRONG...WITH ZODE.
HE WON'T OPEN HIS EYES NO MATTER HOW HARD I SHAKE HIM.
HE NEVER USED TO SLEEP THIS MUCH.
HEY, COME ON, WAKE UP...

WHEN I GET YOU UP, I'M GOING TO TIE A RIBBON AROUND YOUR NECK...
...AND MAKE THE BOW REALLY TIGHT!

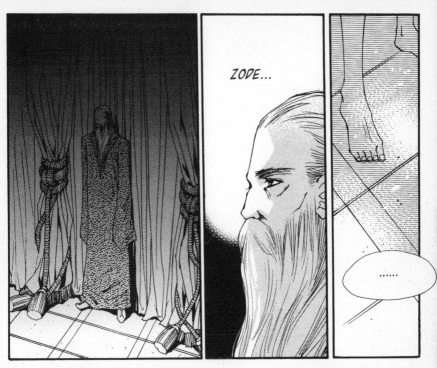

ZODE...

......

DON'T WORRY, HE'S ASLEEP.

I'VE SAID THIS BEFORE, BUT THE BLIND, UNCONDITIONAL LOVE OF YOUR KIND IS TOO MUCH FOR HUMAN BEINGS TO ACCEPT.

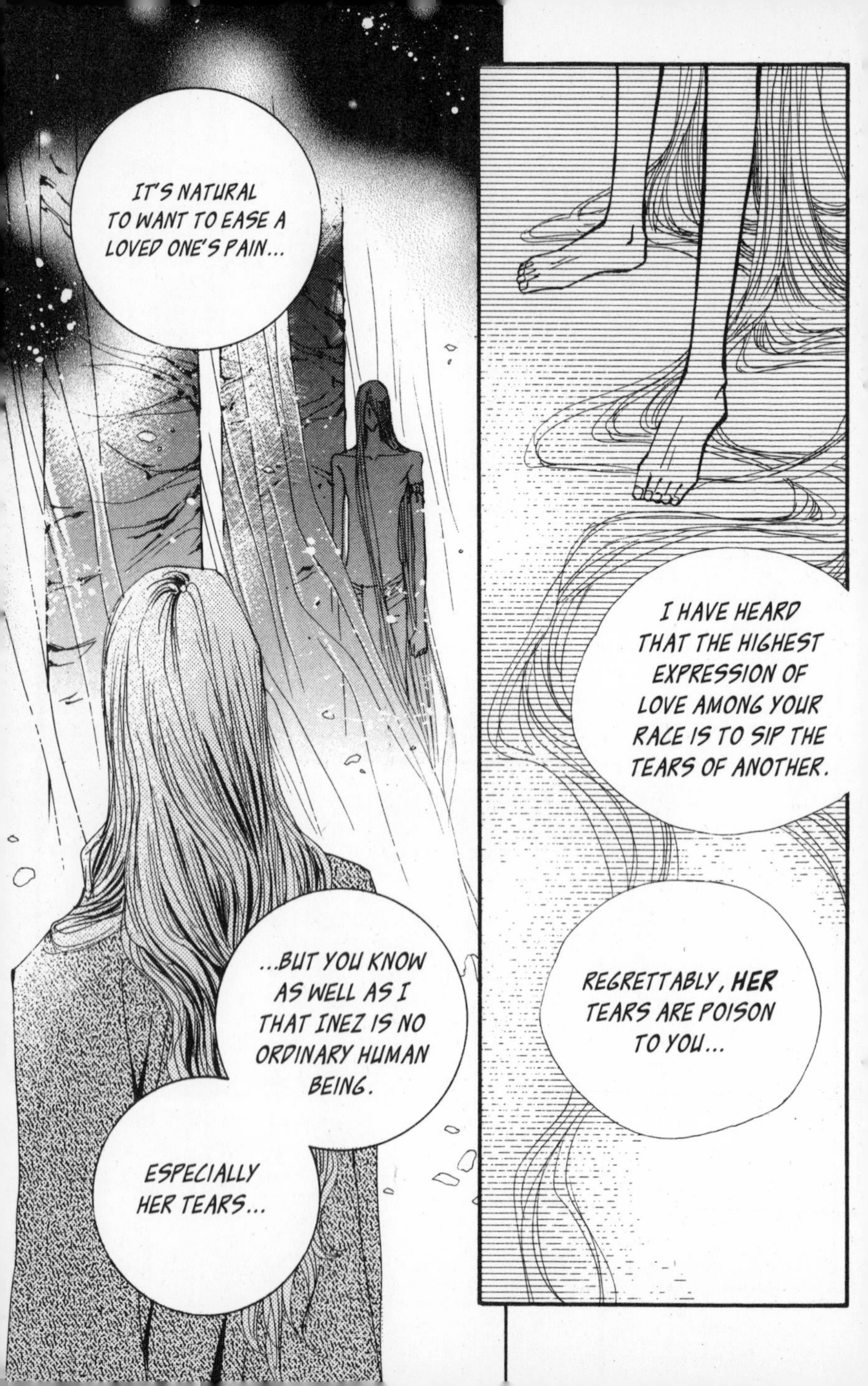
IT'S NATURAL TO WANT TO EASE A LOVED ONE'S PAIN...
...BUT YOU KNOW AS WELL AS I THAT INEZ IS NO ORDINARY HUMAN BEING.
ESPECIALLY HER TEARS...
I HAVE HEARD THAT THE HIGHEST EXPRESSION OF LOVE AMONG YOUR RACE IS TO SIP THE TEARS OF ANOTHER.
REGRETTABLY, **HER** TEARS ARE POISON TO YOU...

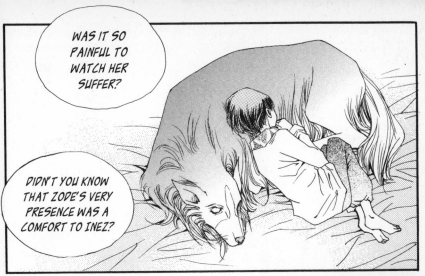

WAS IT SO PAINFUL TO WATCH HER SUFFER?

DIDN'T YOU KNOW THAT ZODE'S VERY PRESENCE WAS A COMFORT TO INEZ?

YET YOU THREW AWAY THAT PHYSICAL FORM.

YOU MUST HAVE KNOWN HOW INEZ WOULD SUFFER AFTER LOSING ZODE.

KNOWING THAT, WHY *DID* YOU DO THAT?

151

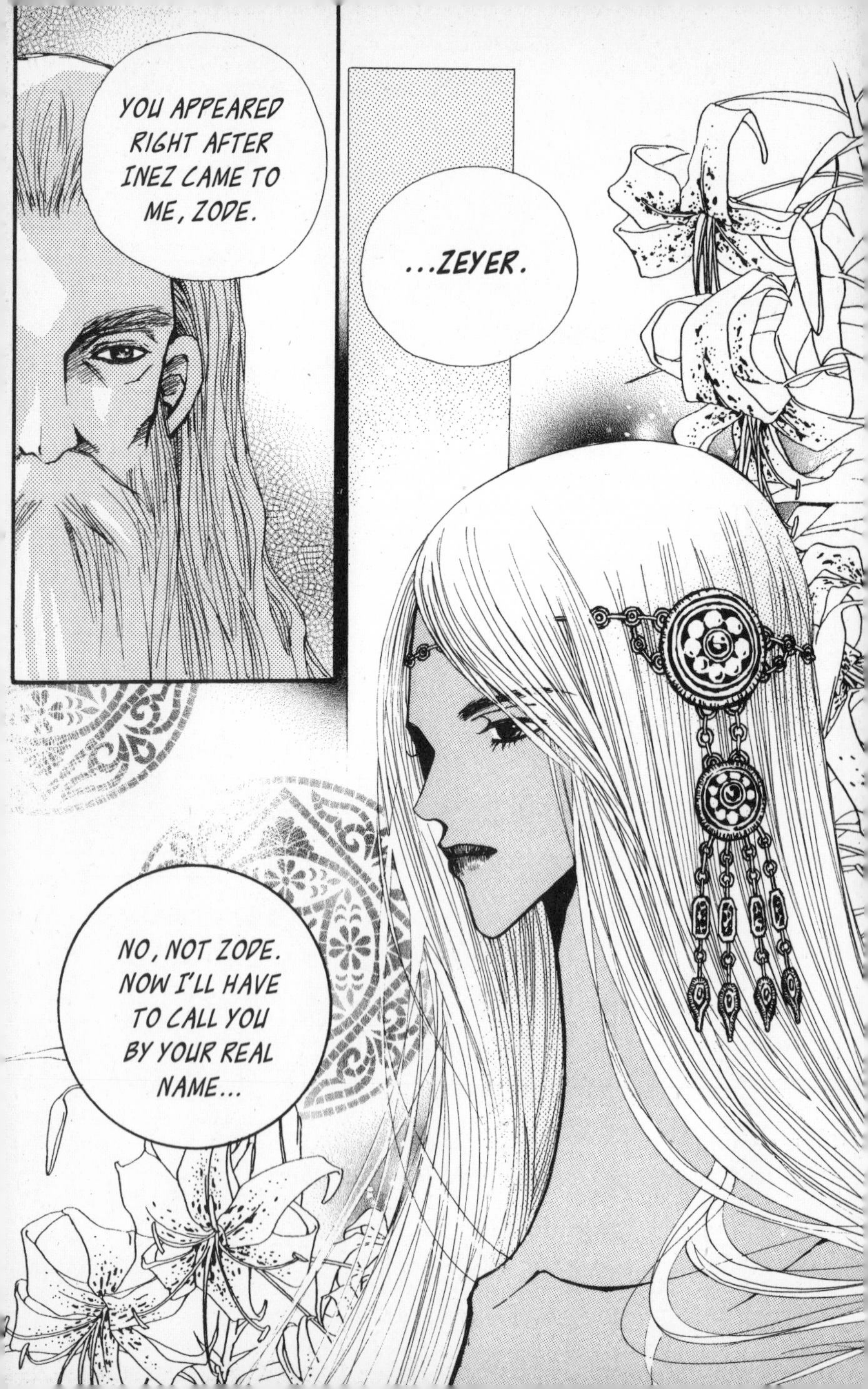
YOU APPEARED RIGHT AFTER INEZ CAME TO ME, ZODE.
...ZEYER.
NO, NOT ZODE. NOW I'LL HAVE TO CALL YOU BY YOUR REAL NAME...

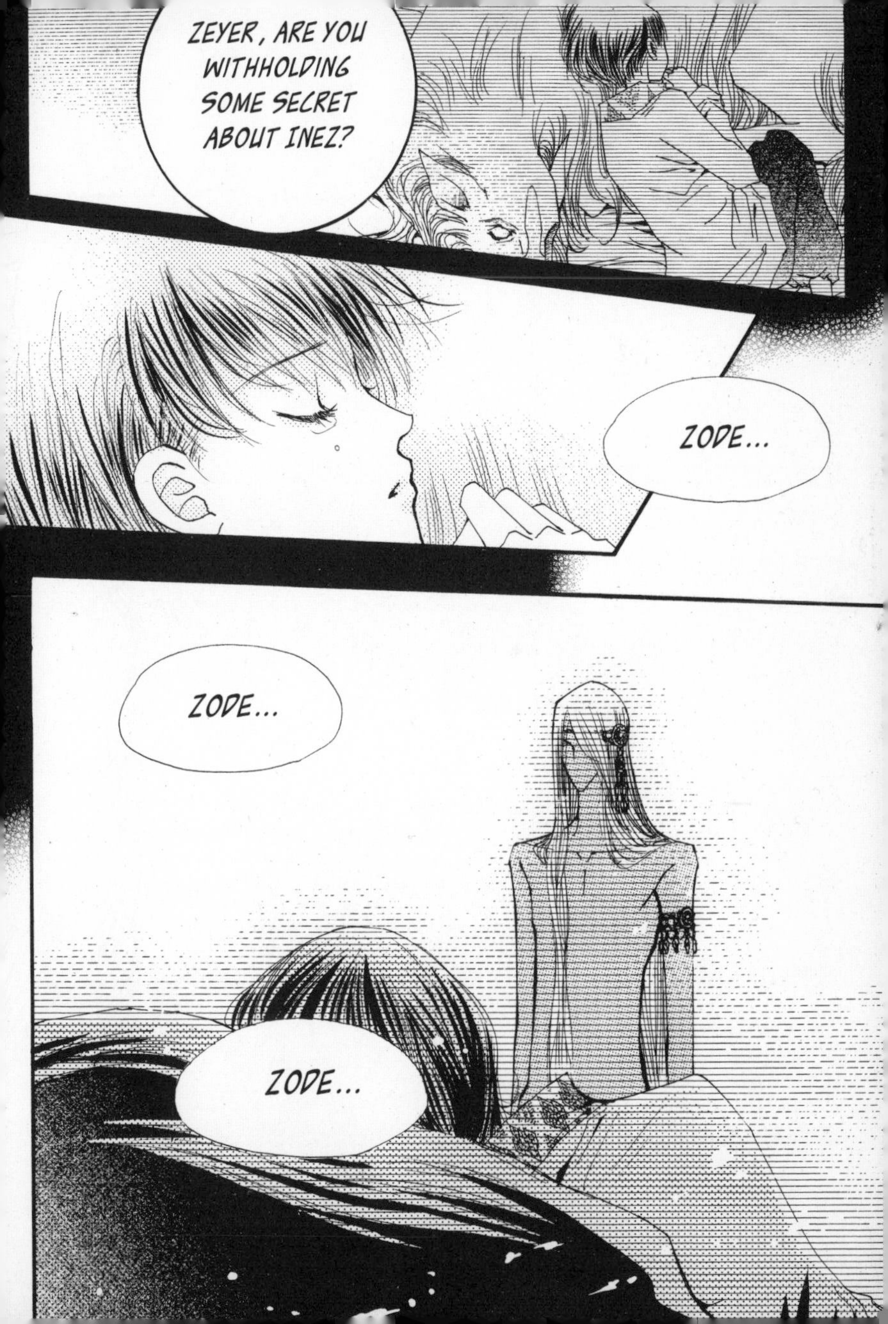
ZEYER, ARE YOU WITHHOLDING SOME SECRET ABOUT INEZ?
ZODE...
ZODE...
ZODE...

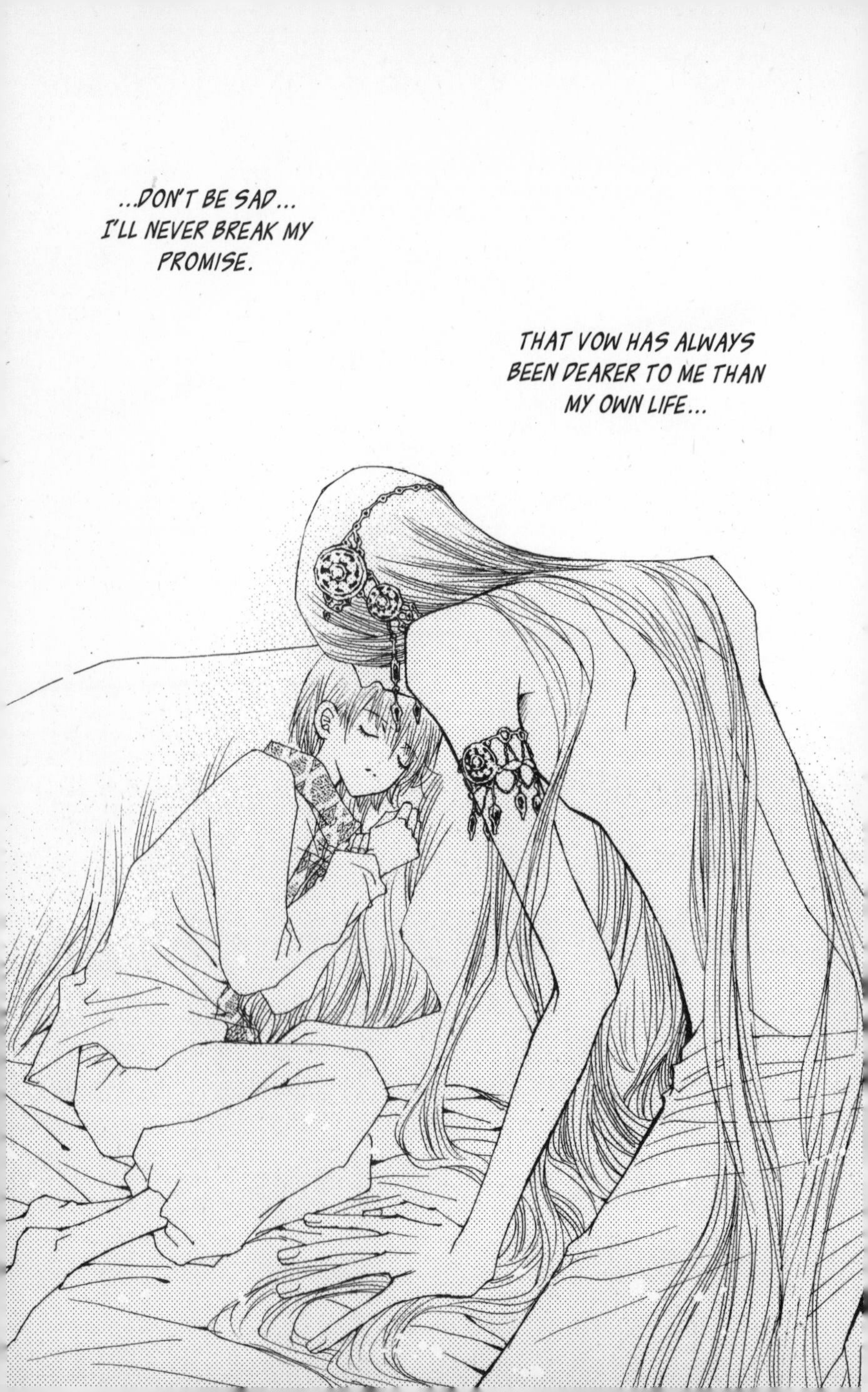
...DON'T BE SAD... I'LL NEVER BREAK MY PROMISE.
THAT VOW HAS ALWAYS BEEN DEARER TO ME THAN MY OWN LIFE...

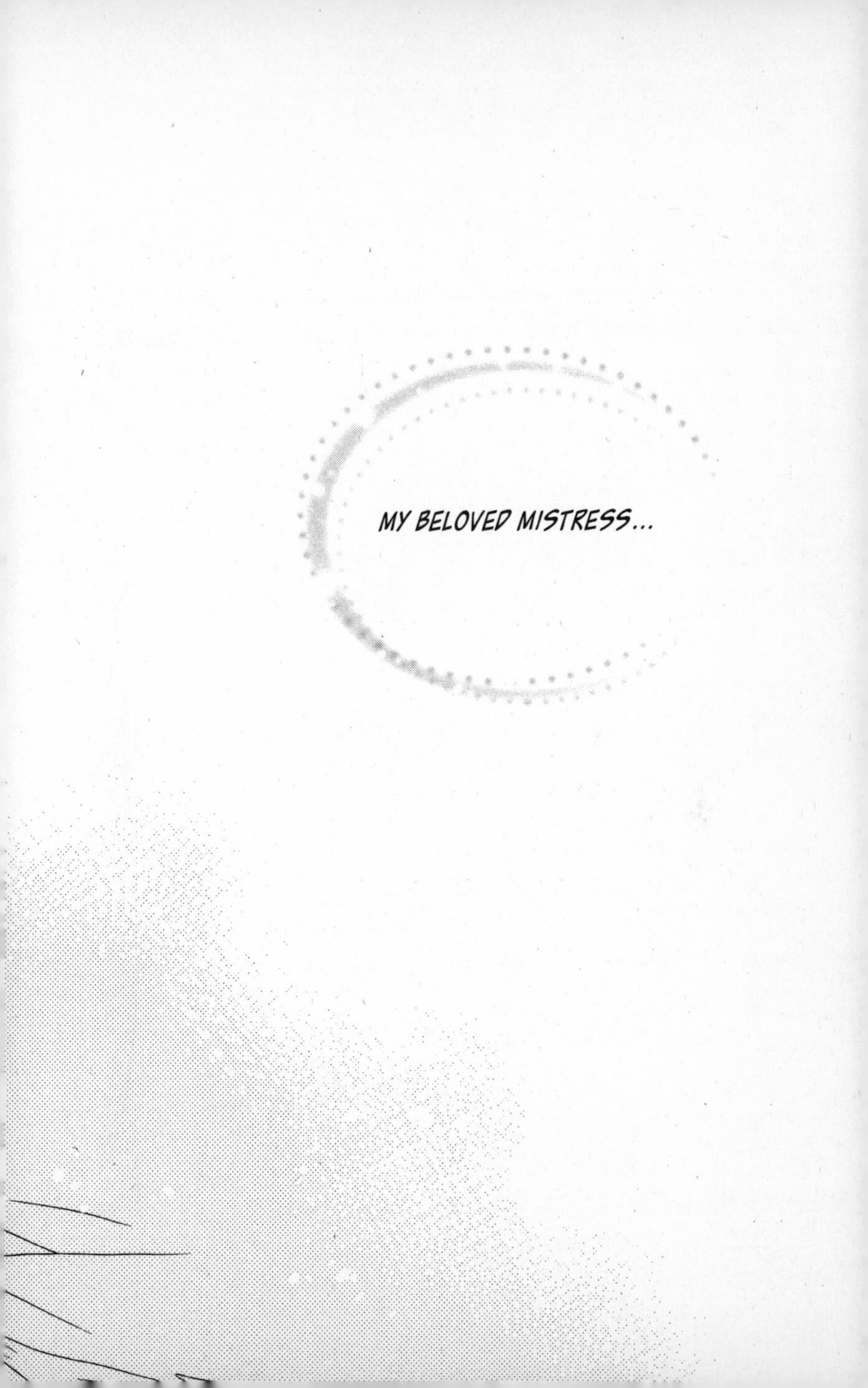
MY BELOVED MISTRESS...

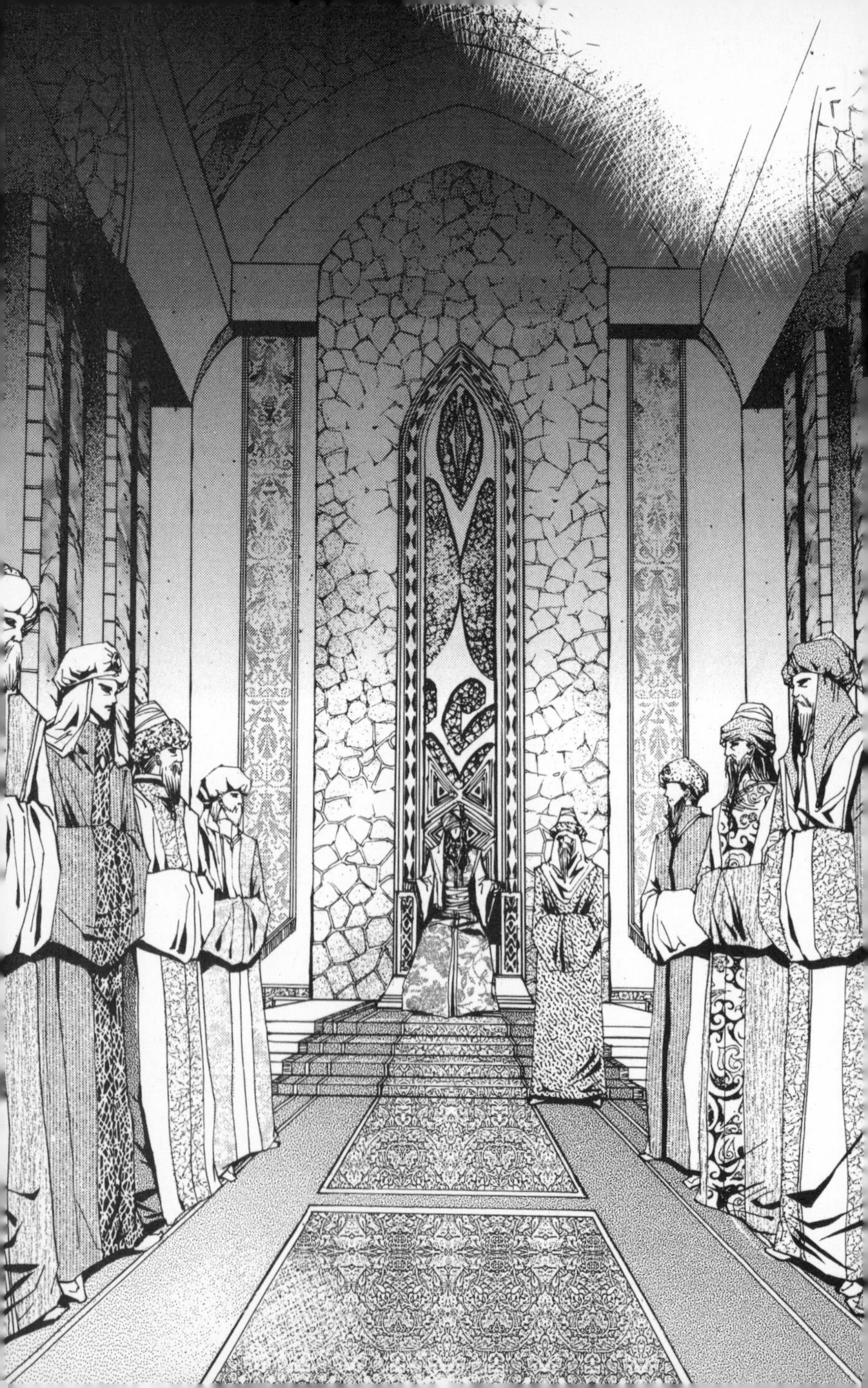

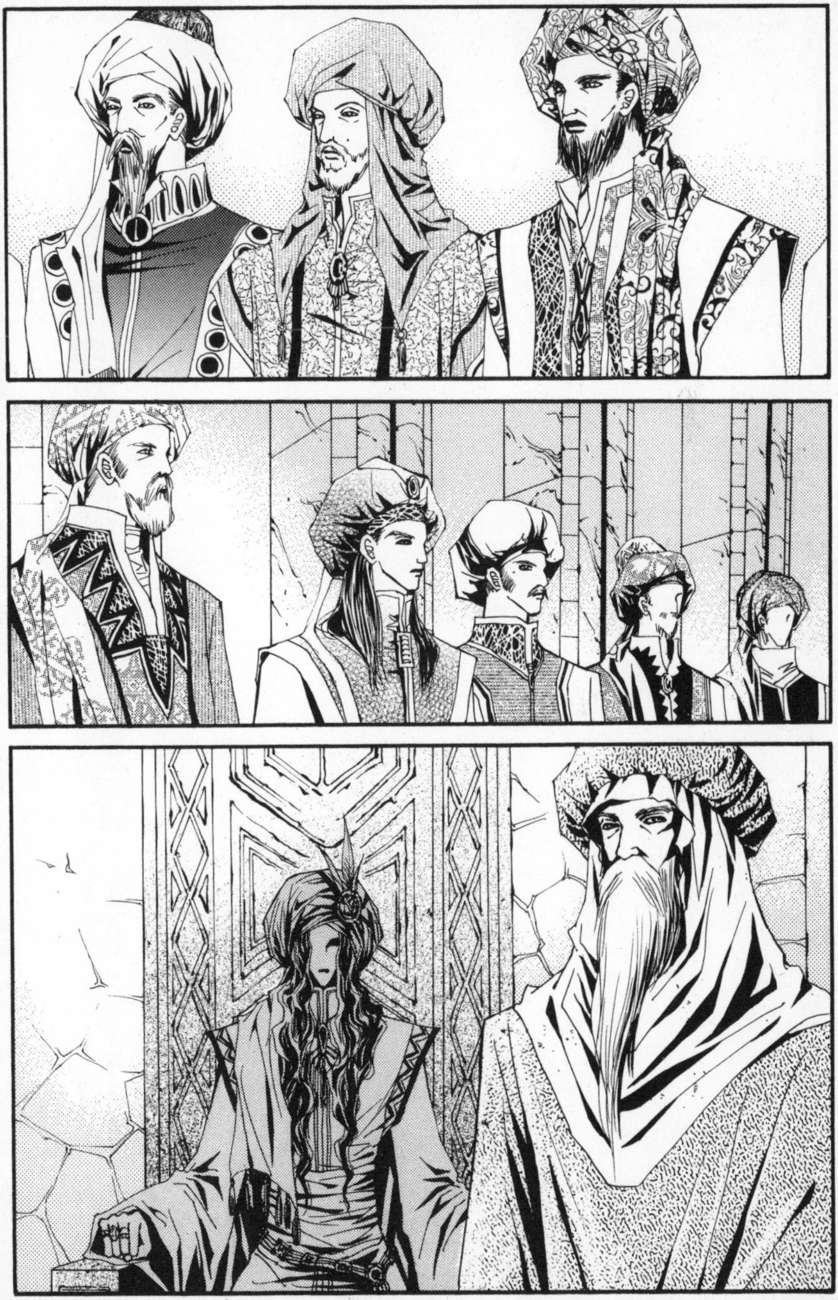

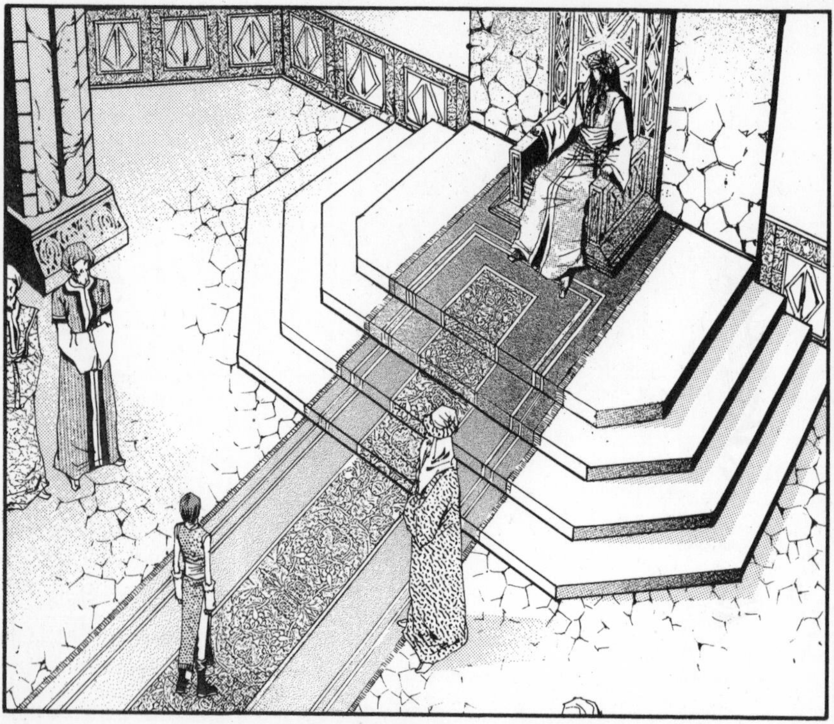

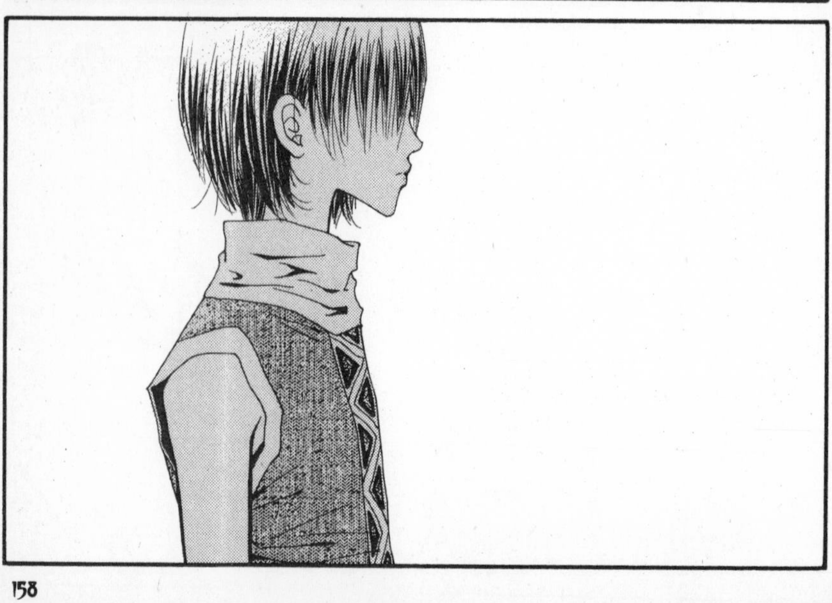

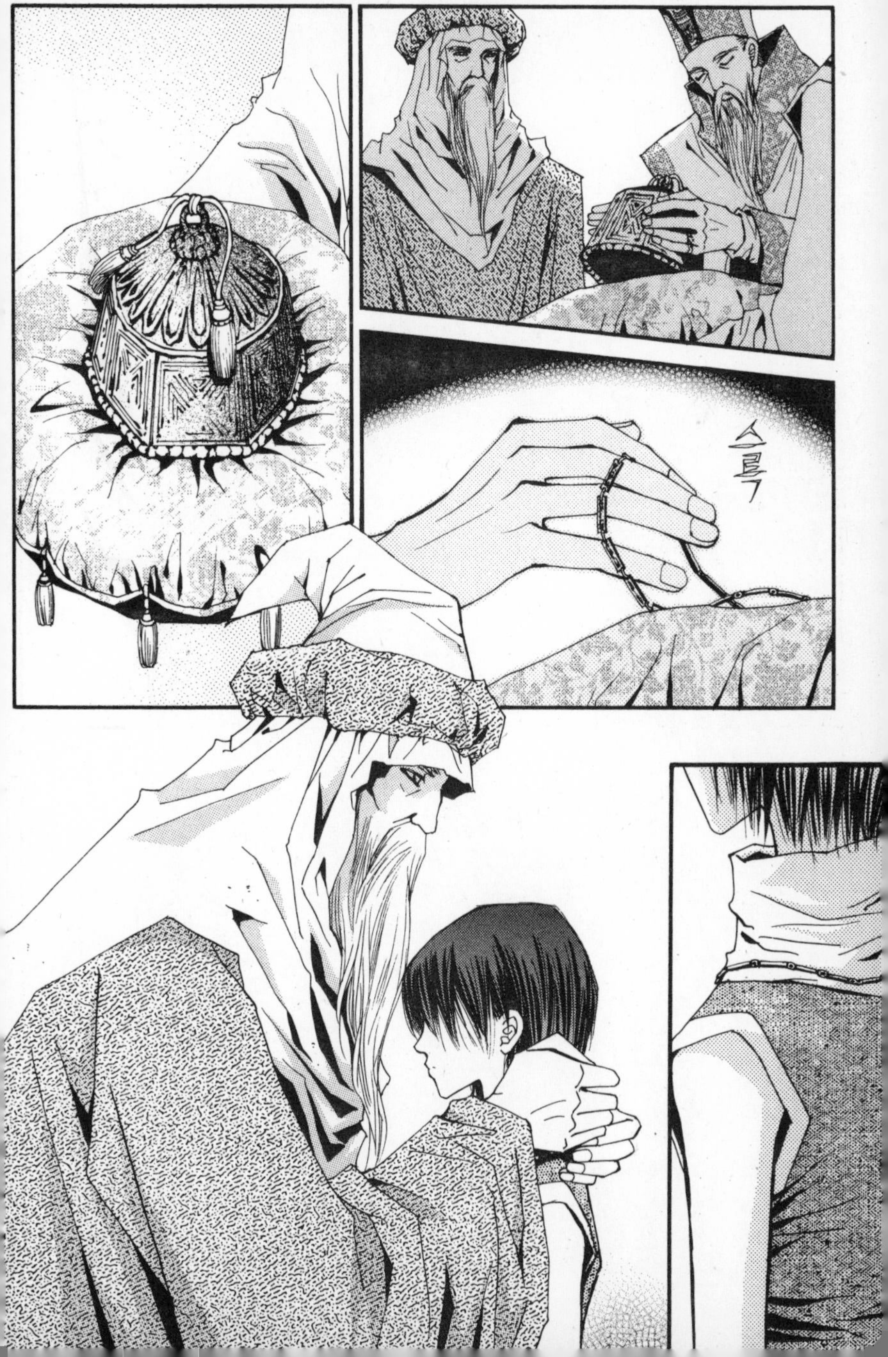
스륵

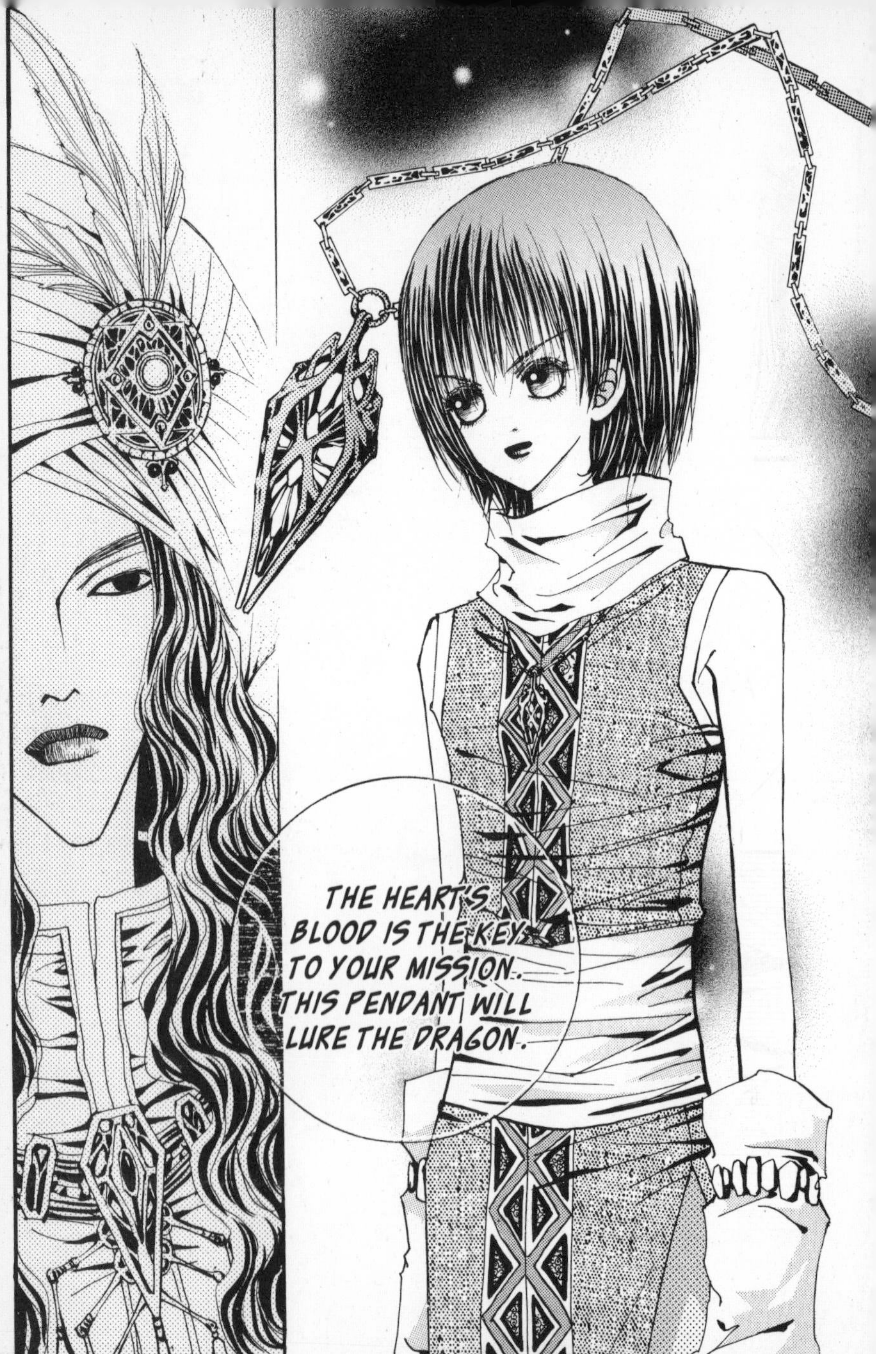
THE HEART'S BLOOD IS THE KEY TO YOUR MISSION. THIS PENDANT WILL LURE THE DRAGON.

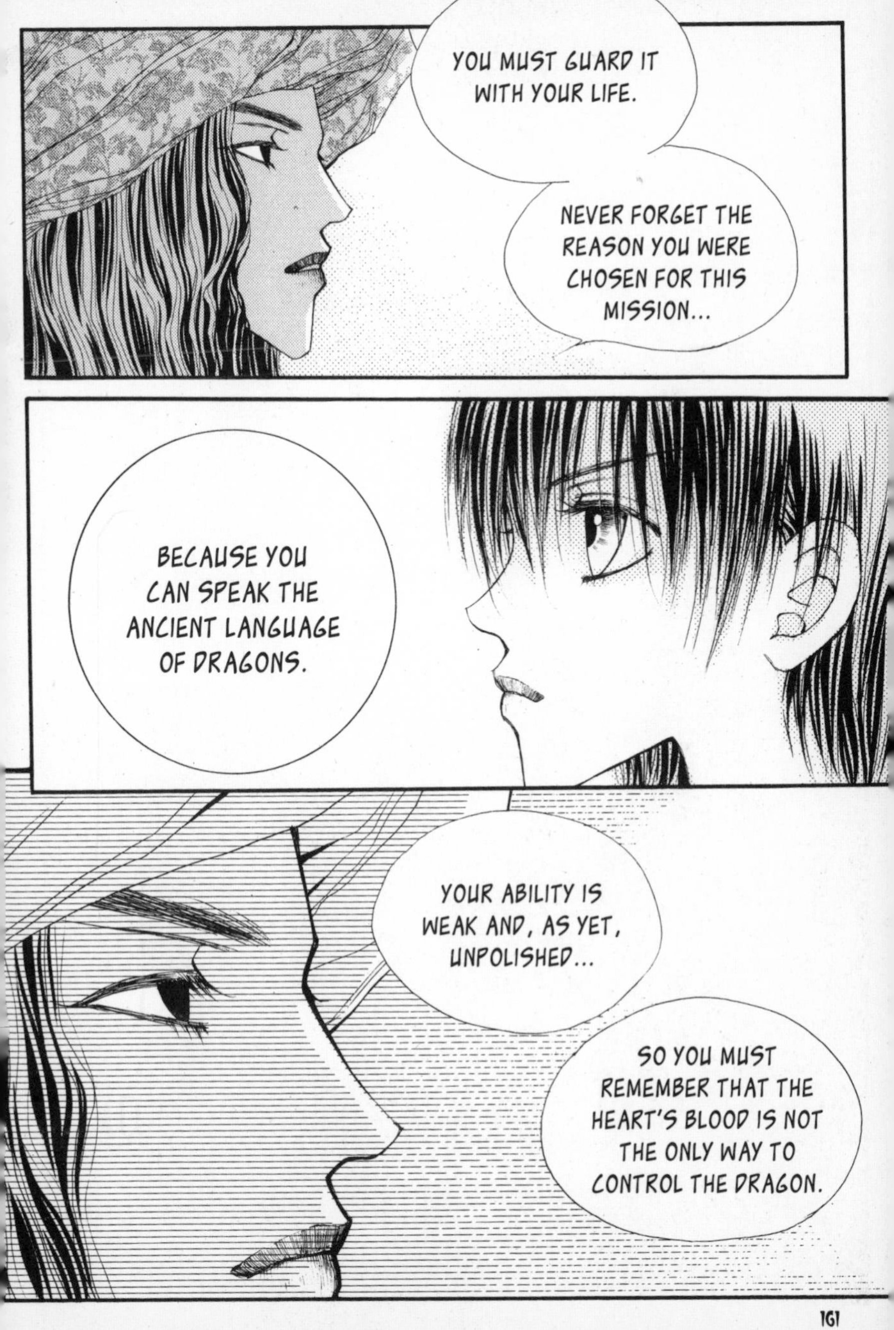
YOU MUST GUARD IT WITH YOUR LIFE.
NEVER FORGET THE REASON YOU WERE CHOSEN FOR THIS MISSION...
BECAUSE YOU CAN SPEAK THE ANCIENT LANGUAGE OF DRAGONS.
YOUR ABILITY IS WEAK AND, AS YET, UNPOLISHED...
SO YOU MUST REMEMBER THAT THE HEART'S BLOOD IS NOT THE ONLY WAY TO CONTROL THE DRAGON.

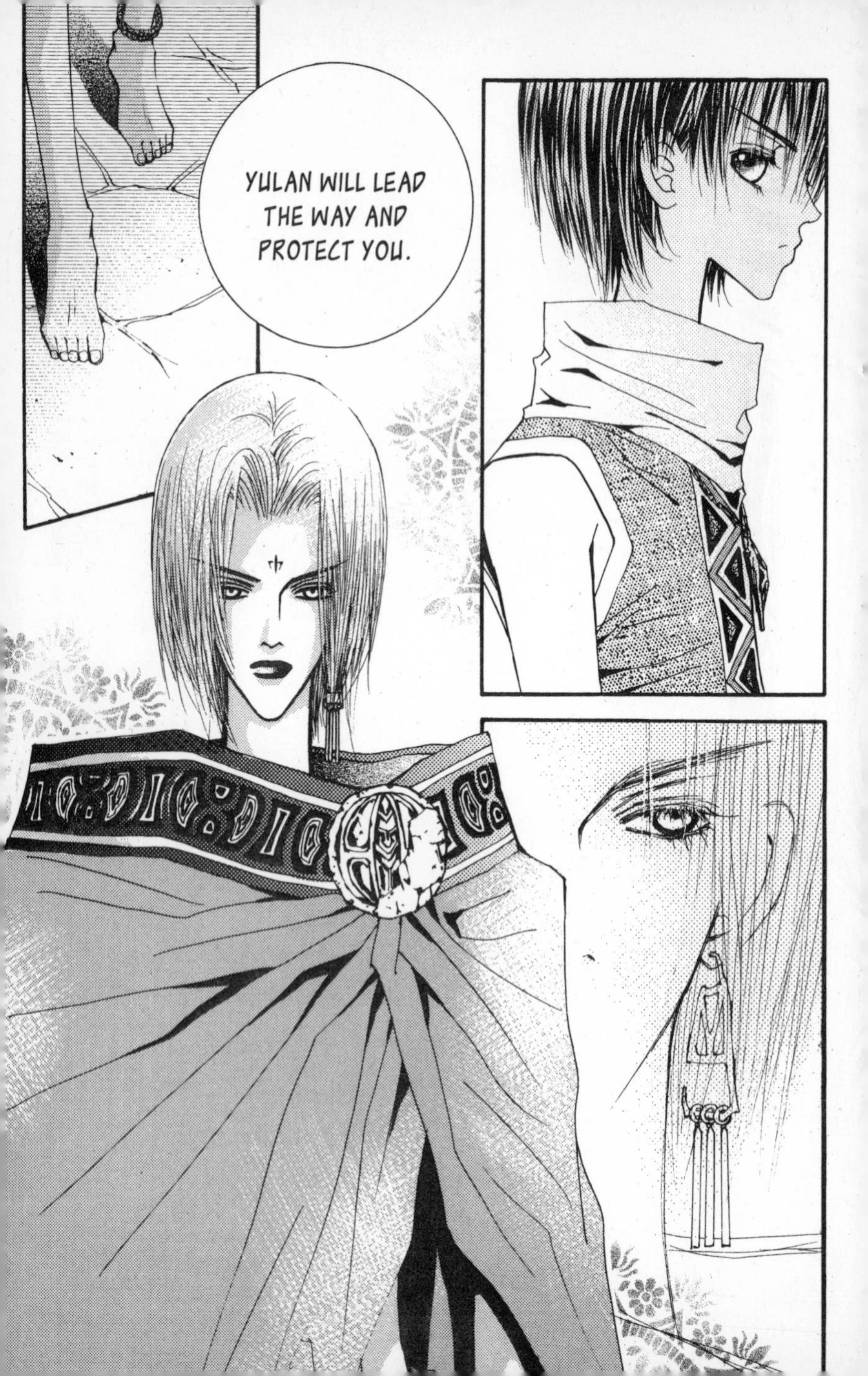
YULAN WILL LEAD THE WAY AND PROTECT YOU.

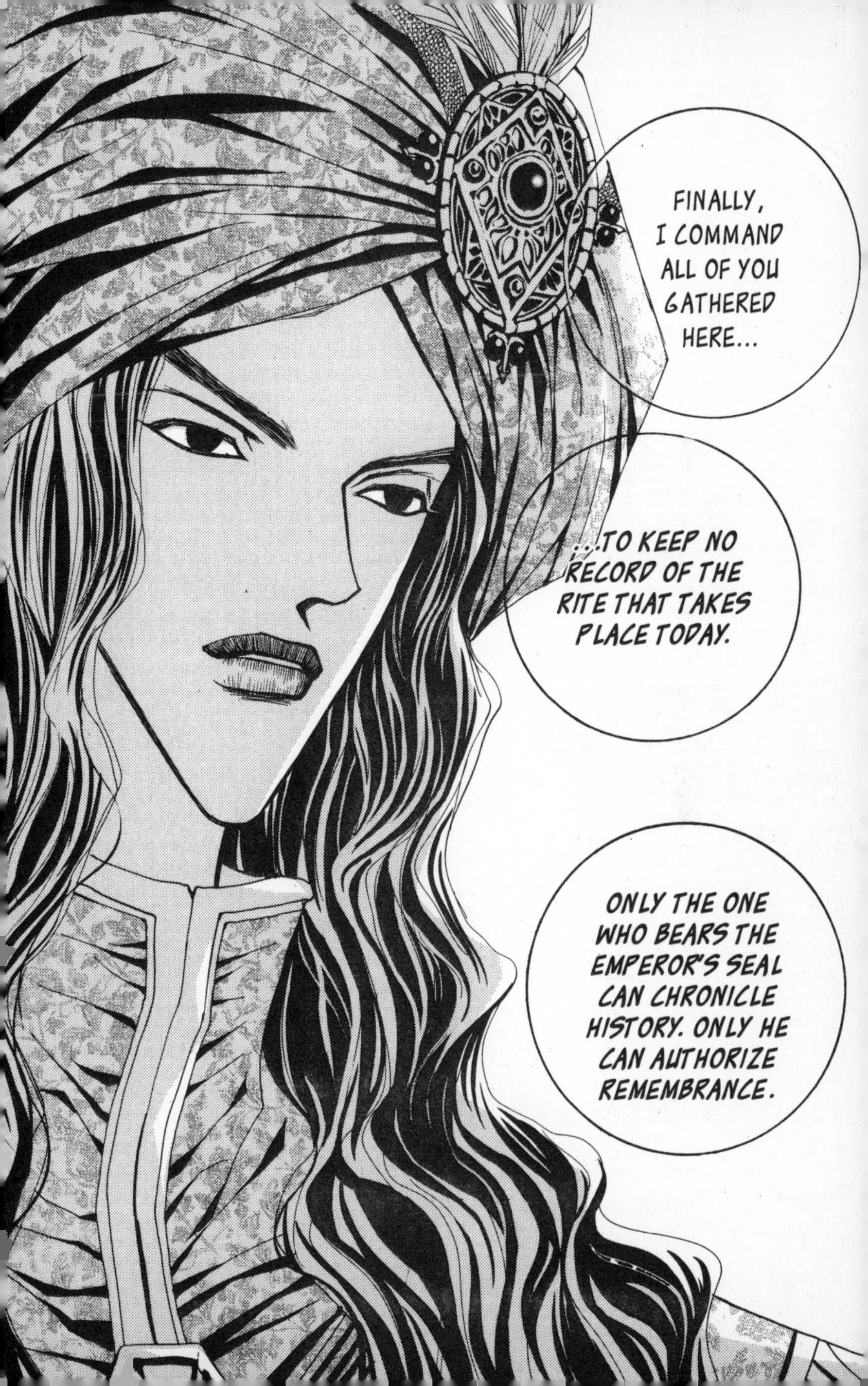
FINALLY, I COMMAND ALL OF YOU GATHERED HERE...
...TO KEEP NO RECORD OF THE RITE THAT TAKES PLACE TODAY.
ONLY THE ONE WHO BEARS THE EMPEROR'S SEAL CAN CHRONICLE HISTORY. ONLY HE CAN AUTHORIZE REMEMBRANCE.

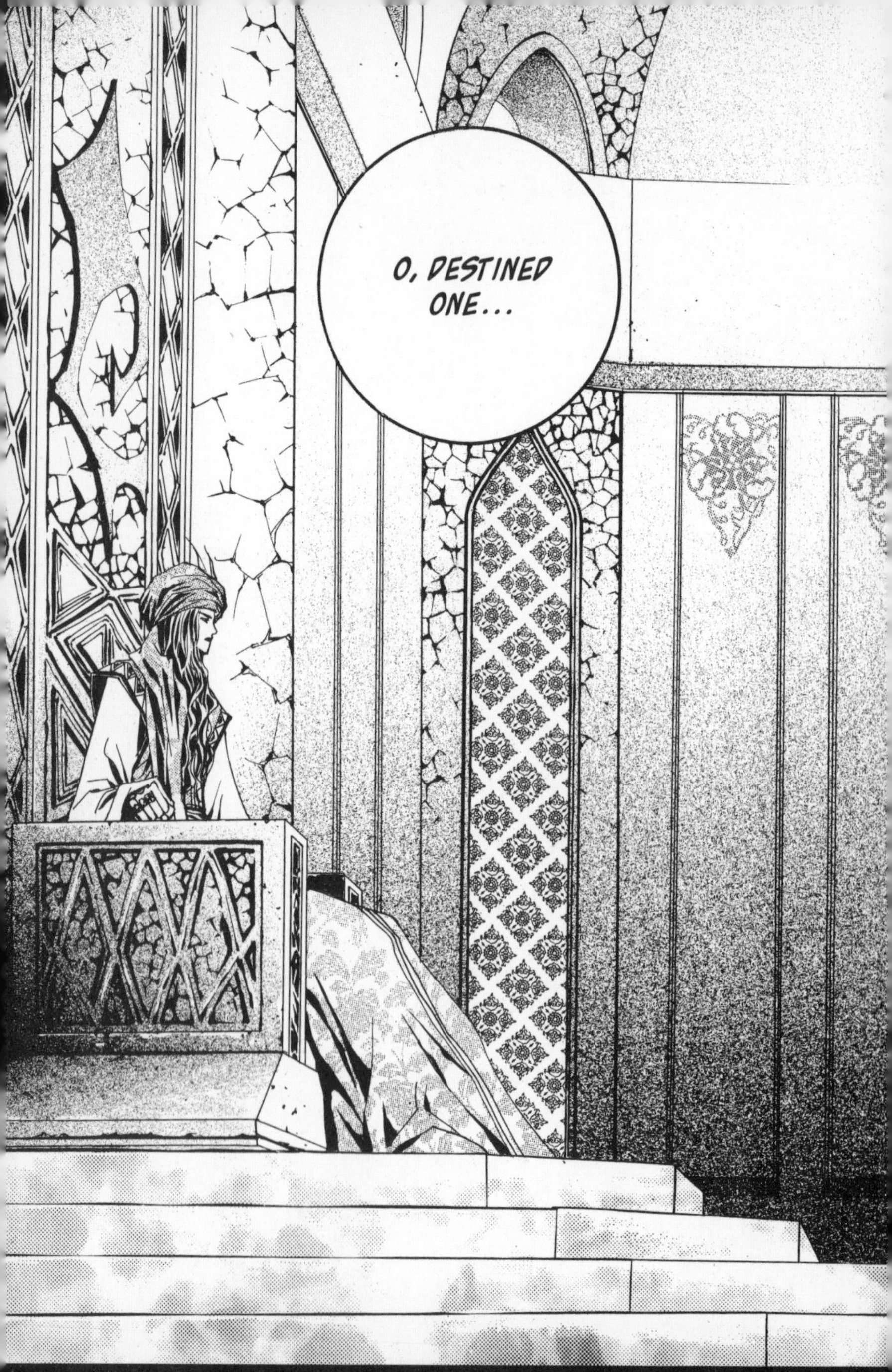
O, DESTINED ONE...

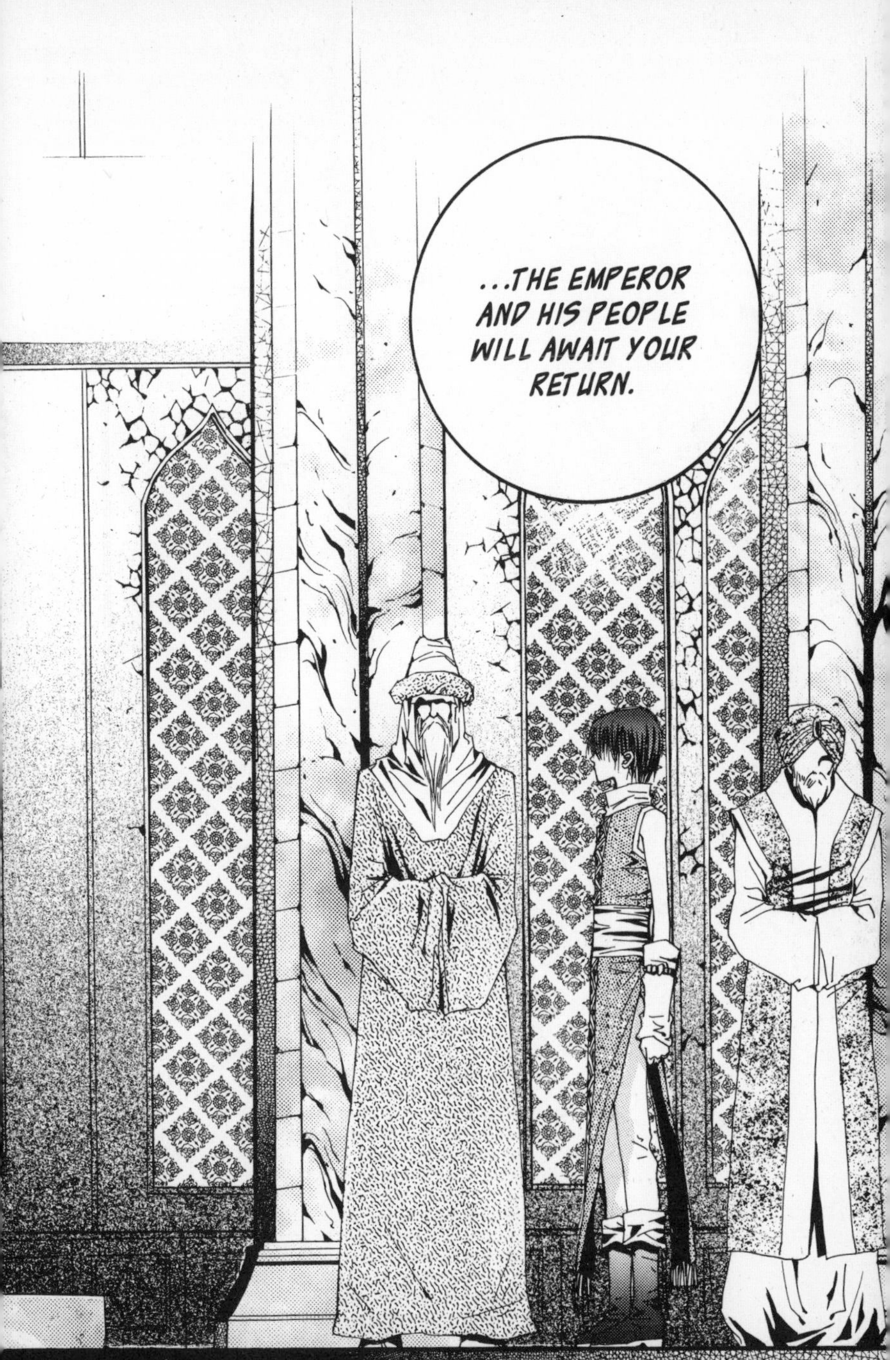
...THE EMPEROR AND HIS PEOPLE WILL AWAIT YOUR RETURN.

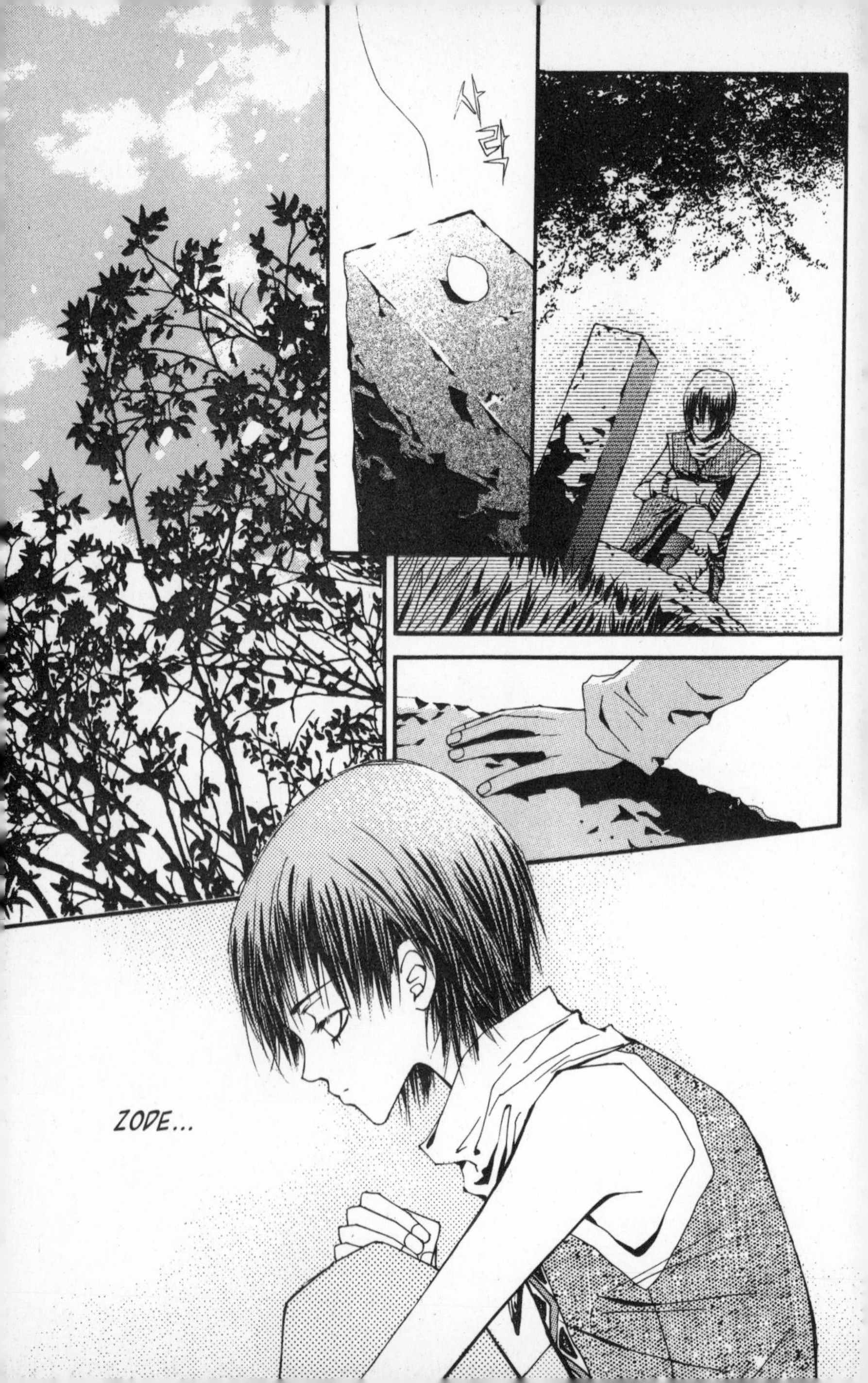
사락
ZODE...

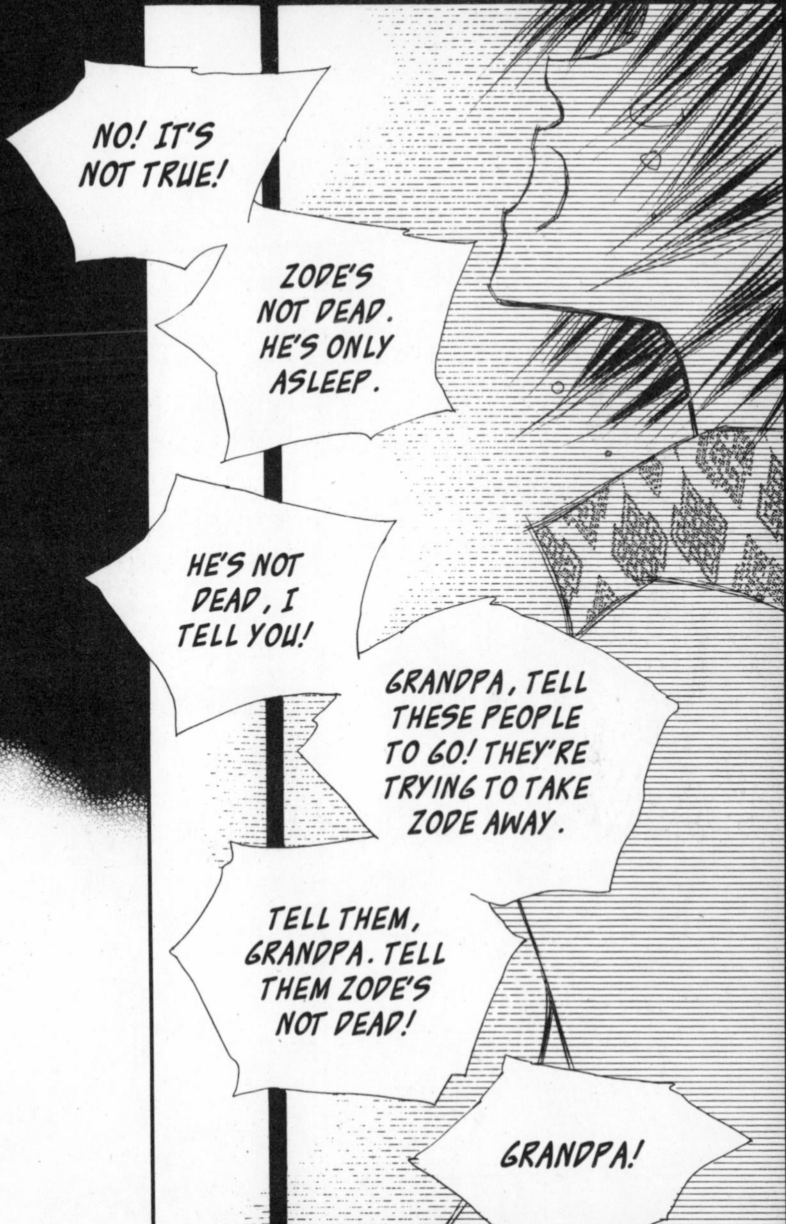
NO! IT'S NOT TRUE!
ZODE'S NOT DEAD. HE'S ONLY ASLEEP.
HE'S NOT DEAD, I TELL YOU!
GRANDPA, TELL THESE PEOPLE TO GO! THEY'RE TRYING TO TAKE ZODE AWAY.
TELL THEM, GRANDPA. TELL THEM ZODE'S NOT DEAD!
GRANDPA!

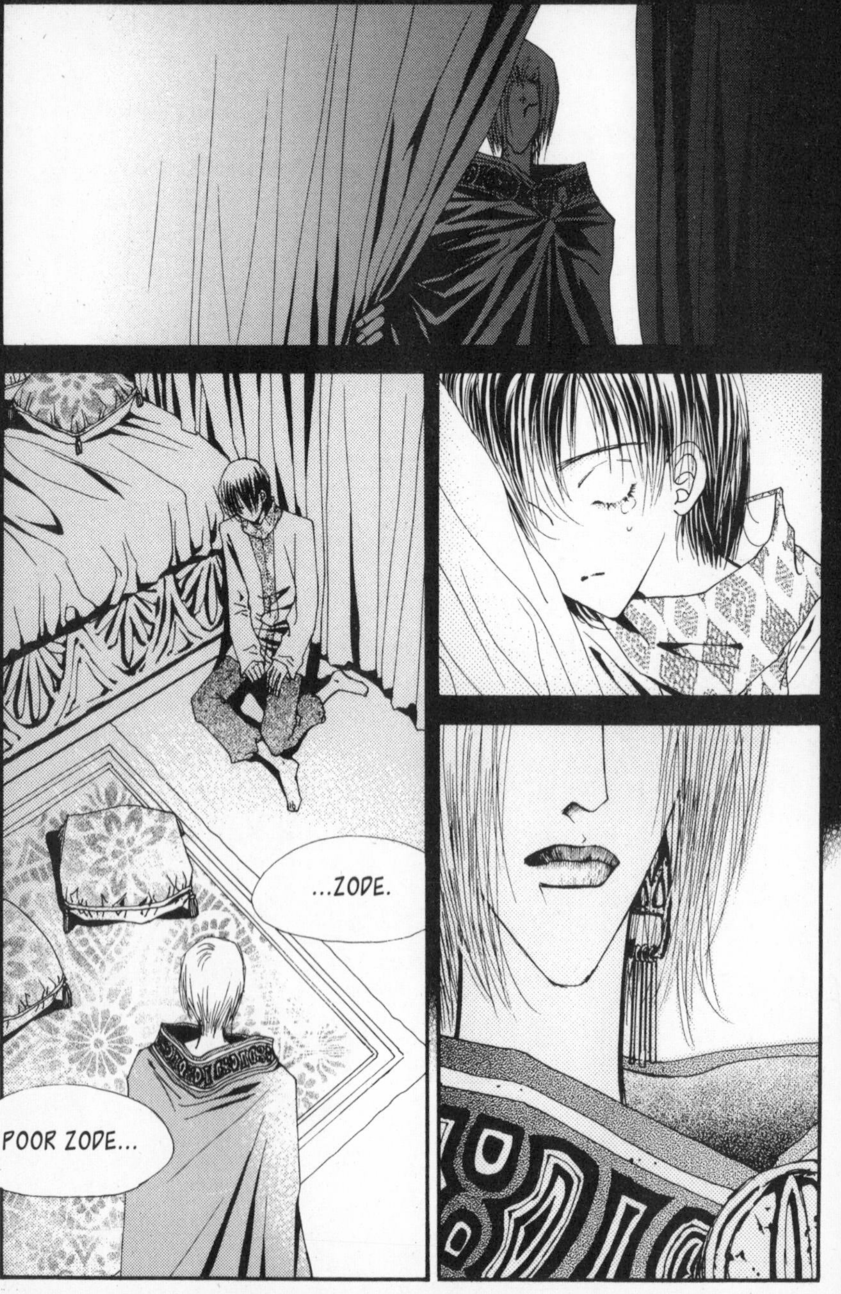
...ZODE.
POOR ZODE...

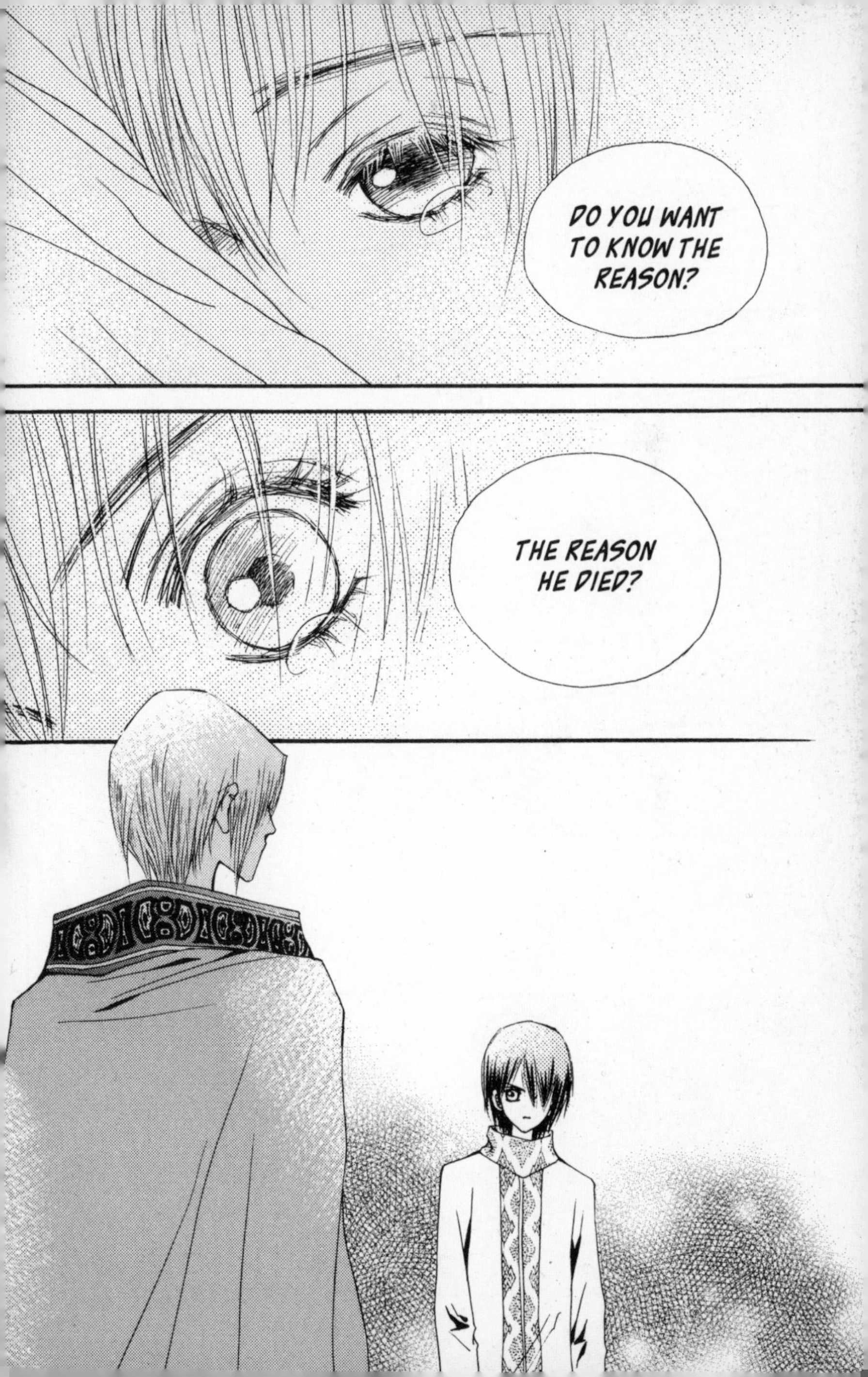
DO YOU WANT TO KNOW THE REASON?
THE REASON HE DIED?

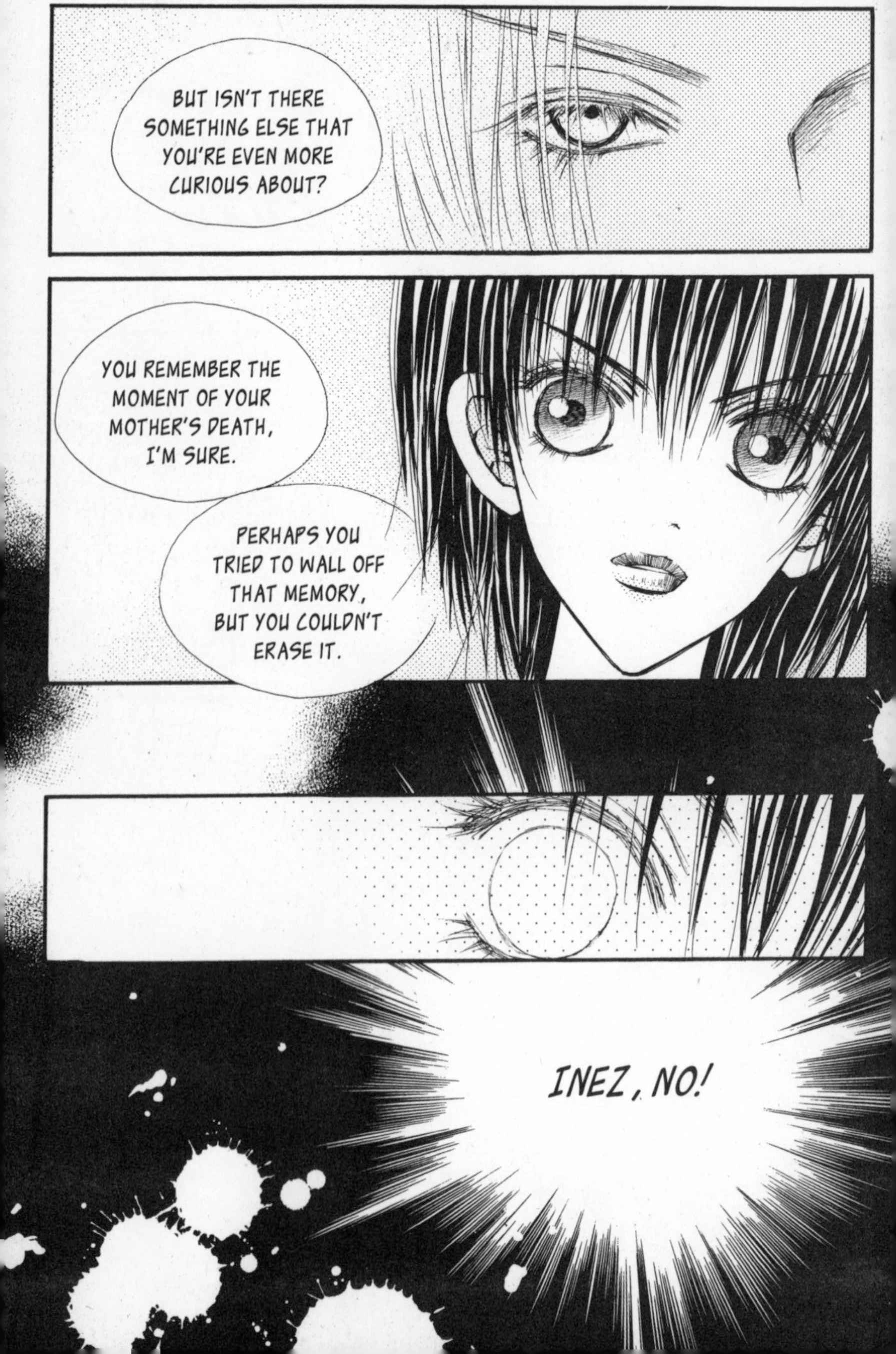
BUT ISN'T THERE SOMETHING ELSE THAT YOU'RE EVEN MORE CURIOUS ABOUT?
YOU REMEMBER THE MOMENT OF YOUR MOTHER'S DEATH, I'M SURE.
PERHAPS YOU TRIED TO WALL OFF THAT MEMORY, BUT YOU COULDN'T ERASE IT.
INEZ, NO!

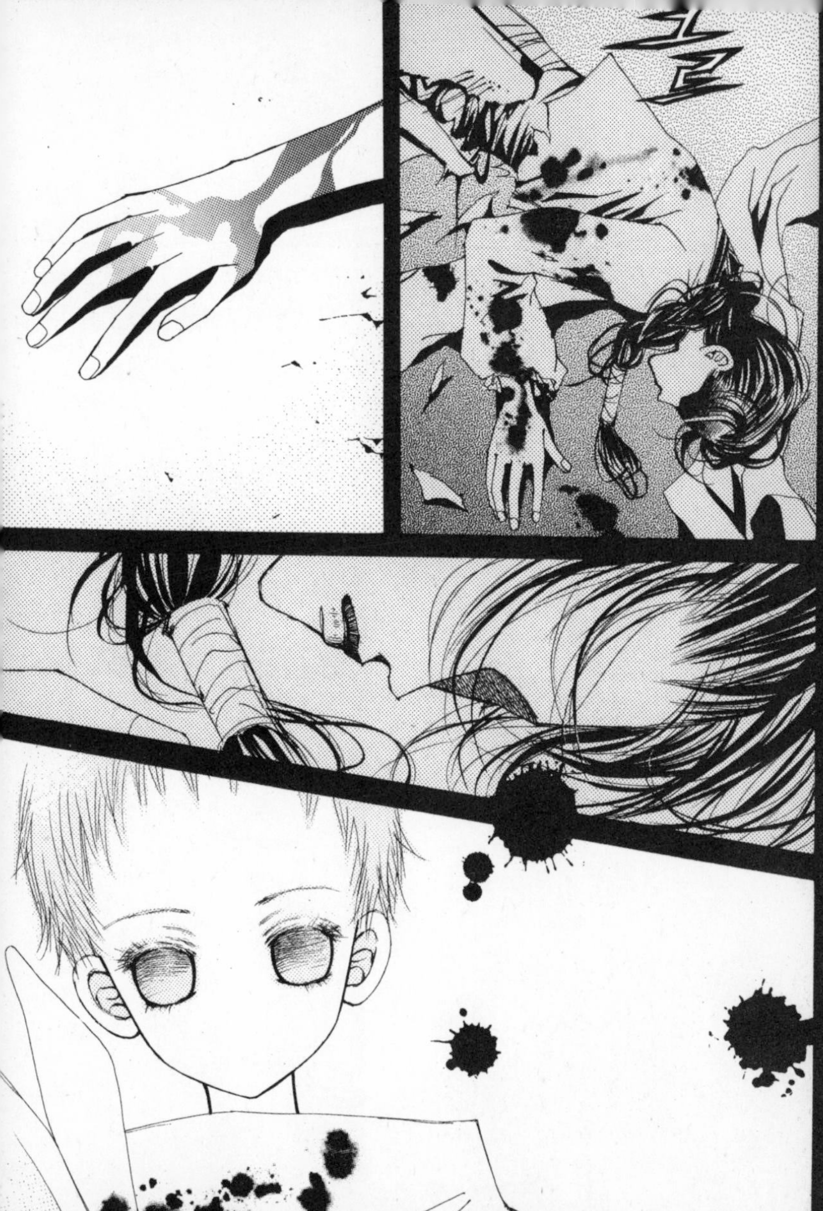

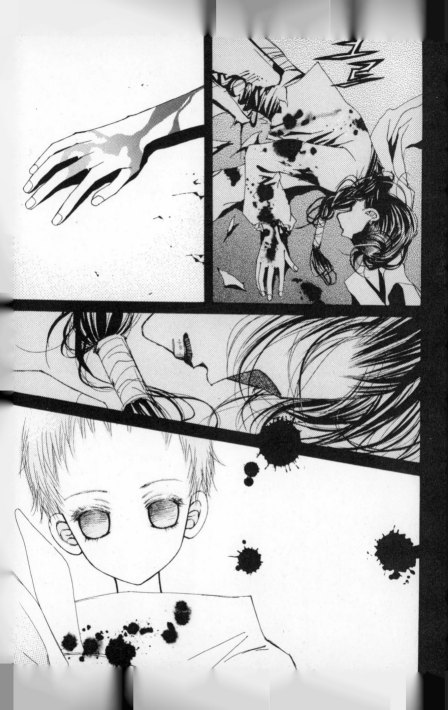

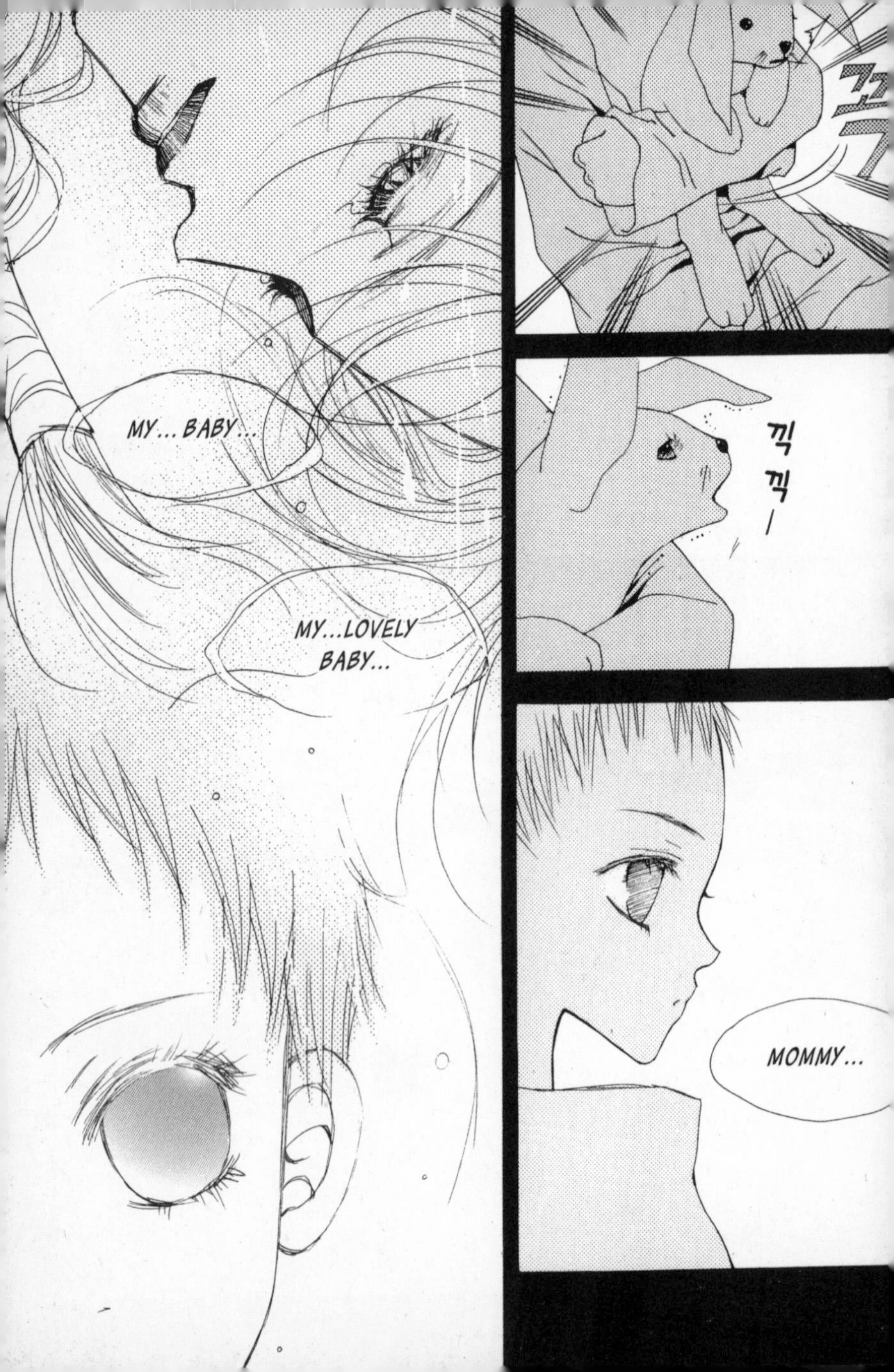
MY... BABY...
MY...LOVELY BABY...
끽 끽
MOMMY...

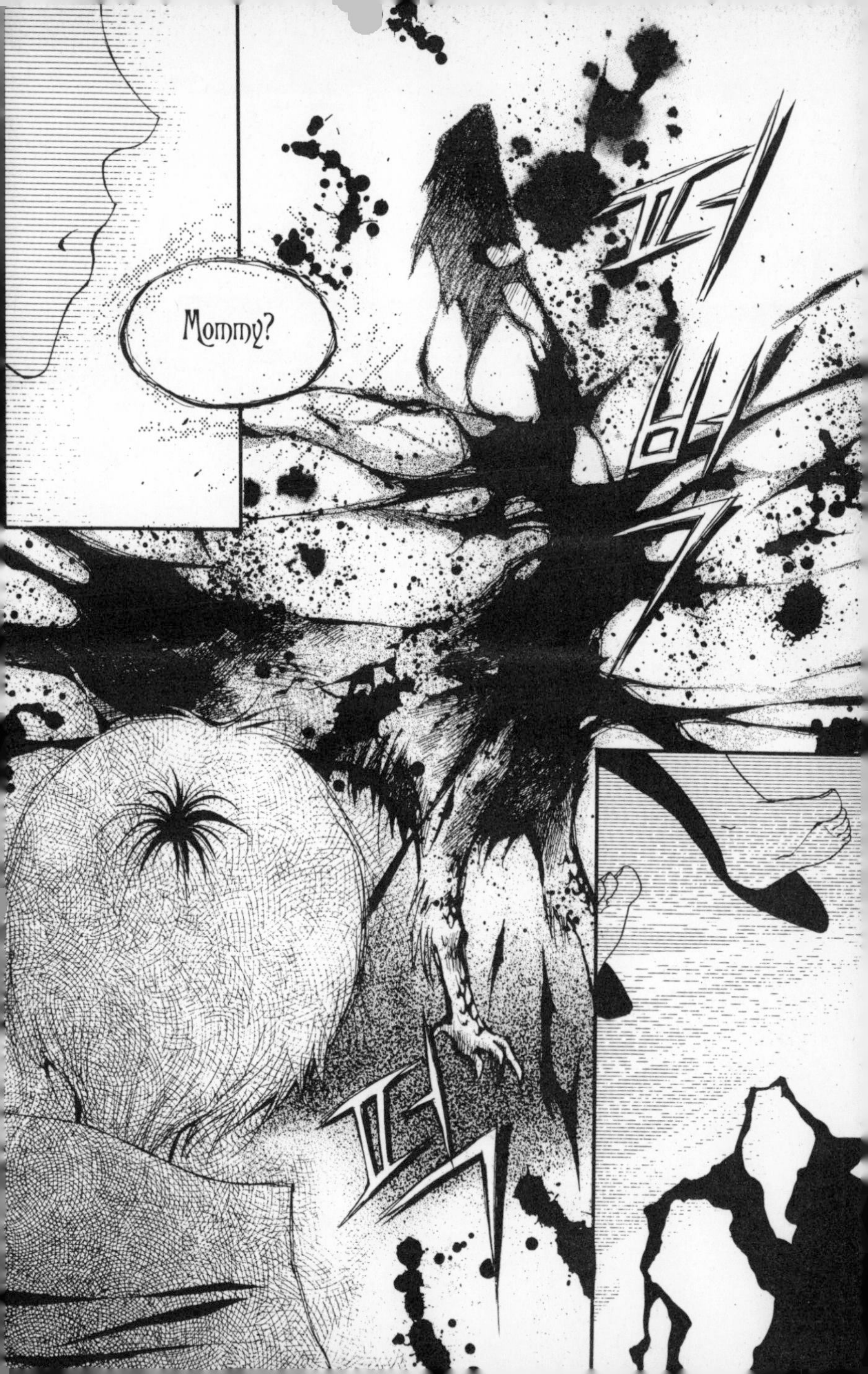
Mommy?

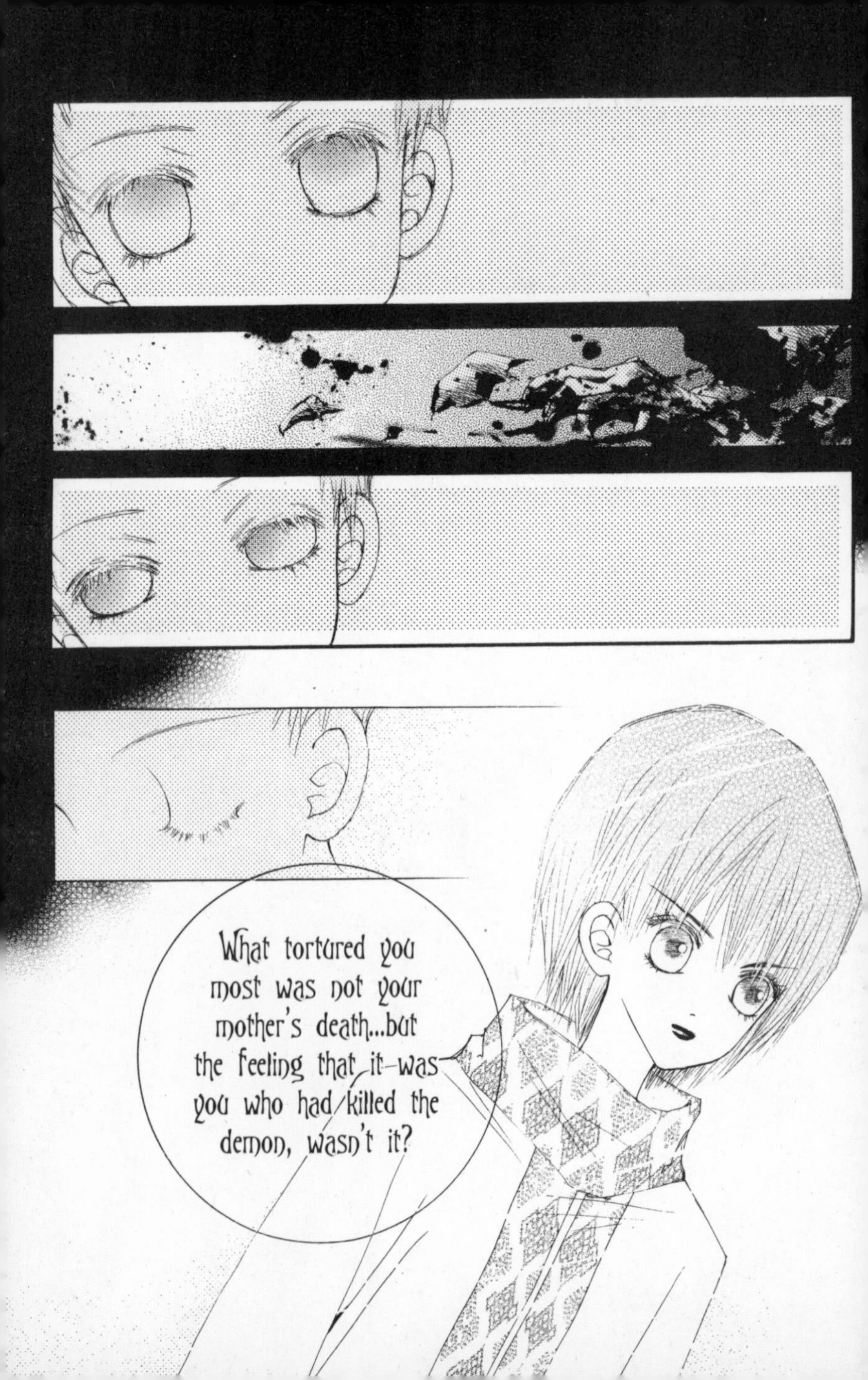
What tortured you most was not your mother's death...but the feeling that it was you who had killed the demon, wasn't it?

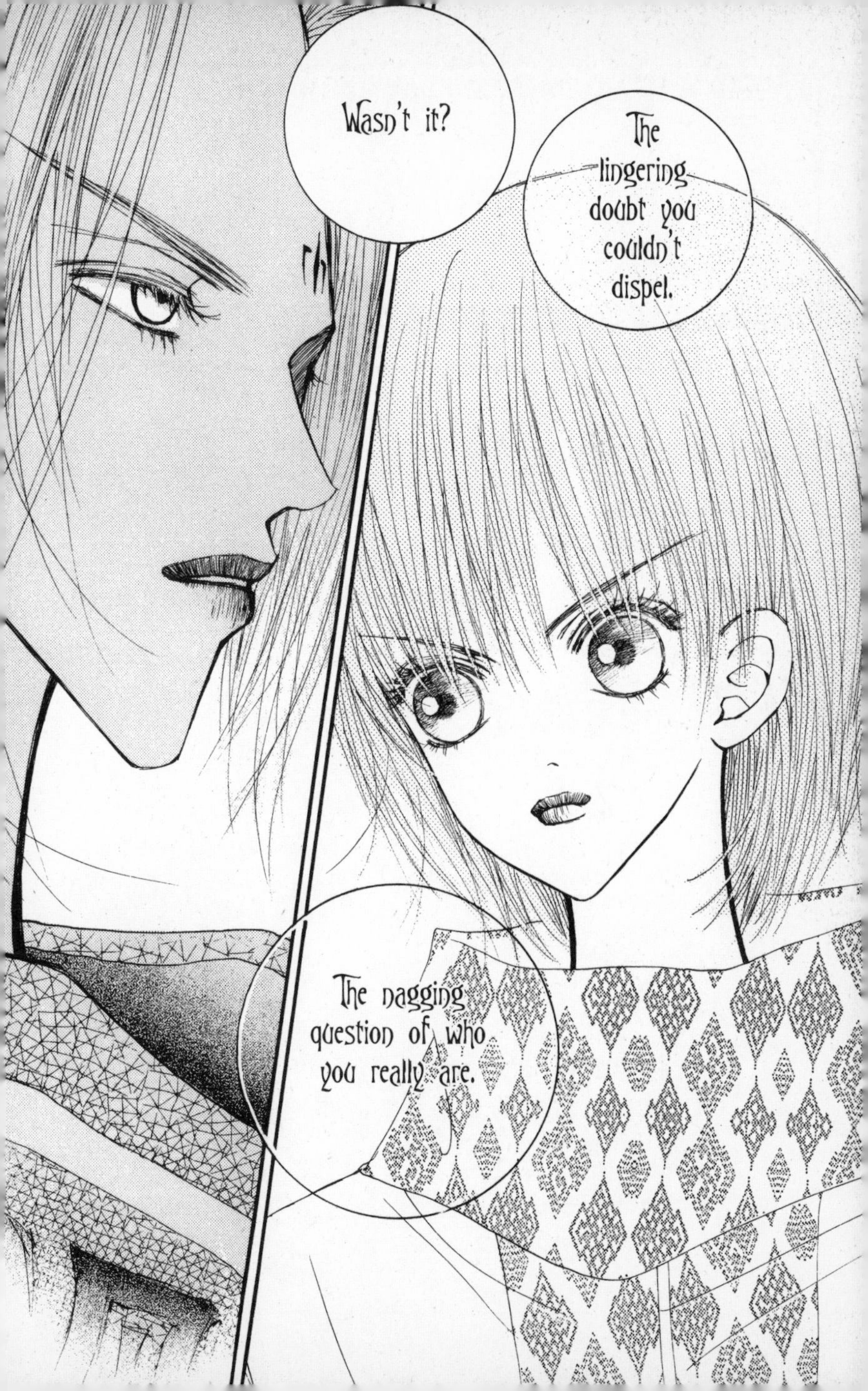
Wasn't it?
The lingering doubt you couldn't dispel.
The nagging question of who you really are.

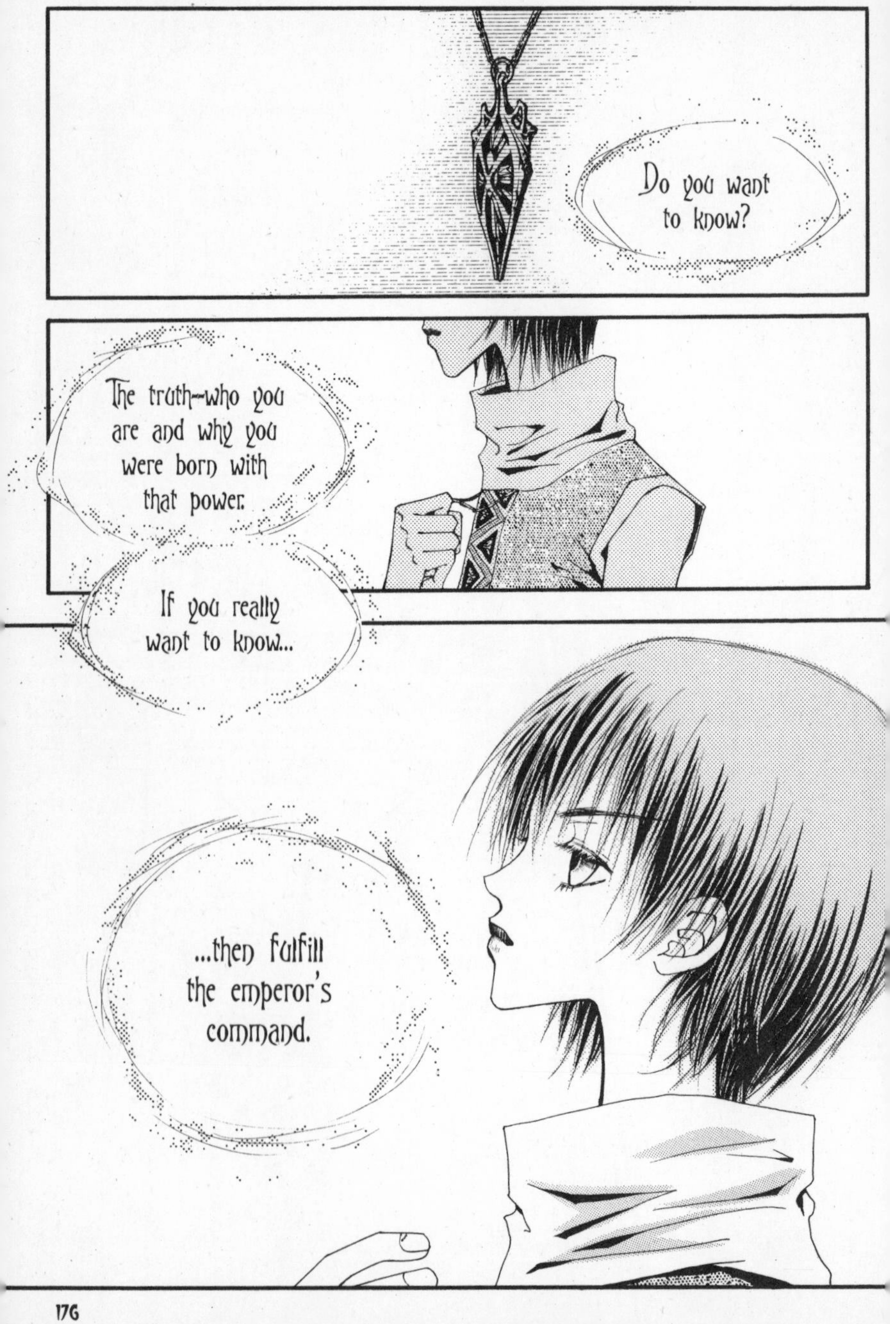
Do you want to know?
The truth--who you are and why you were born with that power.
If you really want to know...
...then fulfill the emperor's command.

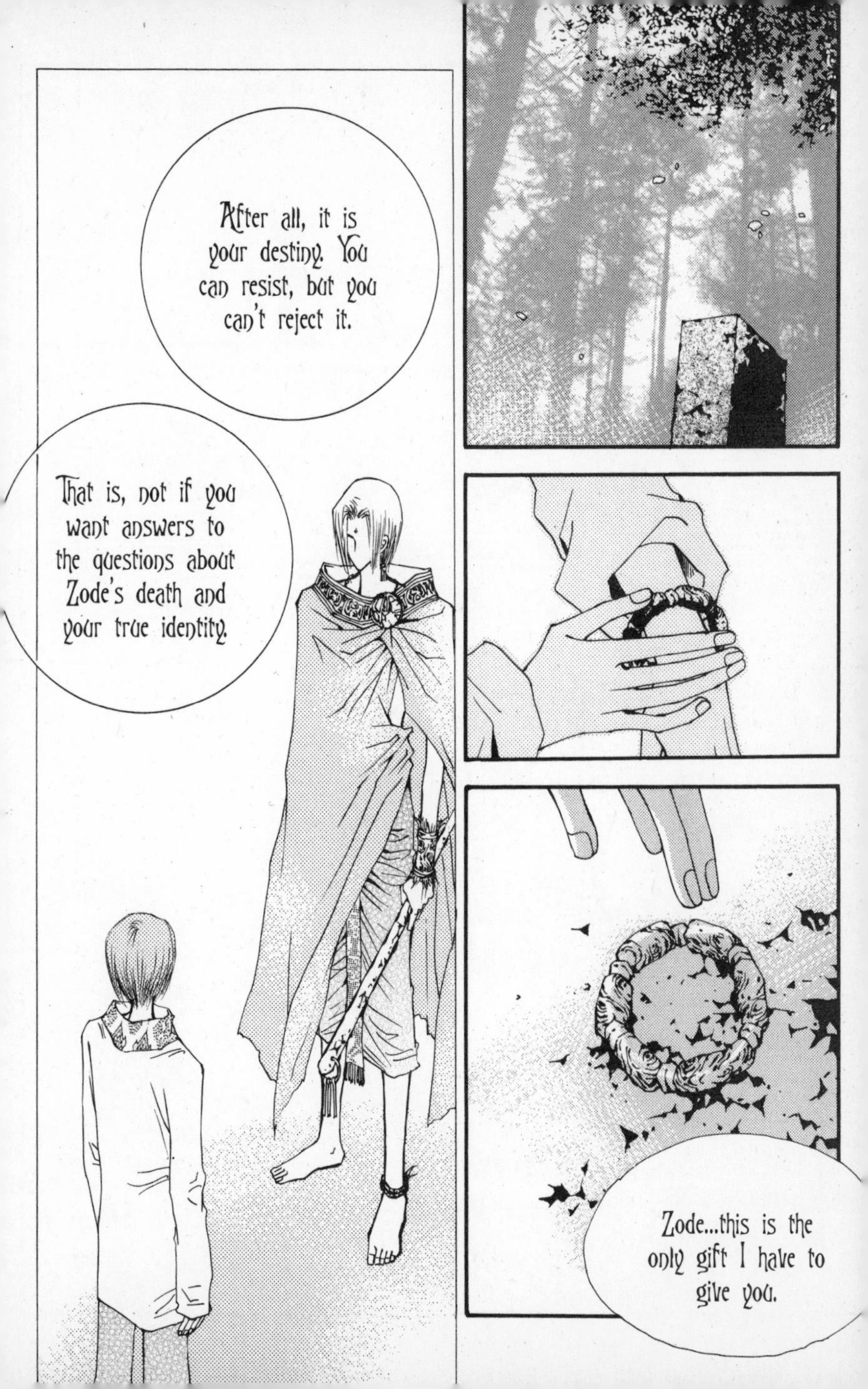
After all, it is your destiny. You can resist, but you can't reject it.
That is, not if you want answers to the questions about Zode's death and your true identity.
Zode...this is the only gift I have to give you.

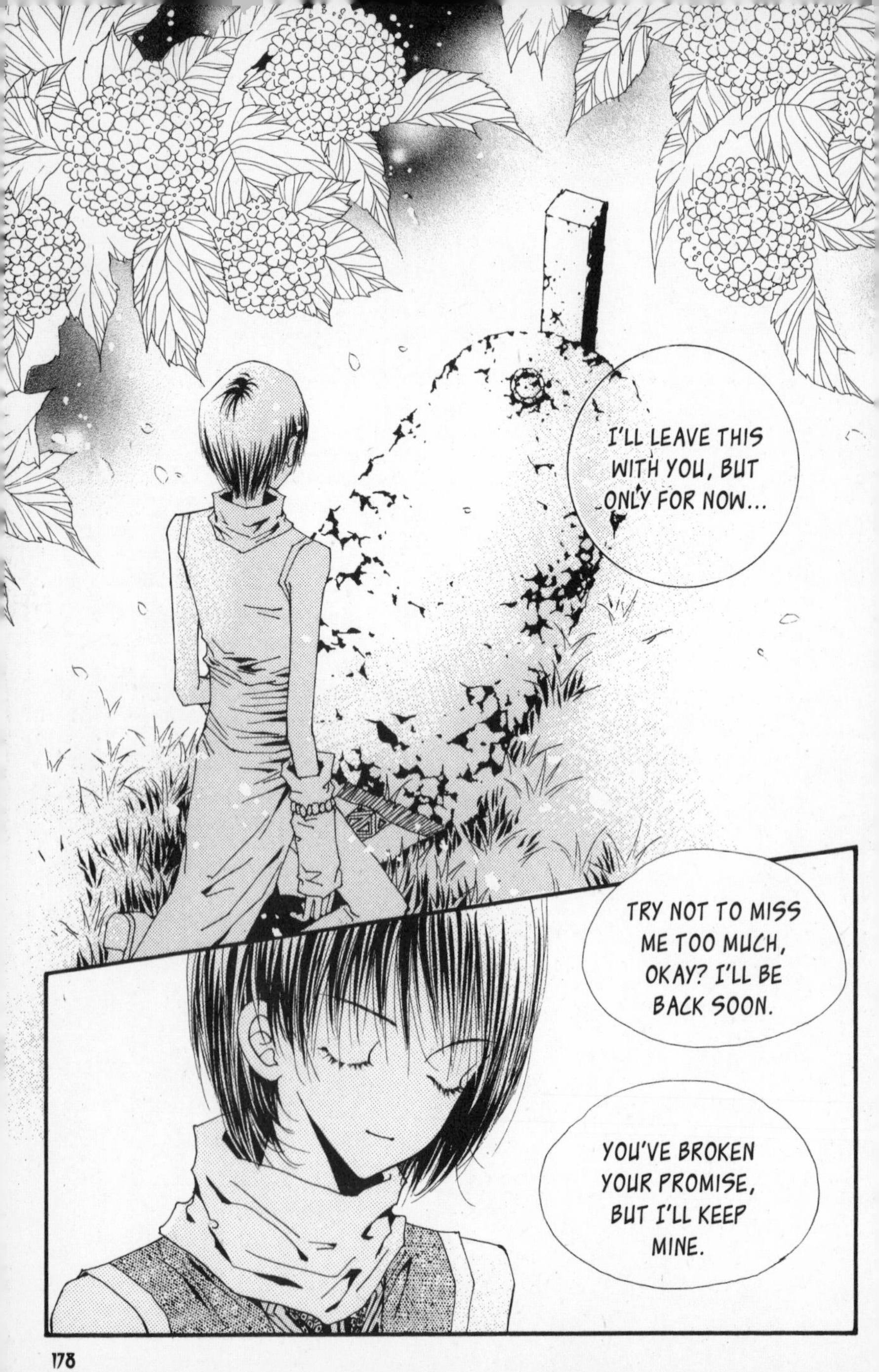
I'LL LEAVE THIS WITH YOU, BUT ONLY FOR NOW...
TRY NOT TO MISS ME TOO MUCH, OKAY? I'LL BE BACK SOON.
YOU'VE BROKEN YOUR PROMISE, BUT I'LL KEEP MINE.

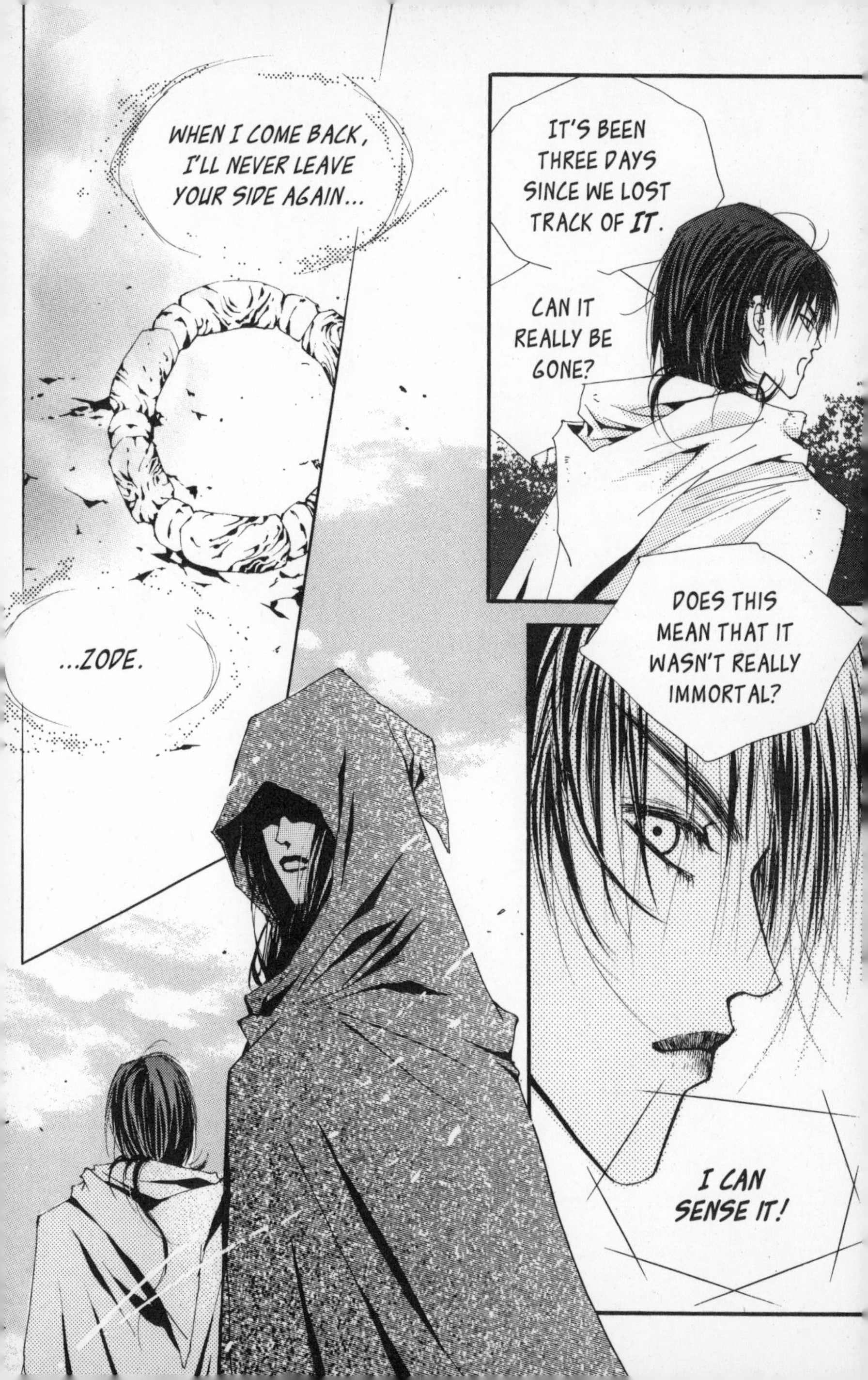
WHEN I COME BACK, I'LL NEVER LEAVE YOUR SIDE AGAIN...
...ZODE.
IT'S BEEN THREE DAYS SINCE WE LOST TRACK OF *IT*.
CAN IT REALLY BE GONE?
DOES THIS MEAN THAT IT WASN'T REALLY IMMORTAL?
I CAN SENSE IT!

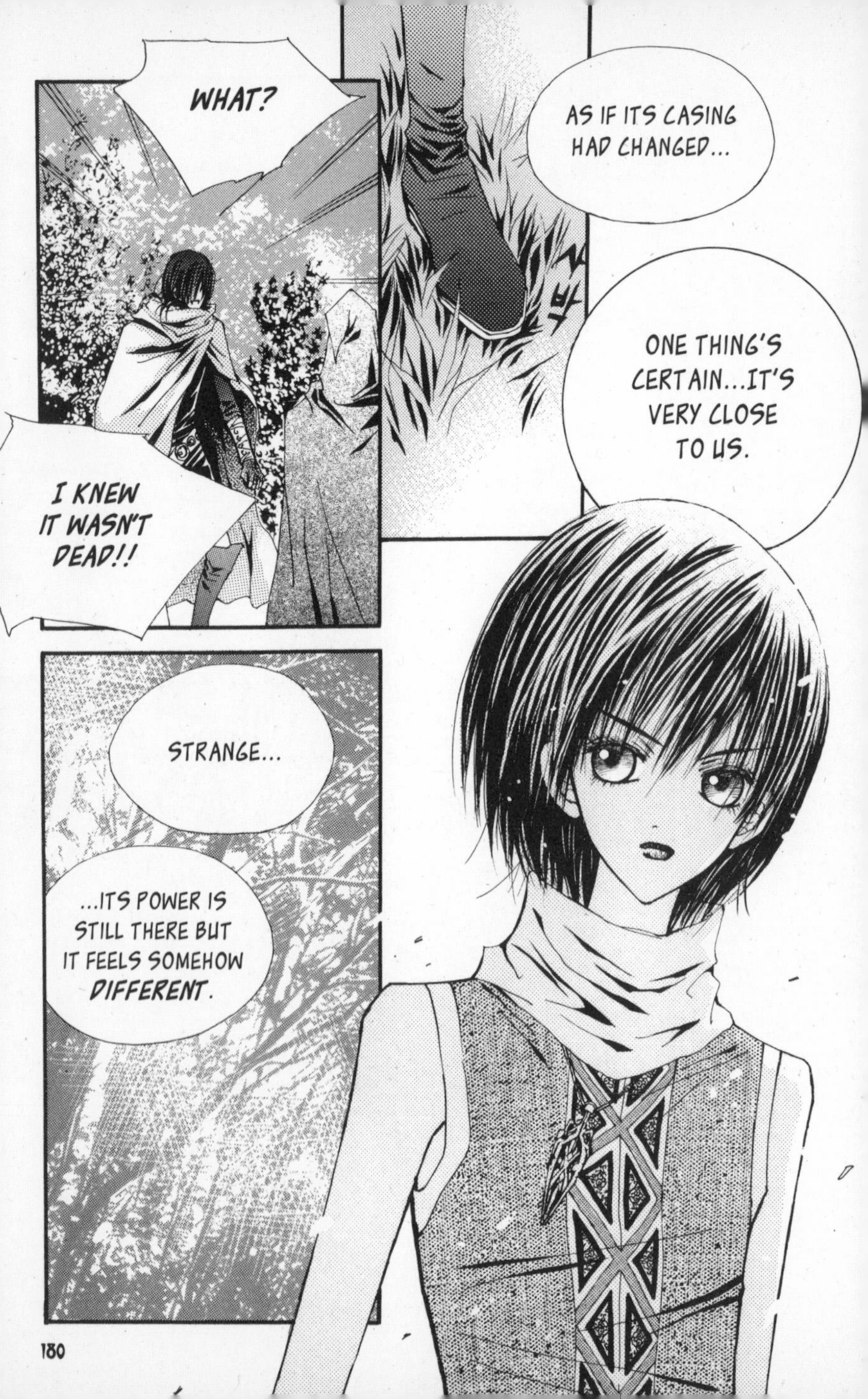
WHAT?
I KNEW IT WASN'T DEAD!!
STRANGE...
...ITS POWER IS STILL THERE BUT IT FEELS SOMEHOW DIFFERENT.
AS IF ITS CASING HAD CHANGED...
ONE THING'S CERTAIN...IT'S VERY CLOSE TO US.

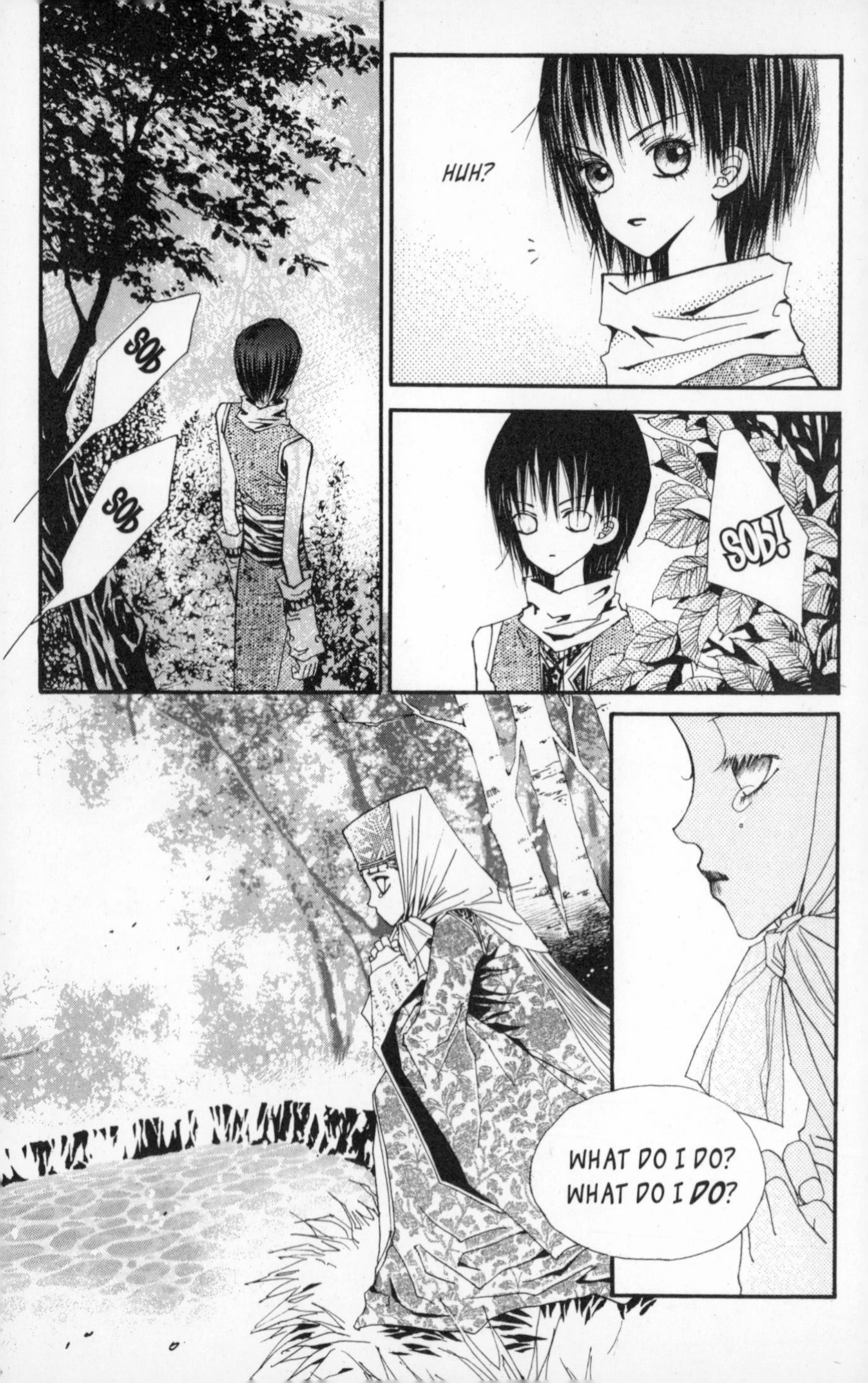
SOB
SOB
HUH?
SOB!
WHAT DO I DO? WHAT DO I DO?

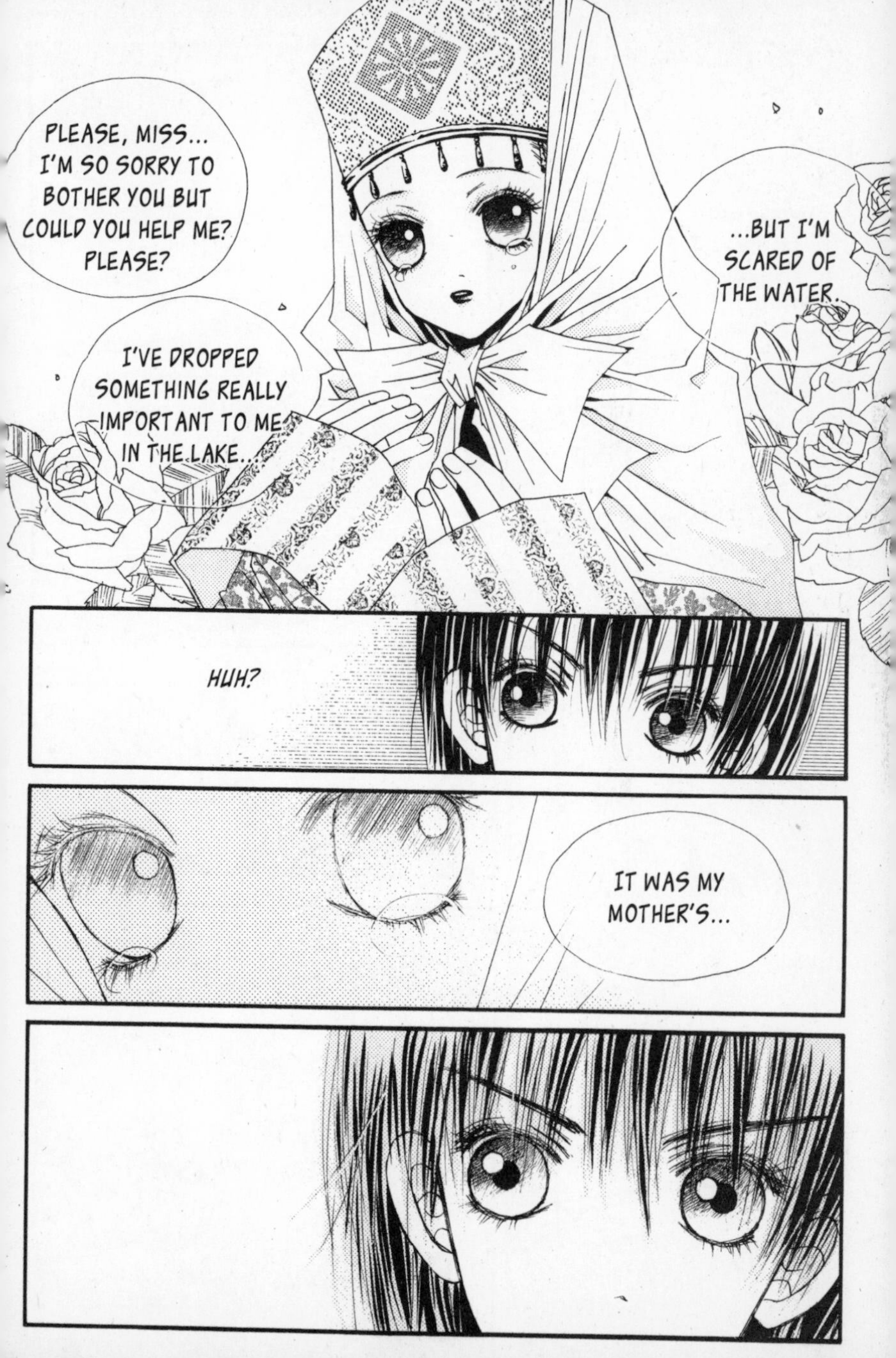
PLEASE, MISS... I'M SO SORRY TO BOTHER YOU BUT COULD YOU HELP ME? PLEASE?
I'VE DROPPED SOMETHING REALLY IMPORTANT TO ME IN THE LAKE...
...BUT I'M SCARED OF THE WATER.
HUH?
IT WAS MY MOTHER'S...

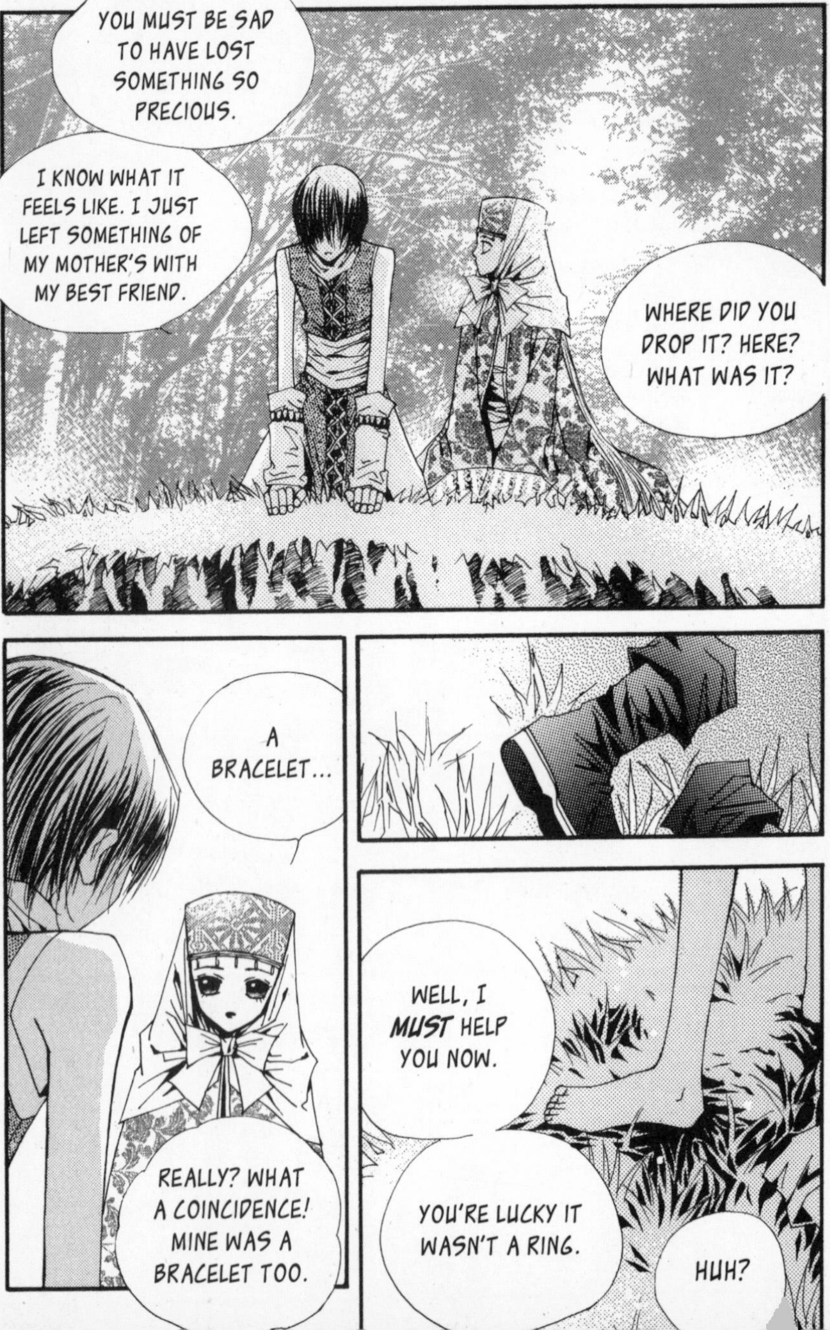
YOU MUST BE SAD TO HAVE LOST SOMETHING SO PRECIOUS.
I KNOW WHAT IT FEELS LIKE. I JUST LEFT SOMETHING OF MY MOTHER'S WITH MY BEST FRIEND.
WHERE DID YOU DROP IT? HERE? WHAT WAS IT?
A BRACELET...
REALLY? WHAT A COINCIDENCE! MINE WAS A BRACELET TOO.
WELL, I *MUST* HELP YOU NOW.
YOU'RE LUCKY IT WASN'T A RING.
HUH?

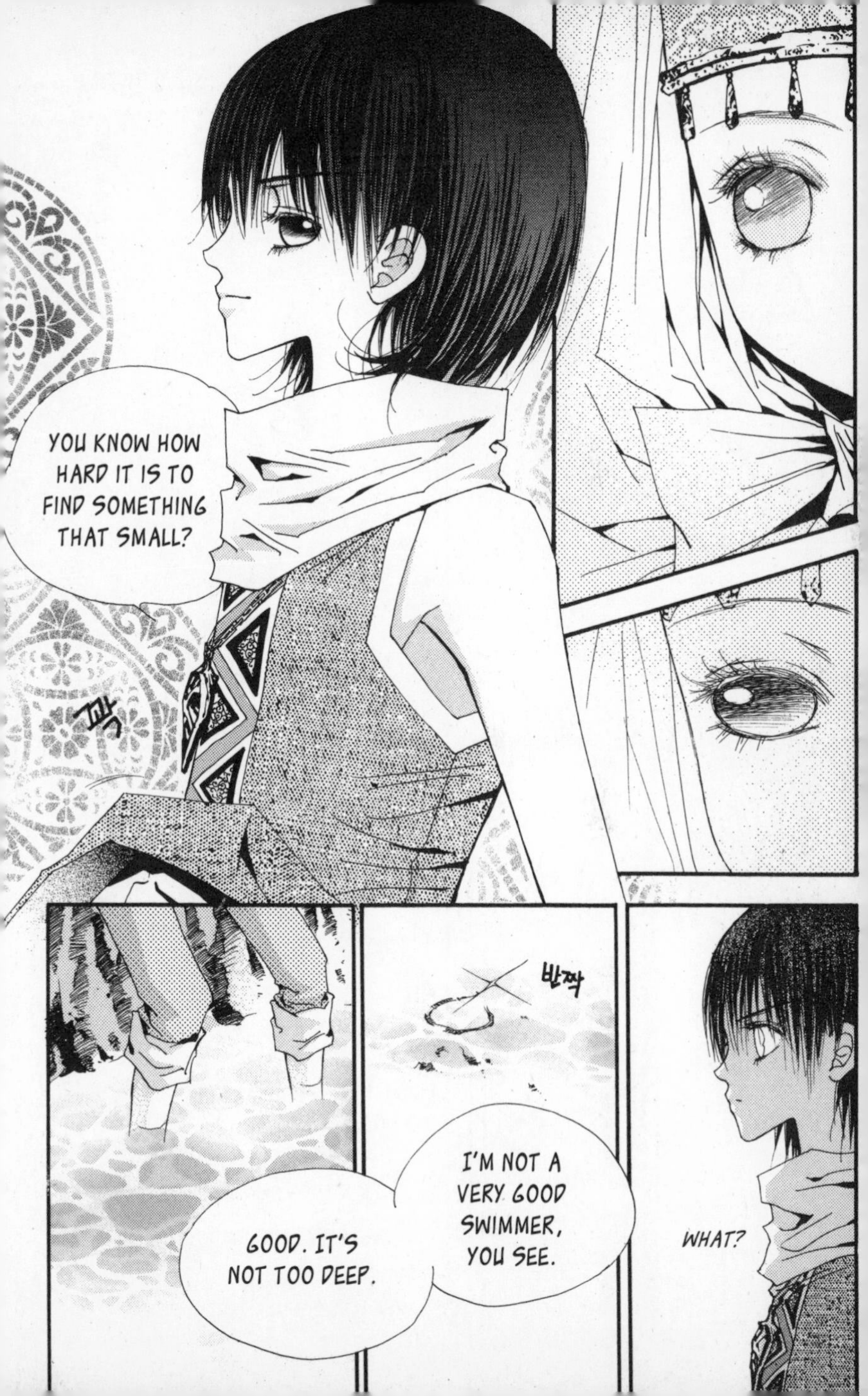
YOU KNOW HOW HARD IT IS TO FIND SOMETHING THAT SMALL?
반짝
GOOD. IT'S NOT TOO DEEP.
I'M NOT A VERY GOOD SWIMMER, YOU SEE.
WHAT?

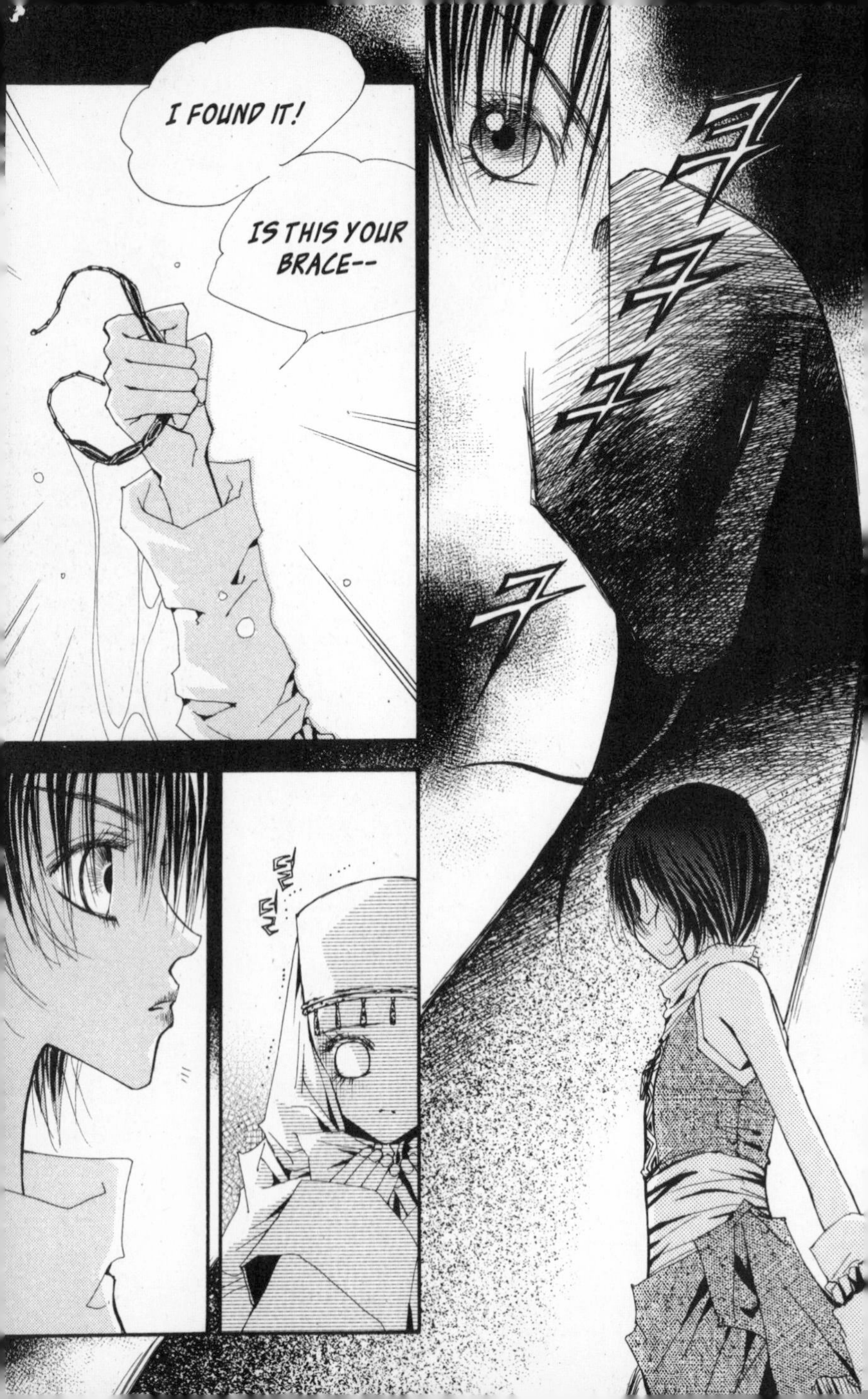
I FOUND IT!
IS THIS YOUR BRACE--

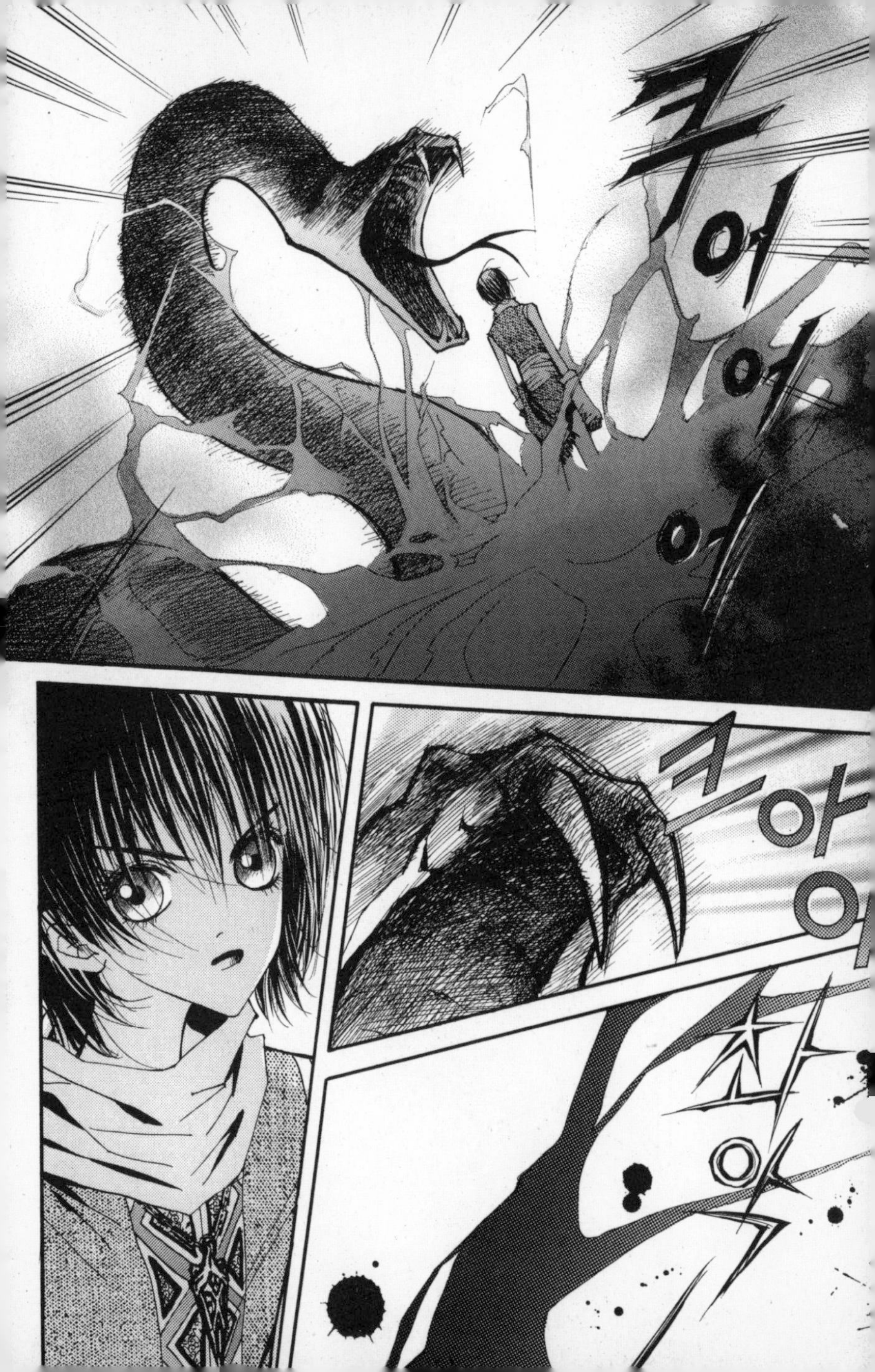
쿠어어어
크아아
촤악

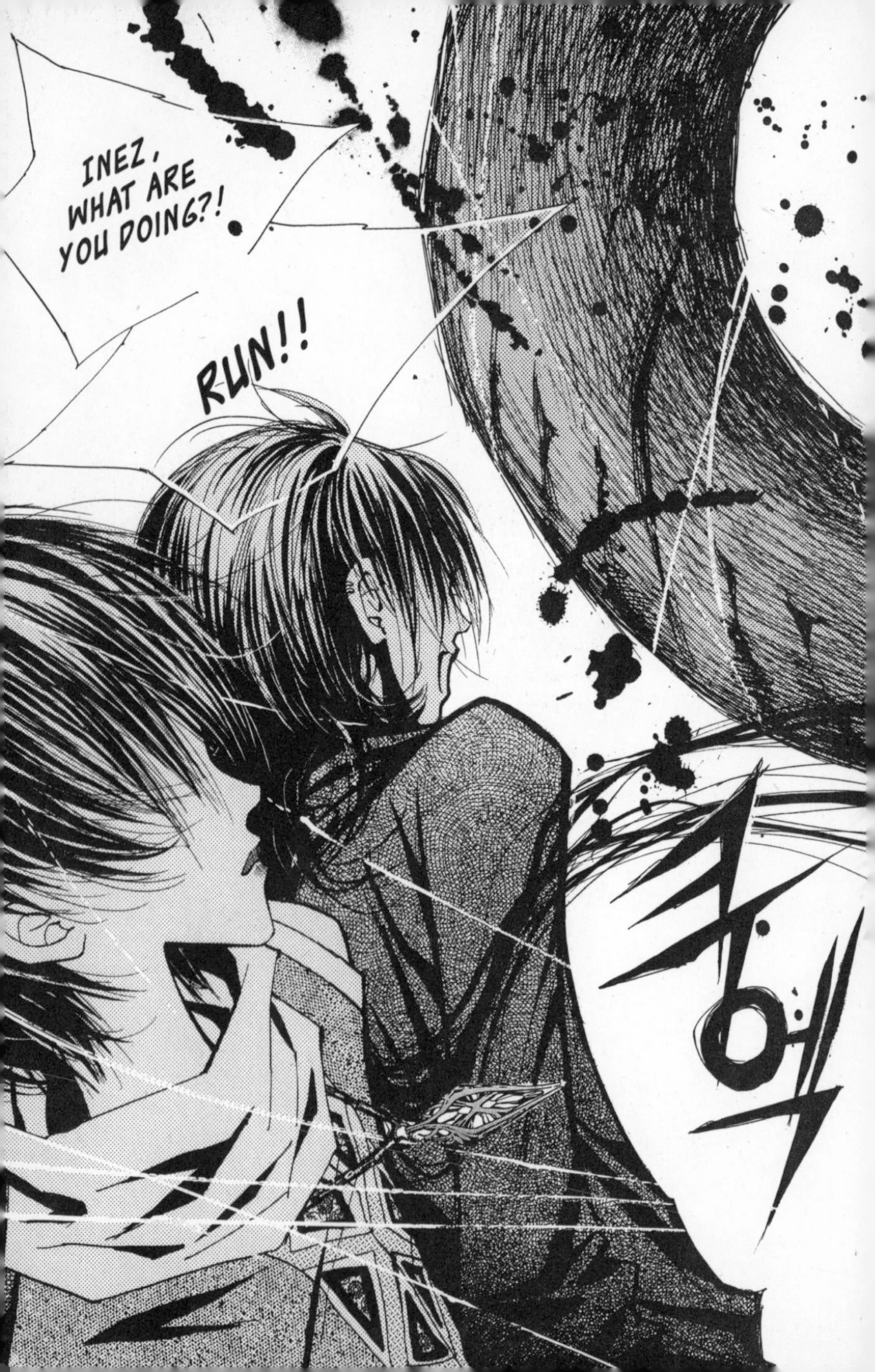
INEZ, WHAT ARE YOU DOING?!
RUN!!

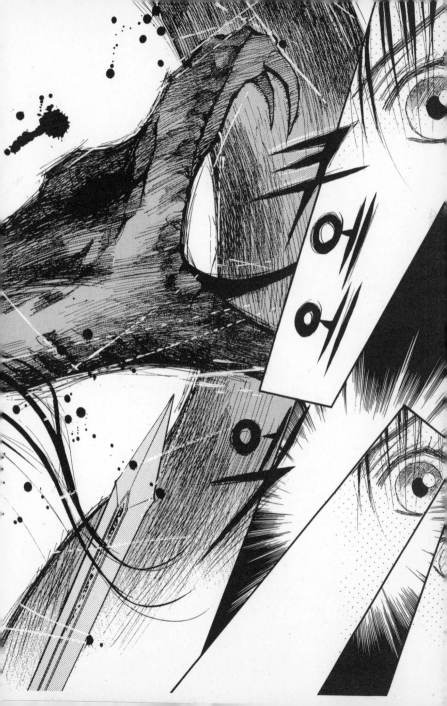

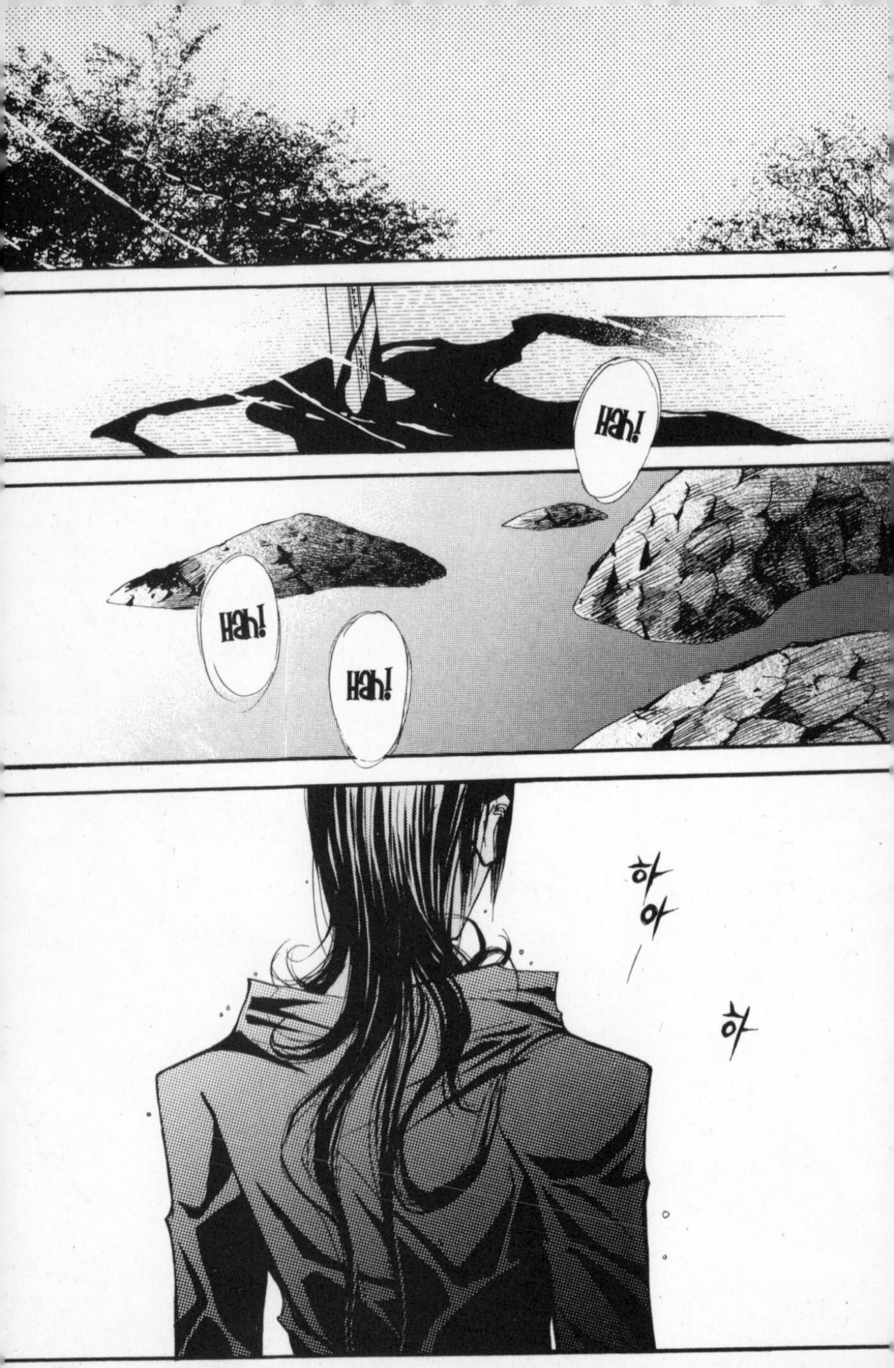
Hah!
Hah!
Hah!
하아— 하

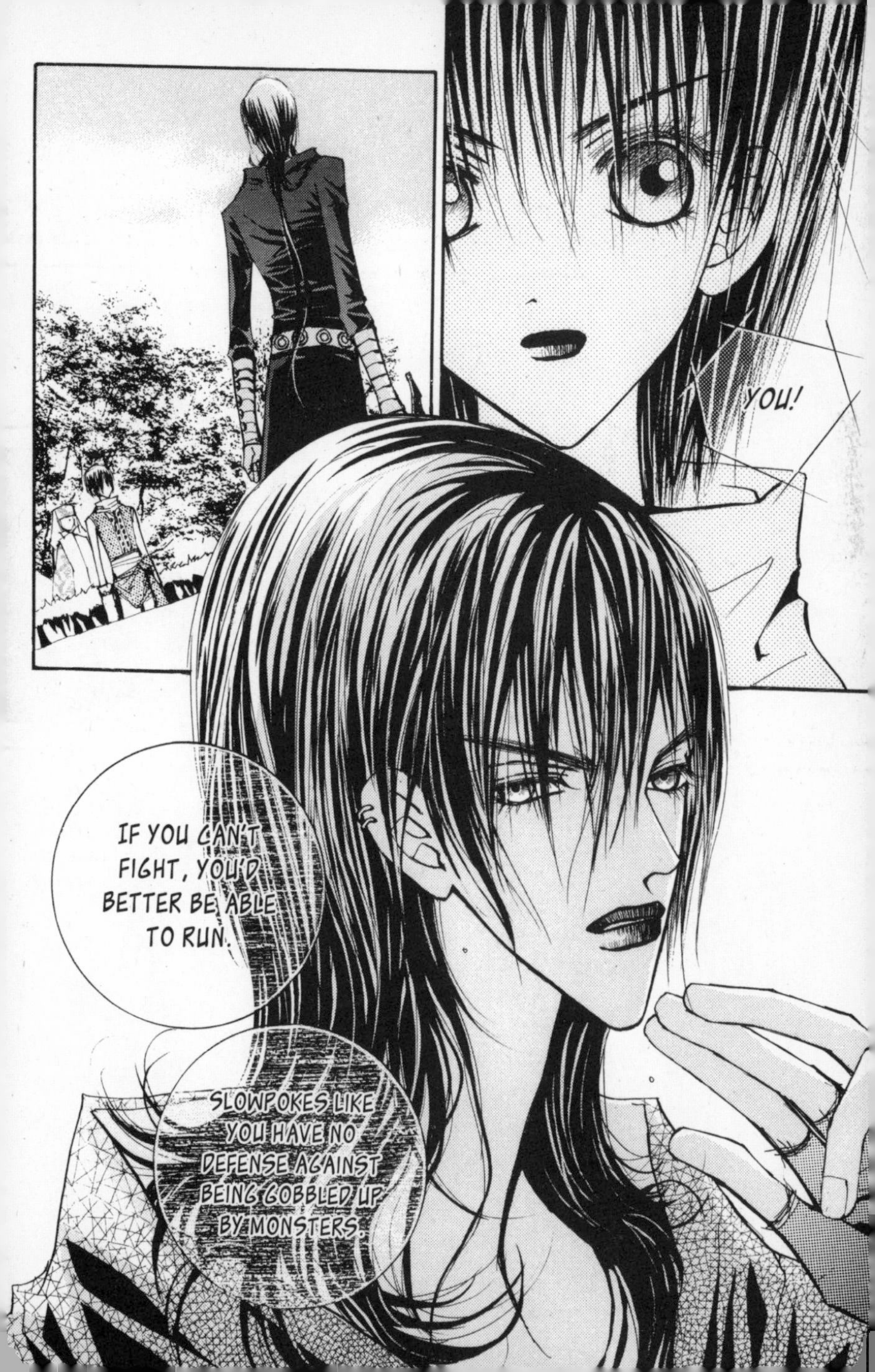
YOU!
IF YOU CAN'T FIGHT, YOU'D BETTER BE ABLE TO RUN.
SLOWPOKES LIKE YOU HAVE NO DEFENSE AGAINST BEING GOBBLED UP BY MONSTERS.

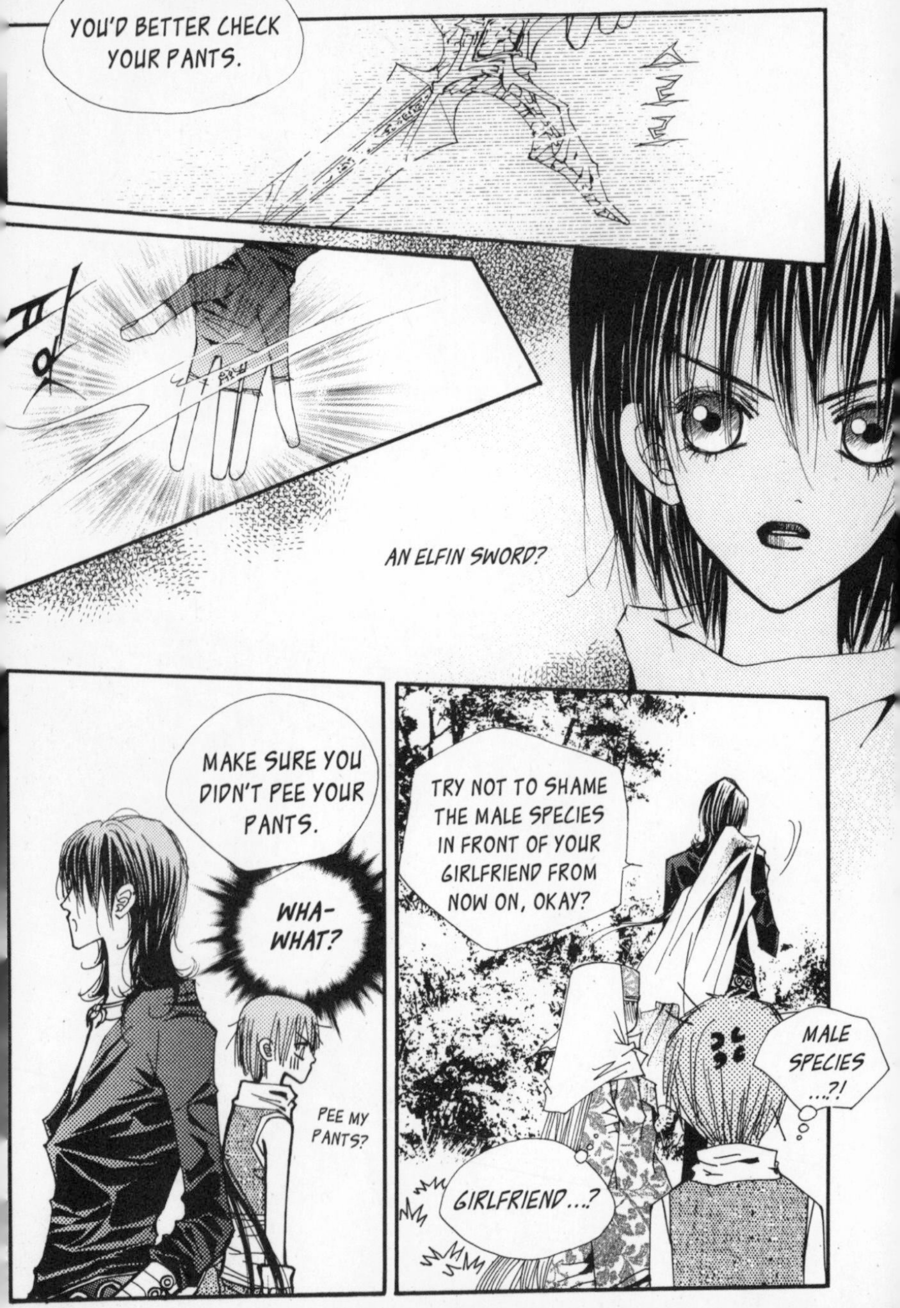
YOU'D BETTER CHECK YOUR PANTS.
AN ELFIN SWORD?
MAKE SURE YOU DIDN'T PEE YOUR PANTS.
WHA- WHAT?
PEE MY PANTS?
TRY NOT TO SHAME THE MALE SPECIES IN FRONT OF YOUR GIRLFRIEND FROM NOW ON, OKAY?
MALE SPECIES ...?!
GIRLFRIEND...?

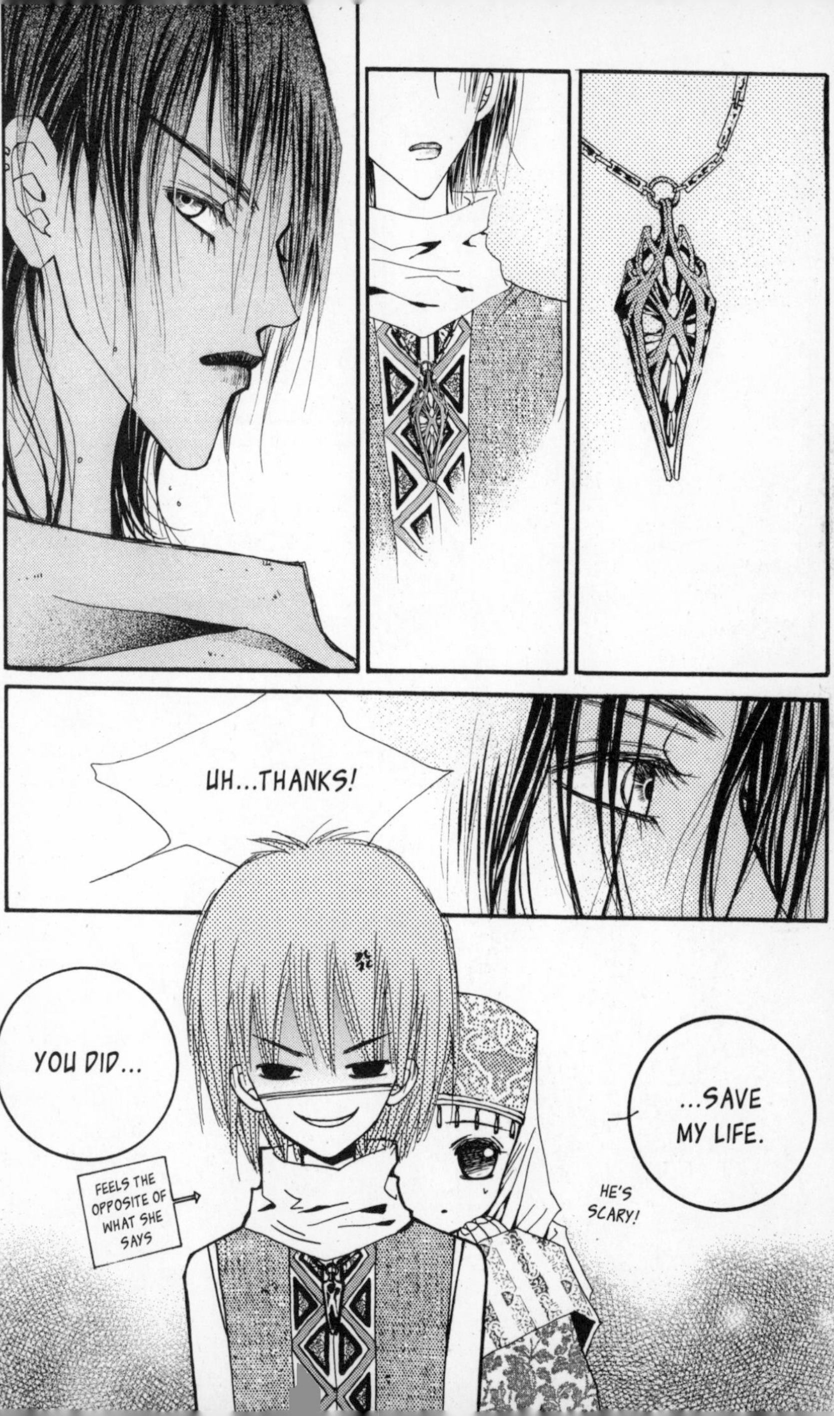
UH...THANKS!
YOU DID...
...SAVE MY LIFE.
FEELS THE OPPOSITE OF WHAT SHE SAYS
HE'S SCARY!

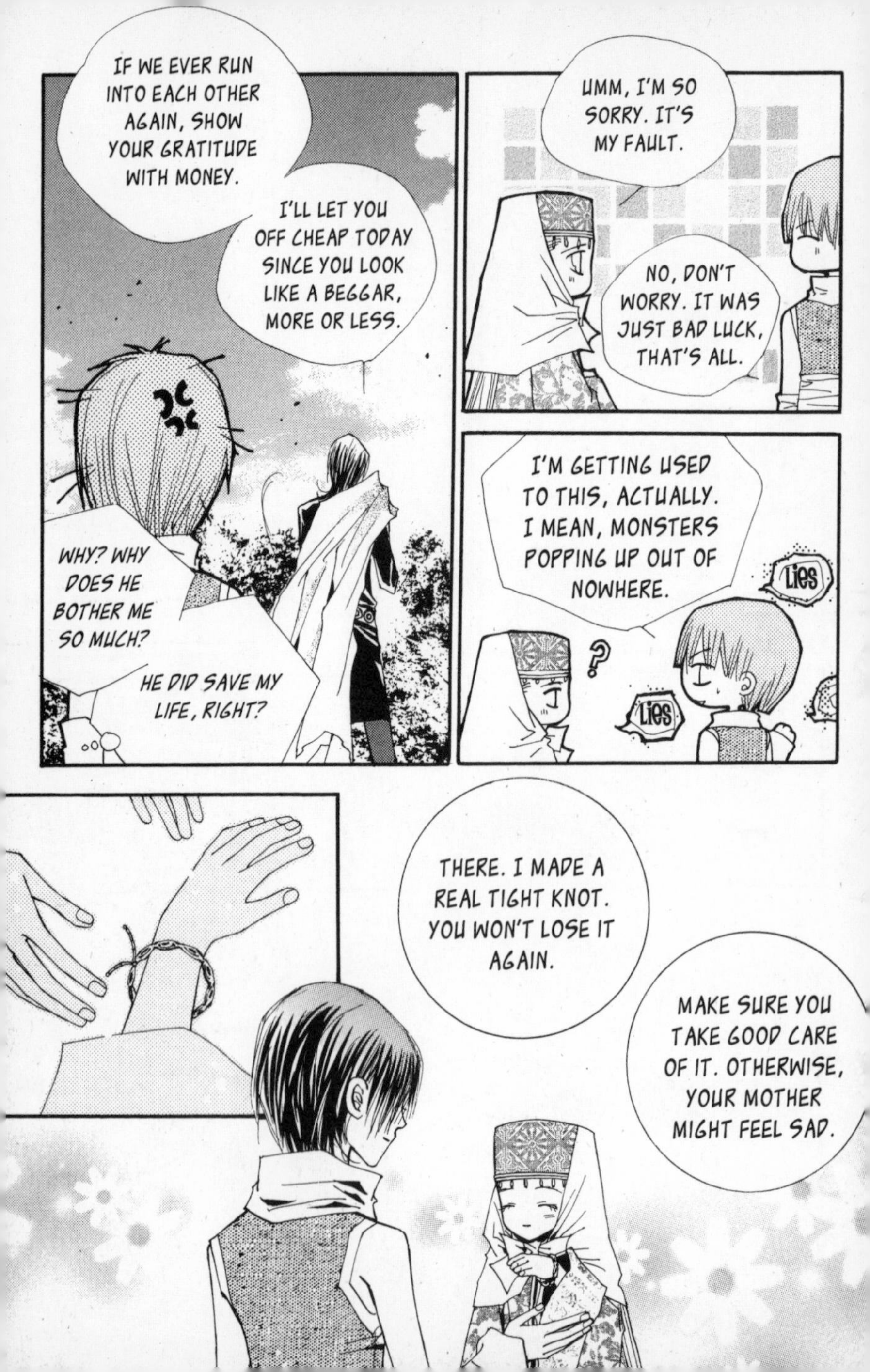
IF WE EVER RUN INTO EACH OTHER AGAIN, SHOW YOUR GRATITUDE WITH MONEY.
I'LL LET YOU OFF CHEAP TODAY SINCE YOU LOOK LIKE A BEGGAR, MORE OR LESS.
WHY? WHY DOES HE BOTHER ME SO MUCH?
HE DID SAVE MY LIFE, RIGHT?
UMM, I'M SO SORRY. IT'S MY FAULT.
NO, DON'T WORRY. IT WAS JUST BAD LUCK, THAT'S ALL.
I'M GETTING USED TO THIS, ACTUALLY. I MEAN, MONSTERS POPPING UP OUT OF NOWHERE.
Lies
?
Lies
THERE. I MADE A REAL TIGHT KNOT. YOU WON'T LOSE IT AGAIN.
MAKE SURE YOU TAKE GOOD CARE OF IT. OTHERWISE, YOUR MOTHER MIGHT FEEL SAD.

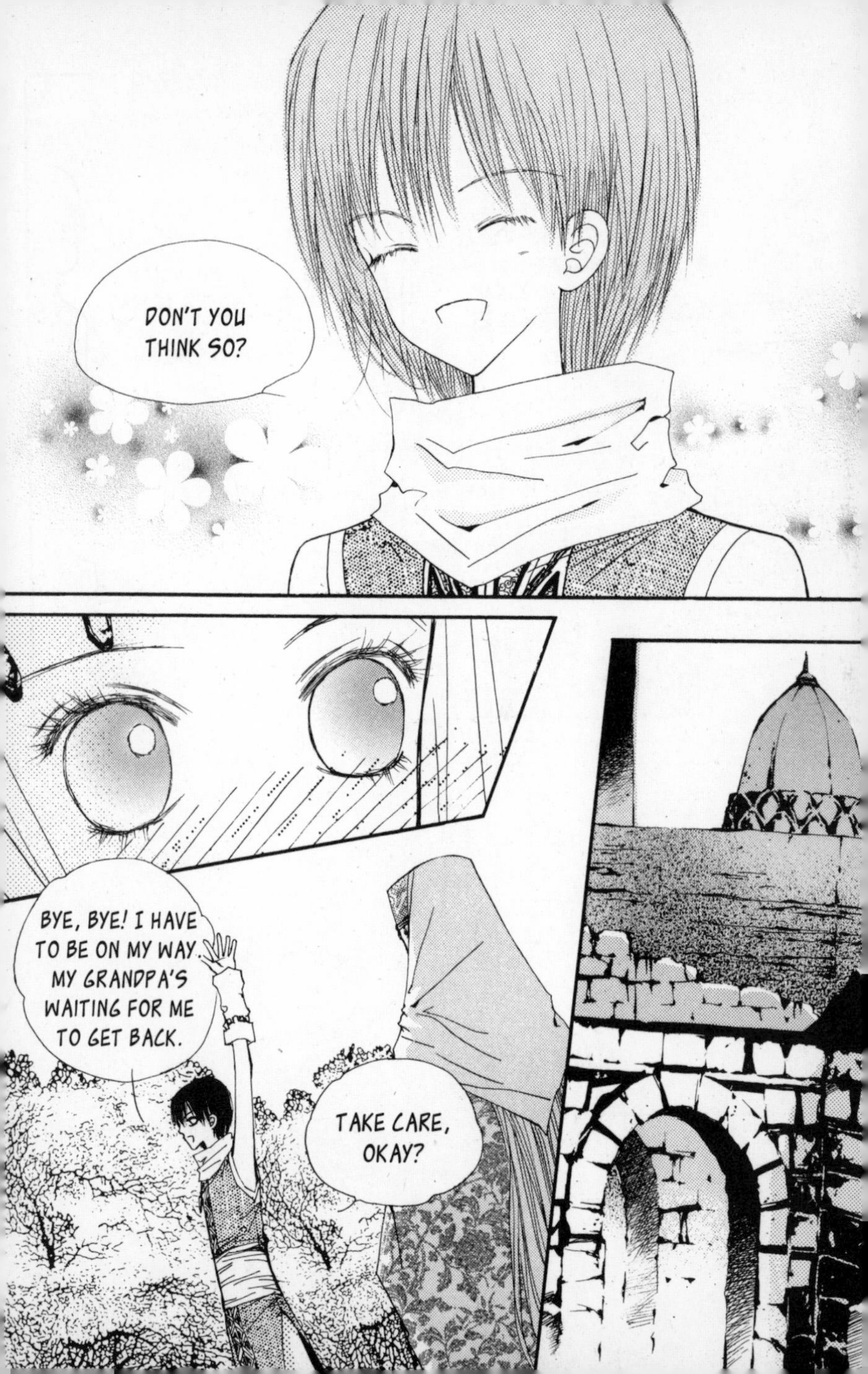
DON'T YOU THINK SO?
BYE, BYE! I HAVE TO BE ON MY WAY. MY GRANDPA'S WAITING FOR ME TO GET BACK.
TAKE CARE, OKAY?

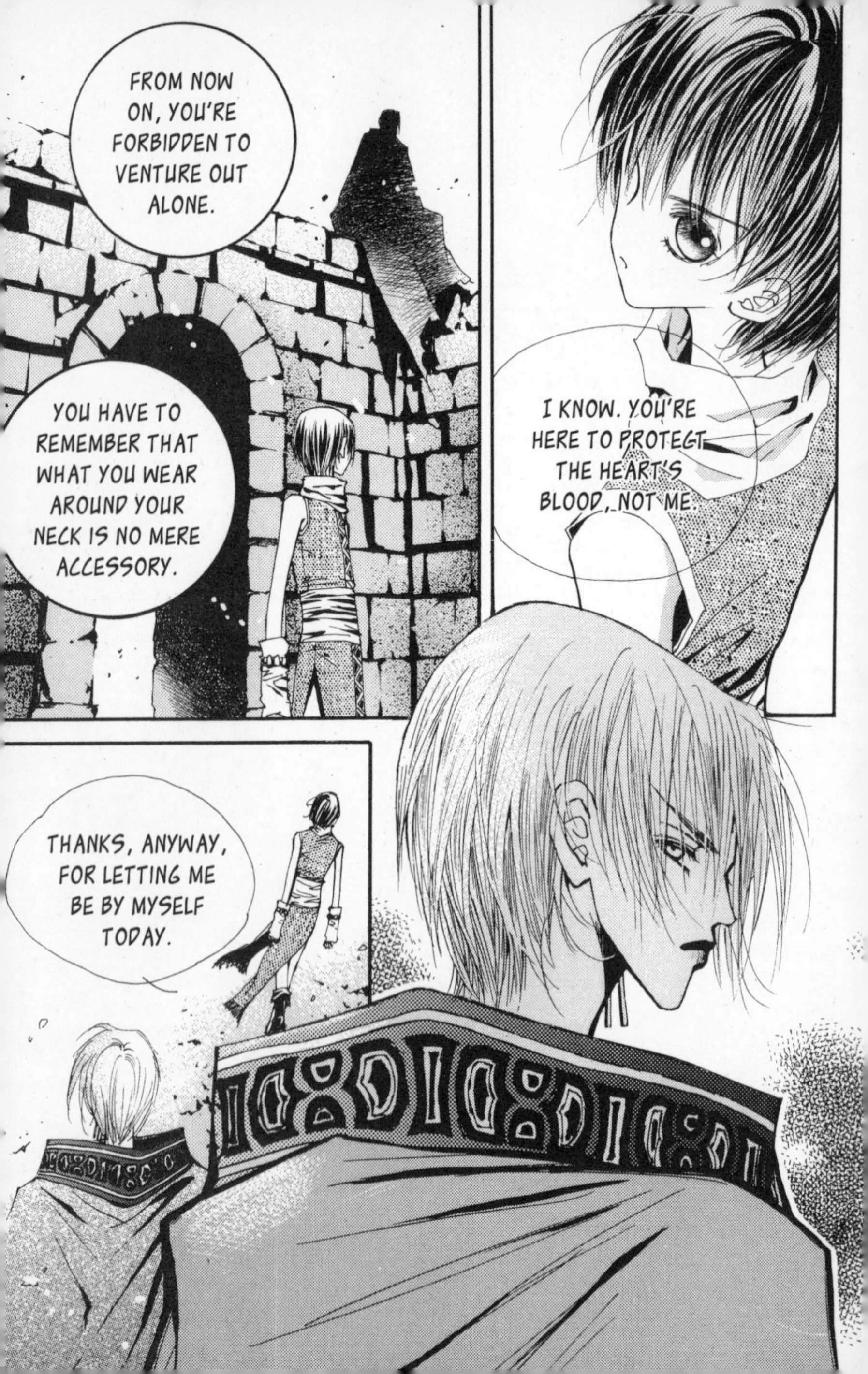
FROM NOW ON, YOU'RE FORBIDDEN TO VENTURE OUT ALONE.
YOU HAVE TO REMEMBER THAT WHAT YOU WEAR AROUND YOUR NECK IS NO MERE ACCESSORY.
I KNOW. YOU'RE HERE TO PROTECT THE HEART'S BLOOD, NOT ME.
THANKS, ANYWAY, FOR LETTING ME BE BY MYSELF TODAY.

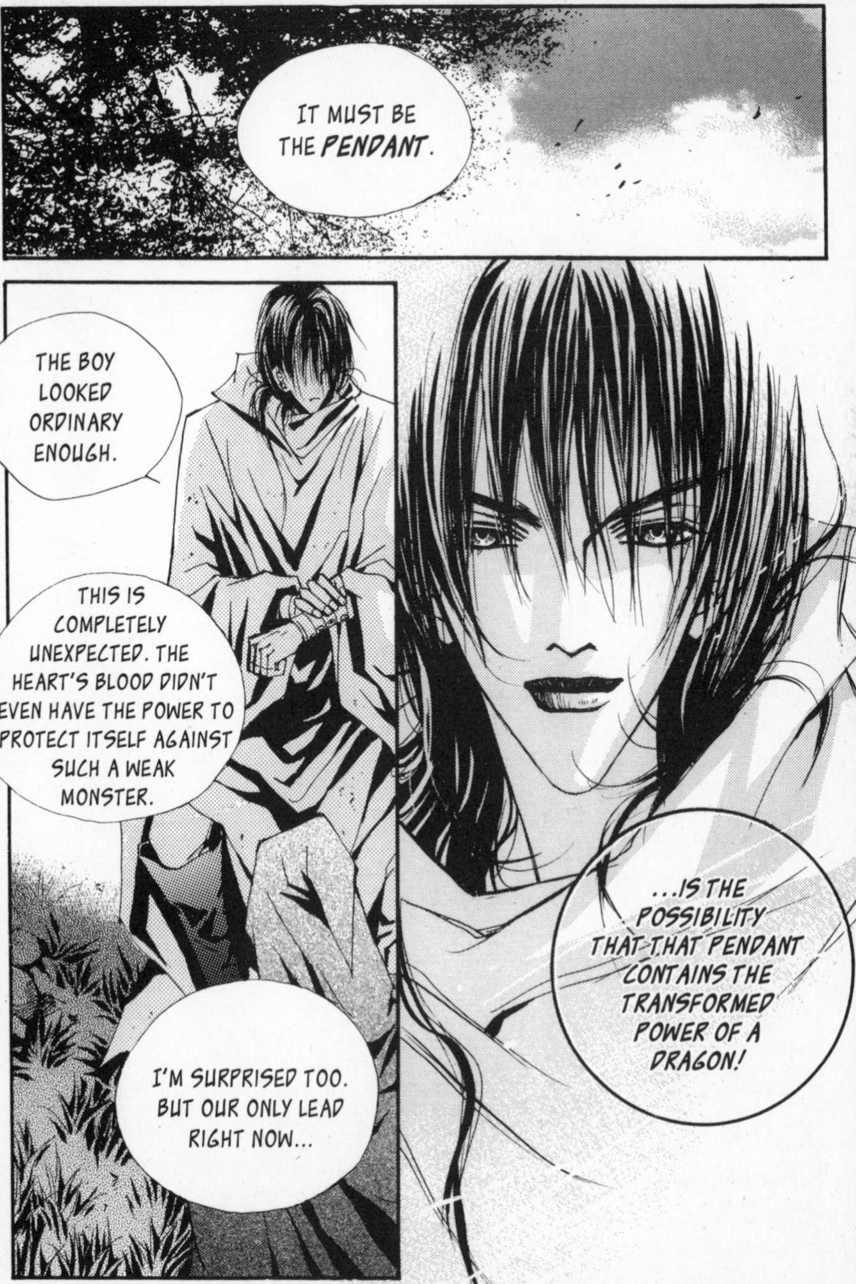
IT MUST BE THE PENDANT.
THE BOY LOOKED ORDINARY ENOUGH.
THIS IS COMPLETELY UNEXPECTED. THE HEART'S BLOOD DIDN'T EVEN HAVE THE POWER TO PROTECT ITSELF AGAINST SUCH A WEAK MONSTER.
I'M SURPRISED TOO. BUT OUR ONLY LEAD RIGHT NOW...
...IS THE POSSIBILITY THAT THAT PENDANT CONTAINS THE TRANSFORMED POWER OF A DRAGON!

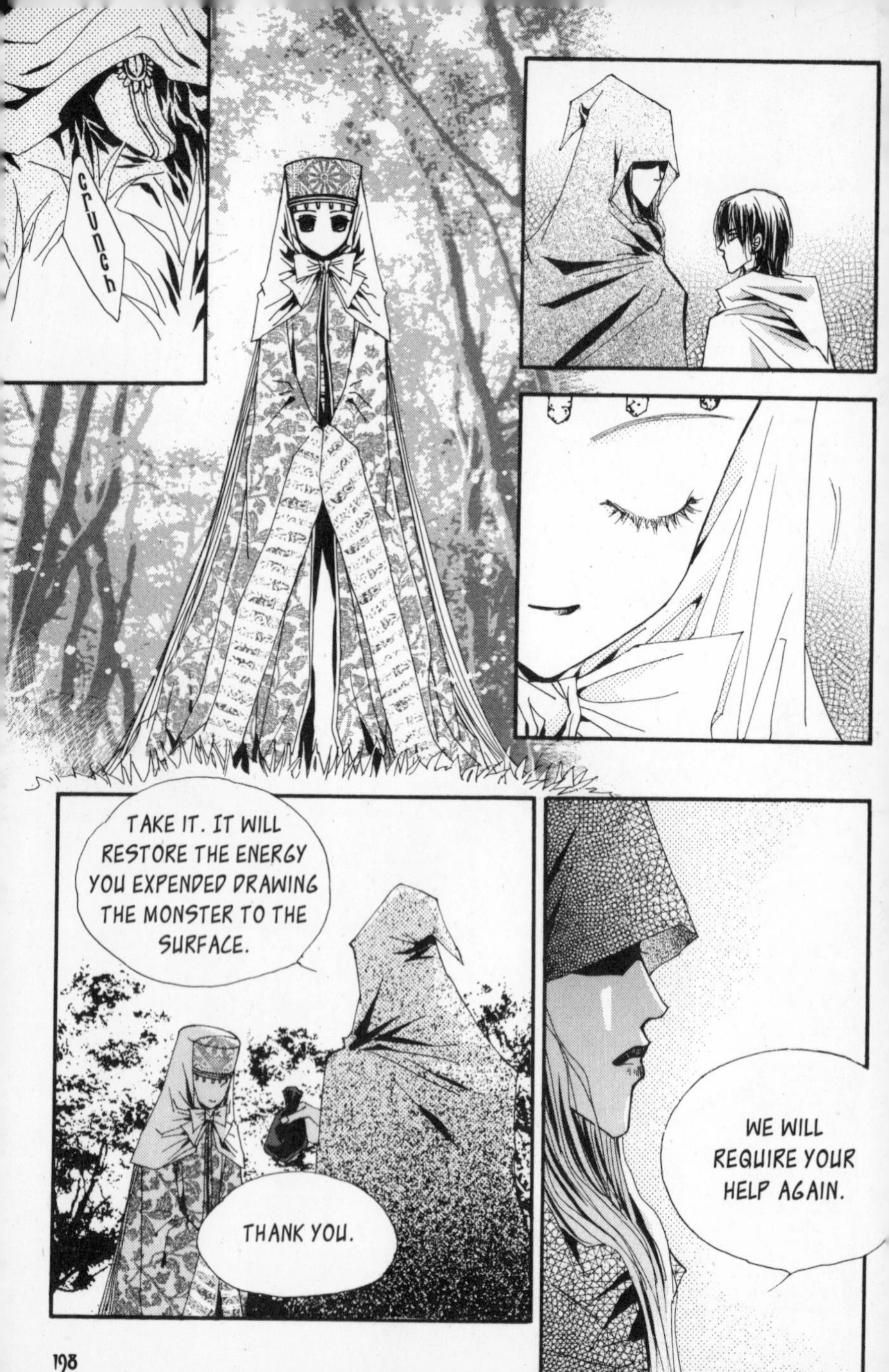
CRUNCH
TAKE IT. IT WILL RESTORE THE ENERGY YOU EXPENDED DRAWING THE MONSTER TO THE SURFACE.
THANK YOU.
WE WILL REQUIRE YOUR HELP AGAIN.

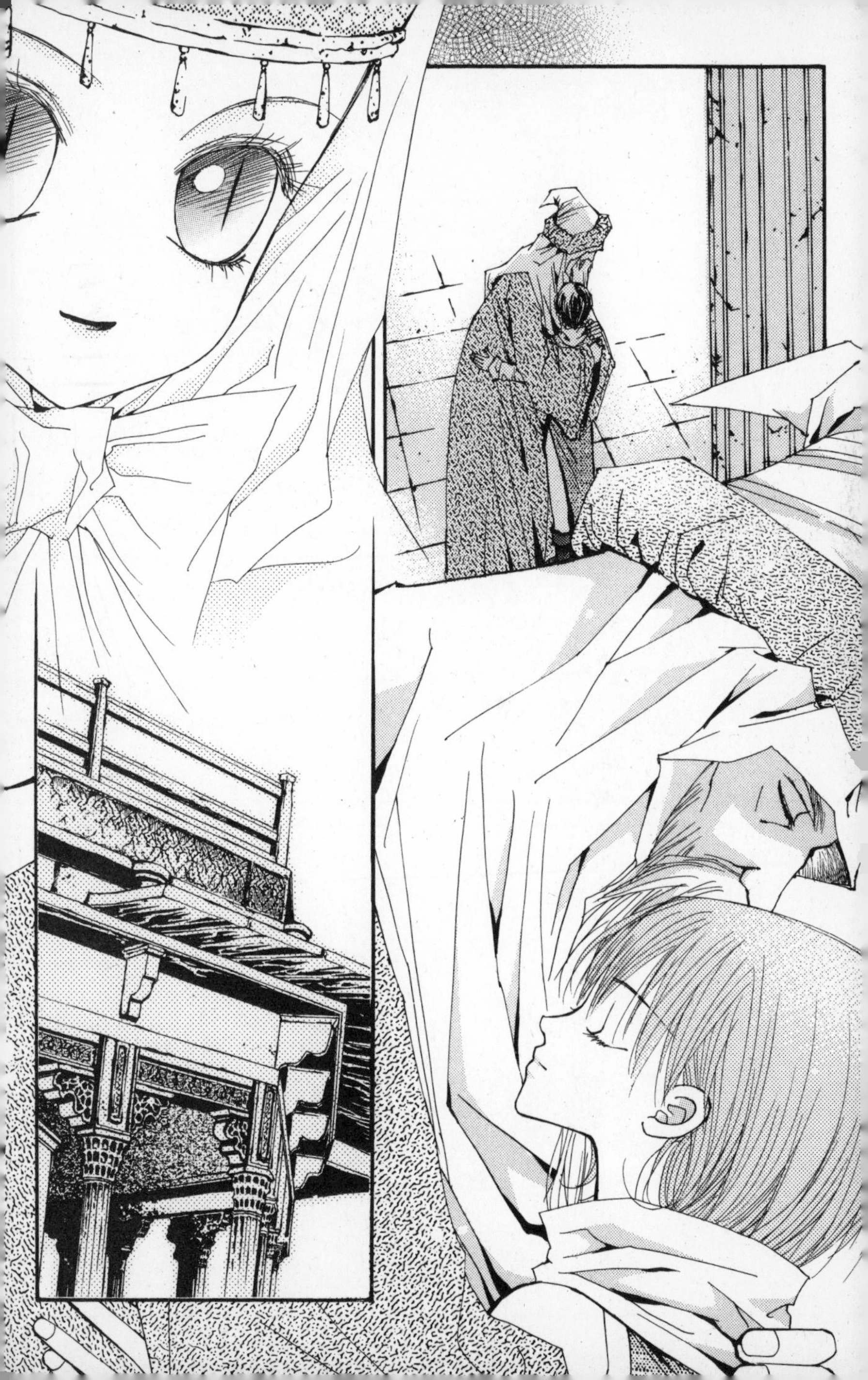

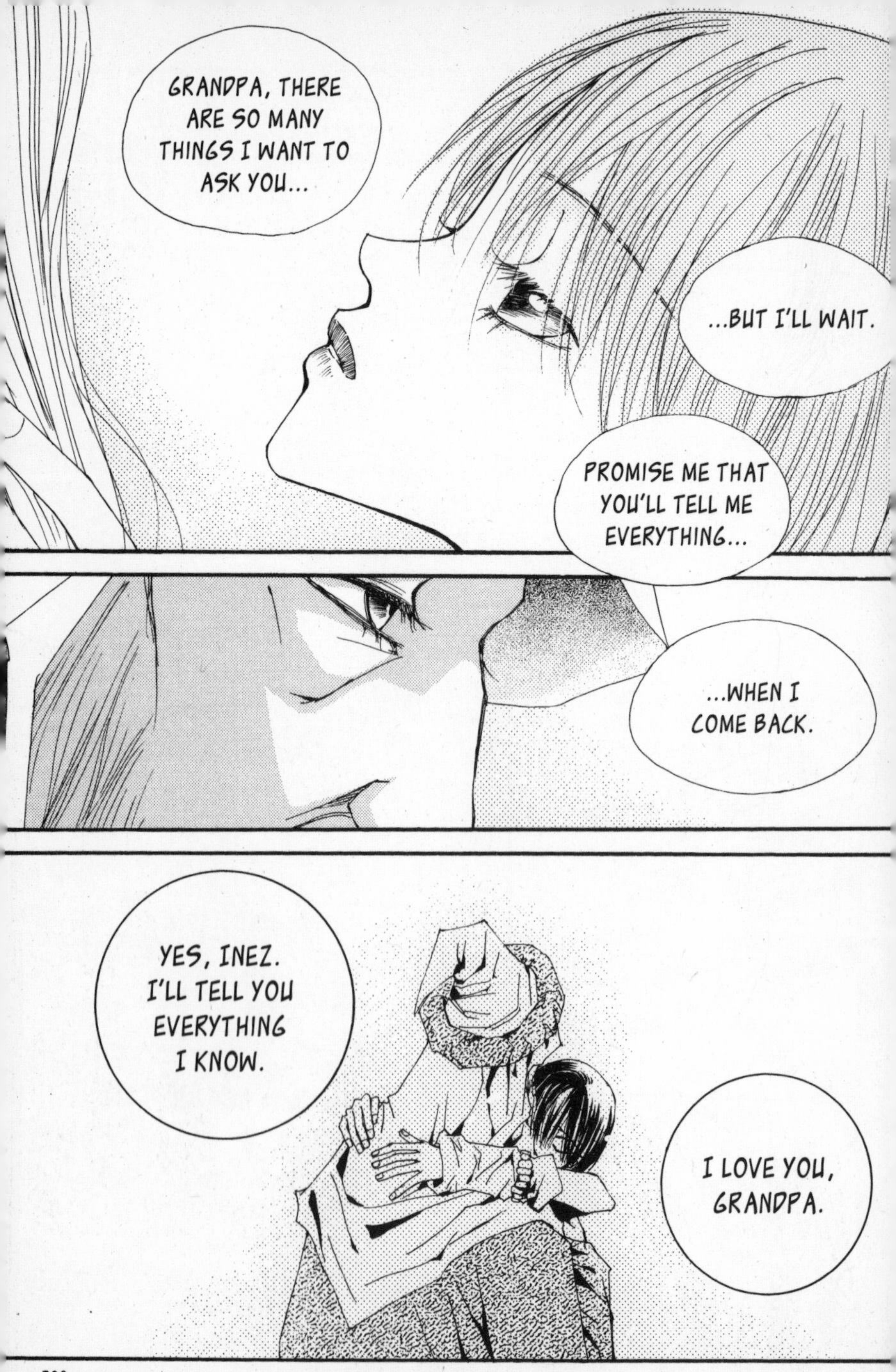
GRANDPA, THERE ARE SO MANY THINGS I WANT TO ASK YOU...
...BUT I'LL WAIT.
PROMISE ME THAT YOU'LL TELL ME EVERYTHING...
...WHEN I COME BACK.
YES, INEZ. I'LL TELL YOU EVERYTHING I KNOW.
I LOVE YOU, GRANDPA.

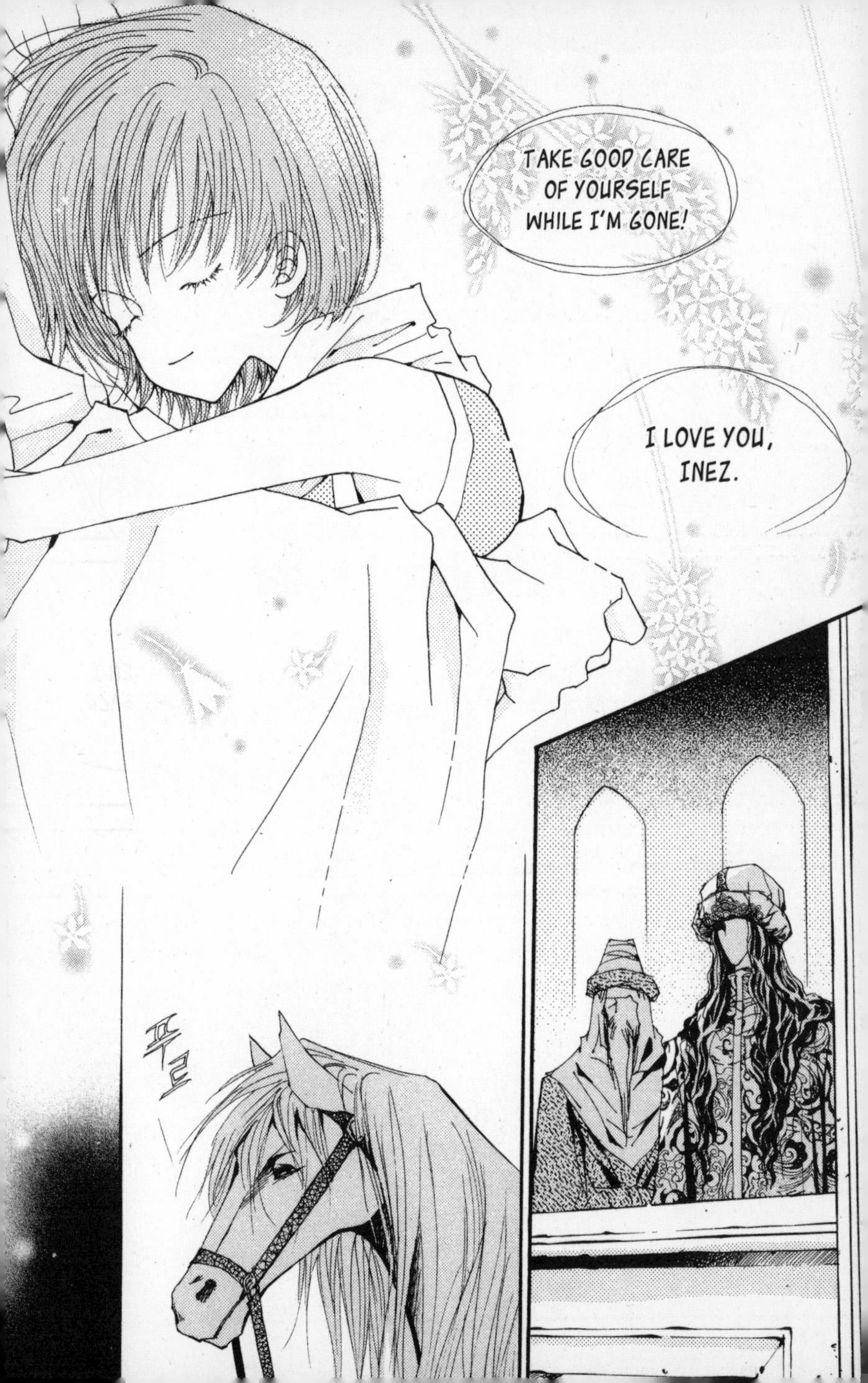
TAKE GOOD CARE OF YOURSELF WHILE I'M GONE!
I LOVE YOU, INEZ.
푸르

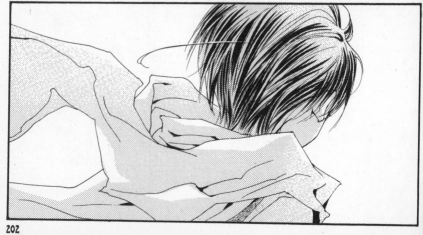

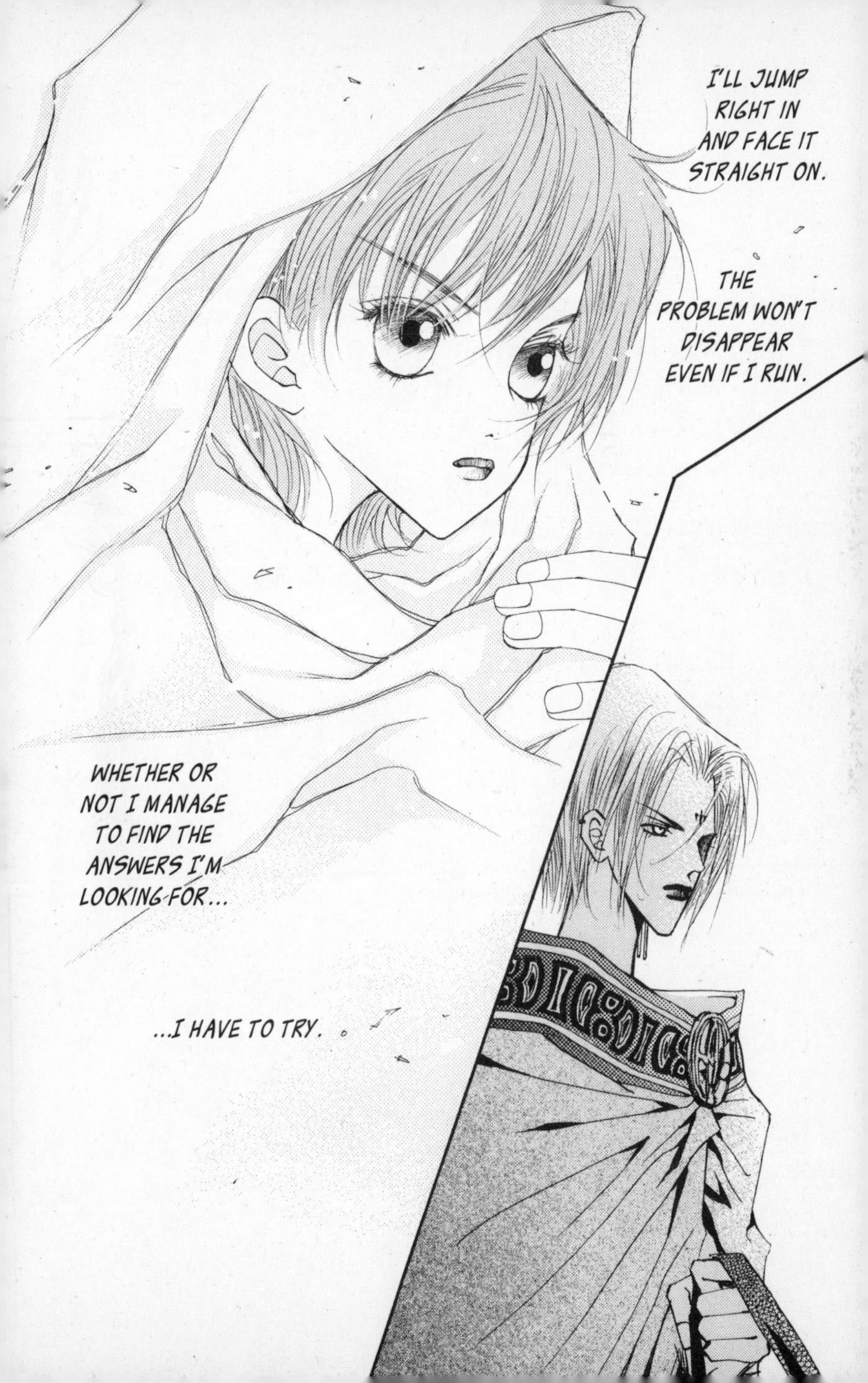
I'LL JUMP RIGHT IN AND FACE IT STRAIGHT ON.
THE PROBLEM WON'T DISAPPEAR EVEN IF I RUN.
WHETHER OR NOT I MANAGE TO FIND THE ANSWERS I'M LOOKING FOR...
...I HAVE TO TRY.

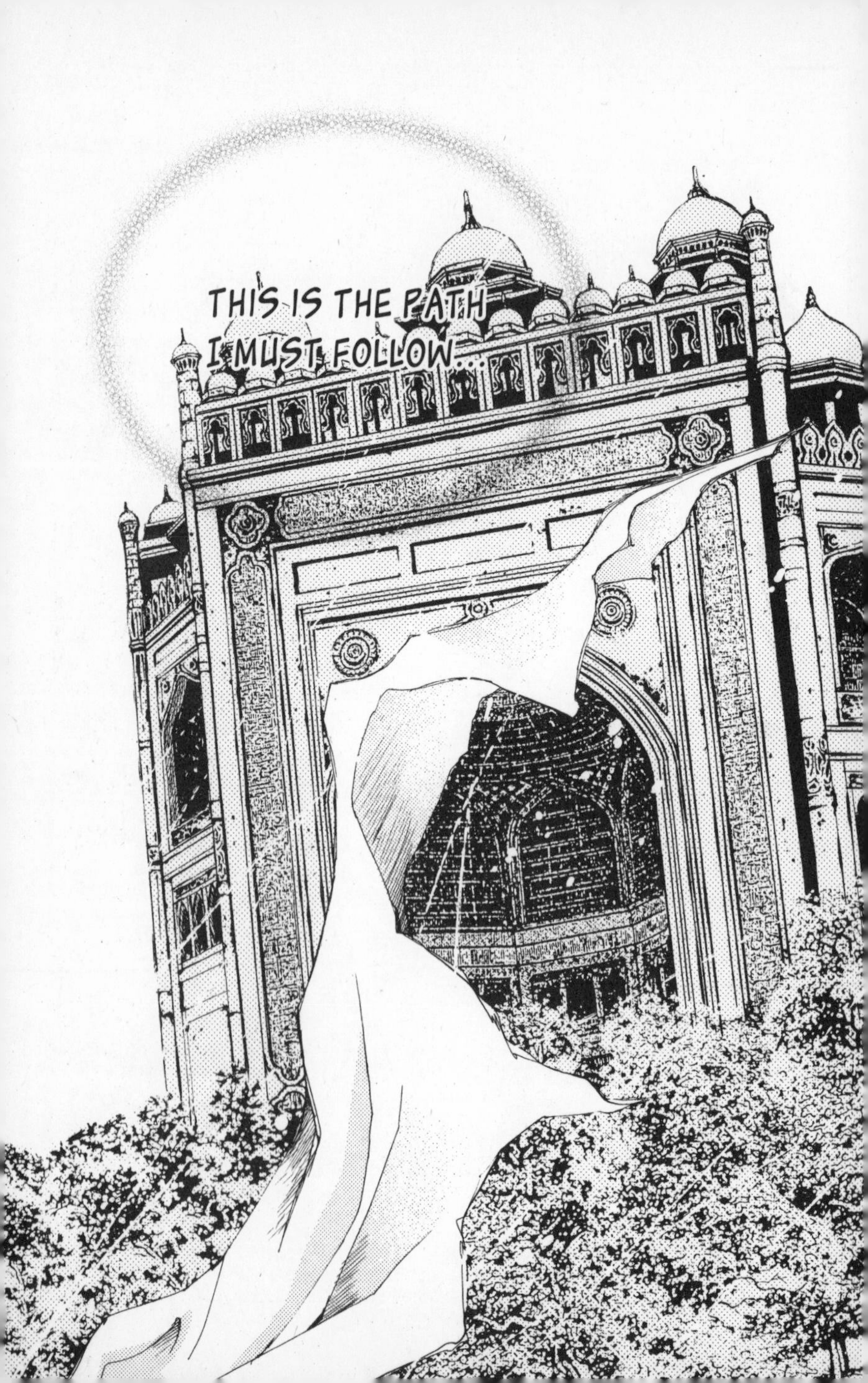
THIS IS THE PATH
I MUST FOLLOW...

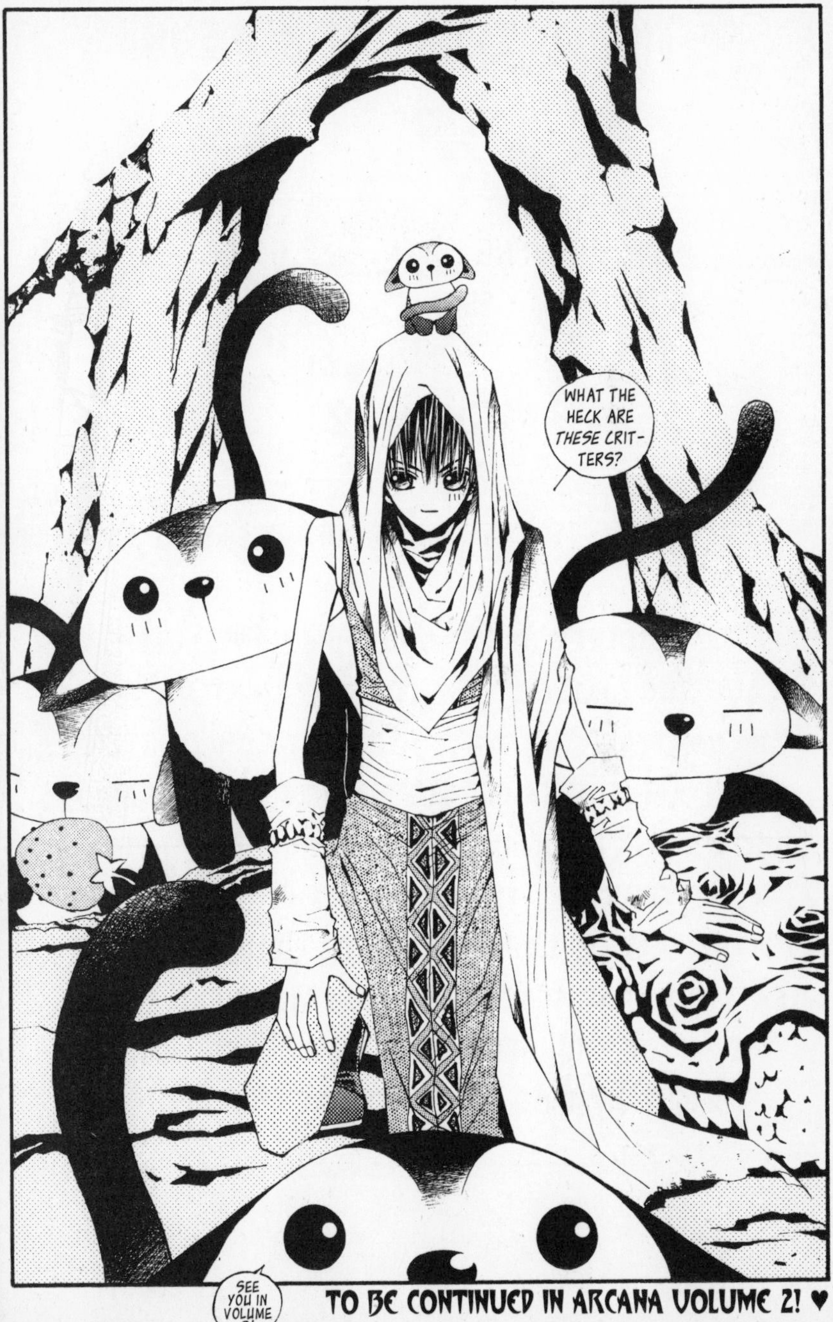
WHAT THE HECK ARE THESE CRIT-TERS?
SEE YOU IN VOLUME 2!

TO BE CONTINUED IN ARCANA VOLUME 2! ♥

THE QUEST CONTINUES IN

ARCANIA

VOLUME 2

THE JOURNEY BEGINS WHEN INEZ AND YULAN
LEAVE THE WALLS OF THE CITY AND VENTURE INTO
UNCHARTED TERRITORY. SOON THEY ENCOUNTER
THE NYAMAS, STRANGE BUT HARMLESS CREATURES
KNOWN FOR THEIR BOUNDLESS CURIOSITY. LATER,
THE MYSTERIOUS KYRETTE MAKES HIMSELF KNOWN
TO THE PAIR OF WARY TRAVELERS, ELICITING MIXED
REACTIONS. AND AFTER AN ELFIN HALF-BREED ENLISTS
THE AID OF THE KIND-HEARTED INEZ, THE MISSION
MIGHT JUST BE OVER BEFORE IT BEGINS!

A Diva Torn from Chaos
A Savior Doomed to Love

Volume 2
Lumination

Ai continues to search for her place in our world on the streets of Tokyo. Using her talent to support herself, Ai signs a contract with a top record label and begins her rise to stardom. But fame is unpredictable—as her talent blooms, all eyes are on Ai. When scandal surfaces, will she burn out in the spotlight of celebrity?

T
TEEN
AGE 13+

Preview the manga at:
www.TOKYOPOP.com/princessai

TOKYOPOP SHOP

WWW.TOKYOPOP.COM/SHOP

HOT NEWS!
Check out the
TOKYOPOP SHOP!
The world's best
collection of manga in
English is now available
online in one place!

ARCANA

TOKYO MEW MEW A LA MODE

MBQ and other
hot titles are
available at
the store that
never closes!

MBQ

WWW.TOKYOPOP.COM/SHOP

0 00000 00000 0

- **LOOK FOR SPECIAL OFFERS**
- **PRE-ORDER UPCOMING RELEASES!**
- **COMPLETE YOUR COLLECTIONS**

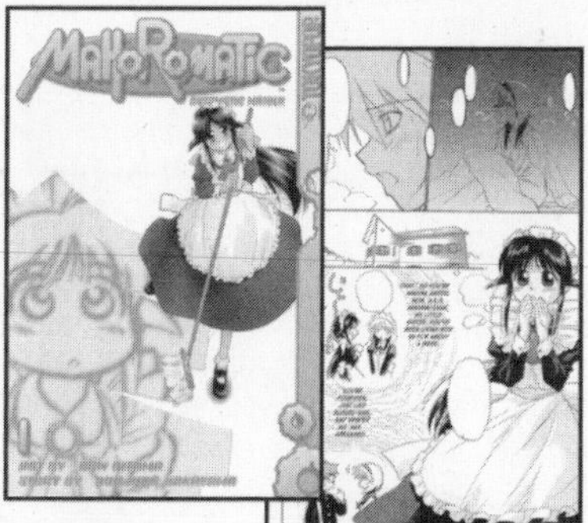

BY BUNJURO NAKAYAMA AND BOW DITAMA

MAHOROMATIC: AUTOMATIC MAIDEN

Mahoro is a sweet, cute, female battle android who decides to go from mopping up alien invaders to mopping up after Suguru Misato, a teenaged orphan boy... and hilarity most definitely ensues. This series has great art and a slick story that easily switches from truly funny to downright heartwarming...but always with a large shadow looming over it. You see, only Mahoro knows that her days are quite literally numbered, and the end of each chapter lets you know exactly how much—or how little—time she has left!

~Rob Tokar, Sr. Editor

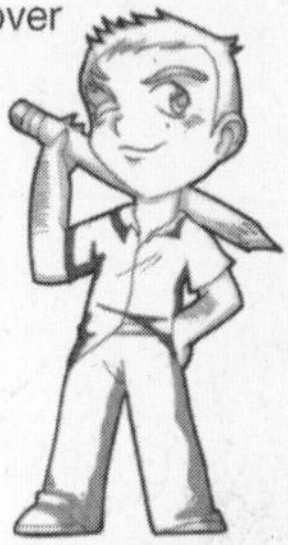

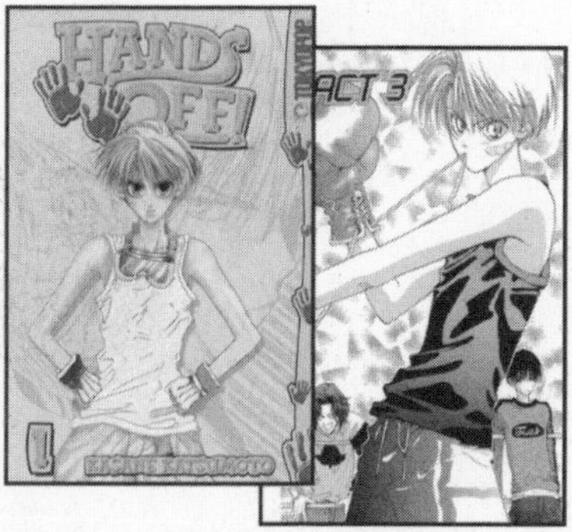
ACT 3

BY KASANE KATSUMOTO

HANDS OFF!

Cute boys with ESP who share a special bond... If you think this is familiar (e.g. *Legal Drug*), well, you're wrong. *Hands Off!* totally stands alone as a unique and thoroughly enjoyable series. Kotarou and Tatsuki's (platonic!) relationship is complex, fascinating and heart-wrenching. Throw in Yuuto, the playboy who can read auras, and you've got a fantastic setup for drama and comedy, with incredible themes of friendship running throughout. Don't be put off by Kotarou's danger-magnet status, either. The episodic stuff gradually changes, and the full arc of the characters' development is well worth waiting for.

~Lillian Diaz-Przybyl, Jr. Editor

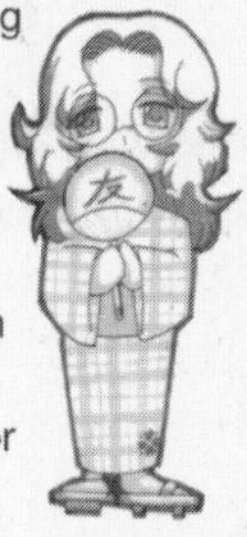

EDITORS' PICKS

TOKYOPOP MANGA SUPPLEMENT

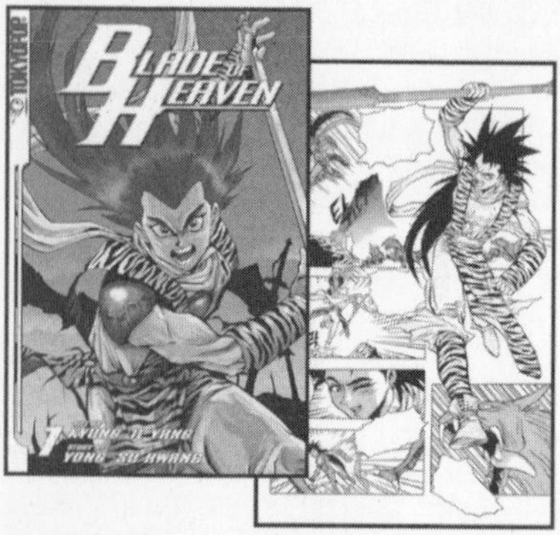
Blade of Heaven
TOKYOPOP

BY YONG-SU HWANG AND KYUNG-IL YANG

BLADE OF HEAVEN

Wildly popular in its homeland of Korea, *Blade of Heaven* enjoys the rare distinction of not only being a hit in its own country, but in Japan and several other countries, as well. On the surface, Yong-Su Hwang and Kyung-Il Yang's fantasy-adventure may look like yet another "Heaven vs. Demons" sword opera, but the story of the mischievous Soma, a pawn caught in a struggle of mythic proportions, is filled with so much humor, pathos, imagination—and yes, action, that it's easy to see why *Blade of Heaven* has been so popular worldwide.

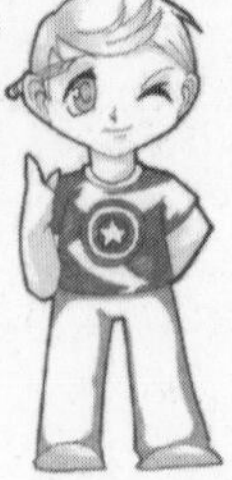

~Bryce P. Coleman, Editor

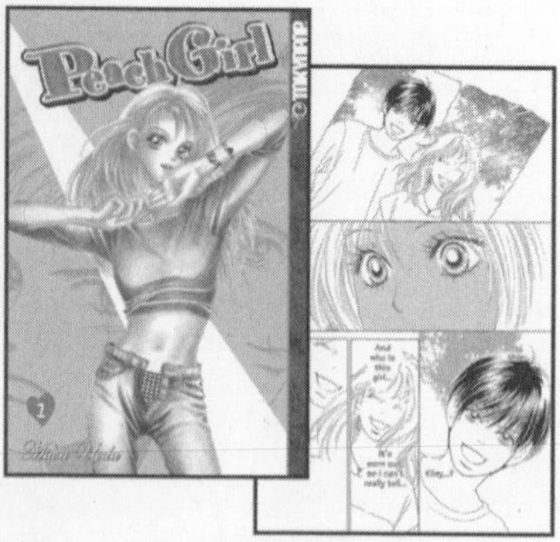
Peach Girl
TOKYOPOP

BY MIWA UEDA

PEACH GIRL

Am I the only person who thinks that *Peach Girl* is just like *The O.C.*? Just imagine Ryan as Toji, Seth as Kiley, Marissa as Momo and Summer as Sae. (The similarities are almost spooky!) Plus, Seth is way into comics and manga—and I'm sure he'd love *Peach Girl*. It has everything that my favorite TV show has and then some—drama, intrigue, romance and lots of will-they-or-won't-they suspense. I love it! *Peach Girl* rules, seriously. If you haven't read it, do so. Now.

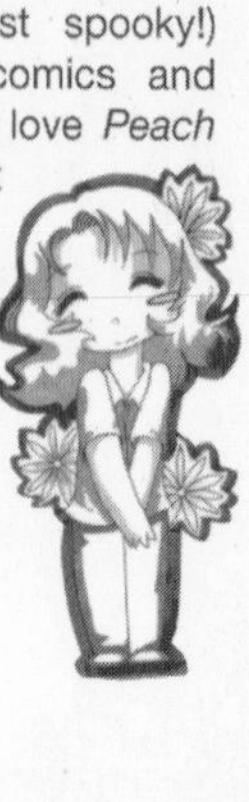

~Julie Taylor, Sr. Editor